ORIGINAL NARRATIVES
OF EARLY AMERICAN HISTORY

REPRODUCED UNDER THE AUSPICES OF THE
AMERICAN HISTORICAL ASSOCIATION

GENERAL EDITOR, J. FRANKLIN JAMESON, PH.D., LL.D., LITT.D.

DIRECTOR OF THE DEPARTMENT OF HISTORICAL RESEARCH IN THE
CARNEGIE INSTITUTION OF WASHINGTON

NARRATIVES OF EARLY VIRGINIA

BRADFORD'S HISTORY OF PLYMOUTH PLANTATION

WINTHROP'S JOURNAL "HISTORY OF NEW ENGLAND"
(2 vols.)

NARRATIVES OF EARLY CAROLINA

NARRATIVES OF EARLY MARYLAND

NARRATIVES OF EARLY PENNSYLVANIA, WEST NEW JERSEY,
AND DELAWARE

NARRATIVES OF NEW NETHERLAND

EARLY ENGLISH AND FRENCH VOYAGES

VOYAGES OF SAMUEL DE CHAMPLAIN

SPANISH EXPLORERS IN THE SOUTHERN UNITED STATES

SPANISH EXPLORATION IN THE SOUTHWEST

NARRATIVES OF THE INSURRECTIONS

NARRATIVES OF THE INDIAN WARS

JOHNSON'S WONDER-WORKING PROVIDENCE

THE JOURNAL OF JASPAR DANCKAERTS

NARRATIVES OF THE NORTHWEST

NARRATIVES OF THE WITCHCRAFT CASES

THE NORTHMEN, COLUMBUS, AND CABOT

ORIGINAL NARRATIVES
OF EARLY AMERICAN HISTORY

No. 11

SPANISH EXPLORERS

IN THE

SOUTHERN UNITED STATES
1528—1543

THE NARRATIVE OF ALVAR NUÑEZ CABEÇA DE VACA

EDITED BY

FREDERICK W. HODGE
OF THE BUREAU OF AMERICAN ETHNOLOGY

THE NARRATIVE OF THE EXPEDITION OF HERNANDO DE SOTO BY THE GENTLEMAN OF ELVAS

EDITED BY

THEODORE H. LEWIS
HONORARY MEMBER OF THE MISSISSIPPI HISTORICAL SOCIETY

THE NARRATIVE OF THE EXPEDITION OF CORONADO, BY PEDRO DE CASTAÑEDA

EDITED BY

FREDERICK W. HODGE

New York
BARNES & NOBLE, INC.

NOTE

ALTHOUGH, in the narrative of the Gentleman of Elvas, the translation by Buckingham Smith has been followed, some corrections have been made in the text, and pains have been taken to set right, in accordance with the Portuguese original at the Lenox Library, the native proper names, on whose interpretation in the Indian languages the identification of localities in many cases depends. If variations from page to page in the spelling of some such names are observed by the reader, they may be assumed to exist in the original.

The three narratives printed in this book are but a small selection from among many scores; for the narratives of Spanish explorers in the southern United States constitute an extensive literature. But if interest and historical importance are both taken into account, it is believed that these three hold an undisputed preëminence among such "relations."

J. F. J.

CONTENTS

THE NARRATIVE OF ALVAR NUÑEZ CABEÇA DE VACA

EDITED BY FREDERICK W. HODGE

		PAGE
THE NARRATIVE OF ALVAR NUÑEZ CABEÇA DE VACA		1
INTRODUCTION		3
Proem		12
Chapter 1.	In which is told when the Armada sailed, and of the Officers and Persons who went in it	14
Chapter 2.	The Coming of the Governor to the Port of Xagua and with a Pilot	18
Chapter 3.	Our Arrival in Florida	19
Chapter 4.	Our Entrance into the Country	20
Chapter 5.	The Governor leaves the Ships	24
Chapter 6.	Our Arrival at Apalache	28
Chapter 7.	The Character of the Country	29
Chapter 8.	We go from Aute	33
Chapter 9.	We leave the Bay of Horses	37
Chapter 10.	The Assault from the Indians	40
Chapter 11.	Of what befell Lope de Oviedo with the Indians	44
Chapter 12.	The Indians bring us Food	45
Chapter 13.	We hear of other Christians	48
Chapter 14.	The Departure of four Christians	49
Chapter 15.	What befell us among the People of Malhado	52
Chapter 16.	The Christians leave the Island of Malhado	55
Chapter 17.	The Coming of Indians with Andrés Dorantes, Castillo, and Estevanico	59
Chapter 18.	The Story Figueroa recounted from Esquivel	63
	Extract from the Letter of the Survivors	68
Chapter 19.	Our Separation by the Indians	70
Chapter 20.	Of our Escape	72
Chapter 21.	Our Cure of some of the Afflicted	74
Chapter 22.	The Coming of other Sick to us the next Day	76
Chapter 23.	Of our Departure after having eaten the Dogs	82
Chapter 24.	Customs of the Indians of that Country	83
Chapter 25.	Vigilance of the Indians in War	85
Chapter 26.	Of the Nations and Tongues	86

PAGE

Chapter 27. We moved away and were well received . . . 88

Chapter 28. Of another strange Custom 91

Chapter 29. The Indians plunder each other 94

Chapter 30. The Fashion of receiving us changes 99

Chapter 31. Of our taking the Way to the Maize 105

Chapter 32. The Indians give us the Hearts of Deer . . . 108

Chapter 33. We see Traces of Christians 112

Chapter 34. Of sending for the Christians 113

Chapter 35. The Chief Alcalde receives us kindly the Night we arrive 116

Chapter 36. Of building Churches in that Land 119

Chapter 37. Of what occurred when I wished to return . . . 121

Chapter 38. Of what became of the Others who went to Indias . 123

THE NARRATIVE OF THE EXPEDITION OF HERNANDO DE SOTO, BY THE GENTLEMAN OF ELVAS

EDITED BY THEODORE H. LEWIS

THE NARRATIVE OF THE EXPEDITION OF HERNANDO DE SOTO, BY THE GENTLEMAN OF ELVAS 127

INTRODUCTION 129

Epigram of Silveira 133

Prefatory Note by the Printer 134

Chapter 1. Who Soto was, and how he came to get the Government of Florida 135

Chapter 2. How Cabeça de Vaca arrived at Court, and gave Account of the Country of Florida; and of the Persons who assembled at Seville to accompany Don Hernando de Soto 136

Chapter 3. How the Portuguese went to Seville, and thence to Sanlúcar; and how the Captains were appointed over the Ships, and the People distributed among them . 138

Chapter 4. How the Adelantado with his People left Spain, going to the Canary Islands, and afterward arrived in the Antillas 139

Chapter 5. Of the Inhabitants there are in the City of Santiago and other Towns of the Island, the Character of the Soil, and of the Fruit 140

Chapter 6. How the Governor sent Doña Ysabel with the Ships from Santiago to Havana, while he with some of the Men went thither by land 142

Chapter 7. How we left Havana and came to Florida, and what other Matters took place 145

PAGE

Chapter 8. Of some Inroads that were made, and how a Christian was found who had been a long time in the possession of a Cacique 148

Chapter 9. How the Christian came to the Land of Florida, who he was, and of what passed at his Interview with the Governor 149

Chapter 10. How the Governor, having sent the Ships to Cuba, marched Inland, leaving one hundred Men at the Port 153

Chapter 11. How the Governor arrived at Caliquen, and thence, taking the Cacique with him, came to Napetaca, where the Indians, attempting to rescue him, had many of their Number killed and captured . . 156

Chapter 12. How the Governor arrived at Palache, and was informed that there was much Gold inland 160

Chapter 13. How the Governor went from Apalache in quest of Yupaha, and what befell him 164

Chapter 14. How the Governor left the Province of Patofa, marching into a Desert Country, where he, with his People, became exposed to great Peril, and underwent severe Privation 169

Chapter 15. How the Governor went from Cutifachiqui in quest of Coça, and what occurred to him on the Journey . 175

Chapter 16. How the Governor left Chiaha, and, having run a Hazard of falling by the Hands of the Indians at Acoste, escaped by his Address: what occurred to him on the Route, and how he came to Coça . 181

Chapter 17. Of how the Governor went from Coça to Tascaluça . 185

Chapter 18. How the Indians rose upon the Governor, and what followed upon that Rising 190

Chapter 19. How the Governor set his Men in order of Battle, and entered the town of Mauilla 192

Chapter 20. How the Governor set out from Mauilla to go to Chicaça, and what befell him 194

Chapter 21. How the Indians returned to attack the Christians, and how the Governor went to Alimamu, and they tarried to give him Battle in the Way 199

Chapter 22. How the Governor went from Quizquiz, and thence to the River Grande 201

Chapter 23. How the Governor went from Aquixo to Casqui, and thence to Pacaha; and how this Country differs from the other 205

Chapter 24. How the Cacique of Pacaha came in Peace, and he of Casqui, having absented himself, returned to excuse his Conduct; and how the Governor made Friendship between the Chiefs 209

PAGE

Chapter 25. How the Governor went from Pacaha to Aquiguate and to Coligoa, and came to Cayas 213

Chapter 26. How the Governor went to visit the Province of Tulla, and what happened to him 217

Chapter 27. How the Governor went from Tulla to Autiamque, where he passed the Winter 221

Chapter 28. How the Governor went from Autiamque to Nilco, and thence to Guachoya 224

Chapter 29. The Message sent to Quigaltam, and the Answer brought back to the Governor, and what occurred the while . 228

Chapter 30. The Death of the Adelantado, Don Hernando de Soto, and how Luys Moscoso de Alvarado was chosen Governor 232

Chapter 31. How the Governor Luys de Moscoso left Guachoya and went to Chaguete, and thence to Aguacay . . 235

Chapter 32. How the Governor went from Aguacay to Naguatex, and what happened to him 238

Chapter 33. How the Cacique of Naguatex came to visit the Governor, and how the Governor went thence, and arrived at Nondacao 240

Chapter 34. How the Governor marched from Nondacao to Soacatino and Guasco, passing through a Wilderness, whence, for want of a Guide and Interpreter, he retired to Nilco 243

Chapter 35. How the Christians returned to Nilco, and thence went to Minoya, where they prepared to build Vessels in which to leave Florida 246

Chapter 36. How Seven Brigantines were built, and the Christians took their Departure from Aminoya 250

Chapter 37. How the Christians, on their Voyage, were attacked in the River, by the Indians of Quigualtam, and what happened 254

Chapter 38. How the Christians were Pursued by the Indians . 257

Chapter 39. How the Christians came to the Sea, what occurred then, and what befell them on the Voyage . . 259

Chapter 40. How the Brigantines lost Sight of each other in a Storm, and afterwards came together at a Kay . 262

Chapter 41. How the Christians arrived at the River Panico . . 264

Chapter 42. How the Christians came to Panico, and of their Reception by the Inhabitants 266

Chapter 43. The Favor the People found in the Viceroy and Residents of Mexico 268

Chapter 44. Which sets forth some of the Diversities and Peculiarities of Florida; and the Fruit, Birds, and Beasts of the Country 270

THE NARRATIVE OF THE EXPEDITION OF CORONADO, BY PEDRO DE CASTAÑEDA

EDITED BY FREDERICK W. HODGE

PAGE

THE NARRATIVE OF THE EXPEDITION OF CORONADO, BY PEDRO DE
CASTAÑEDA 273

INTRODUCTION 275

Preface 281

FIRST PART

Chapter 1. Which treats of the Way we first came to know about
the Seven Cities, and of how Nuño de Guzman made
an Expedition to discover them 285

Chapter 2. Of how Francisco Vazquez Coronado came to be Governor, and the second Account which Cabeza de Vaca
gave 287

Chapter 3. Of how they killed the Negro Estevan at Cibola, and
Friar Marcos returned in Flight 289

Chapter 4. Of how the noble Don Antonio de Mendoza made an
Expedition to discover Cibola 290

Chapter 5. Concerning the Captains who went to Cibola . . 292

Chapter 6. Of how all the Companies collected in Compostela and
set off on the Journey in good Order . . . 293

Chapter 7. Of how the Army reached Chiametla, and the Killing
of the Army-Master, and the other things that happened up to the Arrival at Culiacan 295

Chapter 8. Of how the Army entered the Town of Culiacan and
the Reception it received, and other things which
happened before the Departure 297

Chapter 9. Of how the Army started from Culiacan and the Arrival
of the General at Cibola, and of the Army at Señora
and of other things that happened 298

Chapter 10. Of how the Army started from the Town of Señora,
leaving it inhabited, and how it reached Cibola, and
of what happened to Captain Melchior Diaz on his
Expedition in Search of the Ships and how he discovered the Tison (Firebrand) River . . . 302

Chapter 11. Of how Don Pedro de Tovar discovered Tusayan or
Tutahaco and Don Garcia Lopez de Cardenas saw
the Firebrand River, and the other things that had
happened 306

Chapter 12. Of how people came from Cicuye to Cibola to see the
Christians, and how Hernando de Alvarado went to
see the Cows 310

PAGE

Chapter 13. Of how the General went toward Tutahaco with a few Men and left the Army with Don Tristan, who took it to Tiguex 313

Chapter 14. Of how the Army went from Cibola to Tiguex and what happened to them on the way, on account of the Snow 315

Chapter 15. Of why Tiguex revolted, and how they were punished, without being to Blame for it 317

Chapter 16. Of how they besieged Tiguex and took it and of what happened during the Siege 320

Chapter 17. Of how Messengers reached the Army from the Valley of Señora, and how Captain Melchior Diaz died on the Expedition to the Firebrand River . . . 324

Chapter 18. Of how the General managed to leave the Country in Peace so as to go in Search of Quivira, where the Turk said there was the most Wealth . . . 327

Chapter 19. Of how they started in Search of Quivira and of what happened on the Way 329

Chapter 20. Of how great Stones fell in the Camp, and how they discovered another Ravine, where the Army was divided into two Parts 333

Chapter 21. Of how the Army returned to Tiguex and the General reached Quivira 335

Chapter 22. Of how the General returned from Quivira and of other Expeditions toward the North 339

SECOND PART

WHICH TREATS OF THE HIGH VILLAGES AND PROVINCES AND OF THEIR HABITS AND CUSTOMS, AS COLLECTED BY PEDRO DE CASTANEDA, NATIVE OF THE CITY OF NAJARA

Chapter 1. Of the Province of Culiacan and of its Habits and Customs 344

Chapter 2. Of the Province of Petlatlan and all the Inhabited Country as far as Chichilticalli 346

Chapter 3. Of Chichilticalli and the Desert, of Cibola, its Customs and Habits, and of other things 349

Chapter 4. Of how they live at Tiguex, and of the Province of Tiguex and its Neighborhood 352

Chapter 5. Of Cicuye and the Villages in its Neighborhood, and of how some People came to conquer this Country . . 355

Chapter 6. Which gives the Number of Villages which were seen in the Country of the Terraced Houses, and their Population 358

PAGE

Chapter 7. Which treats of the Plains that were crossed, of the
Cows, and of the People who inhabit them . . . 361
Chapter 8. Of Quivira, of where it is and some Information about it 364

THIRD PART

WHICH DESCRIBES WHAT HAPPENED TO FRANCISCO VAZQUEZ
CORONADO DURING THE WINTER, AND HOW HE GAVE UP THE
EXPEDITION AND RETURNED TO NEW SPAIN

Chapter 1. Of how Don Pedro de Tovar came from Señora with
some Men, and Don Garcia Lopez de Cardenas started
back to New Spain 366
Chapter 2. Of the General's Fall, and of how the Return to New
Spain was ordered 368
Chapter 3. Of the Rebellion at Suya and the Reasons the Settlers
gave for it 370
Chapter 4. Of how Friar Juan de Padilla and Friar Luis remained
in the Country and the Army prepared to return to
Mexico 372
Chapter 5. Of how the Army left the Settlements and marched to
Culiacan, and of what happened on the Way . . 375
Chapter 6. Of how the General started from Culiacan to give the
Viceroy an Account of the Army with which he had
been intrusted 377
Chapter 7. Of the Adventures of Captain Juan Gallego while he
was bringing Reënforcements through the Revolted
Country 379
Chapter 8. Which describes some remarkable things that were seen
on the Plains, with a Description of the Bulls . . 381
Chapter 9. Which treats of the Direction which the Army took, and
of how another more direct Way might be found, if
anyone was to return to that Country 384

SPANISH EXPLORERS IN THE SOUTHERN UNITED STATES

THE NARRATIVE OF ALVAR NUÑEZ CABEZA DE VACA

INTRODUCTION

IN some respects the journey of Alvar Nuñez Cabeza de Vaca and his three companions overland from coast to coast during the eight years from 1528 to 1536 is the most remarkable in the record of American exploration, and as a narrative of suffering and privation the relation here presented perhaps has no equal in the annals of the northern continent.

The author of the narrative was a native of Jeréz de la Frontera, in the province of Cadiz, in southern Spain, but the date of his birth is not known. His father was Francisco de Vera, son of Pedro de Vera, conqueror of the Grand Canary in 1483; his mother, Teresa Cabeza de Vaca, who also was born in Jeréz. Why Alvar Nuñez assumed the matronymic is not known, unless it was with a sense of pride that he desired to perpetuate the name that had been bestowed by the King of Navarre on his maternal ancestor, a shepherd named Martin Alhaja, for guiding the army through a pass that he marked with the skull of a cow (*cabeza de vaca*, literally "cow's head"), thus leading the Spanish army to success in the battle of Las Navas de Tolosa, in July, 1212, which led up to the final conquest of the Moors in Spain.

Having returned to Spain after many years of service in the New World for the Crown, Pámfilo de Narvaez petitioned for a grant; and in consequence the right to conquer and colonize the country between the Rio de las Palmas, in eastern Mexico, and Florida was accorded him. The expedition, consisting of six hundred colonists and soldiers, set sail in five vessels from San Lucar de Barrameda, June 17, 1527, and after various vicissitudes, including the wreck of two ships and the

3

loss of sixty men in a hurricane on the southern coast of Cuba, was finally driven northward by storm, and landed, in April, 1528, at St. Clements Point, near the entrance to Tampa Bay, on the west coast of Florida. Despite the protest of Cabeza de Vaca, who had been appointed treasurer of Rio de las Palmas by the King, Narvaez ordered his ships to skirt the coast in an endeavor to find Pánuco, while the expedition, now reduced to three hundred men by desertions in Santo Domingo, death in the Cuban storm, and the return of those in charge of the ships, started inland in a generally northern course. The fleet searched for the expedition for a year and then sailed to Mexico.

Among the members of the force, in addition to Alvar Nuñez Cabeza de Vaca, were Andrés Dorantes de Carrança, son of Pablo, a native of Béjar del Castañar, in Estremadura, who had received a commission as captain of infantry on the recommendation of Don Alvaro de Zúñiga, Duke of Béjar; Captain Alonzo del Castillo Maldonado, of Salamanca, the son of Doctor Castillo and Aldonza Maldonado; and Estévan, or Estévanico, a blackamoor of Asemmur, or Azamor, on the west coast of Morocco, the slave of Dorantes. With the exception of those who returned with the ships, these four men were the only ones of the entire expedition who ever again entered a civilized community.

Pursuing a generally northerly course, harassed by Indians, and beset with hunger, illness, and treachery in their ranks, Narvaez's party finally reached the head of Appalachee Bay, in the country of the Indians after whom this arm of the Gulf of Mexico takes its name. Looking now to the sea as his only means of escape, Narvaez the incompetent, with neither the proper materials nor the mechanics, set about to build boats to conduct his men out of their trap — craft that were expected to weather such tropical storms as they had already so poorly buffeted with their stouter ships. Every object of metal that the expedition afforded, even to stirrups and spurs, was requisitioned for the manufacture of nails and necessary tools; a rude forge was constructed, with bellows of wood and deer-skins; the native palm supplied tow and covering; the horses were killed and their hides used for water-bottles, while their flesh served the Spaniards for food as the work went on; even the shirts from the very backs of the men were fashioned into sails. Picturing the character of the five boats, laden almost to the gunwales with nearly fifty men each, besides such provisions as could be stowed away, and the untold hardship from thirst after the decay of the horse-hide canteens, the chief wonder is that the motley fleet survived long enough to reach Pensacola Bay. As it passed the mouth of the Mississippi, the current was so swift that fresh water was dipped from the gulf, and the wind so strong that the boats were carried beyond sight of land for three days, and for a time lost sight of each other. For four days more, two of the boats, including that in which was Cabeza de Vaca, drifted within view of each other; but another storm arose, again they were lost to sight, and one by one the occupants succumbed to exhaustion and cast themselves into the bottom of the boat, until Cabeza de Vaca alone was left to steer the flimsy craft in its unknown course. Night came on and the author of our narrative lay down to rest. The next morning, November 6, 1528, the boat was cast ashore on a long narrow island, inhabited by savages, on the Texas coast.

On this "Island of Misfortune" Cabeza de Vaca's party was soon joined by that of one of the other boats, including Dorantes, so that altogether the island harbored about eighty Spaniards. Four men later attempted to reach Pánuco, but all perished but one. During the following winter disease raged among the little colony, reducing it to fifteen. Then the Spaniards became separated, Dorantes and his slave Estévan, now both the slaves of the Indians, were taken to the mainland, whither Cabeza de Vaca, weary of root-digging on the island shore, also escaped, becoming a trader among the Indians, journeying far inland and along the coast from tribe to tribe, for forty or fifty leagues. Every year during the five years that he plied his trade as a dealer in shells, sea-beads, medicine-beans, skins, ochre, and the like, he returned to Malhado, where Lope de Oviedo, and Alvarez, a sick companion, still remained. Finally the latter died, and Cabeza de Vaca and Oviedo again sought the main in the hope of reaching Christian people. Journeying southward along the coast, they crossed the Brazos and other rivers, and finally reached San Antonio Bay. Here Oviedo, owing to ill-treatment by the Indians, deserted Cabeza de Vaca, who shortly after also stole away from the savages and joined Dorantes, Castillo Maldonado, and the Moor (the sole survivors of the party of twelve who had left Malhado years before), whose Indian masters had come down the river, evidently the San Antonio, to gather walnuts.

Once more together, the Christians planned to escape six months hence, when all the Indians from the surrounding country gathered on the southern Texas plains to eat prickly pears. But again were they doomed to disappointment, for although the savages assembled in the tuna fields, a quarrel arose among them (there was "a woman in the case"), which caused the Spaniards to be separated for another year. Their escape was finally accomplished in the manner they had planned; but their departure for the Christian land was not at once effected, by reason of the inhospitable character of the country, which compelled them to sojourn among other Indians until the beginning of another prickly-pear season.

While among the Avavares, with whom the Spaniards lived for eight months, they resumed the treatment of the sick, a practice that had first been forced on them, by the natives of Malhado Island, under threat of starvation. With such success did the

Spaniards, and especially Cabeza de Vaca, meet, that their reputation as healers was sounded far and wide among the tribes, thousands of the natives following them from place to place and showering gifts upon them.

There are few Spanish narratives that are more unsatisfactory to deal with by reason of the lack of directions, distances, and other details, than that of Cabeza de Vaca; consequently there are scarcely two students of the route who agree. His line of travel through Texas was twice crossed by later explorers, — in 1541 by the army of Francisco Vazquez Coronado, on the eastern edge of the Stake Plains, and again in 1582 by Antonio de Espejo, on the Rio Grande below the present El Paso. These data, with the clews afforded by the narrative itself, point strongly to a course from the tuna fields, about thirty leagues inland from San Antonio Bay, to the Rio Colorado and perhaps to the Rio Llano, westward across the lower Pecos to the Rio Grande above the junction of the Conchos, thence in an approximately straight line across Chihuahua and Sonora to the Rio Sonora, where we find Cabeza de Vaca's Village of the Hearts, which Coronado also visited in 1540, at or in the vicinity of the present Ures. Soon after he reached this point traces of the first Christians were seen, and shortly after the Spaniards themselves, in the form of a military body of slave-hunters.

As to the character of our chronicler, he seems to have been an honest, modest, and humane man, who underestimated rather than exaggerated the many strange things that came under his notice, if we except the account of his marvellous healings, even to the revival of the dead. The expedition of Narvaez was in itself a disastrous and dismal failure, reaching "an end alike forlorn and fatal"; but viewed from the standpoint of present-day civilization, the commander deserved his fate. On the other hand, while one might well hesitate to say that the accomplishment of Cabeza de Vaca and his three companions compensated their untold sufferings, the world eventually became the wiser in more ways than one. The northern continent had been penetrated from shore to shore; the waters of the Mississippi and the bison of the plains were now first seen by white men; and some knowledge of the savage tribes had been gleaned for the benefit of those who should come after. There is no blatant announcement of great mineral wealth — a mountain with scoria of iron, some small bags of mica, a quantity of galena, with which the Indians painted their faces, a little turquoise, a few emeralds, and a small copper bell were all. Yet the effect of the remarkable overland journey was to inspire the expedition of Coronado in 1540; and it is not improbable that De Soto, who endeavored to enlist the services of Cabeza de Vaca, may likewise have been stimulated to action.

After the three Spaniards returned to Mexico they united in a report to the Audiencia of Española (Santo Domingo), which is printed in Oviedo's *Historia General y Natural de las Indias* (tomo III., lib. xxxv., ed. 1853). In April, 1537, they embarked for Spain, but the ship in which Dorantes set sail proved to be unseaworthy and returned to Vera Cruz. Invited to the capital by the Viceroy Mendoza, Dorantes was tendered a commission to explore the northern country, but this project was never carried out.

Cabeza de Vaca, in reward for his services, was appointed governor, captain-general, and adelantado of the provinces of Rio de la Plata. Sailing from Cadiz in November, 1540, he reached Brazil in March of the following year. Here he remained seven months, when he sent his vessels ahead to Buenos Ayres and started overland to Asuncion, which he reached in March, 1542, after a remarkable experience in the tropical forests. But the province seems to have needed a man of sterner stuff than Alvar Nuñez, for he soon became the subject of animosity and intrigue, which finally resulted in open rebellion, and his arrest in April, 1543. He was kept under close guard for about two years, when he was sent to Spain, and in 1551 was sentenced to banishment in Africa for eight years — a judgment that does not seem to have been carried out, for after serving probably a year or so in mild captivity at Seville, he was acquitted. He died in 1557.

Of the subsequent career of Castillo little is known. He returned to New Spain, became a citizen of the City of Mexico, married a widow, and was granted half the rents of the Indian town of Tehuacan.

Dorantes, as has been stated, for some reason did not carry out the plan of exploring the north, perhaps because of the projected expedition of Coronado, the way for which was led by Fray Marcos de Niza in 1539 with the negro Estévan as a guide. Dorantes served Mendoza in the conquest of Jalisco, and married Doña María de la Torre, a widow, by whom he had a large family. One of his sons, Balthasar, sometime king's treasurer of Vera Cruz, was born about the middle of the century, and on the death of his father inherited an *encomienda* that produced an income of five thousand pesos a year. Another son, Gaspar, inherited the *encomienda* of the pueblos of Ocava; and another, Melchior, "an *encomienda* of Indians and of very good rents."

Of Estévan there is somewhat more definite information. Well on the road toward the north in 1539, he was sent ahead by Fray Marcos to report the character of the country and its people, and with rattle in hand and accompanied by many Indians of the present Gila River region, entered Háwi-kuh, the first of the Seven Cities of Cíbola. Here Estévan and most of his Indian followers were put to death by the Zuñis; those who escaped fled to Fray Marcos, whose life was threatened but who saved himself by regaling the natives with the contents of his pack.

There was another survivor of the inland expedition of

Narvaez—Juan Ortiz by name. This Spaniard, who had been enticed ashore by the Indians of Florida, led practically the life of a slave, like his countrymen on the Texas main, until 1539, when he was rescued by De Soto, but he died before the expedition returned to civilization.

The *Relacion* of Alvar Nuñez Cabeza de Vaca was first printed at Zamora in 1542, and with slight changes was reprinted, with the first edition of the *Comentarios* on the Rio de la Plata, at Valladolid, in 1555. The *editio princeps* was translated into Italian by Ramusio, in the third volume of his *Navigationi et Viaggi* (Venice, 1556), and this was paraphrased into English by Samuel Purchas in volume IV. of *Purchas His Pilgrimes* (London, 1613, pt. IV., lib. VIII., cap. 1). The *Naufragios* (or *Relacion*) and *Comentarios* were reprinted at Madrid in 1736, preceded by the *Exámen Apologético* of Antonio Ardoino, who seemed to feel it his duty to reply to an Austrian monk named Caspar Plautus, who, in 1621, under the name Philoponus, published a treatise in which he maintained that laymen like Cabeza de Vaca should not be permitted to perform miracles. This edition of the narration of Cabeza de Vaca is included in volume I. of Barcia's *Historiadores Primitivos de las Indias Occidentales*, published at Madrid in 1749. The *Naufragios* of Alvar Nuñez, from the edition of 1555, appears in volume I. of Vedia's *Historiadores Primitivos de Indias* (Madrid, ed. 1852). The letter to the Audiencia of Española, "edited" by Oviedo, has already been alluded to. A "Capitulacion que se tomó con Alvar Nuñez Cabeza de Vaca," dated Madrid, 18 Marzo, 1540, is found in the *Colección de Documentos Inéditos del Archivo de Indias* (tomo XXIII., pp. 8–33, 1875). A *Relación* by Cabeza de Vaca, briefly narrating the story of the expedition until the arrival of its survivors in Espíritu Santo Bay, with his instructions as treasurer, is printed in the *Colección de Documentos de Indias*, XIV. 265–279 (Madrid, 1870). The most recent Spanish edition of the more famous

Relacion reprinted in the following pages forms a part of volume V. of the *Colección de Libros y Documentos referentes á la Historia de América* (Madrid, 1906), which also contains the *Comentarios*.

The single French translation was published as volume VII. of Henri Ternaux-Compans's *Voyages* (Paris, 1837), from the edition of 1555, while the *Commentaires* form volume VI.

In 1851 a translation of the edition of 1555 into English, by (Thomas) Buckingham Smith, under the title *The Narrative of Alvar Nuñez Cabeça de Vaca*, was published privately at Washington by George W. Riggs; and shortly after Mr. Smith's death, in 1871, another edition, with many additions, was published in New York under the editorial supervision of John Gilmary Shea and at the expense of Henry C. Murphy. It is this edition of the *Narrative* that is here reprinted. A paraphrase of the 1851 edition of Smith's translation appears in Henry Kingsley's *Tales of Old Travels* (London, 1869). The first fourteen chapters of W. W. H. Davis's *Spanish Conquest of New Mexico* (Doylestown, Pa., 1869) are also a paraphrase of the same work. Chapters XXX.–XXXVI. of the 1871 edition of Smith, somewhat abridged, were printed in an *Old South Leaflet* (Gen. Ser., No. 39, Boston, 1893). A "Relation of what Befel the Persons who Escaped from the Disasters that Attended the Armament of Captain Pamphilo de Narvaez on the Shores and in the countries of the North," translated and condensed from the letter published by Oviedo, is printed in *The Historical Magazine* (vol. XII., pp. 141, 204, 267, 347; September–December, 1867). The most recent English edition of the Cabeza de Vaca *Relation*, translated from the very rare imprint of 1542 by Mrs. Fanny Bandelier, and edited, with an introduction, by her husband Ad. F. Bandelier, was published in New York, in 1905, under the title, *The Journey of Alvar Nuñez Cabeza de Vaca*, as one of the volumes of the "Trail Makers" series.

F. W. Hodge.

THE NARRATIVE OF CABEZA DE VACA

*Relation that Alvar Nuñez Cabeça de Vaca gave of what befell
the armament in the Indies whither Pánfilo de Narváez
went for Governor from the year 1527 to the year 1536
[1537] when with three comrades he returned and came
to Sevilla.*[1]

PROEM

SACRED CAESARIAN CATHOLIC MAJESTY:

Among the many who have held sway, I think no prince
can be found whose service has been attended with the ardor
and emulation shown for that of your Highness [2] at this time.
The inducement is evident and powerful: men do not pursue
together the same career without motive, and strangers are
observed to strive with those who are equally impelled by
religion and loyalty.

Although ambition and love of action are common to all,
as to the advantages that each may gain, there are great in-
equalities of fortune, the result not of conduct, but only accident, nor caused by the fault of any one, but coming in the
providence of God and solely by His will. Hence to one arises
deeds more signal than he thought to achieve; to another the
opposite in every way occurs, so that he can show no higher
proof of purpose than his effort, and at times even this is so
concealed that it cannot of itself appear.

As for me, I can say in undertaking the march I made on the
main by the royal authority, I firmly trusted that my conduct

---

[1] This heading is taken from the title-page of the edition of 1542. The
edition of 1555, generally followed in this book, has a title-page so phrased
as to cover both the North American and the South American narratives of
the author. The return really took place in 1537.

[2] The Emperor Charles V.

and services would be as evident and distinguished as were those of my ancestors[1] and that I should not have to speak in order to be reckoned among those who for diligence and fidelity in affairs your Majesty honors. Yet, as neither my counsel nor my constancy availed to gain aught for which we set out, agreeably to your interests, for our sins, no one of the many armaments that have gone into those parts has been permitted to find itself in straits great like ours, or come to an end alike forlorn and fatal. To me, one only duty remains, to present a relation of what was seen and heard in the ten years[2] I wandered lost and in privation through many and remote lands. Not merely a statement of positions and distances, animals and vegetation, but of the diverse customs of the many and very barbarous people with whom I talked and dwelt, as well as all other matters I could hear of and discern, that in some way I may avail your Highness. My hope of going out from among those nations was always small, still my care and diligence were none the less to keep in particular remembrance everything, that if at any time God our Lord should will to bring me where I now am, it might testify to my exertion in the royal behalf.

As the narrative is in my opinion of no trivial value to those who in your name go to subdue those countries and bring them to a knowledge of the true faith and true Lord, and under the imperial dominion, I have written this with much exactness; and although in it may be read things very novel and for some persons difficult to believe, nevertheless they may without hesitation credit me as strictly faithful. Better than to exaggerate, I have lessened in all things, and it is sufficient to say the relation is offered to your Majesty for truth. I beg it may be received in the name of homage, since it is the most that one could bring who returned thence naked.

---

[1] He doubtless refers particularly to the services of his grandfather, Pedro de Vera, conqueror of the Canaries, to whom he refers at the close of this work. See the Introduction.

[2] He arrived in Florida with the Narvaez expedition in April, 1528, and reached New Spain overland in April, 1536 — eight years later.

Chapter 1

In which is told when the Armada sailed, and of the officers and persons who went in it.

On the seventeenth day[1] of June, in the year fifteen hundred and twenty-seven, the Governor Pánphilo de Narváez left the port of San Lúcar de Barrameda,[2] authorized and commanded by your Majesty to conquer and govern the provinces of the main, extending from the River Palmas[3] to the cape of Florida. The fleet he took was five ships, in which went six hundred men, a few more or less; the officers (for we shall have to speak of them), were these, with their rank: Cabeça de Vaca, treasurer and high-sheriff; Alonso Enrriquez, comptroller; Alonso de Solis, distributor to your Majesty and assessor; Juan Xuarez,[4] a friar of Saint Francis, commissary, and four more friars of the same order.

We arrived at the island of Santo Domingo, where we tarried near forty-five days, engaged in procuring for ourselves some necessary material, particularly horses. Here we lost from our fleet more than one hundred and forty men, who wished to remain, seduced by the partidos,[5] and advantages held out to them by the people of that country.

[1] The Spanish edition of 1542 has the date June 27.

[2] At the mouth of the Guadalquivir, in the province of Cadiz, Spain; noted as the point of debarkation of Fernão Magalhães, or Magellan, September 20, 1519.

[3] Probably the Rio de Santander, which enters the Gulf of Mexico one hundred miles north of Tampico. The name was later applied to the province that joined the province of Pánuco on the north. The latter was, in general terms, the region drained by the streams that empty into the Gulf about Tampico.

[4] The edition of 1542 has "Juan Gutierrez."

[5] A term often used to designate one of the districts or territories into which a Spanish province was divided for purposes of administration, and having a head pueblo or village ; but here employed to signify the favorable proposals which the colonists made to the deserters from the fleet.

We sailed from the island and arrived at Santiago,[1] a port of Cuba, where, during some days that we remained, the Governor supplied himself further with men, also with arms and horses. It happened there that a gentleman, Vasco Porcallo [2] of Trinidad, which is also on the island,[3] offered to give the Governor some provisions which he had in the town, a hundred leagues from the port of Santiago. Accordingly the Governor set out with all the fleet for Trinidad; but coming to a port half way, called Cabo de Santa Cruz,[4] he thought it well to wait there, and send a vessel to bring the stores. To this end he ordered that a Captain Pantoja [5] should go for them with his ship, and for greater security, that I should accompany him with another. The Governor remained with four ships, having bought one at the island of Santo Domingo.

We having arrived with the two vessels at the port of Trinidad, Captain Pantoja went with Vasco Porcalle (*sic*) to the town, a league off, to receive the provisions, while I remained at sea with the pilots, who said we ought to go thence with the greatest despatch possible, for it was a very bad port in which many vessels were lost. As what there occurred to us was very remarkable, it appears to me not foreign to the purpose with which I write this, to relate it here.

The next morning began to give signs of bad weather; rain commenced falling, and the sea ran so high, that, although I gave the men permission to go on shore, many of them returned to the ship to avoid exposure to the wet and cold, and because the town was a league away. In this time a canoe came off, bringing me a letter from a resident of the place, asking me to come for the needed provisions that were there;

[1] In southeastern Cuba, the Santiago de Cuba that was surrendered to the American forces in the summer of 1898.

[2] Vasco Porcallo de Figueroa afterward became De Soto's lieutenant-general in Florida, but returned to Cuba early in the history of the expedition.

[3] On the southern coast, longitude 80°.

[4] Now Cabo Cruz, longitude 77° 40'.

[5] One Juan Pantoja, captain of crossbowmen and Lord of Ixtlahuaca, accompanied Narvaez on his first expedition to Mexico. If the same as the present Pantoja, which seems likely, he was killed by Sotomayor in a quarrel. See ch. 17.

from which request I excused myself, saying that I could not leave the ships. At noon the canoe returned with another letter, in which I was solicited again with much urging, and a horse was brought for me to ride. I gave the same answer as before, that I could not leave the ships; but the pilots and the people entreated me to go, so that I might hasten the provisions as fast as possible, and we might join the fleet where it lay, for they had great fear lest remaining long in this port, the ships should be lost. For these reasons, I determined to go to the town; but first I left orders with the pilots, that if the south wind, which often wrecks vessels there, came on to blow, and they should find themselves in much danger, to put the ships on shore at some place where the men and horses could be saved. I wished to take some of the men with me for company; but they said the weather was too rainy and cold, and the town too far off; that to-morrow, which was Sunday, they would come, with God's help, and hear mass.

An hour after I left, the sea began to rise very high, and the north wind was so violent that neither the boats dared come to land, nor could the vessels be let drive on shore, because of the head wind, so that the people remained severely laboring against the adverse weather, and under a heavy fall of water all that day and Sunday until dark. At this time, the rain and the tempest had increased to such a degree, there was no less agitation in the town than on the sea; for all the houses and churches fell, and it was necessary in order to move upright, that we should go seven or eight holding on to each other that the wind might not blow us away; and walking in the groves, we had no less fear of the trees than of the houses, as they too were falling and might kill us under them. In this tempest and danger we wandered all night, without finding place or spot where we could remain a half-hour in safety. During the time, particularly from midnight forward, we heard much tumult and great clamor of voices, the sound of timbrels, flutes, and tambourines, as well as other instruments, which lasted until the morning, when the tempest ceased. Nothing so terrible as this storm had been seen in those parts before. I drew up an authenticated account of it, and sent the testimony to your Majesty.

On Monday morning we went down to the harbor, but did not find the ships. The buoys belonging to them were floating on the water; whence we knew the ships were lost, and we walked along the shore to see if any thing could be found of them. As nothing was discovered, we struck into the woods, and, having travelled about a quarter of a league in water, we found the little boat of a ship lodged upon some trees. Ten leagues thence, along the coast, two bodies were found, belonging to my ship, and some lids of boxes; but the persons were so disfigured by beating against the rocks that they could not be recognized. A cloak too was seen, also a coverlet rent in pieces, and nothing more. Sixty persons were lost in the ships, and twenty horses. Those who had gone on shore the day of our arrival, who may have been as many as thirty, were all the survivors of both ships. During some days we were struggling with much hardship and hunger; for the provisions and subsistence were destroyed, and some herds. The country was left in a condition piteous to behold; the trees prostrate, the woods parched, there being neither grass nor leaf.

Thus we lived until the fifth of November, when the Governor arrived with four ships, which had lived through the great storm, having run into a place of safety in good time. The people who came in them, as well as those on shore, were so intimidated by what had passed, that they feared to go on board in the winter, and they besought the Governor to spend it there. Seeing their desire and that it was also the wish of the townspeople, he staid through the season. He gave the ships and people into my charge, that I might go with them to pass the winter at the port of Xagua,[1] twelve leagues thence, where I remained until the twentieth day of February.

[1] The present Jagua, at the entrance to the bay of Cienfuegos.

Chapter 2

*The coming of the Governor to the Port of Xagua and
with a pilot.*

At this time, the Governor arrived with a brigantine
bought in Trinidad, and brought with him a pilot named
Miruelo, who was employed because he said he knew the position of the River Palmas. and had been there, and was a thor-
ough pilot for all the coast of the North. The Governor had
also purchased and left on the shore of Havana another vessel,
of which Alvaro de la Cerda remained in charge, with forty
infantry and twelve cavalry.

The second day after arrival the Governor set sail with
four hundred men and eighty horses, in four ships and a brigantine. The pilot being again on board, put the vessels among
the shoals they call Canarreo,[1] and on the day following we
struck: thus we were situated fifteen days, the keels of our
vessels frequently touching bottom. At the end of this time,
a tempest from the south threw so much water upon the
shoals that we could get off, although not without danger.
We left this place and arrived at Guaniguanico, where another storm overtook us, in which we were at one time near
being lost. At Cape Corrientes [2] we had still another, which
detained us three days. These places being passed, we doubled Cape Sant Anton,[3] and sailed with head winds until we
were within twelve leagues of Havana. Standing in the next
day to enter the harbor, a wind came from the south which
drove us from the land towards the coast of Florida. We
came in sight on Tuesday, the twelfth day of April, and sailed
along the coast. On Holy Thursday we anchored near the

---

[1] Evidently one of the numerous keys between Xagua Bank and the Isle
of Pines.

[2] Southwestern Cuba.

[3] The westernmost point of the island.

shore in the mouth of a bay [1] at the head of which we saw
some houses or habitations of Indians.[2]

Chapter 3

Our arrival in Florida.

On the same day [3] the comptroller, Alonzo Enrriquez,
landed on an island in the bay. He called to the Indians, who
came and remained with him some time; and in barter gave
him fish and several pieces of venison. The day following,
which was Good Friday,[4] the governor debarked with as many
of the people as the boats he brought could contain. When
we came to the *buhíos*,[5] or houses that we had seen, we found
them vacant and abandoned, the inhabitants having fled at
night in their canoes. One of the buhíos was very large;
it could hold more than three hundred persons. The others
were smaller. We found a tinklet of gold among some fish
nets.

The next day [6] the Governor raised ensigns for your Majesty, and took possession of the country in your royal name.[7]
He made known his authority, and was obeyed as governor,

[1] The place of landing is identified as having been about St. Clement's
Point, on the peninsula west of Tampa Bay, on the western coast of Florida.
See Woodbury Lowery, *Spanish Settlements, 1513–1561* (New York, 1901),
p. 177, and App. J.

[2] These were Indians belonging to the Timuquanan, or Timucuan family,
now entirely extinct. The Seminoles were comparatively recent intruders
in the peninsula, except in the extreme northern part.

[3] April 14, 1528.   [4] April 15, 1528.

[5] An Arawak term for house, referring specifically to a dwelling with an
open shed attached. The Spaniards became acquainted with the word in
Santo Domingo. For descriptions of these habitations see Fewkes, " The
Aborigines of Porto Rico and Neighboring Islands," *Twenty-fifth Annual
Report of the Bureau of American Ethnology*, 1906.

[6] April 16, 1528.

[7] For the interesting if farcical formula used in taking possession of a
country in the name of Spain, see Buckingham Smith, *Relation of Alvar
Nuñez Cabeça de Vaca* (ed. 1871), App. III., 215–217, and Lowery, *op. cit.*.
pp. 178–180.

as your Majesty had commanded. At the same time we laid our commissions before him, and he acknowledged them according to their tenor. Then he ordered that the rest of the people and the horses should land. Of the beasts there were only forty-two; by reason of the great storms and the length of time passed at sea, the rest were dead. These few remaining were so lean and fatigued that for the time we could have little service from them. The following day the Indians of the town came and spoke to us; but as we had no interpreter we could not understand what they meant. They made many signs and menaces, and appeared to say we must go away from the country. With this they left us and went off, offering no interruption.

Chapter 4

Our entrance into the country.

The day following, the Governor resolved to make an incursion to explore the land, and see what it might contain. With him went the commissary, the assessor, and myself, with forty men, among them six cavalry, of which we could make little use. We took our way towards the north,[1] until the hour of vespers, when we arrived at a very large bay that appeared to stretch far inland.[2] We remained there that night, and the next day we returned to the place where were our ships and people. The Governor ordered that the brigantine should sail along the coast of Florida and search for the harbor that Miruelo, the pilot, said he knew (though as yet he had failed to find it, and could not tell in what place we were, or where was the port), and that if it were not found, she should steer for Havana and seek the ship of which Alvaro de la Cerda was in command,[3] and, taking provisions, together, they should come to look for us.

After the brigantine left, the same party, with some persons more, returned to enter the land. We kept along the shores

---

[1] Really northeast.

[2] The western arm of Tampa Bay, known as Old Tampa Bay.

[3] With forty men and a dozen horses.

of the bay we had found, and, having gone four leagues, we captured four Indians. We showed them maize, to see if they had knowledge of it, for up to that time we had seen no indication of any. They said they could take us where there was some; so they brought us to their town near by, at the head of the bay, and showed us a little corn not yet fit for gathering.

There we saw many cases, such as are used to contain the merchandise of Castile, in each of them a dead man, and the bodies were covered with painted deer-skins. This appeared to the commissary to be a kind of idolatry, and he burned the cases with the bodies. We also found pieces of linen and of woollen cloth, and bunches of feathers which appeared like those of New Spain.[1] There were likewise traces of gold. Having by signs asked the Indians whence these things came, they motioned to us that very far from there, was a province called Apalachen,[2] where was much gold, and so the same

[1] In the letter addressed by the survivors to the Audiencia of Santo Domingo (Oviedo, *Historia General y Natural de las Indias*, III., cap. i. 583, Madrid, 1853), it is stated that when the natives were asked whence came these intrusive articles, which included also some pieces of shoes, canvas, broadcloth, and iron, they replied by signs that they had taken them from a vessel that had been wrecked in the bay. Compare also cap. vii. 615. It has been suggested that possibly the objects may have come from the vessel which Lucas Vazquez de Ayllon lost in 1526, but as this wreck occurred at the mouth of Cape Fear River, on the southern coast of North Carolina, it does not seem likely that they could have been derived from this source. That natives of the West Indies had intercourse by canoe with Florida, and that an Arawakan colony was early established on the southwest coast of the peninsula, is now well established.

[2] The Apalachee were one of the Muskhogean tribes that occupied northwestern Florida from the vicinity of Pensacola eastward to Ocilla River, their chief seats being in the vicinity of Tallahassee and St. Marks. In 1655 they numbered six or eight thousand, but about the beginning of the eighteenth century they were warred against by the Creeks, instigated by the English of Carolina, and in 1703 and 1704 expeditions by English troops, reinforced by Creek warriors, resulted in the capture and enslavement of about fourteen hundred Apalachee and in practically exterminating the remainder. The town of Apalachicola, on the Savannah River, was inhabited by Apalachee refugees colonized later by the Carolina government, but these were finally merged with the Creeks. Appalachee Bay and the Appalachian Mountains derive their names from this tribe.

abundance in Palachen[1] of everything that we at all cared for.

Taking these Indians for guides, we departed, and travelling ten or twelve leagues[2] we came to a town of fifteen houses. Here a large piece of ground was cultivated in maize then ripe, and we likewise found some already dry. After staying there two days, we returned to where the comptroller tarried with the men and ships, and related to him and the pilots what we had seen, and the information the natives had given.

The next day, the first of May, the Governor called aside the commissary, the comptroller, the assessor, myself, a sailor named Bartolomé Fernandez, and a notary, Hieronymo Alaniz.[3] Being together he said that he desired to penetrate the interior, and that the ships ought to go along the coast until they should come to the port which the pilots believed was very near on the way to the River Palmas. He asked us for our views.

I said it appeared to me that under no circumstances ought we to leave the vessels until they were in a secure and peopled harbor; that he should observe the pilots were not confident, and did not agree in any particular, neither did they know where we were; that, more than this, the horses were in no condition to serve us in such exigencies as might occur. Above all, that we were going without being able to communicate with the Indians by use of speech and without an interpreter, and we could but poorly understand ourselves with them, or learn what we desired to know of the land; that we were about entering a country of which we had no account, and had no knowledge of its character, of what there was in it, or by what people inhabited, neither did we know in what part of it we were; and beside all this, we had not food to sustain us in

---

[1] "Apalachen," as above, in the edition of 1542 (Bandelier translation).

[2] The Spanish league varied greatly, but in these early narratives the judicial league, equivalent to 2.634 English miles, is usually meant. Distances, however, while sometimes paced, were generally loose guesses, as is often shown by the great disparity in the figures given by two or more chroniclers of the same journey.

[3] "Jerónimo de Albaniz" in the edition of 1542 (Bandelier translation).

wandering we knew not whither; that with regard to the stores in the ships, rations could not be given to each man for such a journey, more than a pound of biscuit and another of bacon; that my opinion was, we should embark and seek a harbor and a soil better than this to occupy, since what we had seen of it was desert and poor, such as had never before been discovered in those parts.

To the commissary[1] every thing appeared otherwise. He thought we ought not to embark; but that, always keeping the coast, we should go in search of the harbor, which the pilots stated was only ten or fifteen leagues from there, on the way to Pánuco; and that it was not possible, marching ever by the shore, we should fail to come upon it, because they said it stretched up into the land a dozen leagues; that whichever might first find it should wait for the other; that to embark would be to brave the Almighty after so many adversities encountered since leaving Spain, so many storms, and so great losses of men and ships sustained before reaching there; that for these reasons we should march along the coast until we reached the harbor, and those in the ships should take a like direction until they arrived at the same place.

This plan seemed the best to adopt, to the rest who were present, except the notary, who said that when the ships should be abandoned they ought to be in a known, safe haven, a place with inhabitants; that this done the Governor might advance inland and do what might seem to him proper.

The Governor followed his own judgment and the counsel of others. Seeing his determination, I required him in behalf of your Majesty, not to quit the ships before putting them in port and making them secure; and accordingly I asked a certificate of this under the hand of the notary. The Governor responded that he did but abide by the judgment of the commissary, and of the majority of the officers, and that I had no right to make these requirements of him. He then asked the notary to give him a certificate, that inasmuch as there was no subsistence in that country for the maintenance of a colony,

---

[1] Fray Juan Xuarez.

nor haven for the ships, he broke up the settlement he had placed there, taking its inhabitants in quest of a port and land that should be better. He then ordered the people who were to go with him to be mustered, that they might be victualled with what was needed for the journey. After they had been provided for, he said to me, in the hearing of those present, that since I so much discouraged and feared entering the land, I should sail in charge of the ships and people in them, and form a settlement, should I arrive at the port before him; but from this proposal I excused myself.

After we had separated, the same evening, having said that it did not appear to him that he could entrust the command to any one else, he sent to me to say that he begged I would take it; but finding, notwithstanding he so greatly importuned me, that I still refused, he asked me the cause of my reluctance. I answered that I rejected the responsibility, as I felt certain and knew that he was never more to find the ships, nor the ships him, which might be foreseen in the slender outfit we had for entering the country; that I desired rather to expose myself to the danger which he and the others adventured, and to pass with them what he and they might go through, than to take charge of the ships and give occasion for it to be said I had opposed the invasion and remained behind from timidity, and thus my courage be called in question. I chose rather to risk my life than put my honor in such position. Seeing that what he said to me availed nothing, he begged many persons to reason with me on the subject and entreat me. I answered them in the same way I had him; so he appointed for his lieutenant of the ships an alcalde he had brought with him, whose name was Caravallo.

Chapter 5

The Governor leaves the ships

On Saturday,[1] first of May, the date of this occurrence, the Governor ordered to each man going with him, two pounds of

---

[1] Buckingham Smith has "Sunday," translating *Sábado* ("Sabbath") literally; the Christian Sabbath is the Spanish *Domingo*.

biscuit and half a pound of bacon; and thus victualled we took up our march into the country. The whole number of men was three hundred:[1] among them went the commissary, Friar Juan Xuarez, and another friar, Juan de Palos, three clergymen and the officers. We of the mounted men consisted of forty. We travelled on the allowance we had received fifteen days, without finding any other thing to eat than palmitos,[2] which are like those of Andalusia. In all that time we saw not an Indian, and found neither village nor house. Finally we came to a river,[3] which we passed with great difficulty, by swimming and on rafts. It detained us a day to cross because of the very strong current. Arrived on the other side, there appeared as many as two hundred natives, more or less. The Governor met them, and conversing by signs, they so insulted us with their gestures, that we were forced to break with them.[4] We seized upon five or six, and they took us to their houses half a league off. Near by we found a large quantity of maize in a fit state to be gathered. We gave infinite thanks to our Lord for having succored us in this great extremity, for we were yet young in trials, and besides the weariness in which we came, we were exhausted from hunger.

On the third day after our arrival, the comptroller, the assessor, the commissary and I met, and together besought the Governor to send to look for the sea, that if possible we might find a port, as the Indians stated there was one not a very great way off. He said that we should cease to speak of the sea, for it was remote; but as I chiefly importuned him, he told me to go and look for it, and seek a harbor, to take forty men and to travel on foot. So the next day[5] I left with Captain

[1] The Letter (Oviedo, 584) says two hundred and sixty men afoot and forty horsemen. References to the Letter to the Audiencia of Santo Domingo will henceforth be cited simply as Oviedo, in whose work it appears (see the Introduction).

[2] Buckingham Smith says: "This is the dwarf fan-palm, not the cabbage-palm, to which we often inadvertently apply the diminutive termination *ito*, mispelled *etto*." Smith lived in Florida for many years.

[3] Evidently the Withlacoochee, which enters the Gulf at latitude 29°.

[4] The Spaniards were still among the Timucuan tribes.

[5] May 18, 1528.

Alonzo del Castello [1] and forty men of his company. We marched until noon, when we arrived at some sea sands that appeared to lie a good ways inland. Along this sand we walked for a league and a half,[2] with the water half way up the leg, treading on oysters, which cut our feet badly and made us much trouble, until we reached the river [3] we had before crossed, emptying into this bay. As we could not cross it by reason of our slim outfit for such purpose, we returned to camp and reported what we had discovered. To find out if there was a port and examine the outlet well, it was necessary to repass the river at the place where we had first gone over; so the next day the Governor ordered a captain, Valençuela by name, with sixty men [4] and six cavalry, to cross, and following the river down to the sea, ascertain if there was a harbor. He returned after an absence of two days, and said he had explored the bay, that it was not deeper any where than to the knee, and that he found no harbor. He had seen five or six canoes of Indians passing from one shore to the other, wearing many plumes.

With this information, we left the next day, going ever in quest of Apalache, the country of which the Indians told us, having for our guides those we had taken. We travelled without seeing any natives who would venture to await our coming up with them until the seventeenth day of June, when a chief approached, borne on the back of another Indian, and covered with a painted deer-skin. A great many people attended him, some walking in advance, playing on flutes of reed.[5] In this manner he came to where the Governor stood, and spent an hour with him. By signs we gave him to understand that we were going to Apalachen, and it appeared to us by those he made that he was an enemy to the people of Apalachen, and would go to assist us against them. We gave him beads and hawk-bells, with other articles of barter; and he having pre-

---

[1] Castillo.   [2] Two leagues, according to Oviedo, *op. cit.*, 585.
[3] The Withlacoochee.   [4] Forty men according to Oviedo, 585.
[5] When Hernando de Soto passed through this country eleven years later he also was met by Indians playing flutes.

sented the Governor with the skin he wore, went back, when we followed in the road he took.

That night we came to a wide and deep river with a very rapid current.[1] As we would not venture to cross on rafts, we made a canoe for the purpose, and spent a day in getting over. Had the Indians desired to oppose us, they could well have disputed our passage; for even with their help we had great difficulty in making it. One of the mounted men, Juan Velazquez by name, a native of Cuellar, impatient of detention, entered the river, when the violence of the current casting him from his horse, he grasped the reins of the bridle, and both were drowned. The people of that chief, whose name was Dulchan- chellin, found the body of the beast; and having told us about where in the stream below we should find the corpse, it was sought for. This death caused us much regret, for until now not a man had been lost. The horse afforded supper to many that night.

Leaving that spot, the next day we arrived at the town of the chief, where he sent us maize. During the night one of our men was shot at in a place where we got water, but it pleased God that he should not be hit. The next day we departed, not one of the natives making his appearance, as all had fled. While going on our way a number came in sight, prepared for battle; and though we called to them, they would not return nor await our arrival, but retired following us on the road. The Governor left some cavalry in ambush, which sallying as the natives were about to pass, seized three or four, who thence- forth served as guides. They conducted us through a country very difficult to travel and wonderful to look upon. In it are vast forests, the trees being astonishingly high. So many were fallen on the ground as to obstruct our way in such a manner that we could not advance without much going about and a considerable increase of toil. Many of the standing trees were riven from top to bottom by bolts of lightning which fall in that country of frequent storms and tempests.

We labored on through these impediments until the day after

[1] The Suwannee.

Saint John's,[1] when we came in view of Apalachen, without the inhabitants being aware of our approach. We gave many thanks to God, at seeing ourselves so near, believing true what had been told us of the land, and that there would be an end to our great hardships, caused as much by the length and badness of the way as by our excessive hunger; for although we sometimes found maize, we oftener travelled seven and eight leagues without seeing any; and besides this and the great fatigue, many had galled shoulders from carrying armor on the back; and even more than these we endured. Yet, having come to the place desired, and where we had been informed were much food and gold, it appeared to us that we had already recovered in part from our sufferings and fatigue.

Chapter 6

Our arrival at Apalache.

When we came in view of Apalachen, the Governor ordered that I should take nine cavalry with fifty infantry and enter the town. Accordingly the assessor [2] and I assailed it; and having got in, we found only women and boys there, the men being absent; however these returned to its support, after a little time, while we were walking about, and began discharging arrows at us. They killed the horse of the assessor, and at last taking to flight, they left us.

We found a large quantity of maize fit for plucking, and much dry that was housed; also many deer-skins, and among them some mantelets of thread, small and poor, with which the women partially cover their persons. There were numerous mortars for cracking maize. The town consisted of forty small houses, made low, and set up in sheltered places because of the frequent storms. The material was thatch. They were sur-

---

[1] Saint John the Baptist's Day, June 24. They had been travelling through the jungle for four or five days.

[2] The assessor, or inspector, it will be recalled, was Alonzo de Solis.

rounded by very dense woods, large groves and many bodies
of fresh water, in which so many and so large trees are fallen,
that they form obstructions rendering travel difficult and dangerous.

Chapter 7

The character of the country.

The country where we came on shore to this town and region of Apalachen is for the most part level, the ground of
sand and stiff earth. Throughout are immense trees and open
woods, in which are walnut, laurel, and another tree called
liquid-amber,[1] cedars, savins, evergreen oaks, pines, red-oaks,
and palmitos like those of Spain. There are many lakes, great
and small, over every part of it; some troublesome of fording,
on account of depth and the great number of trees lying
throughout them. Their beds are sand. The lakes in the
country of Apalachen are much larger than those we found
before coming there.[2]

In this province are many maize fields; and the houses
are scattered as are those of the Gelves. There are deer of
three kinds, rabbits, hares, bears, lions, and other wild beasts.
Among them we saw an animal with a pocket on its belly,[3]
in which it carries its young until they know how to seek food,
and if it happen that they should be out feeding and any one
come near, the mother will not run until she has gathered them
in together. The country is very cold.[4] It has fine pastures
for herds. Birds are of various kinds. Geese in great numbers. Ducks, mallards, royal-ducks, fly-catchers, night-herons

---

[1] The sweet-gum, copalm, or alligator tree (*Liquidambar styraciflua*).

[2] Seemingly the lake country in the northern part of Leon and Jefferson
counties, Florida. "Apalachen" town was perhaps on Miccosukee Lake.

[3] The opossum. This is probably the first allusion to this animal. The
name is derived from the Algonquian language of Virginia, having first been
recorded by Captain John Smith.

[4] As it was now late in June, this is not explicable, unless the season
was an unusual one.

and partridges abound. We saw many falcons, gerfalcons, sparrow-hawks, merlins, and numerous other fowl.[1]

Two hours after our arrival at Apalachen, the Indians who had fled from there came in peace to us, asking for their women and children, whom we released; but the detention of a cacique by the Governor produced great excitement, in consequence of which they returned for battle early the next day, and attacked us with such promptness and alacrity that they succeeded in setting fire to the houses in which we were. As we sallied they fled to the lakes near by, because of which and the large maize fields we could do them no injury, save in the single instance of one Indian, whom we killed. The day following, others came against us from a town on the opposite side of the lake, and attacked us as the first had done, escaping in the same way, except one who was also slain.

We were in the town twenty-five days, in which time we made three incursions, and found the country very thinly peopled and difficult to travel for the bad passages, the woods and lakes. We inquired of the cacique we kept and the natives we brought with us, who were the neighbors and enemies of these Indians, as to the nature of the country, the character and condition of the inhabitants, of the food and all other matters concerning it. Each answered apart from the rest, that the largest town in all that region was Apalachen; the people beyond were less numerous and poorer, the land little occupied, and the inhabitants much scattered; that thenceforward were great lakes, dense forests, immense deserts and solitudes. We then asked touching the region towards the south, as to the towns and subsistence in it. They said that in keeping such a direction, journeying nine days, there was a town called Aute,[2] the inhabitants whereof had much maize, beans, and pumpkins, and being near the sea they had fish, and that those people were their friends.

[1] Buckingham Smith thinks it strange that the turkey and the alligator are not particularly mentioned among the fauna of the region.

[2] Most authorities agree that this place was at or near the site of St. Marks, south-southeast of Tallahassee, although the distance seems too short for nine days' travel, as will be seen.

In view of the poverty of the land, the unfavorable accounts of the population and of everything else we heard, the Indians making continual war upon us, wounding our people and horses at the places where they went to drink, shooting from the lakes with such safety to themselves that we could not retaliate, killing a lord of Tescuco, named Don Pedro,[1] whom the commissary brought with him, we determined to leave that place and go in quest of the sea, and the town of Aute of which we were told.

At the termination of the twenty-five days [2] after our arrival we departed,[3] and on the first day got through those lakes and passages without seeing any one, and on the second day we came to a lake difficult of crossing, the water reaching to the paps, and in it were numerous logs. On reaching the middle of it we were attacked by many Indians from behind trees, who thus covered themselves that we might not get sight of them, and others were on the fallen timbers. They drove their arrows with such effect that they wounded many men and horses, and before we got through the lake they took our guide. They now followed, endeavoring to contest the passage; but our coming out afforded no relief, nor gave us any better position; for when we wished to fight them they retired immediately into the lake, whence they continued to wound our men and beasts. The Governor, seeing this, commanded the cavalry to dismount and charge the Indians on foot. Accordingly the comptroller [4] alighting with the rest, attacked them, when they all turned and ran into the lake at hand, and thus the passage was gained.

Some of our men were wounded in this conflict, for whom the good armor they wore did not avail. There were those this day who swore that they had seen two red oaks, each the thickness of the lower part of the leg, pierced through from side to

---

[1] See Buckingham Smith, *Relation of Alvar Nuñez Cabeça de Vaca*, 1871, p. 42, note 7, regarding this Aztec prince of the blood.

[2] "Twenty-six days." Oviedo, 586. The edition of 1542 (Bandelier trans., p. 30) says: "And so we left, arriving there five days after. The first day we travelled across lagunes and trails without seeing a single Indian."

[3] July 19–20, 1528.   [4] Alonzo Enrriquez.

side by arrows; and this is not so much to be wondered at, considering the power and skill with which the Indians are able to project them. I myself saw an arrow that had entered the butt of an elm to the depth of a span.

The Indians we had so far seen in Florida are all archers. They go naked, are large of body, and appear at a distance like giants. They are of admirable proportions, very spare and of great activity and strength. The bows they use are as thick as the arm, of eleven or twelve palms in length, which they will discharge at two hundred paces with so great precision that they miss nothing.

Having got through this passage, at the end of a league we arrived at another of the same character, but worse, as it was longer, being half a league in extent. This we crossed freely, without interruption from the Indians, who, as they had spent on the former occasion their store of arrows, had nought with which they dared venture to engage us. Going through a similar passage the next day, I discovered the trail of persons ahead, of which I gave notice to the Governor, who was in the rear-guard, so that though the Indians came upon us, as we were prepared they did no harm. After emerging upon the plain they followed us, and we went back on them in two directions. Two we killed, and they wounded me and two or three others. Coming to woods we could do them no more injury, nor make them further trouble.

In this manner we travelled eight days. After that occurrence we were not again beset until within a league of the place to which I have said we were going. There, while on our way, the Indians came about us without our suspicion, and fell upon the rear-guard. A hidalgo, named Avellaneda, hearing the cries of his serving boy, went back to give assistance, when he was struck by an arrow near the edge of his cuirass; and so severe was the wound, the shaft having passed almost entirely through his neck, that he presently died. The corpse was carried to Aute, where we arrived at the end of nine days'[1] travel from Apalache. We found all the inhabitants gone and

---

[1] "Eight or nine days." Oviedo, 587.

the houses burned. Maize, beans, and pumpkins were in great plenty, all beginning to be fit for gathering. Having rested two days, the Governor begged me to go and look for the sea, as the Indians said it was near; and we had before discovered it, while on the way, from a very large stream, to which we had given the name of River of the Magdalena.[1]

Accordingly, I set out the next day after, in company with the commissary, Captain Castillo, Andrés Dorantes, seven more on horseback, and fifty on foot. We travelled until the hour of vespers, when we arrived at a road or entrance of the sea. Oysters were abundant, over which the men rejoiced, and we gave thanks to God that he had brought us there. The following morning [2] I sent twenty men to explore the coast and ascertain its direction. They returned the night after, reporting that those creeks and bays were large, and lay so far inland as made it difficult to examine them agreeably to our desires, and that the sea shore was very distant.

These tidings obtained, seeing our slender means, and condition for exploring the coast, I went back to the Governor. On our arrival we found him and many others sick. The Indians had assaulted them the night before, and because of the malady that had come upon them, they had been pushed to extremity. One of the horses had been killed. I gave a report of what I had done, and of the embarrassing nature of the country. We remained there that day.

Chapter 8

We go from Aute.

The next morning [3] we left Aute, and travelled all day before coming to the place I had visited. The journey was extremely arduous. There were not horses enough to carry the sick, who went on increasing in numbers day by day, and we

---

[1] St. Marks River, which flows into St. Marks Bay, at the head of which Aute was situated.

[2] August 1, 1528. [3] August 3, 1528.

knew of no cure. It was piteous and painful to witness our perplexity and distress. We saw on our arrival how small were the means for advancing farther. There was not anywhere to go; and if there had been, the people were unable to move forward, the greater part being ill, and those were few who could be on duty. I cease here to relate more of this, because any one may suppose what would occur in a country so remote and malign, so destitute of all resource, whereby either to live in it or go out of it; but most certain assistance is in God, our Lord, on whom we never failed to place reliance. One thing occurred, more afflicting to us than all the rest, which was, that of the persons mounted, the greater part commenced secretly to plot, hoping to secure a better fate for themselves by abandoning the Governor and the sick, who were in a state of weakness and prostration. But, as among them were many hidalgos and persons of gentle condition, they would not permit this to go on, without informing the Governor and the officers of your Majesty; and as we showed them the deformity of their purpose, and placed before them the moment when they should desert their captain, and those who were ill and feeble, and above all the disobedience to the orders of your Majesty, they determined to remain, and that whatever might happen to one should be the lot of all, without any forsaking the rest.

After the accomplishment of this, the Governor called them all to him, and of each apart he asked advice as to what he should do to get out of a country so miserable, and seek that assistance elsewhere which could not here be found, a third part of the people being very sick, and the number increasing every hour; for we regarded it as certain that we should all become so, and could pass out of it only through death, which from its coming in such a place was to us all the more terrible. These, with many other embarrassments being considered, and entertaining many plans, we coincided in one great project extremely difficult to put in operation, and that was to build vessels in which we might go away. This appeared impossible to every one; we knew not how to construct, nor were there tools, nor iron, nor forge, nor tow, nor resin, nor rigging; finally, no one thing of so many that are necessary, nor any man who had a knowledge of their manufacture; and, above all, there was nothing to eat, while building, for those who should labor. Reflecting on all this, we agreed to think of the subject with more deliberation, and the conversation dropped from that day, each going his way, commending our course to God, our Lord, that he would direct it as should best serve Him.

The next day it was His will that one of the company should come saying that he could make some pipes out of wood, which with deer-skins might be made into bellows; and, as we lived in a time when anything that had the semblance of relief appeared well, we told him to set himself to work. We assented to the making of nails, saws, axes, and other tools of which there was such need, from the stirrups, spurs, crossbows, and the other things of iron there were; and we laid out for support, while the work was going on, that we would make four entries into Aute, with all the horses and men that were able to go, and that on every third day a horse should be killed to be divided among those who labored in the work of the boats and the sick. The incursions were made with the people and horses that were available, and in them were brought back as many as four hundred fanegas[1] of maize; but these were not got without quarrels and contentions with the Indians. We caused many palmitos to be collected for the woof or covering, twisting and preparing it for use in the place of tow for the boats.

We commenced to build on the fourth, with the only carpenter in the company, and we proceeded with so great diligence that on the twentieth day of September five boats were finished, twenty-two cubits in length, each caulked with the fibre of the palmito. We pitched them with a certain resin, made from pine trees by a Greek, named Don Theodoro; from the same husk of the palmito, and from the tails and manes of the horses we made ropes and rigging, from our shirts, sails,

---

[1] About six hundred and forty bushels.

and from the savins growing there we made the oars that
appeared to us requisite. Such was the country into which
our sins had cast us, that only by very great search could we
find stone for ballast and anchors, since in it all we had not seen
one. We flayed the horses, taking the skin from their legs
entire, and tanning them to make bottles wherein to carry
water.

During this time some went gathering shell-fish in the coves
and creeks of the sea, at which employment the Indians twice
attacked them and killed ten men in sight of the camp, without our being able to afford succor. We found their corpses
traversed from side to side with arrows; and for all some had
on good armor, it did not give adequate protection or security
against the nice and powerful archery of which I have spoken.
According to the declaration of our pilots under oath, from the
entrance to which we had given the name Bahía de la Cruz[1]
to this place, we had travelled two hundred and eighty leagues[2]
or thereabout. Over all that region we had not seen a single
mountain, and had no information of any whatsoever.

Before we embarked there died more than forty men of disease and hunger, without enumerating those destroyed by the
Indians. By the twenty-second of the month of September,
the horses had been consumed, one only remaining; and on
that day we embarked in the following order: In the boat of
the Governor went forty-nine men; in another, which he gave
to the comptroller and the commissary, went as many others;
the third, he gave to Captain Alonzo del Castillo and Andrés
Dorantes, with forty-eight men; and another he gave to two
captains, Tellez and Peñalosa, with forty-seven men. The
last was given to the assessor and myself, with forty-nine men.
After the provisions and clothes had been taken in, not over
a span of the gunwales remained above water; and more than
this, the boats were so crowded that we could not move:
so much can necessity do, which drove us to hazard our lives

---

[1] Tampa Bay.
[2] In reality they could not have travelled much more than as many miles
in a straight line from Tampa Bay.

in this manner, running into a turbulent sea, not a single one who went having a knowledge of navigation.[1]

Chapter 9

We leave the Bay of Horses.

The haven we left bears the name of Bahía de Caballos.[2] We passed waist deep in water through sounds without seeing any sign of the coast, and at the close of the seventh day, we came to an island near the main. My boat went first, and from her we saw Indians approaching in five canoes, which they abandoned and left in our hands, finding that we were coming after them. The other boats passed ahead, and stopped at some houses on the island, where we found many dried mullet and roes, which were a great relief in our distress. After taking these we went on, and two leagues thence, we discovered a strait the island makes with the land,[3] which we named Sant Miguel, for having passed through it on his day.[4] Coming out we went to the coast, where with the canoes I had taken, we somewhat improved the boats, making waist-boards and securing them, so that the sides rose two palms above the water. This done we returned to move along the coast in the direction of the River Palmas,[5] our hunger and thirst continually increasing; for our scant subsistence was getting near the end, the water was out, and the bottles made from the legs of the horses having soon rotted, were useless. Sometimes we entered coves and creeks that lay far in, and found them all shallow and dangerous. Thus we journeyed along them thirty days,

---

[1] Consult Garcilasso de la Vega, *La Florida*, 78, 1723, for the finding of the relics of Narvaez by De Soto's expedition in 1539, and see the De Soto narration of the Gentleman of Elvas, later in the present volume.

[2] "Bay of Horses": St. Marks Bay of Appalachee Bay.

[3] The conditions are applicable to the mouth of St. Marks Bay, the two small islands, and the strait between them and the coast.

[4] St. Michael's Day, September 29, 1528.

[5] That is, in a southwesterly direction.

finding occasionally Indian fishermen, a poor and miserable lot.

At the end of this time, while the want of water was great, going near the coast at night we heard the approach of a canoe, for which, so soon as it was in sight, we paused; but it would not meet us, and, although we called, it would neither come nor wait for us. As the night was dark, we did not follow, and kept on our way. When the sun rose we saw a small island, and went to it to find water; but our labor was vain, as it had none. Lying there at anchor, a heavy storm came on, that detained us six days, we not daring to go to sea; and as it was now five days since we had drunk, our thirst was so excessive that it put us to the extremity of swallowing salt water, by which some of the men became so crazed that three or four suddenly died. I state this so briefly, because I do not believe there is any necessity for particularly relating the sufferings and toils amidst which we found ourselves; since, considering the place where we were, and the little hope we had of relief, every one may conceive much of what must have passed.

Although the storm had not ceased, as our thirst increased and the water killed us, we resolved to commend ourselves to God our Lord, and adventure the peril of the sea rather than await the end which thirst made certain. Accordingly we went out by the way we had observed the canoe go the night we came. On this day we were ourselves many times overwhelmed by the waves, and in such jeopardy that there was not one who did not suppose his death inevitable. Thanks be to Him, that in the greatest dangers, He was wont to show us his favor; for at sunset doubling a point made by the land, we found shelter with much calm.[1]

Many canoes came off with Indians who spoke with us and returned, not being disposed to await our arrival. They were of large stature and well formed: they had no bows and arrows. We followed them to their houses near by, at the edge of the water, and jumped on shore. Before their dwellings were many clay pitchers with water, and a large quantity of cooked fish,

[1] Pensacola Bay. The Indians were Choctaws or a closely related tribe.

which the chief of these territories offered to the Governor and then took him to his house. Their dwellings were made of mats, and so far as we observed, were not movable. On entering the house the cacique gave us fish, and we gave him of the maize we brought, which the people ate in our presence. They asked for more and received it, and the Governor presented the cacique with many trinkets. While in the house with him, at the middle hour of night, the Indians fell suddenly upon us, and on those who were very sick, scattered along the shore.[1] They also beset the house in which the Governor was, and with a stone struck him in the face. Those of our comrades present seized the cacique; but his people being near liberated him, leaving in our hands a robe of civet-marten.

These skins are the best, I think, that can be found; they have a fragrance that can be equalled by amber and musk alone, and even at a distance is strongly perceptible. We saw there other skins, but none comparable to these.

Those of us around, finding the Governor wounded, put him into his boat; and we caused others of our people to betake themselves likewise to their boats, some fifty remaining to withstand the natives. They attacked us thrice that night, and with so great impetuosity, that on each occasion they made us retire more than a stone's cast. Not one among us escaped injury: I was wounded in the face. They had not many arrows, but had they been further provided, doubtless they would have done us much harm. In the last onset, the Captains Dorantes, Peñalosa, and Tellez put themselves in ambuscade with fifteen men, and fell upon the rear in such manner that the Indians desisted and fled.

The next morning [2] I broke up more than thirty canoes, which were serviceable for fuel in a north wind in which we were kept all day suffering severe cold, without daring to go to sea, because of the rough weather upon it. This having subsided, we again embarked, and navigated three days.[3] As we brought little water and the vessels were few, we were reduced to the

---

[1] "Killing three men." Oviedo, p. 589.   [2] October 28, 1528.
[3] "Three or four days." Oviedo, p. 589.

last extremity. Following our course, we entered an estuary, and being there we saw Indians approaching in a canoe. We called to them and they came. The Governor, at whose boat they first arrived, asked for water, which they assented to give, asking for something in which they might bring it, when Dorotheo Theodoro, a Greek spoken of before, said that he wished to go with them. The Governor tried to dissuade him, and so did others, but were unable; he was determined to go whatever might betide. Accordingly he went, taking with him a negro, the natives leaving two of their number as hostages. At night the Indians returned with the vessels empty and without the Christians; and when those we held were spoken to by them, they tried to plunge into the sea. Being detained by the men, the Indians in the canoe thereupon fled, leaving us sorrowful and much dejected for our loss.[1]

Chapter 10

The assault from the Indians.

The morning having come, many natives arrived in canoes who asked us for the two that had remained in the boat. The Governor replied that he would give up the hostages when they should bring the Christians they had taken. With the Indians had come five or six chiefs,[2] who appeared to us to be the most comely persons, and of more authority and condition than any we had hitherto seen, although not so large as some others of whom we have spoken. They wore the hair loose and very long, and were covered with robes of marten such as we had before taken. Some of the robes were made up after a strange fashion, with wrought ties of lion skin, making a brave

[1] Biedma's Narrative (*Publications of the Hakluyt Society*, IX. 1–83, 1851) says of the De Soto expedition in 1539: "Having set out for this village [Mavila, Mauvila, Mobile], we found a large river which we supposed to be that which falls into the bay of Chuse [Pensacola Bay]; we learned that the vessels of Narvaez had arrived there in want of water, and that a Christian named Teodoro and an Indian had remained among these Indians: at the same time they showed us a dagger which had belonged to the Christian."

[2] "Three or four," according to the Letter (Oviedo, p. 589), which also gives the number of canoes as twenty.

show. They entreated us to go with them, and said they would give us the Christians, water, and many other things. They continued to collect about us in canoes, attempting in them to take possession of the mouth of that entrance; in consequence, and because it was hazardous to stay near the land, we went to sea, where they remained by us until about mid-day. As they would not deliver our people, we would not give up theirs; so they began to hurl clubs at us and to throw stones with slings, making threats of shooting arrows, although we had not seen among them all more than three or four bows. While thus engaged, the wind beginning to freshen, they left us and went back.

We sailed that day until the middle of the afternoon, when my boat, which was the first, discovered a point made by the land, and against a cape opposite, passed a broad river.[1] I cast anchor near a little island forming the point, to await the arrival of the other boats. The Governor did not choose to come up, and entered a bay near by in which were a great many islets. We came together there, and took fresh water from the sea, the stream entering it in freshet.[2] To parch some of the maize we brought with us, since we had eaten it raw for two days, we went on an island; but finding no wood we agreed to go to the river beyond the point, one league off. By no effort could we get there, so violent was the current on the way, which drove us out, while we contended and strove to gain the land. The north wind, which came from the shore, began to blow so strongly that it forced us to sea without our being able to overcome it. We sounded half a league out, and found with thirty fathoms[3] we could not get bottom; but we were unable to satisfy ourselves that the current was not the cause of failure. Toiling in this manner to fetch the land, we navigated three days, and at the end of this time, a little

---

[1] According to the Letter they travelled two days more before reaching this point of land.

[2] The Mississippi, the waters of which were now seen by white men fourteen years before the "discovery" of the stream by De Soto.

[3] The present normal depth at this distance from the delta is about sixty feet.

before the sun rose, we saw smoke in several places along the shore. Attempting to reach them, we found ourselves in three fathoms of water, and in the darkness we dared not come to land; for as we had seen so many smokes, some surprise might lie in wait, and the obscurity leave us at a loss how to act. We determined therefore to stop until morning.

When day came, the boats had lost sight of each other. I found myself in thirty fathoms. Keeping my course until the hour of vespers, I observed two boats, and drawing near I found that the first I approached was that of the Governor. He asked me what I thought we should do. I told him we ought to join the boat which went in advance, and by no means to leave her; and, the three being together, we must keep on our way to where God should be pleased to lead. He answered saying that could not be done, because the boat was far to sea and he wished to reach the shore; that if I wished to follow him, I should order the persons of my boat to take the oars and work, as it was only by strength of arm that the land could be gained. He was advised to this course by a captain with him named Pantoja, who said that if he did not fetch land that day, in six days more they would not reach it, and in that time they must inevitably famish. Discovering his will I took my oar, and so did every one his, in my boat, to obey it. We rowed until near sunset; but the Governor having in his boat the healthiest of all the men, we could not by any means hold with or follow her. Seeing this, I asked him to give me a rope from his boat, that I might be enabled to keep up with him; but he answered me that he would do much, if they, as they were, should be able to reach the land that night. I said to him, that since he saw the feeble strength we had to follow him, and do what he ordered, he must tell me how he would that I should act. He answered that it was no longer a time in which one should command another; but that each should do what he thought best to save his own life; that he so intended to act; and saying this, he departed with his boat.[1]

---

[1] The selfishness and incompetence of Narvaez, shown throughout the narration, are here further exemplified. His life had more than once been

As I could not follow him, I steered to the other boat at sea, which waited for me, and having come up, I found her to be the one commanded by the Captains Peñalosa and Tellez.

Thus we continued in company, eating a daily allowance of half a handful of raw maize, until the end of four days, when we lost sight of each other in a storm; and such was the weather that only by God's favor we did not all go down. Because of winter and its inclemency, the many days we had suffered hunger, and the heavy beating of the waves, the people began next day to despair in such a manner that when the sun sank, all who were in my boat were fallen one on another, so near to death that there were few among them in a state of sensibility. Of the whole number at this time not five men were on their feet; and when night came, only the master and myself were left, who could work the boat. Two hours after dark, he said to me that I must take charge of her as he was in such condition he believed he should die that night. So I took the paddle, and going after midnight to see if the master was alive he said to me he was rather better, and would take the charge until day. I declare in that hour I would more willingly have died than seen so many people before me in such condition. After the master took the direction of the boat, I lay down a little while; but without repose, for nothing at that time was farther from me than sleep.

Near the dawn of day, it seemed to me I heard the tumbling of the sea; for as the coast was low, it roared loudly. Surprised at this, I called to the master, who answered me that he believed we were near the land. We sounded and found ourselves in seven fathoms. He advised that we should keep to sea until sunrise; accordingly I took an oar and pulled on the land side, until we were a league distant, when we gave her stern to the sea. Near the shore a wave took us, that knocked the boat out of water the distance of the throw of a

spared through the self-sacrifice of his men, yet he now thought more of saving himself, with the aid of his hardy crew, than of lending a hand to his weakened companions.

crowbar,[1] and from the violence with which she struck, nearly all the people who were in her like dead, were roused to consciousness. Finding themselves near the shore, they began to move on hands and feet, crawling to land into some ravines. There we made fire, parched some of the maize we brought, and found rain water. From the warmth of the fire the people recovered their faculties, and began somewhat to exert themselves. The day on which we arrived was the sixth of November [1528].

Chapter 11

Of what befell Lope de Oviedo with the Indians.

After the people had eaten, I ordered Lope de Oviedo, who had more strength and was stouter than any of the rest, to go to some trees that were near by, and climbing into one of them to look about and try to gain knowledge of the country. He did as I bade, and made out that we were on an island.[2] He saw that the land was pawed up in the manner that ground is wont to be where cattle range, whence it appeared to him that this should be a country of Christians; and thus he reported to us. I ordered him to return and examine much more particularly, and see if there were any roads that were worn, but without going far, because there might be danger.

He went, and coming to a path, took it for the distance of half a league, and found some huts, without tenants, they having gone into the field.[3] He took from these an earthen pot, a little dog, some few mullets, and returned. As it appeared to us he was gone a long time, we sent two men that they should look to see what might have happened. They met him near by, and saw that three Indians with bows and ar-

---

[1] *Juego de herradura*, a game played with an iron bar, often a crowbar, which is grasped at the middle and cast as far as possible.

[2] See p. 57, note 2.

[3] As this was the root-digging season, the word *campo* in the original evidently refers to the digging "grounds" in the shoal water, and not to "woods" as Mr. Smith interpreted it.

rows followed and were calling to him, while he, in the same
way, was beckoning them on. Thus he arrived where we
were, the natives remaining a little way back, seated on the
shore. Half an hour after, they were supported by one hundred other Indian bowmen,[1] who if they were not large, our
fears made giants of them. They stopped near us with the
first three. It were idle to think that any among us could
make defence, for it would have been difficult to find six that
could rise from the ground. The assessor and I went out and
called to them, and they came to us. We endeavored the best
we could to encourage them and secure their favor. We gave
them beads and hawk-bells, and each of them gave me an
arrow, which is a pledge of friendship. They told us by signs
that they would return in the morning and bring us something
to eat, as at that time they had nothing.[2]

Chapter 12

The Indians bring us food.

At sunrise the next day, the time the Indians appointed,
they came according to their promise, and brought us a large
quantity of fish with certain roots, some a little larger than walnuts, others a trifle smaller, the greater part got from under
the water and with much labor. In the evening they returned and brought us more fish and roots. They sent their
women and children to look at us, who went back rich with
the hawk-bells and beads given them, and they came afterwards on other days, returning as before. Finding that we
had provision, fish, roots, water, and other things we asked
for, we determined to embark again and pursue our course.
Having dug out our boat from the sand in which it was buried,
it became necessary that we should strip, and go through

---

[1] "Two hundred archers with holes in their ears in which were joints
of cane." Oviedo, p. 590.

[2] For an account of these Indians, see ch. 14, p. 50, 51.

great exertion to launch her, we being in such a state that things very much lighter sufficed to make us great labor.

Thus embarked, at the distance of two crossbow shots in the sea we shipped a wave that entirely wet us. As we were naked, and the cold was very great, the oars loosened in our hands, and the next blow the sea struck us, capsized the boat. The assessor [1] and two others held fast to her for preservation, but it happened to be far otherwise; the boat carried them over, and they were drowned under her. As the surf near the shore was very high, a single roll of the sea threw the rest into the waves and half drowned upon the shore of the island, without our losing any more than those the boat took down. The survivors escaped naked as they were born, with the loss of all they had; and although the whole was of little value, at that time it was worth much, as we were then in November, the cold was severe, and our bodies were so emaciated the bones might be counted with little difficulty, having become the perfect figures of death. For myself I can say that from the month of May passed, I had eaten no other thing than maize, and sometimes I found myself obliged to eat it unparched; for although the beasts were slaughtered while the boats were building, I could never eat their flesh, and I did not eat fish ten times. I state this to avoid giving excuses, and that every one may judge in what condition we were. Besides all these misfortunes, came a north wind upon us, from which we were nearer to death than life. Thanks be to our Lord that, looking among the brands we had used there, we found sparks from which we made great fires. And thus were we asking mercy of Him and pardon for our transgressions, shedding many tears, and each regretting not his own fate alone, but that of his comrades about him.

At sunset, the Indians thinking that we had not gone, came to seek us and bring us food; but when they saw us thus, in a plight so different from what it was before, and so extraordinary, they were alarmed and turned back. I went toward them and called, when they returned much frightened.

[1] Alonzo de Solis.

I gave them to understand by signs that our boat had sunk and three of our number had been drowned. There, before them, they saw two of the departed, and we who remained were near joining them. The Indians, at sight of what had befallen us, and our state of suffering and melancholy destitution, sat down among us, and from the sorrow and pity they felt, they all began to lament so earnestly that they might have been heard at a distance, and continued so doing more than half an hour. It was strange to see these men, wild and untaught, howling like brutes over our misfortunes. It caused in me as in others, an increase of feeling and a livelier sense of our calamity.

The cries having ceased, I talked with the Christians, and said that if it appeared well to them, I would beg these Indians to take us to their houses. Some, who had been in New Spain, replied that we ought not to think of it; for if they should do so, they would sacrifice us to their idols. But seeing no better course, and that any other led to a nearer and more certain death, I disregarded what was said, and besought the Indians to take us to their dwellings. They signified that it would give them delight, and that we should tarry a little, that they might do what we asked. Presently thirty men loaded themselves with wood and started for their houses, which were far off,[1] and we remained with the others until near night, when, holding us up, they carried us with all haste. Because of the extreme coldness of the weather, lest any one should die or fail by the way, they caused four or five very large fires to be placed at intervals, and at each they warmed us; and when they saw that we had regained some heat and strength, they took us to the next so swiftly that they hardly let us touch our feet to the ground. In this manner we went as far as their habitations, where we found that they had made a house for us with many fires in it. An hour after our arrival, they

---

[1] As he does not speak of crossing water, the dwellings of these Indians were doubtless those seen by Lope de Oviedo on the island, where they lived from October until March, for the purpose of obtaining the roots from the shoal water, as well as fish and oysters.

began to dance and hold great rejoicing, which lasted all
night, although for us there was no joy, festivity nor sleep,
awaiting the hour they should make us victims. In the morning they again gave us fish and roots, showing us such hospitality that we were reassured, and lost somewhat the fear of
sacrifice.

Chapter 13

We hear of other Christians.

This day I saw a native with an article of traffic I knew
was not one we had bestowed; and asking whence it came, I
was told by signs that it had been given by men like ourselves
who were behind. Hearing this I sent two Indians, and with
them two Christians to be shown those persons. They met
near by,[1] as the men were coming to look after us; for the
Indians of the place where they were, gave them information
concerning us. They were Captains Andrés Dorantes and
Alonzo del Castillo, with all the persons of their boat. Having
come up they were surprised at seeing us in the condition we
were, and very much pained at having nothing to give us, as
they had brought no other clothes than what they had on.

Thus together again, they related that on the fifth day of
that month,[2] their boat had capsized a league and a half [3] from
there, and they escaped without losing any thing. We all
agreed to refit their [our] boat, that those of us might go in
her who had vigor sufficient and disposition to do so, and the
rest should remain until they became well enough to go, as
they best might, along the coast until God our Lord should
be pleased to conduct us alike to a land of Christians. Directly as we arranged this, we set ourselves to work. Before
we threw the boat out into the water, Tavera, a gentleman of

---

[1] This would seem to indicate that Dorantes' boat was cast ashore on the
same island.

[2] November, 1528.   Dorantes' boat was therefore cast ashore the day
before the landing of Cabeza de Vaca's party.

[3] About four miies.

our company, died; and the boat, which we thought to use, came to its end, sinking from unfitness to float.

As we were in the condition I have mentioned, the greater number of us naked, and the weather boisterous for travel, and to cross rivers and bays by swimming, and we being entirely without provisions or the means of carrying any, we yielded obedience to what necessity required, to pass the winter in the place where we were. We also agreed that four men of the most robust should go on to Panunco,[1] which we believed to be near, and if, by Divine favor, they should reach there, they could give information of our remaining on that island, and of our sorrows and destitution. These men were excellent swimmers. One of them was Alvaro Fernandez, a Portuguese sailor and carpenter, the second was named Mendez, the third Figueroa, who was a native of Toledo, and the fourth Astudillo, a native of Çafra. They took with them an Indian of the island of Auia.[2]

Chapter 14

The departure of four Christians.

The four Christians being gone, after a few days such cold and tempestuous weather succeeded that the Indians could not pull up roots, the cane weirs in which they took fish no longer yielded any thing, and the houses being very open, our people began to die. Five Christians, of a mess [quartered] on the coast, came to such extremity that they ate their dead; the body of the last one only was found unconsumed. Their names were Sierra, Diego Lopez, Corral, Palacios and Gonçalo Ruiz. This produced great commotion among the Indians

[1] Pánuco, previously referred to.

[2] The edition of 1542 omits the last two words. *Auia* has been regarded as the native name of Malhado Island, but this is seemingly an error, otherwise Cabeza de Vaca would in all probability have mentioned the nativity of the Indian in later speaking (ch. 17) of his death from cold and hunger. Herrera says: "the island of Cuba," which seems more probable.

giving rise to so much censure that had they known it in season to have done so, doubtless they would have destroyed any survivor, and we should have found ourselves in the utmost perplexity. Finally, of eighty men who arrived in the two instances, fifteen only remained alive.

After this, the natives were visited by a disease of the bowels, of which half their number died. They conceived that we had destroyed them,[1] and believing it firmly, they concerted among themselves to dispatch those of us who survived. When they were about to execute their purpose, an Indian who had charge of me, told them not to believe we were the cause of those deaths, since if we had such power we should also have averted the fatality from so many of our people, whom they had seen die without our being able to minister relief, already very few of us remaining, and none doing hurt or wrong, and that it would be better to leave us unharmed. God our Lord willed that the others should heed this opinion and counsel, and be hindered in their design.

To this island we gave the name Malhado.[2] The people[3] we found there are large and well formed; they have no other arms than bows and arrows, in the use of which they are very dexterous. The men have one of their nipples bored from side to side, and some have both, wearing a cane in each, the length of two palms and a half, and the thickness of two fingers. They have the under lip also bored, and wear in it a piece of cane the breadth of half a finger. Their women are accustomed to great toil. The stay they make on the island is from October to the end of February. Their subsistence then is the root I have spoken of, got from under the water in November and December. They have weirs of cane and take fish only in this season; afterwards they live on the roots. At the end of February, they go into other parts to seek food; for then the root is beginning to grow and is not food.

Those people love their offspring the most of any in the

---

[1] That is, the Indians believed the Christians to be sorcerers.

[2] "Misfortune," "ill-fate."

[3] The Capoques, or Cahoques, and the Hans. See ch. 26.

world, and treat them with the greatest mildness.[1] When it occurs that a son dies, the parents and kindred weep as does everybody; the wailing continuing for him a whole year. They begin before dawn every day, the parents first and after them the whole town. They do the same at noon and at sunset. After a year of mourning has passed, the rites of the dead are performed; then they wash and purify themselves from the stain of smoke. They lament all the deceased in this manner, except the aged, for whom they show no regret, as they say that their season has passed, they having no enjoyment, and that living they would occupy the earth and take aliment from the young. Their custom is to bury the dead, unless it be those among them who have been physicians. These they burn. While the fire kindles they are all dancing and making high festivity, until the bones become powder. After the lapse of a year the funeral honors are celebrated, every one taking part in them, when that dust is presented in water for the relatives to drink.[2]

Every man has an acknowledged wife. The physicians are allowed more freedom: they may have two or three wives, among whom exist the greatest friendship and harmony. From the time a daughter marries, all that he who takes her to wife kills in hunting or catches in fishing, the woman brings to the house of her father, without daring to eat or take any part of it, and thence victuals are taken to the husband. From that time neither her father nor mother enters his house, nor can he enter theirs, nor the houses of their children; and if by chance they are in the direction of meeting, they turn aside, and pass the distance of a crossbow shot from each other, carrying the head low the while, the eyes cast on the ground; for they hold it improper to see or to speak to

[1] This is characteristic of all Indians, who punish their children very rarely.

[2] Nevertheless these same people were so horrified by the uncanny action of the Spaniards who ate their dead companions that they sought to put them to death. It should be noted that the Attacapan and probably the Karankawan tribes of the Texas coast, to which the people of Malhado Island may have belonged, were reputed to be cannibals.

each other.[1] But the woman has liberty to converse and communicate with the parents and relatives of her husband. The custom exists from this island the distance of more than fifty leagues inland.

There is another custom, which is, when a son or brother dies, at the house where the death takes place they do not go after food for three months, but sooner famish, their relatives and neighbors providing what they eat. As in the time we were there a great number of the natives died, in most houses there was very great hunger, because of the keeping of this their custom and observance; for although they who sought after food worked hard, yet from the severity of the season they could get but little; in consequence, the Indians who kept me, left the island, and passed over in canoes to the main, into some bays where are many oysters. For three months in the year they eat nothing besides these, and drink very bad water.[2] There is great want of wood: mosquitos are in great plenty. The houses are of mats, set up on masses of oyster shells, which they sleep upon, and in skins, should they accidentally possess them. In this way we lived until April [1529], when we went to the seashore, where we ate blackberries all the month, during which time the Indians did not omit to observe their *areitos* [3] and festivities.

Chapter 15

What befell us among the people of Malhado.

On an island of which I have spoken, they wished to make us physicians without examination or inquiring for diplomas. They cure by blowing upon the sick, and with that breath and

---

[1] Tabu of the mother-in-law by a young man is quite common among the Indians, but refusal to see or to speak to the wife's father is very rare.

[2] On their food, compare Oviedo, p. 592.

[3] An *areito*, or *areyto*, was a dance ceremony of the Arawak Indians of the West Indies in which their traditions were recounted in chants. Like *buhío*, previously mentioned, the word was now carried to the continent.

the imposing of hands they cast out infirmity. They ordered that we also should do this, and be of use to them in some way. We laughed at what they did, telling them it was folly, that we knew not how to heal. In consequence, they withheld food from us until we should practise what they required. Seeing our persistence, an Indian told me I knew not what I uttered, in saying that what he knew availed nothing; for stones and other matters growing about in the fields have virtue, and that passing a pebble along the stomach would take away pain and restore health, and certainly then we who were extraordinary men must possess power and efficacy over all other things. At last, finding ourselves in great want we were constrained to obey; but without fear lest we should be blamed for any failure or success.

Their custom is, on finding themselves sick to send for a physician, and after he has applied the cure, they give him not only all they have, but seek among their relatives for more to give. The practitioner scarifies over the seat of pain, and then sucks about the wound. They make cauteries with fire, a remedy among them in high repute, which I have tried on myself and found benefit from it. They afterwards blow on the spot, and having finished, the patient considers that he is relieved.

Our method was to bless the sick, breathing upon them, and recite a Pater-noster and an Ave-Maria, praying with all earnestness to God our Lord that he would give health and influence them to make us some good return. In his clemency he willed that all those for whom we supplicated, should tell the others that they were sound and in health, directly after we made the sign of the blessed cross over them. For this the Indians treated us kindly; they deprived themselves of food that they might give to us, and presented us with skins and some trifles.

So protracted was the hunger we there experienced, that many times I was three days without eating. The natives also endured as much; and it appeared to me a thing impossible that life could be so prolonged, although afterwards I found myself in greater hunger and necessity, which I shall speak of farther on.

The Indians who had Alonzo del Castillo, Andrés Dorantes, and the others that remained alive, were of a different tongue and ancestry from these,[1] and went to the opposite shore of the main to eat oysters, where they staid until the first day of April, when they returned. The distance is two leagues in the widest part. The island is half a league in breadth and five leagues in length.[2]

The inhabitants of all this region go naked. The women alone have any part of their persons covered, and it is with a wool [3] that grows on trees. The damsels dress themselves in deer-skin. The people are generous to each other of what they possess. They have no chief. All that are of a lineage keep together. They speak two languages; those of one are called Capoques, those of the other, Han.[4] They have a custom when they meet, or from time to time when they visit, of remaining half an hour before they speak, weeping; [5] and, this over, he that is visited first rises and gives the other all he has, which is received, and after a little while he carries it away, and often goes without saying a word. They have

---

[1] These were evidently the Hans, of whom he speaks later.
[2] See p. 57, note 2.   [3] Spanish moss.

[4] Important as it is in affording evidence of the route of Cabeza de Vaca and his companions, it is not possible, with our present knowledge of the former tribes of the coast region of Texas, to identify with certainty the various Indians mentioned by the narrator. Whether the names given by him are those which the natives applied to themselves or are those given by other tribes is unknown, and as no remnant of this once considerable coast population now exists, the only hope of the ultimate determination of these Indians lies in the historical archives of Texas, Mexico, and Spain. The two languages and stocks represented on the island of Malhado — the Capoque and the Han — would seem to apply to the Karankawan and Attacapan families respectively. The Capoques (called Cahoques on p. 87) are seemingly identical with the Cocos who lived with the Mayayes on the coast between the Brazos and Colorado Rivers in 1778, and with the Cokés, who as late as 1850 are described as a branch of the Koronks (Karankawa). Of the Han people nothing more definite is known than that which is here recorded.

[5] Compare Barcia, *Ensayo*, 263, 1723, and Gatschet in *Archaeological and Ethnological Papers of the Peabody Museum*, Harvard University, 1891, for references to these "weepers."

other strange customs; but I have told the principal of them, and the most remarkable, that I may pass on and further relate what befell us.

Chapter 16

The Christians leave the island of Malhado.

After Dorantes and Castillo returned to the island, they brought together the Christians, who were somewhat separated, and found them in all to be fourteen. As I have said, I was opposite on the main, where my Indians had taken me, and where so great sickness had come upon me, that if anything before had given me hopes of life, this were enough to have entirely bereft me of them.

When the Christians heard of my condition, they gave an Indian the cloak of marten skins we had taken from the cacique, as before related, to pass them over to where I was that they might visit me. Twelve of them crossed; for two were so feeble that their comrades could not venture to bring them. The names of those who came were Alonzo del Castillo, Andrés Dorantes, Diego Dorantes, Valdevieso,[1] Estrada, Tostado, Chaves, Gutierrez, Asturiano a clergyman, Diego de Huelva, Estevanico the black, and Benitez; and when they reached the main land, they found another, who was one of our company, named Francisco de Leon. The thirteen together followed along the coast. So soon as they had come over, my Indians informed me of it, and that Hieronymo de Alvaniz[2] and Lope de Oviedo remained on the island. But sickness prevented me from going with my companions or even seeing them.

I was obliged to remain with the people belonging to the island[3] more than a year, and because of the hard work they put upon me and the harsh treatment, I resolved to flee from

---

[1] Diego Dorantes and Pedro de Valdivieso were cousins of Andrés Dorantes. See p. 69.

[2] Called also Alaniz — the notary.   [3] The Capoques.

them and go to those of Charruco, who inhabit the forests
and country of the main, the life I led being insupportable.
Besides much other labor, I had to get out roots from below
the water, and from among the cane where they grew in the
ground. From this employment I had my fingers so worn
that did a straw but touch them they would bleed. Many of
the canes are broken, so they often tore my flesh, and I had
to go in the midst of them with only the clothing on I have
mentioned.

Accordingly, I put myself to contriving how I might get
over to the other Indians, among whom matters turned somewhat more favorably for me. I set to trafficking, and strove
to make my employment profitable in the ways I could best
contrive, and by that means I got food and good treatment.
The Indians would beg me to go from one quarter to another
for things of which they have need; for in consequence of in-
cessant hostilities, they cannot traverse the country, nor make
many exchanges. With my merchandise and trade I went
into the interior as far as I pleased, and travelled along the
coast forty or fifty leagues. The principal wares were cones and
other pieces of sea-snail, conchs used for cutting, and fruit
like a bean of the highest value among them, which they use
as a medicine and employ in their dances and festivities.
Among other matters were sea-beads. Such were what I
carried into the interior; and in barter I got and brought
back skins, ochre with which they rub and color the face, hard
canes of which to make arrows, sinews, cement and flint for the
heads, and tassels of the hair of deer that by dyeing they make
red. This occupation suited me well; for the travel allowed
me liberty to go where I wished, I was not obliged to work,
and was not a slave. Wherever I went I received fair treatment, and the Indians gave me to eat out of regard to my
commodities. My leading object, while journeying in this
business, was to find out the way by which I should go forward, and I became well known. The inhabitants were
pleased when they saw me, and I had brought them what
they wanted; and those who did not know me sought and

desired the acquaintance, for my reputation. The hardships that I underwent in this were long to tell, as well of peril and privation as of storms and cold. Oftentimes they overtook me alone and in the wilderness; but I came forth from them all by the great mercy of God our Lord. Because of them I avoided pursuing the business in winter, a season in which the natives themselves retire to their huts and ranches, torpid and incapable of exertion.

I was in this country nearly six years,[1] alone among the Indians, and naked like them. The reason why I remained so long, was that I might take with me the Christian, Lope de Oviedo, from the island; Alaniz, his companion, who had been left with him by Alonzo del Castillo, and by Andrés Dorantes, and the rest, died soon after their departure; and to get the survivor out from there, I went over to the island every year, and entreated him that we should go, in the best way we could contrive, in quest of Christians. He put me off every year, saying in the next coming we would start. At last I got him off, crossing him over the bay, and over four rivers in the coast,[2] as he could not swim. In this way we

---

[1] From 1528 to 1533.

[2] The identification of Malhado Island is a difficult problem. On general principles Galveston Island would seem to supply the conditions, in that it more likely would have been inhabited by two distinct tribes, perhaps representing distinct linguistic families, as it is known to have been occupied by Indians (the Karankawa) at a later period, besides having the smaller island or islands behind it. But its size and the other conditions are not in favor of the identification, for its length is at least twice as great as that of Malhado, as given in the narrative, and it is also more than two leagues from its nearest end to the first stream that the Spaniards crossed after departing from the island (Oviedo, p. 593). Mr. James Newton Baskett suggests that the so-called Velasco Island, next south of Galveston Island, better fulfils the requirements, as indeed it does topographically, except for the fact that it is really a peninsula. Aside from this, it possesses all the physical features,—length and width, distance from the first stream to the southward, and having the necessary island or islands (Mud and San Luis) off its northern shore. Accepting Mr. Baskett's determination, it is not difficult to account for the four streams, "very large and of rapid current," one of which flowed directly into the gulf. Following the journey of the Spaniards from the island, down the coast, in April, when the streams were swollen by flood, the first river was crossed in two leagues after they had reached the mainland. This was evidently Oyster Creek. Three leagues farther was another river, running so power-

went on with some Indians, until coming to a bay a league in width, and everywhere deep. From the appearance we supposed it to be that which is called Espiritu Sancto. We met some Indians on the other side of it, coming to visit ours, who told us that beyond them were three men like us, and gave their names. We asked for the others, and were told that they were all dead of cold and hunger; that the Indians farther on, of whom they were, for their diversion had killed Diego Dorantes, Valdevieso, and Diego de Huelva,[1] because they left one house for another; and that other Indians, their neighbors with whom Captain Dorantes now was, had in consequence of a dream, killed Esquivel and Mendez.[2] We asked

fully that one of the rafts was driven to sea more than a league. This fully agrees with the Brazos, which indeed is the only large stream of the landlocked Texas coast that flows directly into the gulf. Four leagues still farther they reached another river, where the boat of the comptroller and the commissary was found. From this fact it may be assumed that this stream also flowed into the open gulf, a condition satisfied by Caney Creek. The San Bernardo may well have escaped notice in travelling near the coast, from the fact that it flows into Cedar Lake. Five or six leagues more brought them to another large river (the Colorado), which the Indians carried them across in a canoe; and in four days they reached the bay of Espíritu Santo (La Vaca Bay?). "The bay was broad, nearly a league across. The side toward Pánuco [the south] forms a point running out nearly a quarter of a league, having on it some large white sand-stacks which it is reasonable to suppose can be descried from a distance at sea, and were consequently thought to mark the River Espíritu Santo." After two days of exertion they succeeded in crossing the bay in a broken canoe; and at the end of twelve leagues they came to a small bay not more than the breadth of a river. Here they found Figueroa, the only survivor of the four who had attempted to return to Mexico. The distance from Malhado Island is given as sixty leagues, consequently the journey from the Colorado to the bay now reached, which seems to be no other than San Antonio Bay, covered thirty-two to thirty-three leagues. Lofty sand dunes, such as those seen on what we regard as perhaps La Vaca Bay, occur on San Antonio Bay. See *United States Coast Survey Report* for 1859, p. 325. The western shore of the bay is a bluff or bank of twenty feet. "At one place on this side, a singular range of sand-hills, known as the Sand-mounds, approaches the shore. The highest peak is about seventy-five feet above the bay."

[1] These were all members of Dorantes' party who visited Cabeza de Vaca when he was ill on the mainland. See p. 55.

[2] Esquivel was one of the party under Enrriquez the comptroller; Mendez was one of the good swimmers who started from the island in the hope of reaching Pánuco.

how the living were situated, and they answered that they were very ill used, the boys and some of the Indian men being very idle, out of cruelty gave them many kicks, cuffs, and blows with sticks; that such was the life they led.

We desired to be informed of the country ahead, and of the subsistence: they said there was nothing to eat, and that it was thin of people, who suffered of cold, having no skins or other things to cover them. They told us also if we wished to see those three Christians, two days from that time the Indians who had them would come to eat walnuts a league from there on the margin of that river; and that we might know what they told us of the ill usage to be true, they slapped my companion and beat him with a stick, and I was not left without my portion. Many times they threw lumps of mud at us, and every day they put their arrows to our hearts, saying that they were inclined to kill us in the way that they had destroyed our friends. Lope Oviedo, my comrade, in fear said that he wished to go back with the women of those who had crossed the bay with us, the men having remained some distance behind. I contended strongly against his returning, and urged my objections; but in no way could I keep him. So he went back, and I remained alone with those savages. They are called Quevenes,[1] and those with whom he returned, Deaguanes.[2]

Chapter 17

The coming of Indians with Andrés Dorantes, Castillo, and Estevanico.

Two days after Lope de Oviedo left, the Indians who had Alonzo del Castillo and Andrés Dorantes, came to the place of which we had been told, to eat walnuts. These are ground with a kind of small grain, and this is the subsistence of the

---

[1] *Guevenes* in the edition of 1542 (Bandelier translation). There is reason to believe that these people may have been identical with the Cohani, who lived west of the Colorado River of Texas in the first quarter of the nineteenth century. [2] *Doguenes* in ch. 26.

people two months in the year without any other thing; but even the nuts they do not have every season, as the tree produces in alternate years. The fruit is the size of that in Galicia; the trees are very large and numerous.

An Indian told me of the arrival of the Christians, and that if I wished to see them I must steal away and flee to the point of a wood to which he directed me, and that as he and others, kindred of his, should pass by there to visit those Indians, they would take me with them to the spot where the Christians were. I determined to attempt this and trust to them, as they spoke a language distinct from that of the others. I did so, and the next day they left, and found me in the place that had been pointed out, and accordingly took me with them.

When I arrived near their abode, Andrés Dorantes came out to see who it could be, for the Indians had told him that a Christian was coming. His astonishment was great when he saw me, as they had for many a day considered me dead, and the natives had said that I was. We gave many thanks at seeing ourselves together, and this was a day to us of the greatest pleasure we had enjoyed in life. Having come to where Castillo was, they inquired of me where I was going. I told them my purpose was to reach the land of Christians, I being then in search and pursuit of it. Andrés Dorantes said that for a long time he had entreated Castillo and Estevanico to go forward; but that they dared not venture, because they knew not how to swim, and greatly dreaded the rivers and bays they should have to cross, there being many in that country. Thus the Almighty had been pleased to preserve me through many trials and diseases, conducting me in the end to the fellowship of those who had abandoned me, that I might lead them over the bays and rivers that obstructed our progress. They advised me on no account to let the natives know or have a suspicion of my desire to go on, else they would destroy me; and that for success it would be necessary for me to remain quiet until the end of six months, when comes the season in which these Indians go to another part of the country to eat prickly pears.[1] People would arrive from parts farther on, bringing bows to barter and for exchange, with whom, after making our escape, we should be able to go on their return. Having consented to this course, I remained. The prickly pear is the size of a hen's egg, vermillion and black in color, and of agreeable flavor. The natives live on it three months in the year, having nothing beside.

I was given as a slave to an Indian, with whom was Dorantes. He was blind of one eye, as were also his wife and sons, and likewise another who was with him; so that of a fashion they were all blind. These are called Marians;[2] Castillo was with another neighboring people, called Yguases.[3]

While here the Christians related to me how they had left the island of Malhado, and found the boat in which the comptroller and the friars had sailed, bottom up on the seashore; and that going along crossing the rivers, which are four,[4] very large and of rapid current, their boats[5] were swept away and carried to sea, where four of their number were drowned; that thus they proceeded until they crossed the bay, getting over it with great difficulty, and fifteen leagues thence they came to another. By the time they reached this, they had lost two companions in the sixty leagues they travelled, and those remaining were nearly dead, in all the while having eaten nothing but crabs and rockweed.[6] Arrived at this bay, they found Indians eating mulberries, who, when they saw them, went to a cape opposite. While contriving and seeking for some means to cross the bay, there came over to them an Indian, and a Christian whom they recognized to be Figueroa,

---

[1] The fruit of the *Opuntia* cactus, of which there are about two hundred species.

[2] *Mariames* in ch. 26, and in the edition of 1542. These people are not identified. They were possibly of Karankawan or Coahuiltecan affinity, but there is no direct evidence of this.

[3] *Iguaces* in the edition of 1542. [4] See p. 57, note 2.

[5] Rafts built for the purpose of crossing the streams.

[6] *Yerba pedrera*: "Of which glass is made in Spain." Oviedo, p. 593. Doubtless kelp. It was burned and from the product glass and soap were formerly manufactured. It is still a source of manufacture of carbonate of soda and iodine.

one of the four we had sent forward from the island of Malhado. He there recounted how he and his companions had got as far as that place, when two of them and an Indian [1] died of cold and hunger, being exposed in the most inclement of seasons. He and Mendez were taken by the Indians, and while with them his associate fled, going as well as he could in the direction of Pánuco, and the natives pursuing, put him to death.

While living with these Indians, Figueroa learned from them that there was a Christian among the Mariames, who had come over from the opposite side, and he found him among the Quevenes. This was Hernando de Esquivel, a native of Badajoz, who had come in company with the commissary. From him Figueroa learned the end to which the Governor, the comptroller, and the others had come. Esquivel told him that the comptroller and the friars had upset their boat at the confluence of the rivers,[2] and that the boat of the Governor, moving along the coast, came with its people to land. Narváez went in the boat until arriving at that great bay, where he took in the people, and, crossing them to the opposite point, returned for the comptroller, the friars, and the rest. And he related that being disembarked, the Governor had recalled the commission the comptroller held as his lieutenant, assigning the duties to a captain with him named Pantoja: that Narváez stayed the night in his boat, not wishing to come on shore, having a cockswain with him and a page who was unwell, there being no water nor anything to eat on board; that at midnight, the boat having only a stone for anchor, the north wind blowing strongly took her unobserved to sea, and they never knew more of their commander.

The others then went along the coast, and as they were arrested by a wide extent of water, they made rafts with much labor, on which they crossed to the opposite shore. Going on, they arrived at a point of woods on the banks of the water

---

[1] Alvaro Fernandez, the Portuguese sailor and carpenter; Astudillo, the native of Zafra; and the Indian from the island of "Auia" (Cuba).

[2] The Mississippi delta.

where were Indians, who, as they saw them coming, put their houses [1] into their canoes and went over to the opposite side. The Christians, in consideration of the season, for it was now the month of November, stopped at this wood, where they found water and fuel, some crabs and shell-fish. They began, one by one, to die of cold and hunger; and, more than this, Pantoja, who was Lieutenant-Governor, used them severely, which Soto-Mayor (the brother of Vasco Porcallo, of the island of Cuba), who had come with the armament as camp-master, not being able to bear, had a struggle with him, and, giving him a blow with a club, Pantoja was instantly killed.

Thus did the number go on diminishing. The living dried the flesh of them that died; and the last that died was Soto-Mayor, when Esquivel preserved his flesh, and, feeding on it, sustained existence until the first of March, when an Indian of those that had fled, coming to see if they were alive, took Esquivel with him. While he was in the possession of the native, Figueroa saw him, and learned all that had been related. He besought Esquivel to come with him, that together they might pursue the way to Pánuco; to which Esquivel would not consent, saying that he had understood from the friars that Pánuco had been left behind: [2] so he remained there and Figueroa went to the coast where he was accustomed to live.

Chapter 18

The story Figueroa recounted from Esquivel.

This account was all given by Figueroa, according to the relation he received from Esquivel, and from him through the others it came to me; whence may be seen and understood the fate of the armament, and the individual fortunes of the greater part of the people. Figueroa said, moreover, that if

---

[1] Doubtless consisting of mats fastened to a framework.

[2] That is, he supposed that he was then somewhere on the coast of central Mexico.

the Christians should at any time go in that direction, it were possible they might see Esquivel, for he knew that he had fled from the Indian with whom he was, to the Mariames, who were neighbors. After Figueroa had finished telling the story, he and the Asturian made an attempt to go to other Indians farther on; but as soon as they who had the Christians discovered it, they followed, and beating them severely, stripped the Asturian and shot an arrow through his arm. They finally escaped by flight.

The other Christians remained, and prevailed on the Indians to receive them as slaves. In their service they were abused as slaves never were, nor men in any condition have ever been. Not content with frequently buffeting them, striking them with sticks, and pulling out their beard for amusement, they killed three of the six for only going from one house to another. These were the persons I have named before: Diego Dorantes, Valdivieso, and Diego de Huelva: and the three that remained looked forward to the same fate. Not to endure this life, Andrés Dorantes fled, and passed to the Mariames, the people among whom Esquivel tarried. They told him that having had Esquivel there, he wished to run away because a woman dreamed that a son of hers would kill him; and that they followed after, and slew him. They showed Dorantes his sword, beads, and book, with other things that had been his.[1]

Thus in obedience to their custom they take life, destroying even their male children on account of dreams. They cast away their daughters at birth, and cause them to be eaten by dogs. The reason of their doing this, as they state, is because all the nations of the country are their foes; and as they have unceasing war with them, if they were to marry away their daughters, they would so greatly multiply their enemies that they must be overcome and made slaves; thus they prefer to destroy all, rather than that from them should come a single enemy. We asked why they did not themselves marry them;

---

[1] See the extracts from the letter of the survivors (preserved by Oviedo) appended to this chapter.

and they said it would be a disgustful thing to marry among relatives, and far better to kill than to give them either to their kindred or to their foes.

This is likewise the practice of their neighbors the Yguazes, but of no other people of that country. When the men would marry, they buy the women of their enemies: the price paid for a wife is a bow, the best that can be got, with two arrows: if it happens that the suitor should have no bow, then a net a fathom in length and another in breadth. They kill their male children, and buy those of strangers. The marriage state continues no longer than while the parties are satisfied, and they separate for the slightest cause. Dorantes was among this people, and after a few days escaped.

Castillo and Estevanico went inland to the Yguazes. This people are universally good archers and of a fine symmetry, although not so large as those we left. They have a nipple and a lip bored.[1] Their support is principally roots, of two or three kinds, and they look for them over the face of all the country. The food is poor and gripes the persons who eat it. The roots require roasting two days: many are very bitter, and withal difficult to be dug. They are sought the distance of two or three leagues, and so great is the want these people experience, that they cannot get through the year without them. Occasionally they kill deer, and at times take fish; but the quantity is so small and the famine so great, that they eat spiders and the eggs of ants, worms, lizards, salamanders, snakes, and vipers that kill whom they strike; and they eat earth and wood, and all that there is, the dung of deer, and other things that I omit to mention; and I honestly believe that were there stones in that land they would eat them. They save the bones of the fishes they consume, of snakes and other animals, that they may afterwards beat them together and eat the powder. The men bear no burthens, nor carry anything of weight; such are borne by women and old men who are of the least esteem. They have not so

---

[1] Evidently for the insertion of canes, as was the custom of the Capoques and Hans of the island of Malhado.

great love for their children as those we have before spoken of.[1] Some among them are accustomed to sin against nature. The women work very hard, and do a great deal; of the twenty-four hours they have only six of repose; the rest of the night they pass in heating the ovens to bake those roots they eat. At daybreak they begin to dig them, to bring wood and water to their houses and get in readiness other things that may be necessary. The majority of the people are great thieves; for though they are free to divide with each other, on turning the head, even a son or a father will take what he can. They are great liars, and also great drunkards, which they became from the use of a certain liquor.[2]

These Indians are so accustomed to running, that without rest or fatigue they follow a deer from morning to night. In this way they kill many. They pursue them until tired down, and sometimes overtake them in the race. Their houses are of matting, placed upon four hoops. They carry them on the back, and remove every two or three days in search of food. Nothing is planted for support. They are a merry people, considering the hunger they suffer; for they never cease, notwithstanding, to observe their festivities and *areytos*. To them the happiest part of the year is the season of eating prickly pears ; they have hunger then no longer, pass all the time in dancing, and eat day and night. While these last, they squeeze out the juice, open and set them to dry, and when dry they are put in hampers like figs. These they keep to eat on their way back. The peel is beaten to powder.

It occurred to us many times while we were among this people, and there was no food, to be three or four days without eating, when they, to revive our spirits, would tell us not to be sad, that soon there would be prickly pears when we should eat a plenty and drink of the juice, when our bellies would be very big and we should be content and joyful, having no hun-

---

[1] The Capoques of Malhado Island.

[2] It is not improbable that the liquor was made from the peyote, or mescal button, still used by the Kiowa, Comanche, and others to produce stupefaction. See Mooney in *Seventeenth Report of the Bureau of American Ethnology*, 1898.

ger. From the time they first told us this, to that at which
the earliest were ripe enough to be eaten, was an interval of
five or six months; so having tarried until the lapse of this
period, and the season had come, we went to eat the fruit.

We found mosquitos of three sorts, and all of them abundant in every part of the country. They poison and inflame,
and during the greater part of the summer gave us great
annoyance. As a protection we made fires, encircling the
people with them, burning rotten and wet wood to produce
smoke without flame. The remedy brought another trouble,
and the night long we did little else than shed tears from the
smoke that came into our eyes, besides feeling intense heat
from the many fires, and if at any time we went out for repose to the seaside and fell asleep, we were reminded with
blows to make up the fires. The Indians of the interior have
a different method, as intolerable, and worse even than the
one I have spoken of, which is to go with brands in the hand
firing the plains and forests within their reach, that the mosquitos may fly away, and at the same time to drive out lizards and other like things from the earth for them to eat.

They are accustomed also to kill deer by encircling them
with fires. The pasturage is taken from the cattle by burning, that necessity may drive them to seek it in places where
it is desired they should go. They encamp only where there
are wood and water; and sometimes all carry loads of these
when they go to hunt deer, which are usually found where
neither is to be got. On the day of their arrival, they kill
the deer and other animals which they can, and consume all
the water and all the wood in cooking and on the fires they
make to relieve them of mosquitos. They remain the next
day to get something to sustain them on their return; and
when they go, such is their state from those insects that they
appear to have the affliction of holy Lazarus. In this way do
they appease their hunger, two or three times in the year,
at the cost I have mentioned. From my own experience, I
can state there is no torment known in this world that can
equal it.

Inland are many deer, birds, and beasts other than those I have spoken of. Cattle [1] come as far as here. Three times I have seen them and eaten of their meat. I think they are about the size of those in Spain. They have small horns like the cows of Morocco; the hair is very long and flocky like the merino's. Some are tawny, others black. To my judgment the flesh is finer and fatter than that of this country. Of the skins of those not full grown the Indians make blankets, and of the larger they make shoes and bucklers. They come as far as the sea-coast of Florida, from a northerly direction, ranging through a tract of more than four hundred leagues; and throughout the whole region over which they run, the people who inhabit near, descend and live upon them, distributing a vast many hides into the interior country.

[Buckingham Smith introduces the following translation from the *Letter* (Oviedo, pp. 594–598) as throwing important light on the occurrences related in the foregoing chapter. F. W. H.]

"Thus ended the account of Figueroa, without his being able to add more to it, than that Esquivel was about there in the possession of some natives, and they might see him in a little while; but a month afterwards, it was known that he no longer lived, for having gone from the natives, they had followed after and put him to death. Figueroa tarried a few moments, long enough to relate the sad news. The Indian who brought him would not permit him to remain. Asturiano, the clergyman, and a young man being the only ones who could swim, accompanied them for the purpose of returning with fish which they were promised, as likewise that they should be brought back over that bay; but when the Indians found them at their houses, they would neither bring them nor let them return; on the contrary, they put their houses into their canoes and took the two Christians with them, saying that they would soon come back. . . .

"The eight companions remained that day to appease their hunger, and the next morning they saw two Indians of a rancho coming over the water to place their dwellings on the hither side. The purpose was to live on blackberries that grow in some places along the

---

[1] This is the first printed reference to the bison.

coast, which they seek at a season they know full well, and although precarious, they promise a food that supports life. They called to the Indians, who came as to persons they thought lightly of, taking some part of what they possessed almost by force. The Christians besought the natives to set them over, which they did in a canoe, taking them to their houses near by, and at dark gave them a small quantity of fish. They went out the next day for more, and returned at night, giving them a part of what they had caught. The day following they moved off with the Christians and never after were the two seen whom the other Indians had taken away.

"At last the natives, weary of seeking food for their guests, turned away five, that they should go to some Indians who they said were to be found in another bay, six leagues farther on. Alonzo del Castillo went there with Pedro de Valdivieso, cousin of Andrés Dorantes, and another, Diego de Huelva, where they remained a long time; the two others went down near the coast, seeking relief, where they died, as Dorantes states, who found the bodies, one of whom, Diego Dorantes, was his cousin. The two hidalgos and the negro remaining in that rancho, sufficed for the use of the natives, to bring back-loads of wood and water as slaves. After three or four days however, these likewise were turned off, when for some time they wandered about lost, without hope of relief; and going naked among marshes, having been previously despoiled one night of their clothing, they came upon those dead.

"They continued the route until they found some Indians, with whom Andrés Dorantes remained. A cousin of his, one of the three who had gone on to the bay where they stopped, came over from the opposite shore, and told him that the swimmers who went from them had passed in that direction, having their clothes taken from them and they much bruised about the head with sticks because they would not remain; still though beaten and stripped, they had gone on for the sake of the oath they had taken, never to stop even if death stood in the path, before coming to a country of Christians. Dorantes states that he saw in the rancho where he was, the clothes belonging to the clergyman and to one of the swimmers, with a breviary or prayer book. Valdivieso returned, and a couple of days afterwards was killed, because he wished to flee, and likewise in a little time Diego de Huelva, because he forsook one lodge-house for another.

"The Christians were there made slaves, forced with more cruelty to serve than the Moor would have used. Besides going stark naked and bare-footed over the coast burning in summer like fire, their continual occupation was bringing wood and water on the back, or whatever the Indians needed, and dragging canoes over inundated grounds in hot weather.

"These natives eat nothing the year round but fish, and of that not much. They experience far less hunger however, than the inhabitants inland among whom the Spaniards afterwards lived. The food often fails, causing frequent removals, or otherwise they starve. . . . They have finger nails that for any ordinary purpose are knives, and are their principal arms among themselves. . . .

"The Spaniards lived here fourteen months, from May to the May ensuing of the year 1530, and to the middle of the month of August, when Andrés Dorantes, being at a point that appeared most favorable for going, commended himself to God, and went off at midday. . . . Castillo tarried among that hard people a year and a half later, until an opportunity presented for starting; but on arriving he found only the negro; Dorantes, finding these Indians unbearably cruel, had gone back more than twenty leagues to a river near the bay of Espíritu Sancto, among those who had killed Esquivel, the solitary one that had escaped from the boats of the Governor and Alonzo Enrriques, slain, as they were told, because a woman had dreamed some absurdity. The people of this country have belief in dreams, their only superstition. On account of them they will even kill their children; and this hidalgo Dorantes states, that in the course of four years he had been a witness to the killing or burying alive of eleven or twelve young males, and rarely do they let a girl live. . . .

"Andrés Dorantes passed ten months among this people, enduring much privation with continual labor, and in fear of being killed. . . ."

Chapter 19

Our separation by the Indians.

When the six months were over, I had to spend with the Christians to put in execution the plan we had concerted, the Indians went after prickly pears, the place at which they grew being thirty leagues off; [1] and when we approached the point of flight, those among whom we were, quarrelled about a woman. After striking with fists, beating with sticks and bruising heads in great anger, each took his lodge and went

---

[1] In an article on the wanderings of Cabeza de Vaca, by Ponton and McFarland (*Texas Historical Association Quarterly*, I. 176, map, 1898), the northern limit of the cactus belt is placed on a line extending irregularly westward from the mouth of the Colorado River of Texas.

his way, whence it became necessary that the Christians should also separate, and in no way could we come together until another year.

In this time I passed a hard life, caused as much by hunger as ill usage. Three times I was obliged to run from my masters, and each time they went in pursuit and endeavored to slay me; but God our Lord in his mercy chose to protect and preserve me; and when the season of prickly pears returned, we again came together in the same place. After we had arranged our escape, and appointed a time, that very day the Indians separated and all went back. I told my comrades I would wait for them among the prickly-pear plants until the moon should be full. This day was the first of September,[1] and the first of the moon; and I said that if in this time they did not come as we had agreed, I would leave and go alone. So we parted, each going with his Indians. I remained with mine until the thirteenth day of the moon, having determined to flee to others when it should be full.

At this time Andrés Dorantes arrived with Estevanico and informed me that they had left Castillo with other Indians near by, called Lanegados;[2] that they had encountered great obstacles and wandered about lost; that the next day the Indians, among whom we were, would move to where Castillo was, and were going to unite with those who held him and become friends, having been at war until then, and that in this way we should recover Castillo.

---

[1] 1534. Cabeza de Vaca had evidently lost his reckoning (perhaps during his illness), as the date of the new moon in this year was September 8.

[2] *Anagados* in the 1542 edition. The tribe cannot be identified, although it may be well known under some other name. *Anegado* is Spanish for "overflowed," "inundated," but it is by no means certain that the Spaniards applied this name to them. Buckingham Smith suggests that they may have been the Nacadoch (Nacogdoches), but this does not seem probable, as the latter tribe lived very far to the northeast of the point where the Spaniards now were, that is, some thirty leagues inland from the coast between latitude 28° and 29°. The name sounds more like *Năddáko*, the designation which the Anadarcos give themselves. This Caddoan tribe, when first known, lived high up on the Brazos and the Trinity, but in 1812 their village was on the Sabine. They are now incorporated with the Caddo in Oklahoma.

We had thirst all the time we ate the pears, which we quenched with their juice. We caught it in a hole made in the earth, and when it was full we drank until satisfied. It is sweet, and the color of must. In this manner they collect it for lack of vessels. There are many kinds of prickly pears, among them some very good, although they all appeared to me to be so, hunger never having given me leisure to choose, nor to reflect upon which were the best.

Nearly all these people drink rain-water, which lies about in spots. Although there are rivers, as the Indians never have fixed habitations, there are no familiar or known places for getting water. Throughout the country are extensive and beautiful plains with good pasturage; and I think it would be a very fruitful region were it worked and inhabited by civilized men. We nowhere saw mountains.

These Indians told us that there was another people next in advance of us, called Camones,[1] living towards the coast, and that they had killed the people who came in the boat of Peñalosa and Tellez, who arrived so feeble that even while being slain they could offer no resistance, and were all destroyed. We were shown their clothes and arms, and were told that the boat lay there stranded. This, the fifth boat, had remained till then unaccounted for. We have already stated how the boat of the Governor had been carried out to sea, and that of the comptroller and the friars had been cast away on the coast, of which Esquevel[2] narrated the fate of the men. We have once told how the two boats in which Castillo, I, and Dorantes came, foundered near the Island of Malhado.

Chapter 20

Of our escape.

The second day after we had moved, we commended ourselves to God and set forth with speed, trusting, for all the

---

[1] *Camoles* in ch. 26. They evidently lived toward the northeast, north of Malhado Island; unidentified.

[2] Esquivel.

lateness of the season and that the prickly pears were about
ending, with the mast which remained in the woods [field],
we might still be enabled to travel over a large territory.
Hurrying on that day in great dread lest the Indians should
overtake us, we saw some smokes, and going in the direction
of them we arrived there after vespers, and found an Indian.
He ran as he discovered us coming, not being willing to wait
for us. We sent the negro [1] after him, when he stopped, seeing
him alone. The negro told him we were seeking the people
who made those fires. He answered that their houses were
near by, and he would guide us to them. So we followed him.
He ran to make known our approach, and at sunset we saw
the houses. Before our arrival, at the distance of two crossbow shots from them, we found four Indians, who waited for
us and received us well. We said in the language of the
Mariames, that we were coming to look for them. They were
evidently pleased with our company, and took us to their
dwellings. Dorantes and the negro were lodged in the house
of a physician,[2] Castillo and myself in that of another.

These people speak a different language, and are called
Avavares.[3] They are the same that carried bows to those
with whom we formerly lived,[4] going to traffic with them, and
although they are of a different nation and tongue, they
understand the other language. They arrived that day with
their lodges, at the place where we found them. The community directly brought us a great many prickly pears, having
heard of us before, of our cures, and of the wonders our Lord
worked by us, which, although there had been no others, were
adequate to open ways for us through a country poor like
this, to afford us people where oftentimes there are none, and
to lead us through immediate dangers, not permitting us to
be killed, sustaining us under great want, and putting into

[1] Estévanico.
[2] A shaman, or "medicine-man."
[3] *Chavavares* in ch. 26, in which it is said that they joined the Mariames.
Their affinity is unknown. The statement that the Spaniards are again
among these tribes suggests that they were now pursuing a northerly direction.
[4] The Mariames. See note to ch. 26, respecting these tribes.

those nations the heart of kindness, as we shall relate hereafter.

Chapter 21

Our cure of some of the afflicted.

That same night of our arrival, some Indians came to Castillo and told him that they had great pain in the head, begging him to cure them. After he made over them the sign of
the cross, and commended them to God, they instantly said
that all the pain had left, and went to their houses bringing
us prickly pears, with a piece of venison, a thing to us little
known. As the report of Castillo's performances spread, many
came to us that night sick, that we should heal them, each
bringing a piece of venison, until the quantity became so great
we knew not where to dispose of it. We gave many thanks
to God, for every day went on increasing his compassion and
his gifts. After the sick were attended to, they began to dance
and sing, making themselves festive, until sunrise; and because of our arrival, the rejoicing was continued for three days.

When these were ended, we asked the Indians about the
country farther on, the people we should find in it, and of the
subsistence there. They answered us, that throughout all the
region prickly-pear plants abounded; but the fruit was now
gathered and all the people had gone back to their houses.
They said the country was very cold, and there were few skins.
Reflecting on this, and that it was already winter, we resolved
to pass the season with these Indians.

Five days after our arrival, all the Indians went off, taking
us with them to gather more prickly pears, where there were
other peoples speaking different tongues. After walking five
days in great hunger, since on the way was no manner of
fruit, we came to a river [1] and put up our houses. We then
went to seek the product of certain trees, which is like peas.
As there are no paths in the country, I was detained some

---

[1] This may have been the San Antonio or the San Marcos-Guadalupe.

time. The others returned, and coming to look for them in the dark I got lost. Thank God I found a burning tree, and in the warmth of it I passed the cold of that night. In the morning, loading myself with sticks, and taking two brands with me, I returned to seek them. In this manner I wandered five days, ever with my fire and load; for if the wood had failed me where none could be found, as many parts are without any, though I might have sought sticks elsewhere, there would have been no fire to kindle them. This was all the protection I had against cold, while walking naked as I was born. Going to the low woods near the rivers, I prepared myself for the night, stopping in them before sunset. I made a hole in the ground and threw in fuel which the trees abundantly afforded, collected in good quantity from those that were fallen and dry. About the whole I made four fires, in the form of a cross, which I watched and made up from time to time. I also gathered some bundles of the coarse straw that there abounds, with which I covered myself in the hole. In this way I was sheltered at night from cold. On one occasion while I slept, the fire fell upon the straw, when it began to blaze so rapidly that notwithstanding the haste I made to get out of it, I carried some marks on my hair of the danger to which I was exposed. All this while I tasted not a mouthful, nor did I find anything I could eat. My feet were bare and bled a good deal. Through the mercy of God, the wind did not blow from the north in all this time, otherwise I should have died.

At the end of the fifth day I arrived on the margin of a river,[1] where I found the Indians, who with the Christians, had considered me dead, supposing that I had been stung by a viper. All were rejoiced to see me, and most so were my companions. They said that up to that time they had struggled with great hunger, which was the cause of their not having sought me. At night, all gave me of their prickly pears, and the next morning we set out for a place where they were

---

[1] Presumably the river last mentioned, where they had erected their shelters.

in large quantity, with which we satisfied our great craving, the Christians rendering thanks to our Lord that He had ever given us His aid.

Chapter 22

The coming of other sick to us the next day.

The next day morning, many Indians came, and brought five persons who had cramps and were very unwell. They came that Castillo might cure them. Each offered his bow and arrows, which Castillo received. At sunset he blessed them, commending them to God our Lord, and we all prayed to Him the best we could to send health; for that He knew there was no other means, than through Him, by which this people would aid us, so we could come forth from this unhappy existence. He bestowed it so mercifully, that, the morning having come, all got up well and sound, and were as strong as though they never had a disorder. It caused great admiration, and inclined us to render many thanks to God our Lord, whose goodness we now clearly beheld, giving us firm hopes that He would liberate and bring us to where we might serve Him. For myself I can say that I ever had trust in His providence that He would lead me out from that captivity, and thus I always spoke of it to my companions.

The Indians having gone and taken their friends with them in health, we departed for a place at which others were eating prickly pears. These people are called Cuthalchuches [1] and Malicones, who speak different tongues. Adjoining them were others called Coayos and Susolas, who were on the opposite side, others called Atayos,[2] who were at war with the Su-

---

[1] Cultalchulches in ch. 26 (q. v.), and in the edition of 1542.

[2] These were possibly the Adai, or Adaize, although their country was in northeastern Texas, about Red River and the Sabine; nevertheless they may have wandered very far during the prickly-pear season. There is evidence that in 1792, fourteen families of the Adai migrated to a region south of San Antonio de Béjar, where they were merged with the tribes living thereabout. The main body, although greatly reduced, did not leave their

solas, exchanging arrow shots daily. As through all the country they talked only of the wonders which God our Lord
worked through us, persons came from many parts to seek
us that we might cure them. At the end of the second day
after our arrival, some of the Susolas came to us and besought
Castillo that he would go to cure one wounded and others
sick, and they said that among them was one very near his
end. Castillo was a timid practitioner, most so in serious
and dangerous cases, believing that his sins would weigh, and
some day hinder him in performing cures. The Indians told
me to go and heal them, as they liked me; they remembered
that I had ministered to them in the walnut grove when they
gave us nuts and skins, which occurred when I first joined
the Christians. So I had to go with them, and Dorantes accompanied me with Estevanico. Coming near their huts, I
perceived that the sick man we went to heal was dead. Many
persons were around him weeping, and his house was prostrate,
a sign that the one who dwelt in it is no more.[1] When I arrived I found his eyes rolled up, and the pulse gone, he having all the appearances of death, as they seemed to me and as
Dorantes said. I removed a mat with which he was covered,
and supplicated our Lord as fervently as I could, that He
would be pleased to give health to him, and to the rest that
might have need of it. After he had been blessed and breathed
upon many times, they brought me his bow, and gave me a
basket of pounded prickly pears.

The natives took me to cure many others who were sick of
a stupor, and presented me two more baskets of prickly pears,
which I gave to the Indians who accompanied us. We then
went back to our lodgings. Those to whom we gave the fruit
tarried, and returned at night to their houses, reporting that

old home until the nineteenth century, when the remnant, who had been
missionized, were incorporated with their kindred the Caddo.

[1] It is not uncommon for all the possessions of an Indian, including his
dwelling, to be destroyed at the time of his death. In recent times this custom
has had the tendency, as among the Navahos, for example, to cause them
to adhere to their simple aboriginal form of dwellings instead of to go to the
trouble of erecting substantial houses that might have to be demolished.

he who had been dead and for whom I wrought before them,
had got up whole and walked, had eaten and spoken with them
and that all to whom I had ministered were well and much
pleased. This caused great wonder and fear, and throughout
the land the people talked of nothing else. All to whom the
fame of it reached, came to seek us that we should cure them
and bless their children.

When the Cuthalchuches, who were in company with our
Indians, were about to return to their own country, they left
us all the prickly pears they had, without keeping one: they
gave us flints of very high value there, a palm and a half in
length, with which they cut. They begged that we would
remember them and pray to God that they might always be
well, and we promised to do so. They left, the most satisfied
beings in the world, having given us the best of all they had.

We remained with the Avavares eight months, reckoned
by the number of moons. In all this time people came to
seek us from many parts, and they said that most truly we
were children of the sun. Dorantes and the negro to this time
had not attempted to practise; but because of the great solicitation made by those coming from different parts to find us, we
all became physicians, although in being venturous and bold
to attempt the performance of any cure, I was the most remarkable. No one whom we treated, but told us he was left
well; and so great was the confidence that they would become
healed if we administered to them, they even believed that
whilst we remained none of them could die. These and the
rest of the people behind, related an extraordinary circumstance, and by the way they counted, there appeared to be
fifteen or sixteen years since it occurred.

They said that a man wandered through the country whom
they called Badthing; he was small of body and wore beard,
and they never distinctly saw his features. When he came
to the house where they lived, their hair stood up and they
trembled. Presently a blazing torch shone at the door, when
he entered and seized whom he chose, and giving him three
great gashes in the side with a very sharp flint, the width of

the hand and two palms in length, he put his hand through them, drawing forth the entrails, from one of which he would cut off a portion more or less, the length of a palm, and throw it on the embers. Then he would give three gashes to an arm, the second cut on the inside of an elbow, and would sever the limb. A little after this, he would begin to unite it, and putting his hands on the wounds, these would instantly become healed. They said that frequently in the dance he appeared among them, sometimes in the dress of a woman, at others in that of a man; that when it pleased him he would take a buhío,[1] or house, and lifting it high, after a little he would come down with it in a heavy fall. They also stated that many times they offered him victuals, but that he never ate: they asked him whence he came and where was his abiding place, and he showed them a fissure in the earth and said that his house was there below. These things they told us of, we much laughed at and ridiculed; and they seeing our incredulity, brought to us many of those they said he had seized; and we saw the marks of the gashes made in the places according to the manner they had described. We told them he was an evil one, and in the best way we could, gave them to understand, that if they would believe in God our Lord, and become Christians like us, they need have no fear of him, nor would he dare to come and inflict those injuries, and they might be certain he would not venture to appear while we remained in the land. At this they were delighted and lost much of their dread. They told us that they had seen the Asturian and Figueroa with people farther along the coast, whom we had called those of the figs.[2]

They are all ignorant of time, either by the sun or moon, nor do they reckon by the month or year; they better know and understand the differences of the seasons, when the fruits come to ripen, where the fish resort,[3] and the position of the

---

[1] See page 19, note 5.   [2] See chap. 26.

[3] Buckingham Smith prefers this meaning for *i en tiempo que muere el Pescado* to "by the time when the fish die," or "at times at which the fishes die."

stars, at which they are ready and practised. By these we were ever well treated. We dug our own food and brought our loads of wood and water. Their houses and also the things we ate, are like those of the nation from which we came, but they suffer far greater want, having neither maize, acorns, nor nuts. We always went naked like them, and covered ourselves at night with deer-skins.

Of the eight months we were among this people, six we supported in great want, for fish are not to be found where they are. At the expiration of the time, the prickly pears began to ripen,[1] and I and the negro went, without these Indians knowing it, to others farther on, a day's journey distant, called Maliacones.[2] At the end of three days, I sent him to bring Castillo and Dorantes, and they having arrived, we all set out with the Indians who were going to get the small fruit of certain trees on which they support themselves ten or twelve days whilst the prickly pears are maturing. They joined others called Arbadaos,[3] whom we found to be very weak, lank, and swollen, so much so as to cause us great astonishment. We told those with whom we came, that we wished to stop with these people, at which they showed regret and went back by the way they came; so we remained in the field near the houses of the Indians, which when they observed, after talking among themselves they came up together, and each of them taking one of us by the hand, led us to their dwellings. Among them we underwent greater hunger than with the others; we ate daily not more than two handfuls of the prickly pears, which were green and so milky they burned our mouths. As there was lack of water, those who ate suffered great thirst. In our extreme want we bought two dogs, giv-

[1] That is, until the summer of 1535.

[2] See ch. 27: "By the coast live those called Quitoks, and in front inward on the main are the Chavavares, to whom adjoin the Maliacones, the Cultalchulches and others called Susolas and the Comos." This would seem to indicate that he was journeying in a generally northward or northwestward direction.

[3] The name suggests the Bidai, a Caddoan tribe that lived at a later period west of the Trinity, about latitude 31°, but this locality does not agree with the narrative.

ing in exchange some nets, with other things, and a skin I used to cover myself.

I have already stated that throughout all this country we went naked, and as we were unaccustomed to being so, twice a year we cast our skins like serpents. The sun and air produced great sores on our breasts and shoulders, giving us sharp pain; and the large loads we had, being very heavy, caused the cords to cut into our arms. The country is so broken and thickset, that often after getting our wood in the forests, the blood flowed from us in many places, caused by the obstruction of thorns and shrubs that tore our flesh wherever we went. At times, when my turn came to get wood, after it had cost me much blood, I could not bring it out either on my back or by dragging. In these labors my only solace and relief were in thinking of the sufferings of our Redeemer, Jesus Christ, and in the blood He shed for me, in considering how much greater must have been the torment He sustained from the thorns, than that I there received.

I bartered with these Indians in combs that I made for them and in bows, arrows, and nets. We made mats, which are their houses, that they have great necessity for; and although they know how to make them, they wish to give their full time to getting food, since when otherwise employed they are pinched with hunger. Sometimes the Indians would set me to scraping and softening skins; and the days of my greatest prosperity there, were those in which they gave me skins to dress. I would scrape them a very great deal and eat the scraps, which would sustain me two or three days. When it happened among these people, as it had likewise among others whom we left behind, that a piece of meat was given us, we ate it raw; for if we had put it to roast, the first native that should come along would have taken it off and devoured it; and it appeared to us not well to expose it to this risk; besides we were in such condition it would have given us pain to eat it roasted, and we could not have digested it so well as raw. Such was the life we spent there; and the meagre subsistence

G

we earned by the matters of traffic which were the work of our hands.

Chapter 23

Of our departure after having eaten the dogs.

After eating the dogs, it seemed to us we had some strength to go forward; and so commending ourselves to God our Lord, that He would guide us, we took our leave of the Indians. They showed us the way to others, near by, who spoke their language. While on our journey, rain fell, and we travelled the day in wet. We lost our way and went to stop in an extensive wood. We pulled many leaves of the prickly pear, which we put at night in an oven we made, and giving them much heat, by the morning they were in readiness. After eating, we put ourselves under the care of the Almighty and started. We discovered the way we had lost. Having passed the wood, we found other houses, and coming up to them, we saw two women with some boys walking in the forest, who were frightened at the sight of us and fled, running into the woods to call the men. These arriving, stopped behind trees to look at us. We called to them, and they came up with much timidity. After some conversation they told us that food was very scarce with them; that near by were many houses of their people to which they would guide us. We came at night where were fifty dwellings. The inhabitants were astonished at our appearance, showing much fear. After becoming somewhat accustomed to us, they reached their hands to our faces and bodies, and passed them in like manner over their own.

We stayed there that night, and in the morning the Indians brought us their sick, beseeching us that we would bless them. They gave us of what they had to eat, the leaves of the prickly pear and the green fruit roasted. As they did this with kindness and good will, and were happy to be without anything to eat, that they might have food to give us, we tarried

some days. While there, others came from beyond, and when
they were about to depart, we told our entertainers that we
wished to go with those people. They felt much uneasiness
at this, and pressed us warmly to stay: however, we took our
leave in the midst of their weeping, for our departure weighed
heavily upon them.

Chapter 24

Customs of the Indians of that country.

From the Island of Malhado to this land, all the Indians
whom we saw have the custom from the time in which their
wives find themselves pregnant, of not sleeping with them until
two years after they have given birth. The children are suckled
until the age of twelve years, when they are old enough to get
support for themselves. We asked why they reared them in
this manner; and they said because of the great poverty of the
land, it happened many times, as we witnessed, that they were
two or three days without eating, sometimes four, and consequently, in seasons of scarcity, the children were allowed to
suckle, that they might not famish; otherwise those who lived
would be delicate, having little strength.

If any one chance to fall sick in the desert, and cannot keep
up with the rest, the Indians leave him to perish, unless it be
a son or a brother; him they will assist, even to carrying on
their back. It is common among them all to leave their wives
when there is no conformity, and directly they connect themselves with whom they please. This is the course of the men
who are childless; those who have children remain with their
wives and never abandon them. When they dispute and quarrel in their towns, they strike each other with the fists, fighting
until exhausted, and then separate. Sometimes they are
parted by the women going between them; the men never
interfere. For no disaffection that arises do they resort to
bows and arrows. After they have fought, or had out their
dispute, they take their dwellings and go into the woods, living

apart from each other until their heat has subsided. When no longer offended and their anger is gone, they return. From that time they are friends as if nothing had happened; nor is it necessary that any one should mend their friendships, as they in this way again unite them. If those that quarrel are single, they go to some neighboring people, and although these should be enemies, they receive them well and welcome them warmly, giving them so largely of what they have, that when their animosity cools, and they return to their town, they go rich.

They are all warlike, and have as much strategy for protecting themselves against enemies as they could have were they reared in Italy in continual feuds. When they are in a part of the country where their enemies may attack them, they place their houses on the skirt of a wood, the thickest and most tangled they can find, and near it make a ditch in which they sleep. The warriors are covered by small pieces of stick through which are loop-holes; these hide them and present so false an appearance, that if come upon they are not discovered. They open a very narrow way, entering into the midst of the wood, where a spot is prepared on which the women and children sleep. When night comes they kindle fires in their lodges, that should spies be about, they may think to find them there; and before daybreak they again light those fires. If the enemy comes to assault the houses, they who are in the ditch make a sally; and from their trenches do much injury without those who are outside seeing or being able to find them. When there is no wood in which they can take shelter in this way, and make their ambuscades, they settle on open ground at a place they select, which they invest with trenches covered with broken sticks, having apertures whence to discharge arrows. These arrangements are made for night.

While I was among the Aguenes,[1] their enemies coming suddenly at midnight, fell upon them, killed three and wounded many, so that they ran from their houses to the fields before them. As soon as these ascertained that their assailants had withdrawn, they returned to pick up all the arrows the others

[1] Elsewhere called Doguenes.

had shot, and following after them in the most stealthy manner possible, came that night to their dwellings without their presence being suspected. At four o'clock in the morning the Aguenes attacked them, killed five, and wounded numerous others, and made them flee from their houses, leaving their bows with all they possessed. In a little while came the wives of the Quevenes [1] to them and formed a treaty whereby the parties became friends. The women, however, are sometimes the cause of war. All these nations, when they have personal enmities, and are not of one family, assassinate at night, waylay, and inflict gross barbarities on each other.

Chapter 25

Vigilance of the Indians in war.

They are the most watchful in danger of any people I ever knew. If they fear an enemy they are awake the night long, each with a bow at his side and a dozen arrows. He that would sleep tries his bow, and if it is not strung, he gives the turn necessary to the cord. They often come out from their houses, bending to the ground in such manner that they cannot be seen, looking and watching on all sides to catch every object. If they perceive anything about, they are at once in the bushes with their bows and arrows, and there remain until day, running from place to place where it is needful to be, or where they think their enemies are. When the light has come, they unbend their bows until they go out to hunt. The strings are the sinews of deer.

The method they have of fighting, is bending low to the earth, and whilst shot at they move about, speaking and leaping from one point to another, thus avoiding the shafts of their enemies. So effectual is their manœuvring that they can receive very little injury from crossbow or arquebus; they rather scoff at them; for these arms are of little value employed in

---

[1] Guevenes in the edition of 1542.

open field, where the Indians move nimbly about. They are proper for defiles and in water; everywhere else the horse will best subdue, being what the natives universally dread.[1] Whosoever would fight them must be cautious to show no fear, or desire to have anything that is theirs; while war exists they must be treated with the utmost rigor; for if they discover any timidity or covetousness, they are a race that well discern the opportunities for vengeance, and gather strength from any weakness of their adversaries. When they use arrows in battle and exhaust their store, each returns his own way, without the one party following the other, although the one be many and the other few, such being their custom. Oftentimes the body of an Indian is traversed by the arrow; yet unless the entrails or the heart be struck, he does not die but recovers from the wound.

I believe these people see and hear better, and have keener senses than any other in the world. They are great in hunger, thirst, and cold, as if they were made for the endurance of these more than other men, by habit and nature.

Thus much I have wished to say, beyond the gratification of that desire men have to learn the customs and manners of each other, that those who hereafter at some time find themselves amongst these people, may have knowledge of their usages and artifices, the value of which they will not find inconsiderable in such event.

Chapter 26

Of the nations and tongues.

I desire to enumerate the natives and tongues that exist from those of Malhado to the farthest Cuchendados there are. Two languages are found in the island; the people of one are called

---

[1] Cabeza de Vaca is now evidently recalling the experience of Narvaez's men in Florida.

Cahoques,[1] of the other, Han. On the tierra-firme, over against the island, is another people, called Chorruco, who take their names from the forests where they live. Advancing by the shores of the sea, others inhabit who are called the Doguenes, and opposite them others by the name of Mendica. Farther along the coast are the Quevenes, and in front of them on the main, the Mariames; and continuing by the coast are other called Guaycones; and in front of them, within on the main, the Yguazes. At the close of these are the Atayos; and in their rear others, the Acubadaos, and beyond them are many in the same direction. By the coast live those called Quitoks, and in front inward on the main are the Chavavares, to whom adjoin the Maliacones, the Cultalchulches and others called Susolas, and the Comos; and by the coast farther on are the Camoles; and on the same coast in advance are those whom we called People of the Figs.

They all differ in their habitations, towns and tongues. There is a language in which calling to a person, for "look here" they say "Arre aca," and to a dog "Xo." [2] Everywhere they produce stupefaction with a smoke, and for that they will give whatever they possess. They drink a tea made from leaves of a tree like those of the oak, which they toast in a pot; and after these are parched, the vessel, still remaining on the fire, is filled with water. When the liquor has twice boiled, they pour it into a jar, and in cooling it use the half of a gourd. So soon as it is covered thickly with froth, it is drunk as warm as can be supported; and from the time it is taken out of the pot until it is used they are crying aloud: "Who wishes to

---

[1] In the 1542 edition these tribal names are similarly spelled except in the case of Capoques, Charruco, Deguenes, Yeguaces, Decubadaos (for Acubadaos), Quitoles (for Quitoks), Chauauares, and Camolas. None of these Indians have thus far been conclusively identified with later historical tribes, with the possible exception of the Atayos and the Quevenes. See p. 76, note 2, and p. 59, note 1.

[2] In the 1542 edition, as given by Mrs. Bandelier, "Among them is a language wherein they call men *mira aca, arraca,* and dogs *xo.*" Compare *háka,* "sit down," in Karankawa (Gatschet, *Karankawa Indians,* Cambridge, Mass., 1891, p. 80). In the above it would appear as if the Spanish *mira* had been regarded as a part of the Indian exclamation.

drink?" When the women hear these cries, they instantly stop, fearing to move; and although they may be heavily laden, they dare do nothing further. Should one of them move, they dishonor her, beating her with sticks, and greatly vexed, throw away the liquor they have prepared; while they who have drunk eject it, which they do readily and without pain. The reason they give for this usage is, that when they are about to drink, if the women move from where they hear the cry, something pernicious enters the body in that liquid, shortly producing death. At the time of boiling, the vessel must be covered; and if it should happen to be open when a woman passes, they use no more of that liquid, but throw it out. The color is yellow. They are three days taking it, eating nothing in the time, and daily each one drinks an arroba and a half.[1]

When the women have their indisposition, they seek food only for themselves, as no one else will eat of what they bring. In the time I was thus among these people, I witnessed a diabolical practice; a man living with another, one of those who are emasculate and impotent. These go habited like women, and perform their duties, use the bow, and carry heavy loads. Among them we saw many mutilated in the way I describe. They are more muscular than other men, and taller: they bear very weighty burthens.

Chapter 27

We moved away and were well received.

After parting with those we left weeping,[2] we went with the others to their houses and were hospitably received by the

---

[1] The tree from which the so-called "black drink" is made is *Ilex cassine*, and the custom of preparing and partaking of the liquid (known also as Carolina tea) was general among the tribes of the South, including the Gulf coast. The drink was known among the Catawbas as *yaupon*, among the Creeks as *ássi-lupútski*, the latter signifying "small leaves," commonly abbreviated *ássi*, whence the name of the celebrated Seminole chief *Osceola*, i.e., "Black-drink Hallooer," or "Black-drink Singer." The partaking of the black drink was an important part of the *puskita*, or *busk*, ceremony among the Creeks.

[2] The Arbadaos or Acubadaos. See chs. 22, 23.

people in them. They brought their children to us that we might touch their hands, and gave us a great quantity of the flour of mezquiquez.[1] The fruit while hanging on the tree, is very bitter and like unto the carob; when eaten with earth it is sweet and wholesome. The method they have of preparing it is this: they make a hole of requisite depth in the ground, and throwing in the fruit, pound it with a club the size of the leg, a fathom and a half in length, until it is well mashed. Besides the earth that comes from the hole, they bring and add some handfuls, then returning to beat it a little while longer. Afterward it is thrown into a jar, like a basket, upon which water is poured until it rises above and covers the mixture. He that beats it tastes it, and if it appears to him not sweet, he asks for earth to stir in, which is added until he finds it sweet. Then all sit round, and each putting in a hand, takes out as much as he can. The pits and hulls are thrown upon a skin, whence they are taken by him who does the pounding, and put into the jar whereon water is poured as at first, whence having expressed the froth and juice, again the pits and husks are thrown upon the skin. This they do three or four times to each pounding. Those present, for whom this is a great banquet, have their stomachs greatly distended by the earth and water they swallow. The Indians made a protracted festival of this sort on our account, and great *areitos*[2] during the time we remained.

When we proposed to leave them, some women of another people came there who lived farther along. They informed us whereabout were their dwellings, and we set out for them, although the inhabitants entreated us to remain for that day, because the houses whither we were going were distant, there was no path to them, the women had come tired, and would the next day go with us refreshed and show us the way. Soon after we had taken our leave, some of the women, who had come on together from the same town, followed behind us. As

[1] The mesquite (*Prosopis juliflora*). The beans are still extensively used as food by the Indians of southern Arizona and northern Mexico.

[2] See p. 52, note 3.

there are no paths in the country we presently got lost, and thus travelled four leagues, when, stopping to drink, we found the women in pursuit of us at the water, who told us of the great exertion they had made to overtake us. We went on taking them for guides, and passed over a river towards evening, the water reaching to the breast. It might be as wide as that at Seville; its current was very rapid.[1]

At sunset we reached a hundred Indian habitations. Before we arrived, all the people who were in them came out to receive us, with such yells as were terrific, striking the palms of their hands violently against their thighs. They brought us gourds bored with holes and having pebbles in them, an instrument for the most important occasions, produced only at the dance or to effect cures, and which none dare touch but those who own them. They say there is virtue in them, and because they do not grow in that country, they come from heaven; nor do they know where they are to be found, only that the rivers bring them in their floods.[2] So great were the fear and distraction of these people, some to reach us sooner than others that they might touch us, they pressed us so closely that they lacked little of killing us; and without letting us put our feet to the ground, carried us to their dwellings. We were so crowded upon by numbers, that we went into the houses they had made for us. On no account would we consent that they should rejoice over us any more that night. The night long they passed in singing and dancing among themselves; and the next day they brought us all the people of the town, that we should touch and bless them in the way we had done to others among whom we had been. After this performance they presented many arrows to some women of the other town who had accompanied theirs.

The next day we left, and all the people of the place went with us; and when we came to the other Indians we were as

---

[1] Probably the Colorado River. Buckingham Smith remarks that the Guadalquivir at Seville is about a hundred paces in width.

[2] The Pueblo Indians of New Mexico have cultivated gourds for use as rattles and receptacles, especially dippers, from time immemorial. If the Pecos

well received as we had been by the last. They gave us of
what they had to eat, and the deer they had killed that day.
Among them we witnessed another custom, which is this:
they who were with us took from him who came to be cured,
his bow and arrows, shoes and beads if he wore any, and then
brought him before us, that we should heal him. After being
attended to, he would go away highly pleased, saying that he
was well. So we parted from these Indians, and went to others
by whom we were welcomed. They brought us their sick,
which, we having blessed, they declared were sound; he who
was healed, believed we could cure him; and with what the
others to whom we had administered would relate, they made
great rejoicing and dancing, so that they left us no sleep.

Chapter 28

Of another strange custom.

Leaving these Indians, we went to the dwellings of numerous others. From this place began another novel custom,
which is, that while the people received us very well, those who
accompanied us began to use them so ill as to take their goods
and ransack their houses, without leaving anything. To witness this unjust procedure gave us great concern, inflicted too
on those who received us hospitably; we feared also that it
might provoke offence, and be the cause of some tumult between them; but, as we were in no condition to make it better,
or to dare chastise such conduct, for the present we had to bear
with it, until a time when we might have greater authority
among them. They, also, who lost their effects, noticing
our dejection, attempted to console us by saying that we should
not be grieved on this account, as they were so gratified at

were the stream, or one of the streams, whence the gourds were derived, they
might have come from the pueblo of Pecos, southeast of the present Santa
Fé; if from the Rio Grande, they might have come from various villages
along that river and its tributaries in the north. See p. 95, note 1.

having seen us, they held their properties to be well bestowed, and that farther on they would be repaid by others who were very rich.

On all the day's travel we received great inconvenience from the many persons following us. Had we attempted to escape we could not have succeeded, such was their haste in pursuit, in order to touch us. So great was the importunity for this privilege, we consumed three hours in going through with them that they might depart. The next day all the inhabitants were brought before us. The greater part were clouded of an eye, and others in like manner were entirely blind, which caused in us great astonishment. They are a people of fine figure, agreeable features, and whiter than any of the many nations we had seen until then.

Here we began to see mountains; they appeared to come in succession from the North Sea, and, according to the information the Indians gave us, we believe they rise fifteen leagues from the sea.[1] We set forth in a direction towards them with these Indians, and they guided us by the way of some kindred of theirs; for they wished to take us only where were their relations, and were not willing that their enemies should come to such great good, as they thought it was to see us. After we arrived they that went with us plundered the others; but as the people there knew the fashion, they had hidden some things before we came; and having welcomed us with great festivity and rejoicing, they brought out and presented to us what they had concealed. These were beads, ochre, and some little bags of silver.[2] In pursuance of custom, we directly gave them to

[1] Probably the escarpment that extends from Austin to Eagle Pass. The Colorado (which was probably the wide, deep stream previously encountered) was crossed seemingly below the present Austin. It should be remembered that the information regarding the point at which the mountains commenced to rise was given by Indians whose language the Spaniards could not understand. At any rate, the fact that the latter believed the mountains to rise fifteen leagues from the sea would tend to indicate that the direction they had been following was a northerly one. See the statement in the following paragraph of the text.

[2] According to Oviedo (p. 617): "This is an error of the printer, and should read 'little bags of margarite [pearl-mica],' instead of silver." Buck-

the Indians who came with us, which, when they had received, they began their dances and festivities, sending to call others from a town near by, that they also might see us.

In the afternoon they all came and brought us beads and bows, with trifles of other sort, which we also distributed. Desiring to leave the next day, the inhabitants all wished to take us to others, friends of theirs, who were at the point of the ridge, stating that many houses were there, and people who would give us various things. As it was out of our way, we did not wish to go to them, and took our course along the plain near the mountains, which we believed not to be distant from the coast [1] where the people are all evil disposed, and we considered it preferable to travel inland; [2] for those of the interior are of a better condition and treated us mildly, and we felt sure that we should find it more populous and better provisioned. Moreover, we chose this course because in traversing the country we should learn many particulars of it, so that should God our Lord be pleased to take any of us thence, and lead us to the land of Christians, we might carry that information and news of it. As the Indians saw that we were determined not to go where they would take us, they said that in the direction we would go, there were no inhabitants, nor any prickly pears nor other thing to eat, and begged us to tarry there that day; we accordingly did so. They directly sent two of their number to seek for people in the direction that we wished to go; and the next day we left, taking with us several of the Indians. The women went carrying water, and so great was our authority that no one dared drink of it without our permission.

Two leagues from there we met those who had gone out, and they said that they had found no one; at which the Indians seemed much disheartened, and began again to entreat

ingham Smith translates Oviedo's *margarita*, " pearls," and Cabeza de Vaca's *margarita* (ch. 29) as " marquesite." It may be added that magnetic iron ore of the highest quality occurs in Mason County, Texas.

[1] In the face of such an assertion it is difficult to conceive that the Spaniards had been journeying directly westward, away from the coast.

[2] That is, they decided to change their course from northward to a more westward direction.

us to go by way of the mountains. We did not wish to do so, and they, seeing our disposition, took their leave of us with much regret, and returned down the river to their houses, while we ascended along by it. After a little time we came upon two women with burthens, who put them down as they saw us, and brought to us, of what they carried. It was the flour of maize. They told us that farther up on that river we should find dwellings, a plenty of prickly pears and of that meal. We bade them farewell: they were going to those whom we had left.

We walked until sunset, and arrived at a town of some twenty houses, where we were received with weeping and in great sorrow; for they already knew that wheresoever we should come, all would be pillaged and spoiled by those who accompanied us. When they saw that we were alone, they lost their fear, and gave us prickly pears with nothing more. We remained there that night, and at dawn, the Indians who had left us the day before, broke upon their houses. As they came upon the occupants unprepared and in supposed safety, having no place in which to conceal anything, all they possessed was taken from them, for which they wept much. In consolation the plunderers told them that we were children of the sun and that we had power to heal the sick and to destroy; and other lies even greater than these, which none knew how to tell better than they when they find it convenient. They bade them conduct us with great respect, advised that they should be careful to offend us in nothing, give us all they might possess, and endeavor to take us where people were numerous; and that wheresoever they arrived with us, they should rob and pillage the people of what they have, since this was customary.

Chapter 29

The Indians plunder each other.

After the Indians had told and shown these natives well what to do, they left us together and went back. Remembering the instruction, they began to treat us with the same awe and reverence that the others had shown. We travelled with them three days, and they took us where were many inhabitants. Before we arrived, these were informed of our coming by the others, who told them respecting us all that the first had imparted, adding much more; for these people are all very fond of romance, and are great liars, particularly so where they have any interest. When we came near the houses all the inhabitants ran out with delight and great festivity to receive us. Among other things, two of their physicians gave us two gourds, and thenceforth we carried these with us, and added to our authority a token highly reverenced by Indians.[1] Those who accompanied us rifled the houses; but as these were many and the others few, they could not carry off what they took, and abandoned more than the half.

From here we went along the base of the ridge, striking inland more than fifty leagues, and at the close we found upwards of forty houses. Among the articles given us, Andrés Dorantes received a hawk-bell of copper, thick and large, figured with a face, which the natives had shown, greatly prizing it. They told him that they had received it from others, their neighbors; we asked them whence the others had obtained it, and they said it had been brought from the northern direction, where there was much copper, which was highly esteemed. We concluded that whencesoever it came there was a foundry, and that work was done in hollow form.[2]

We departed the next day, and traversed a ridge seven leagues in extent. The stones on it are scoria of iron.[3] At night we arrived at many houses seated on the banks of a very beautiful river.[4] The owners of them came half way out on

---

[1] The possession of one of these "medicine" rattles was not improbably one of the causes of the death of Estévanico at the hands of the Zuñis of Cibola in 1539. See the Introduction, and compare p. 90, note 2; p. 117, note 2.

[2] See p. 97, note 1.

[3] See pp. 92–93, note 2, regarding the occurrence of magnetic iron in Mason County, where it is found in great quantities, but is yet unworked.

[4] Perhaps the Llano, a branch of the Colorado, or possibly they had met the Colorado again. See p. 90, note 1.

the road to meet us, bringing their children on their backs. They gave us many little bags of margarite [1] and pulverized galena,[2] with which they rub the face. They presented us many beads, and blankets of cowhide, loading all who accompanied us with some of every thing they had. They eat prickly pears and the seed of pine. In that country are small pine trees,[3] the cones like little eggs; but the seed is better than that of Castile, as its husk is very thin, and while green is beaten and made into balls, to be thus eaten. If the seed be dry, it is pounded in the husk, and consumed in the form of flour.

Those who there received us, after they had touched us went running to their houses and directly returned, and did not stop running, going and coming, to bring us in this manner many things for support on the way. They fetched a man to me and stated that a long time since he had been wounded by an arrow in the right shoulder, and that the point of the shaft was lodged above his heart, which, he said, gave him much pain, and in consequence, he was always sick. Probing the wound I felt the arrow-head, and found it had passed through the cartilage. With a knife I carried, I opened the breast to the place, and saw the point was aslant and troublesome to take out. I continued to cut, and, putting in the point of the knife, at last with great difficulty I drew the head forth. It was very large. With the bone of a deer, and by virtue of my calling, I made two stitches that threw the blood over me, and with hair from a skin I stanched the flow. They asked me for the arrow-head after I had taken it out, which I gave, when the whole town came to look at it. They sent it into the back country that the people there might view it. In consequence of this operation they had many of their customary dances

[1] See p. 92, note 2. In the edition of 1542 the text here says *silver*.

[2] Lead is found in Texas in the trans-Pecos region. The mineral resources of the state have not yet been well exploited.

[3] Doubtless the nut pine (*Pinus edulis*). Cabeza de Vaca evidently here aims to describe the character of this tree and its fruit without necessarily asserting that the tree was found growing very far east of the Pecos. In the valley of the latter stream it is more or less prolific.

and festivities. The next day I cut the two stitches and the Indian was well. The wound I made appeared only like a seam in the palm of the hand. He said he felt no pain or sensitiveness in it whatsoever. This cure gave us control throughout the country in all that the inhabitants had power, or deemed of any value, or cherished. We showed them the hawk-bell we brought, and they told us that in the place whence that had come, were buried many plates of the same material; it was a thing they greatly esteemed, and where it came from were fixed habitations.[1] The country we considered to be on the South Sea, which we had ever understood to be richer than the one of the North.

We left there, and travelled through so many sorts of people, of such diverse languages, the memory fails to recall them. They ever plundered each other, and those that lost, like those that gained, were fully content.[2] We drew so many followers

[1] The allusion is probably to Mexico rather than to a northern country, as previously asserted by the Indians. See the second preceding paragraph.

[2] Of this exchange of gifts, or perhaps we may call it plunder, there was an echo a few years later, when Coronado and his army were traversing the eastern part of the Staked Plain, under the guidance of the "Turk," in search of Quivira, in 1541. Before sending the army back, and while among the ravines of western Texas, Rodrigo Maldonado was sent forward to explore, and in four days reached a deep ravine in the bottom of which was a village that Cabeza de Vaca had visited, on which account (see p. 332) "they presented Don Rodrigo with a pile of tanned skins and other things." An unfair distribution being threatened, the men rushed upon the skins and took possession without further ado. "The women and some others were left crying, because they thought that the strangers were not going to take anything, but would bless them as Cabeza de Vaca and Dorantes had done *when they passed through here.*" Captain Jaramillo does not mention this occurrence in his narrative (*Fourteenth Report of the Bureau of American Ethnology*, p. 588), but he speaks of reaching a settlement of Indians, in advance of that, according to the narrations, of which Castañeda speaks, "among whom there was an old blind man with a beard, who gave us to understand by signs which he made, that he had seen four others like us many days before, whom he had seen near there and rather more toward New Spain [Mexico], and we so understood him, and presumed that it was Dorantes and Cabeza de Vaca and those whom I have mentioned." Although we do not have here conclusive evidence that Cabeza de Vaca actually visited the village or villages mentioned, there is no question that he must have been in this vicinity, and as the evidence is strong that the Rio Colorado was the ravined stream alluded to, there is little likelihood that Cabeza de Vaca's route lay far below that river.

K

that we had not use for their services. While on our way through these vales, every Indian carried a club three palms in length, and kept on the alert. On raising a hare, which animals are abundant, they surround it directly and throw numerous clubs at it with astonishing precision. Thus they cause it to run from one to another; so that, according to my thinking, it is the most pleasing sport which can be imagined, as oftentimes the animal runs into the hand. So many did they give us that at night when we stopped we had eight or ten back-loads apiece.[1] Those having bows were not with us; they dispersed about the ridge in pursuit of deer; and at dark came bringing five or six for each of us, besides quail, and other game. Indeed, whatever they either killed or found, was put before us, without themselves daring to take anything until we had blessed it, though they should be expiring of hunger, they having so established the rule, since marching with us.

The women carried many mats, of which the men made us houses, each of us having a separate one, with all his attendants. After these were put up, we ordered the deer and hares to be roasted, with the rest that had been taken. This was done by means of certain ovens made for the purpose. Of each we took a little and the remainder we gave to the principal personage of the people coming with us, directing him to divide it among the rest. Every one brought his portion to us, that we might breathe upon and give it our benediction; for not until then did they dare eat any of it. Frequently we were accompanied by three or four thousand persons, and as we had to breathe upon and sanctify the food and drink for each, and grant permission to do the many things they would come to ask, it may be seen how great was the annoyance. The women first brought us prickly pears, spiders, worms, and whatever else they could gather; for even were they famishing, they would eat nothing unless we gave it them.

In company with these, we crossed a great river coming

---

[1] The Pueblo Indians of New Mexico have similar communal rabbit-hunts, in which the animals are killed with a curved stick shaped somewhat like a boomerang.

from the north,[1] and passing over some plains thirty leagues in extent, we found many persons coming a long distance to receive us, who met us on the road over which we were to travel, and welcomed us in the manner of those we had left.

Chapter 30

The fashion of receiving us changes.

From this place was another method of receiving us, as respects the pillage. Those who came out in the ways to bring us presents were not plundered; but on our coming into their houses, themselves offered us all they had, as well as the houses. We gave the things to the chief personages who accompanied us, that they should divide them; those who were despoiled always followed us until coming to a populous country, where they might repair their loss. They would tell those among whom we came, to retain everything and make no concealment, as nothing could be done without our knowledge, and we might cause them to die, as the sun revealed everything to us. So great was their fear that during the first days they were with us, they continually trembled, without daring even to speak, or raise their eyes to the heavens. They guided us through more than fifty leagues of desert, over rough mountains, which being dry were without game, and in consequence we suffered much from hunger.[2]

At the termination we forded a very large river, the water

[1] Evidently the Pecos. This is the first stream mentioned as flowing from the north.

[2] Eighty leagues would probably be a reasonable estimate of the distance from the Pecos to the Rio Grande, which the travellers had now reached. It would seem strange that no mention is made of the cañon of the latter stream (which hereabouts flows through a territory four thousand feet above sea level), were it not for the fact that they had become thoroughly inured to suffering and hard travelling; nevertheless, the terribly rough country through which they had just been guided from stream to stream is commented on, while the fact that the Rio Grande here "flows between some ridges" is mentioned farther on.

coming up to our breasts. From this place, many of the people began to sicken from the great privation and labor they had undergone in the passage of those ridges, which are sterile and difficult in the extreme. They conducted us to certain plains at the base of the mountains, where people came to meet us from a great distance, and received us as the last had done, and gave so many goods to those who came with us, that the half were left because they could not be carried. I told those who gave, to resume the goods that they might not lie there and be lost; but they answered they could in no wise do so, as it was not their custom after they had bestowed a thing to take it back;[1] so considering the articles no longer of value, they were left to perish.

We told these people that we desired to go where the sun sets; and they said inhabitants in that direction were remote. We commanded them to send and make known our coming; but they strove to excuse themselves the best they could, the people being their enemies, and they did not wish to go to them. Not daring to disobey, however, they sent two women, one of their own, the other a captive from that people; for the women can negotiate even though there be war. We followed them, and stopped at a place where we agreed to wait. They tarried five days; and the Indians said they could not have found anybody.

We told them to conduct us towards the north; and they answered, as before, that except afar off there were no people in that direction, and nothing to eat, nor could water be found.[2] Notwithstanding all this, we persisted, and said we desired to go in that course. They still tried to excuse themselves in the best manner possible. At this we became offended, and one night I went out to sleep in the woods apart from them; but directly they came to where I was, and remained all night without sleep, talking to me in great fear, telling me how terrified they were, beseeching us to be no longer angry, and said

---

[1] An assertion quite contrary to the popular belief in "Indian gifts."

[2] The Indians were evidently endeavoring to compel the Spaniards to remain among them as long as possible.

that they would lead us in the direction it was our wish to go, though they knew they should die on the way.

Whilst we still feigned to be displeased lest their fright should leave them, a remarkable circumstance happened, which was that on the same day many of the Indians became ill, and the next day eight men died. Abroad in the country, wheresoever this became known, there was such dread that it seemed as if the inhabitants would die of fear at sight of us. They besought us not to remain angered, nor require that more of them should die. They believed we caused their death by only willing it, when in truth it gave us so much pain that it could not be greater; for, beyond their loss, we feared they might all die, or abandon us of fright, and that other people thenceforward would do the same, seeing what had come to these. We prayed to God, our Lord, to relieve them; and from that time the sick began to get better.

We witnessed one thing with great admiration, that the parents, brothers, and wives of those who died had great sympathy for them in their suffering; but, when dead, they showed no feeling, neither did they weep nor speak among themselves, make any signs, nor dare approach the bodies until we commanded these to be taken to burial.

While we were among these people, which was more than fifteen days, we saw no one speak to another, nor did we see an infant smile: the only one that cried they took off to a distance, and with the sharp teeth of a rat they scratched it from the shoulders down nearly to the end of the legs. Seeing this cruelty, and offended at it, I asked why they did so: they said for chastisement, because the child had wept in my presence. These terrors they imparted to all those who had lately come to know us, that they might give us whatever they had; for they knew we kept nothing, and would relinquish all to them. This people were the most obedient we had found in all the land, the best conditioned, and, in general, comely.

The sick having recovered, and three days having passed since we came to the place, the women whom we sent away returned, and said they had found very few people; nearly all had gone for cattle, being then in the season. We ordered the convalescent to remain and the well to go with us, and that at the end of two days' journey those women should go with two of our number to fetch up the people, and bring them on the road to receive us. Consequently, the next morning the most robust started with us. At the end of three days' travel we stopped, and the next day Alonzo del Castillo set out with Estevanico the negro, taking the two women as guides. She that was the captive led them to the river which ran between some ridges,[1] where was a town at which her father lived; and these habitations were the first seen, having the appearance and structure of houses.[2]

Here Castillo and Estevanico arrived, and, after talking with the Indians, Castillo returned at the end of three days to the spot where he had left us, and brought five or six of the people. He told us he had found fixed dwellings of civilization, that the inhabitants lived on beans and pumpkins,[3] and that he had seen maize. This news the most of anything delighted us, and for it we gave infinite thanks to our Lord. Castillo told us the negro was coming with all the population to wait for us in the road not far off. Accordingly we left, and, having travelled a league and a half, we met the negro and the people coming to

[1] *The* river was the Rio Grande, to which they had now returned. The description of the topography is in accordance with the facts.

[2] The substantial character of the houses was noted also by Antonio de Espejo, toward the close of 1582, on his journey northward to New Mexico. Espejo speaks of these Indians, the Jumanos, or Patarabueyes, as occupying five villages from about the junction of the Conchos northward up the Rio Grande for twelve days' journey, and as numbering ten thousand souls — but Espejo's estimates of population are always greatly exaggerated. More important is his statement that the Jumanos knew something of Christianity which they had gleaned years before from three Christians and a negro, whom he naturally believed to have been "Alvaro Nuñez Cabeza de Vaca, y Dorantes, y Castillo Maldonado, y un negro," who had made their escape from Narvaez's fleet. This is one of the few definite points of the narrative that can be established without question. See *Coleccion de Documentos Inéditos relativos . . . de América y Oceanía*, XV. 107 (1871).

[3] *Melones* in the edition of 1542. Bandelier has no doubt that a species of squash is meant.

receive us. They gave us beans, many pumpkins, calabashes,[1] blankets of cowhide and other things. As this people and those who came with us were enemies,[2] and spoke not each other's language, we discharged the latter, giving them what we received, and we departed with the others. Six leagues from there, as the night set in we arrived at the houses, where great festivities were made over us. We remained one day, and the next set out with these Indians. They took us to the settled habitations of others,[3] who lived upon the same food.

From that place onward was another usage. Those who knew of our approach did not come out to receive us on the road as the others had done, but we found them in their houses, and they had made others for our reception. They were all seated with their faces turned to the wall, their heads down, the hair brought before their eyes, and their property placed in a heap in the middle of the house. From this place they began to give us many blankets of skin; and they had nothing they did not bestow. They have the finest persons of any people we saw, of the greatest activity and strength, who best understood us and intelligently answered our inquiries. We called them the Cow nation, because most of the cattle killed are slaughtered in their neighborhood, and along up that river for over fifty leagues they destroy great numbers.[4]

They go entirely naked after the manner of the first we saw. The women are dressed with deer-skin, and some few men,

[1] . . . "beans and many squashes to eat, gourds to carry water in" (ed. of 1542, Bandelier translation).

[2] That is, the Jumanos and probably the Tobosos respectively. The captive woman evidently belonged to the latter tribe.

[3] Apparently other settlements of the Jumanos, as mentioned in the above note. The Spaniards were now going up the Rio Grande.

[4] Although they resided in permanent habitations at this time, the Jumanos lived east of the Rio Grande, in New Mexico, a century later and practised the habits of the buffalo-hunting plains tribes rather than those of sedentary Indians. The "neighborhood" was evidently not the immediate vicinity, and the stream alluded to seems much more likely to have been the Pecos than the Rio Grande, the former having been named Rio de las Vacas by Espejo in 1583. On this point see the opening paragraph of the following chapter.

mostly the aged, who are incapable of fighting. The country
is very populous. We asked how it was they did not plant
maize. They answered it was that they might not lose what
they should put in the ground; that the rains had failed for two
years in succession, and the seasons were so dry the seed had
everywhere been taken by the moles, and they could not venture to plant again until after water had fallen copiously. They
begged us to tell the sky to rain, and to pray for it, and we said
we would do so. We also desired to know whence they got the
maize, and they told us from where the sun goes down; there it
grew throughout the region, and the nearest was by that path.
Since they did not wish to go thither, we asked by what direction we might best proceed, and bade them inform us concerning
the way; they said the path was along up by that river towards
the north, for otherwise in a journey of seventeen days we
should find nothing to eat, except a fruit they call *chacan*, that
is ground between stones, and even then it could with difficulty
be eaten for its dryness and pungency, — which was true.
They showed it to us there, and we could not eat it. They informed us also that, whilst we travelled by the river upward, we
should all the way pass through a people that were their enemies, who spoke their tongue, and, though they had nothing to
give us to eat, they would receive us with the best good will,
and present us with mantles of cotton, hides, and other articles
of their wealth.[1] Still it appeared to them we ought by no
means to take that course.

Doubting what it would be best to do, and which way we
should choose for suitableness and support, we remained two
days with these Indians, who gave us beans and pumpkins for
our subsistence. Their method of cooking is so new that for
its strangeness I desire to speak of it; thus it may be seen and
remarked how curious and diversified are the contrivances and

---

[1] The Pueblo Indians of New Mexico are here referred to. Later Spanish
explorers found cotton garments in abundance in their country. The statement here that the Jumanos spoke the same tongue as some of the Pueblos
is significant, and accounts in a measure for the affiliation of the Jumanos
with the Piros when missions were established by the Franciscans among these
two tribes east of the Rio Grande, in New Mexico, in 1629.

ingenuity of the human family. Not having discovered the use of pipkins, to boil what they would eat, they fill the half of a large calabash with water, and throw on the fire many stones of such as are most convenient and readily take the heat. When hot, they are taken up with tongs of sticks and dropped into the calabash until the water in it boils from the fervor of the stones. Then whatever is to be cooked is put in, and until it is done they continue taking out cooled stones and throwing in hot ones. Thus they boil their food.[1]

Chapter 31

Of our taking the way to the maize.

Two days being spent while we tarried, we resolved to go in search of the maize. We did not wish to follow the path leading to where the cattle are, because it is towards the north, and for us very circuitous, since we ever held it certain that going towards the sunset we must find what we desired.

Thus we took our way, and traversed all the country until coming out at the South Sea. Nor was the dread we had of the sharp hunger through which we should have to pass (as in verity we did, throughout the seventeen days' journey of which the natives spoke) sufficient to hinder us. During all that time, in ascending by the river, they gave us many coverings of cowhide; but we did not eat of the fruit. Our sustenance each day was about a handful of deer-suet, which we had a long time been used to saving for such trials. Thus we passed the entire journey of seventeen days, and at the close we crossed the river [2] and travelled other seventeen days.

As the sun went down, upon some plains that lie between

---

[1] This was not an uncommon practice, especially among the non-sedentary tribes who could not readily transport pottery from place to place. The name *Assiniboin*, meaning "stone Sioux," abbreviated to "Stonies," is derived from this custom. Tightly woven baskets and wooden bowls were also used for the purpose.

[2] Probably the Rio Santa Maria, in Chihuahua.

chains of very great mountains,[1] we found a people who for the
third part of the year eat nothing but the powder of straw, and,
that being the season when we passed, we also had to eat of it,
until reaching permanent habitations, where was abundance of
maize brought together.[2] They gave us a large quantity in
grain and flour, pumpkins, beans, and shawls of cotton. With
all these we loaded our guides, who went back the happiest
creatures on earth. We gave thanks to God, our Lord, for
having brought us where we had found so much food.

Some houses are of earth, the rest all of cane mats. From
this point we marched through more than a hundred leagues of
country, and continually found settled domicils, with plenty of
maize and beans. The people gave us many deer and cotton
shawls better than those of New Spain, many beads and certain
corals found on the South Sea, and fine turquoises that come
from the north. Indeed they gave us every thing they had.
To me they gave five emeralds[3] made into arrow-heads, which
they use at their singing and dancing. They appeared to be
very precious. I asked whence they got these; and they said
the stones were brought from some lofty mountains that stand
toward the north, where were populous towns and very large
houses, and that they were purchased with plumes and the
feathers of parrots.

Among this people the women are treated with more deco-
rum than in any part of the Indias we had visited. They wear
a shirt of cotton that falls as low as the knee, and over it half
sleeves with skirts reaching to the ground, made of dressed
deer-skin.[4] It opens in front and is brought close with straps
of leather. They soap this with a certain root[5] that cleanses
well, by which they are enabled to keep it becomingly. Shoes
are worn. The people all came to us that we should touch and
bless them, they being very urgent, which we could accomplish

---

[1] The Sierra Madre.

[2] The numerous villages of the Opata and cognate tribes of Sonora.

[3] Bandelier (p. 156) believes that there may have been malachites.

[4] For the clothing of the Opata Indians, see Castañeda's narration in
this volume.

[5] Amole, the root of the yucca.

only with great labor, for sick and well all wished to go with a benediction. Many times it occurred that some of the women who accompanied us gave birth; and so soon as the children were born the mothers would bring them to us that we should touch and bless them.

These Indians ever accompanied us until they delivered us to others; and all held full faith in our coming from heaven. While travelling, we went without food all day until night, and we ate so little as to astonish them. We never felt exhaustion, neither were we in fact at all weary, so inured were we to hardship. We possessed great influence and authority: to preserve both, we seldom talked with them. The negro was in constant conversation; he informed himself about the ways we wished to take, of the towns there were, and the matters we desired to know.

We passed through many and dissimilar tongues. Our Lord granted us favor with the people who spoke them, for they always understood us, and we them. We questioned them, and received their answers by signs, just as if they spoke our language and we theirs; for, although we knew six languages, we could not everywhere avail ourselves of them, there being a thousand differences.

Throughout all these countries the people who were at war immediately made friends, that they might come to meet us, and bring what they possessed. In this way we left all the land at peace, and we taught all the inhabitants by signs, which they understood, that in heaven was a Man we called God, who had created the sky and the earth; Him we worshipped and had for our master; that we did what He commanded and from His hand came all good; and would they do as we did, all would be well with them. So ready of apprehension we found them that, could we have had the use of language by which to make ourselves perfectly understood, we should have left them all Christians. Thus much we gave them to understand the best we could. And afterward, when the sun rose, they opened their hands together with loud shouting towards the heavens, and then drew them down all over their bodies. They did the

same again when the sun went down. They are a people of
good condition and substance, capable in any pursuit.

Chapter 32

The Indians give us the hearts of deer.

In the town where the emeralds were presented to us the
people gave Dorantes over six hundred open hearts of deer.
They ever keep a good supply of them for food, and we called
the place Pueblo de los Corazones.[1] It is the entrance into
many provinces on the South Sea. They who go to look for
them, and do not enter there, will be lost. On the coast is no
maize: the inhabitants eat the powder of rush and of straw,
and fish that is caught in the sea from rafts, not having canoes.
With grass and straw the women cover their nudity. They are
a timid and dejected people.[2]

We think that near the coast by way of those towns through
which we came are more than a thousand leagues of inhabited
country, plentiful of subsistence. Three times the year it is
planted with maize and beans. Deer are of three kinds; one
the size of the young steer of Spain. There are innumerable
houses, such as are called *bahíos*.[3] They have poison from a
certain tree the size of the apple. For effect no more is necessary than to pluck the fruit and moisten the arrow with it, or, if
there be no fruit, to break a twig and with the milk do the like.
The tree is abundant and so deadly that, if the leaves be bruised
and steeped in some neighboring water, the deer and other
animals drinking it soon burst.[4]

[1] Town of the Hearts, at or near the present Ures, on the Rio Sonora.
The place became celebrated in 1540, when Coronado's army passed
through the country. See the Castañeda narration in this volume.

[2] These were the Seri, Guaymas, Upanguaymas, and Tepoca tribes.
The Seri particularly have ever been noted for their warlike character, but
Cabeza de Vaca does not here speak from personal knowledge.

[3] That is, in the West Indies, see p. 19, note 5.

[4] See the Castañeda narration, p.326, *post;* and compare the *Rudo Ensayo*
(*ca.* 1763), p. 64, 1863, which says: "*Mago,* in the Opata language, is a

We were in this town three days. A day's journey[1] farther
was another town,[2] at which the rain fell heavily while we were
there, and the river became so swollen we could not cross it,
which detained us fifteen days. In this time Castillo saw the
buckle of a sword-belt on the neck of an Indian and stitched
to it the nail of a horseshoe. He took them, and we asked the
native what they were: he answered that they came from
heaven. We questioned him further, as to who had brought
them thence: they all responded that certain men who wore
beards like us had come from heaven and arrived at that river,
bringing horses, lances, and swords, and that they had lanced
two Indians. In a manner of the utmost indifference we could
feign, we asked them what had become of those men. They
answered us that they had gone to sea, putting their lances
beneath the water, and going themselves also under the water;
afterwards that they were seen on the surface going towards the
sunset. For this we gave many thanks to God our Lord. We
had before despaired of ever hearing more of Christians. Even
yet we were left in great doubt and anxiety, thinking those people were merely persons who had come by sea on discoveries.
However, as we had now such exact information, we made
greater speed, and, as we advanced on our way, the news of the
Christians continually grew. We told the natives that we were
going in search of that people, to order them not to kill nor
make slaves of them, nor take them from their lands, nor do
other injustice. Of this the Indians were very glad.

We passed through many territories and found them all vacant: their inhabitants wandered fleeing among the mountains,
without daring to have houses or till the earth for fear of Christians. The sight was one of infinite pain to us, a land very

small tree, very green, luxuriant, and beautiful to the eye; but it contains
a deadly juice which flows upon making a slight incision in the bark. The
natives rub their arrows with it, and for this reason they call it arrow herb;
but at present they use very little."

[1] Twelve leagues, and the same distance from the Gulf of California,
according to the last paragraph of this chapter.

[2] Perhaps at or in the vicinity of the present Hermosillo, Sonora,
although the distance is greater than that given later.

fertile and beautiful, abounding in springs and streams, the hamlets deserted and burned, the people thin and weak, all fleeing or in concealment. As they did not plant, they appeased their keen hunger by eating roots and the bark of trees. We bore a share in the famine along the whole way; for poorly could these unfortunates provide for us, themselves being so reduced they looked as though they would willingly die. They brought shawls of those they had concealed because of the Christians, presenting them to us; and they related how the Christians at other times had come through the land, destroying and burning the towns, carrying away half the men, and all the women and the boys, while those who had been able to escape were wandering about fugitives. We found them so alarmed they dared not remain anywhere. They would not nor could they till the earth, but preferred to die rather than live in dread of such cruel usage as they received. Although these showed themselves greatly delighted with us, we feared that on our arrival among those who held the frontier, and fought against the Christians, they would treat us badly, and revenge upon us the conduct of their enemies; but, when God our Lord was pleased to bring us there, they began to dread and respect us as the others had done, and even somewhat more, at which we no little wondered. Thence it may at once be seen that, to bring all these people to be Christians and to the obedience of the Imperial Majesty, they must be won by kindness, which is a way certain, and no other is.

They took us to a town on the edge of a range of mountains, to which the ascent is over difficult crags. We found many people there collected out of fear of the Christians. They received us well, and presented us all they had. They gave us more than two thousand back-loads of maize, which we gave to the distressed and hungered beings who guided us to that place. The next day we despatched four messengers through the country, as we were accustomed to do, that they should call together all the rest of the Indians at a town distant three days' march. We set out the day after with all the people. The tracks of the Christians and marks where they slept were continually seen. At mid-day we met our messengers, who told us they had found no Indians, that they were roving and hiding in the forests, fleeing that the Christians might not kill nor make them slaves; the night before they had observed the Christians from behind trees, and discovered what they were about, carrying away many people in chains.

Those who came with us were alarmed at this intelligence; some returned to spread the news over the land that the Christians were coming; and many more would have followed, had we not forbidden it and told them to cast aside their fear, when they reassured themselves and were well content. At the time we had Indians with us belonging a hundred leagues behind, and we were in no condition to discharge them, that they might return to their homes. To encourage them, we stayed there that night; the day after we marched and slept on the road. The following day those whom we had sent forward as messengers guided us to the place where they had seen Christians. We arrived in the afternoon, and saw at once that they told the truth. We perceived that the persons were mounted, by the stakes to which the horses had been tied.

From this spot, called the river Petutan,[1] to the river to which Diego de Guzmán came,[2] where we heard of Christians, may be as many as eighty leagues; thence to the town where the rains overtook us, twelve leagues, and that is twelve leagues from the South Sea.[3] Throughout this region, wheresoever the mountains extend, we saw clear traces of gold and lead, iron, copper, and other metals. Where the settled habitations are, the climate is hot; even in January the weather is very warm. Thence toward the meridian, the country unoccupied to the North Sea is unhappy and sterile. There we underwent great

---

[1] Petatlan; so also in the edition of 1542. This is the Rio Sinaloa. See Castañeda's narration of the Coronado expedition, part 2, ch. 2, *post*.

[2] See the note on Guzman in the Castañeda relation. The narrative is here slightly confused, as the town at which they first heard of Christians was the one in which they were overtaken by the rain, according to Cabeza de Vaca's previous statement in this chapter.

[3] The Gulf of California. As he did not go to the coast, however, his estimate is considerably below the actual distance.

and incredible hunger. Those who inhabit and wander over it are a race of evil inclination and most cruel customs. The people of the fixed residences [1] and those beyond regard silver and gold with indifference, nor can they conceive of any use for them.

Chapter 33

We see traces of Christians.

When we saw sure signs of Christians, and heard how near we were to them, we gave thanks to God our Lord for having chosen to bring us out of a captivity so melancholy and wretched. The delight we felt let each one conjecture, when he shall remember the length of time we were in that country, the suffering and perils we underwent. That night I entreated my companions that one of them should go back three days' journey after the Christians who were moving about over the country, where we had given assurance of protection. Neither of them received this proposal well, excusing themselves because of weariness and exhaustion; and although either might have done better than I, being more youthful and athletic, yet seeing their unwillingness, the next morning I took the negro with eleven Indians, and, following the Christians by their trail, I travelled ten leagues, passing three villages, at which they had slept.

The day after I overtook four of them on horseback, who were astonished at the sight of me, so strangely habited as I was, and in company with Indians.[2] They stood staring at me a length of time, so confounded that they neither hailed me nor drew near to make an inquiry. I bade them take me to their chief: accordingly we went together half a league to the place where was Diego de Alcaraz, their captain.[3]

---

[1] The Jumanos, previously mentioned.

[2] There were twenty horsemen according to the *Letter* (Oviedo, p. 612).

[3] Alcaraz later served as a lieutenant under Diaz in the Coronado expedition. Castañeda characterizes him as a weakling.

After we had conversed, he stated to me that he was completely undone; he had not been able in a long time to take any Indians; he knew not which way to turn, and his men had well begun to experience hunger and fatigue. I told him of Castillo and Dorantes, who were behind, ten leagues off, with a multitude that conducted us. He thereupon sent three cavalry to them, with fifty of the Indians who accompanied him. The negro returned to guide them, while I remained. I asked the Christians to give me a certificate of the year, month, and day I arrived there, and of the manner of my coming, which they accordingly did. From this river[1] to the town of the Christians, named San Miguel,[2] within the government of the province called New Galicia, are thirty leagues.

Chapter 34

Of sending for the Christians.

Five days having elapsed, Andrés Dorantes and Alonzo del Castillo arrived with those who had been sent after them. They brought more than six hundred persons of that community, whom the Christians had driven into the forests, and who had wandered in concealment over the land. Those who accompanied us so far had drawn them out, and given them to the Christians, who thereupon dismissed all the others they had brought with them. Upon their coming to where I was, Alcaraz begged that we would summon the people of the towns on the margin of the river, who straggled about under cover of the woods, and order them to fetch us something to eat. This last was unnecessary, the Indians being ever diligent to bring us all they could. Directly we sent our messengers to call them, when there came six hundred souls, bringing us all the maize in their possession. They fetched it in certain pots, closed with

---

[1] Evidently the Rio Sinaloa.
[2] San Miguel Culiacan. See Castañeda's narration.

i

clay, which they had concealed in the earth. They brought us whatever else they had; but we, wishing only to have the provision, gave the rest to the Christians, that they might divide among themselves. After this we had many high words with them; for they wished to make slaves of the Indians we brought.

In consequence of the dispute, we left at our departure many bows of Turkish shape we had along with us and many pouches. The five arrows with the points of emerald were forgotten among others, and we lost them. We gave the Christians a store of robes of cowhide and other things we brought. We found it difficult to induce the Indians to return to their dwellings, to feel no apprehension and plant maize. They were willing to do nothing until they had gone with us and delivered us into the hands of other Indians, as had been the custom; for, if they returned without doing so, they were afraid they should die, and, going with us, they feared neither Christians nor lances. Our countrymen became jealous at this, and caused their interpreter to tell the Indians that we were of them, and for a long time we had been lost; that they were the lords of the land who must be obeyed and served, while we were persons of mean condition and small force. The Indians cared little or nothing for what was told them; and conversing among themselves said the Christians lied: that we had come whence the sun rises, and they whence it goes down; we healed the sick, they killed the sound; that we had come naked and barefooted, while they had arrived in clothing and on horses with lances; that we were not covetous of anything, but all that was given to us we directly turned to give, remaining with nothing; that the others had the only purpose to rob whomsoever they found, bestowing nothing on any one.

In this way they spoke of all matters respecting us, which they enhanced by contrast with matters concerning the others, delivering their response through the interpreter of the Spaniards. To other Indians they made this known by means of one among them through whom they understood us. Those who speak that tongue we discriminately call Primahaitu,

which is like saying Vasconyados.[1] We found it in use over
more than four hundred leagues of our travel, without another
over that whole extent. Even to the last, I could not convince
the Indians that we were of the Christians; and only with great
effort and solicitation we got them to go back to their residences.
We ordered them to put away apprehension, establish their
towns, plant and cultivate the soil.

From abandonment the country had already grown up
thickly in trees. It is, no doubt, the best in all these Indias,
the most prolific and plenteous in provisions. Three times in
the year it is planted. It produces great variety of fruit, has
beautiful rivers, with many other good waters. There are ores
with clear traces of gold and silver. The people are well disposed: they serve such Christians as are their friends, with
great good will. They are comely, much more so than the
Mexicans. Indeed, the land needs no circumstance to make it
blessed.

The Indians, at taking their leave, told us they would do
what we commanded, and would build their towns, if the Christians would suffer them; and this I say and affirm most posi-
tively, that, if they have not done so, it is the fault of the
Christians.

After we had dismissed the Indians in peace, and thanked
them for the toil they had supported with us, the Christians
with subtlety sent us on our way under charge of Zebreros, an
alcalde, attended by two men. They took us through forests
and solitudes, to hinder us from intercourse with the natives,
that we might neither witness nor have knowledge of the act
they would commit. It is but an instance of how frequently
men are mistaken in their aims; we set about to preserve the
liberty of the Indians and thought we had secured it, but the
contrary appeared; for the Christians had arranged to go and

[1] Evidently intended for *Pimahaitu*, through misunderstanding. These
tribes who lived in permanent habitations, from the village of the Corazones
(Hearts) to Culiacan, were all of the Piman family, and consequently spoke
related languages. The Pima do not call themselves *Pima*, but *O-otam*,
"men," "people." *Pima* means "no"; *pimahaitu*, "no thing." The term
Vasconyados, or *Vascongados*, refers to the Biscayans.

spring upon those we had sent away in peace and confidence. They executed their plan as they had designed, taking us through the woods, wherein for two days we were lost, without water and without way. Seven of our men died of thirst, and we all thought to have perished. Many friendly to the Christians in their company were unable to reach the place where we got water the second night, until the noon of next day. We travelled twenty-five leagues, little more or less, and reached a town of friendly Indians. The alcalde left us there, and went on three leagues farther to a town called Culiacan where was Melchior Diaz, principal alcalde and captain of the province.[1]

Chapter 35

The chief alcalde receives us kindly the night we arrive.

The *alcalde mayor* knew of the expedition, and, hearing of our return, he immediately left that night and came to where we were. He wept with us, giving praises to God our Lord for having extended over us so great care. He comforted and entertained us hospitably. In behalf of the Governor, Nuño de Guzman and himself, he tendered all that he had, and the service in his power. He showed much regret for the seizure, and the injustice we had received from Alcaraz and others. We were sure, had he been present, what was done to the Indians and to us would never have occurred.

The night being passed, we set out the next day for Anhacan. The chief alcalde besought us to tarry there, since by so doing we could be of eminent service to God and your Majesty; the deserted land was without tillage and everywhere badly wasted, the Indians were fleeing and concealing themselves in the thickets, unwilling to occupy their towns; we were to send and call them, commanding them in behalf of

---

[1] For the later career of this officer, see Castañeda's narration. Melchior Diaz was a man of very different stamp to Guzman, Alcaraz, and Zebreros (or Cebreros), so far as his treatment of the Indians is concerned.

God and the King, to return to live in the vales and cultivate the soil.

To us this appeared difficult to effect. We had brought no native of our own, nor of those who accompanied us according to custom, intelligent in these affairs. At last we made the attempt with two captives, brought from that country, who were with the Christians we first overtook. They had seen the people who conducted us, and learned from them the great authority and command we carried and exercised throughout those parts, the wonders we had worked, the sick we had cured, and the many things besides we had done. We ordered that they, with others of the town, should go together to summon the hostile natives among the mountains and of the river Petachan,[1] where we had found the Christians, and say to them they must come to us, that we wished to speak with them. For the protection of the messengers, and as a token to the others of our will, we gave them a gourd of those we were accustomed to bear in our hands, which had been our principal insignia and evidence of rank,[2] and with this they went away.

The Indians were gone seven days, and returned with three chiefs of those revolted among the ridges, who brought with them fifteen men, and presented us beads, turquoises, and feathers. The messengers said they had not found the people of the river where we appeared, the Christians having again made them run away into the mountains. Melchior Diaz told the interpreter to speak to the natives for us; to say to them we came in the name of God, who is in heaven; that we had travelled about the world many years, telling all the people we found that they should believe in God and serve Him; for He was the Master of all things on the earth, benefiting and rewarding the virtuous, and to the bad giving perpetual punishment of fire; that, when the good die, He takes them to heaven, where none ever die, nor feel cold, nor hunger, nor thirst, nor

---

[1] Petatlan — the Rio Sinaloa.
[2] Evidently one of those obtained in Texas and which the Indians there so highly regarded. See p. 90, note 2; p. 95, note 1.

any inconvenience whatsoever, but the greatest enjoyment possible to conceive; that those who will not believe in Him, nor obey His commands, He casts beneath the earth into the company of demons, and into a great fire which is never to go out, but always torment; that, over this, if they desired to be Christians and serve God in the way we required, the Christians would cherish them as brothers and behave towards them very kindly; that we would command they give no offence nor take them from their territories, but be their great friends. If the Indians did not do this, the Christians would treat them very hardly, carrying them away as slaves into other lands.[1]

They answered through the interpreter that they would be true Christians and serve God. Being asked to whom they sacrifice and offer worship, from whom they ask rain for their corn-fields and health for themselves, they answered of a man that is in heaven. We inquired of them his name, and they told us Aguar; and they believed he created the whole world, and the things in it. We returned to question them as to how they knew this; they answered their fathers and grandfathers had told them, that from distant time had come their knowledge, and they knew the rain and all good things were sent to them by him. We told them that the name of him of whom they spoke we called Dios; and if they would call him so, and would worship him as we directed, they would find their welfare. They responded that they well understood, and would do as we said. We ordered them to come down from the mountains in confidence and peace, inhabit the whole country and construct their houses: among these they should build one for God, at its entrance place a cross like that which we had there present; and, when Christians came among them, they should go out to receive them with crosses in their hands, without bows or any arms, and take them to their dwellings, giving of what they have to eat, and the Christians would do them no injury, but be their friends; and the Indians told us they would do as we had commanded.

---

[1] Among the Indians of this region who were carried away into captivity were the Yaqui, who have been hostile to the whites to this day.

The captain having given them shawls and entertained
them, they returned, taking the two captives who had been
used as emissaries. This occurrence took place before the
notary, in the presence of many witnesses.

Chapter 36

Of building churches in that land.

As soon as these Indians went back, all those of that province who were friendly to the Christians, and had heard of us,
came to visit us, bringing beads and feathers. We commanded
them to build churches and put crosses in them: to that time
none had been raised; and we made them bring their principal
men to be baptized.

Then the captain made a covenant with God, not to invade
nor consent to invasion, nor to enslave any of that country and
people, to whom we had guaranteed safety; that this he would
enforce and defend until your Majesty and the Governor Nuño
de Guzman, or the Viceroy in your name, should direct what
would be most for the service of God and your Highness.

When the children had been baptized, we departed for the
town of San Miguel. So soon as we arrived, April 1, 1536,
came Indians, who told us many people had come down from
the mountains and were living in the vales; that they had
made churches and crosses, doing all we had required. Each
day we heard how these things were advancing to a full im-
provement.

Fifteen days of our residence having passed, Alcaraz got
back with the Christians from the incursion, and they related
to the captain the manner in which the Indians had come down
and peopled the plain; that the towns were inhabited which
had been tenantless and deserted, the residents, coming out to
receive them with crosses in their hands, had taken them to
their houses, giving of what they had, and the Christians had
slept among them over night. They were surprised at a thing

so novel; but, as the natives said they had been assured of safety, it was ordered that they should not be harmed, and the Christians took friendly leave of them.

God in His infinite mercy is pleased that in the days of your Majesty, under your might and dominion, these nations should come to be thoroughly and voluntarily subject to the Lord, who has created and redeemed us. We regard this as certain, that your Majesty is he who is destined to do so much, not difficult to accomplish; for in the two thousand leagues we journeyed on land, and in boats on water, and in that we travelled unceasingly for ten months after coming out of captivity, we found neither sacrifices nor idolatry.

In the time, we traversed from sea to sea; and from information gathered with great diligence, there may be a distance from one to another at the widest part, of two thousand leagues; and we learned that on the coast of the South Sea there are pearls and great riches, and the best and all the most opulent countries are near there.

We were in the village of San Miguel until the fifteenth day of May.[1] The cause of so long a detention was, that from thence to the city of Compostela, where the Governor Nuño de Guzman resided, are a hundred leagues of country, entirely devastated and filled with enemies, where it was necessary we should have protection. Twenty mounted men went with us for forty leagues, and after that six Christians accompanied us, who had with them five hundred slaves. Arrived at Compostela, the Governor entertained us graciously and gave us of his clothing for our use. I could not wear any for some time, nor could we sleep anywhere else but on the ground. After ten or twelve days we left for Mexico, and were all along on the way well entertained by Christians. Many came out on the roads to gaze at us, giving thanks to God for having saved us from so many calamities. We arrived at Mexico on Sunday, the day before the vespers of Saint Iago,[2] where we were handsomely treated by the Viceroy and the Marquis del

---

[1] 1536.

[2] The day of Saint James the Apostle — July 25, 1536.

Valle,[1] and welcomed with joy. They gave us clothing and proffered whatsoever they had. On the day of Saint Iago was a celebration, and a joust of reeds with bulls.

Chapter 37

Of what occurred when I wished to return.

When we had rested two months in Mexico, I desired to return to these kingdoms;[2] and being about to embark in the month of October, a storm came on, capsizing the ship, and she was lost. In consequence I resolved to remain through the winter; because in those parts it is a boisterous season for navigation. After that had gone by, Dorantes and I left Mexico, about Lent, to take shipping at Vera Cruz. We remained waiting for a wind until Palm Sunday, when we went on board, and were detained fifteen days longer for a wind. The ship leaked so much that I quitted her, and went to one of two other vessels that were ready to sail, but Dorantes remained in her.

On the tenth day of April,[3] the three ships left the port, and sailed one hundred and fifty leagues. Two of them leaked a great deal; and one night the vessel I was in lost their company. Their pilots and masters, as afterwards appeared, dared not proceed with the other vessels so, and without telling us of their intentions, or letting us know aught of them, put back to the port they had left. We pursued our voyage, and on the fourth day of May we entered the harbor of Havana, in the island of Cuba. We remained waiting for the other vessels, believing them to be on their way, until the second of June, when we sailed, in much fear of falling in with Frenchmen, as they had a few days before taken three Spanish vessels. Having arrived at the island of Bermuda, we were struck by one of those storms that overtake those who pass there, according to what they state who sail thither.

[1] The Viceroy Mendoza and Cortés.   [2] Spain.   [3] 1537.

All one night we considered ourselves lost; and we were thankful that when morning was come, the storm ceased, and we could go on our course.

At the end of twenty-nine days after our departure from Havana, we had sailed eleven hundred leagues, which are said to be thence to the town of the Azores. The next morning, passing by the island called Cuervo,[1] we fell in with a French ship. At noon she began to follow, bringing with her a caravel captured from the Portuguese, and gave us chase. In the evening we saw nine other sail; but they were so distant we could not make out whether they were Portuguese or of those that pursued us. At night the Frenchman was within shot of a lombard from our ship, and we stole away from our course in the dark to evade him, and this we did three or four times. He approached so near that he saw us and fired. He might have taken us, or, at his option could leave us until the morning. I remember with gratitude to the Almighty when the sun rose, and we found ourselves close with the Frenchman, that near us were the nine sail we saw the evening before, which we now recognized to be of the fleet of Portugal. I gave thanks to our Lord for escape from the troubles of the land and perils of the sea. The Frenchman, so soon as he discovered their character, let go the caravel he had seized with a cargo of negroes and kept as a prize, to make us think he was Portuguese, that we might wait for him. When he cast her off, he told the pilot and the master of her, that we were French and under his convoy. This said, sixty oars were put out from his ship, and thus with these and sail he commenced to flee, moving so fast it was hardly credible. The caravel being let go, went to the galleon, and informed the commander that the other ship and ours were French. As we drew nigh the galleon, and the fleet saw we were coming down upon them, they made no doubt we were, and putting themselves in order of battle, bore up for us, and when near we hailed them. Discovering that we were friends, they found that they were mocked in permitting the corsair to

[1] Corvo.

escape, by being told that we were French and of his company.

Four caravels were sent in pursuit. The galleon drawing near, after the salutation from us, the commander, Diego de Silveira, asked whence we came and what merchandise we carried, when we answered that we came from New Spain, and were loaded with silver and gold. He asked us how much there might be; the captain told him we carried three thousand *castellanos*. The commander replied: "In honest truth you come very rich, although you bring a very sorry ship and a still poorer artillery. By Heaven, that renegade whoreson Frenchman has lost a good mouthful. Now that you have escaped, follow me, and do not leave me that I may, with God's help, deliver you in Spain."

After a little time, the caravels that pursued the Frenchman returned, for plainly he moved too fast for them; they did not like either, to leave the fleet, which was guarding three ships that came laden with spices. Thus we reached the island of Terceira, where we reposed fifteen days, taking refreshment and awaiting the arrival of another ship coming with a cargo from India, the companion of the three of which the armada was in charge. The time having run out, we left that place with the fleet, and arrived at the port of Lisbon on the ninth of August, on the vespers of the day of our master Saint Lawrence,[1] in the year one thousand five hundred and thirty-seven.

That what I have stated in my foregoing narrative is true, I subscribe with my name.

CABEZA DE VACA.

The narrative here ended is signed with his name and arms.

Chapter 38

Of what became of the others who went to Indias.

Since giving this circumstantial account of events attending the voyage to Florida, the invasion, and our going out thence

[1] The day of Saint Lawrence (San Lorenzo) is August 10.

until the arrival in these realms, I desire to state what became
of the ships and of the people who remained with them. I
have not before touched on this, as we were uninformed until
coming to New Spain, where we found many of the persons,
and others here in Castile, from whom we learned everything
to the latest particular.

At the time we left, one of the ships had already been lost
on the breakers, and the three others were in considerable
danger, having nearly a hundred souls on board and few stores.
Among the persons were ten married women, one of whom
had told the Governor many things that afterwards befell
him on the voyage. She cautioned him before he went inland
not to go, as she was confident that neither he nor any going
with him could ever escape; but should any one come back
from that country, the Almighty must work great wonders in
his behalf, though she believed few or none would return.
The Governor said that he and his followers were going to
fight and conquer nations and countries wholly unknown,
and in subduing them he knew that many would be slain;
nevertheless, that those who survived would be fortunate,
since from what he had understood of the opulence of that
land, they must become very rich. And further he begged
her to inform him whence she learned those things that had
passed, as well as those she spoke of, that were to come; she
replied that in Castile a Moorish woman of Hornachos had
told them to her, which she had stated to us likewise before
we left Spain, and while on the passage many things happened
in the way she foretold.

After the Governor had made Caravallo, a native of Cuenca
de Huete, his lieutenant and commander of the vessels and
people, he departed, leaving orders that all diligence should
be used to repair on board, and take the direct course to Pánuco, keeping along the shore closely examining for the harbor,
and having found it, the vessels should enter there and await
our arrival. And the people state, that when they had be-
taken themselves to the ships, all of them looking at that
woman, they distinctly heard her say to the females, that

well, since their husbands had gone inland, putting their persons in so great jeopardy, their wives should in no way take more account of them, but ought soon to be looking after whom they would marry, and that she should do so. She did accordingly: she and others married, or became the concubines of those who remained in the ships.

After we left, the vessels made sail, taking their course onward; but not finding the harbor, they returned. Five leagues below the place at which we debarked, they found the port, the same we discovered when we saw the Spanish cases containing dead bodies, which were of Christians.[1] Into this haven and along this coast, the three ships passed with the other ship that came from Cuba, and the brigantine, looking for us nearly a year, and not finding us, they went to New Spain.

The port of which we speak is the best in the world. At the entrance are six fathoms of water and five near the shore. It runs up into the land seven or eight leagues. The bottom is fine white sand. No sea breaks upon it nor boisterous storm, and it can contain many vessels. Fish is in great plenty. There are a hundred leagues to Havana, a town of Christians in Cuba, with which it bears north and south. The north-east wind ever prevails and vessels go from one to the other, returning in a few days; for the reason that they sail either way with it on the quarter.

As I have given account of the vessels, it may be well that I state who are, and from what parts of these kingdoms come, the persons whom our Lord has been pleased to release from these troubles. The first is Alonzo del Castillo Maldonado, native of Salamanca, son of Doctor Castillo and Doña Aldonça Maldonado. The second is Andrés Dorantes, son of Pablo Dorantes, native of Béjar, and citizen of Gibraleon. The third is Alvar Nuñez Cabeça de Vaca, son of Francisco de Vera, and grandson of Pedro de Vera who conquered the Canaries, and his mother was Doña Tereça Cabeça de Vaca, native of

---

[1] Tampa Bay, Florida.

Xeréz de la Frontera. The fourth, called Estevanico, is an Arabian black, native of Açamor.

THE END

The present tract was imprinted in the very magnificent, noble and very ancient City of Zamora, by the honored residents Augustin de Paz and Juan Picardo, partners, printers of books, at the cost and outlay of the virtuous Juan Pedro Musetti, book merchant of Medina del Campo, having been finished the sixth day of the month of October, in the year one thousand five hundred and forty-two of the birth of our Saviour Jesus Christ.[1]

[1] Colophon of the first edition.

THE NARRATIVE OF THE EXPEDITION OF HERNANDO DE SOTO, BY THE GENTLEMAN OF ELVAS

INTRODUCTION

In the early annals of the exploration, conquest, and settlement of the territory of the United States none are to be found to which more interest is attached than to the expedition of Hernando de Soto through the Gulf States. History, tradition, and poetry are indissolubly linked with his name. Counties, towns, and lakes have been named after him, and tradition attaches his name to many localities far removed from the line of his march.

In the narrative of the expedition we get our first geographical knowledge of the interior of the states of Florida, Georgia, North and South Carolina, Tennessee, Alabama, Mississippi, Arkansas, Texas, and the Indian Territory. The Spaniards while on their minor expeditions among the Indians may also have entered the states of Missouri and Louisiana, but of this there is no certainty.

The earliest history of the great Indian tribes or nations residing in the above-named states is related by these narratives, the expedition having traversed the territory of the Timuguas, Cherokees, the various divisions or tribes of the Muskogee or Creek confederacy, the Choctaws, Chickasaws, Quapaws or Arkansas, several branches of the great Pani nation, and some other tribes that are not so easily identified. In the narratives are also to be found the first descriptions of the habits, manners, and customs of the native tribes met with. Their towns, villages, houses, temples, granaries, bridges, canoes, banners, arms, wearing apparel, and culinary implements are also described.

The first published narrative was written by a gentleman from the town of Elvas, in Portugal, who joined the expedition and participated in its trials and privations, and in the weary but memorable march through what was then known as Florida. If he was one of those Portuguese who are named in the book as having started from Elvas, the inference may be drawn from the wording of the narrative that he was named Alvaro Fernandez. His narrative was written after his return from the expedition, and is evidently not based upon a diary, or even field-notes, but seemingly was drawn entirely from memory. His descriptions are somewhat vague, the localities sometimes indefinite, the distances sometimes confused, and there are some palpable errors. The lengthy addresses of the caciques belong to romance rather than to history; at least, they are open to grave suspicion that they were manufactured for the occasion. Nevertheless, when the narrative is considered as a whole, it is decidedly the best full account that has been handed down to us. It records the first discovery and navigation of the Mississippi River, the death of its discoverer, De Soto, the building of the first sea-going vessels — brigantines — by Moscoso, the first voyage down "the great river," and the arrival in Mexico of the remnants of the once powerful expedition. The narrative, taken in connection with that of Ranjel, preserved in Oviedo's *Historia General y Natural de las Indias* (Seville, 1547), supplies almost a daily record of the events as they occurred.

The Gentleman of Elvas having been an eye-witness, and his narrative being the best one that has been preserved, it must be taken as a basis for laying down the route of the expedition. The abridged journal of Ranjel, De Soto's private secretary, should also be accepted as a standard, especially as to dates and the order in which the towns and provinces are named. The narrative of Biedma, the factor of the expedition,[1] although written after his arrival in Mexico, supplies

[1] First printed by Buckingham Smith in his *Coleccion de varios Documentos para la Historia de la Florida* (London, 1857).

some additional information. It furnishes the only clue as
to the direction pursued by Moscoso, after leaving Guachoya,
and therefore contains valuable auxiliary evidence. The account written by Garcilaso de la Vega, "the Inca," *Florida
del Ynca* (Lisbon, 1605), is principally based upon the oral
statements of a noble Spaniard who accompanied Soto as a
volunteer, and the written but illiterate reports of two common soldiers, Alonzo de Carmona and Juan Coles. After elimi-
nating all the overdrawn, flowery, and fanciful portions of
the account, there is a residue consisting, in part, of misplaced
towns, provinces, and events, together with occasional dupli-
cations of descriptions. Of the remainder, only such portions
as conform to, or do not conflict with, the other narratives are
worthy of consideration. By combining the geographical,
topographical, and descriptive portions of the narratives, and
exploring the probable and possible sections of the route, the
present writer has succeeded in identifying a number of points
visited by Soto and his followers. A detailed description of
the places identified will be found in the *Publications of the
Mississippi Historical Society* (VI. 449–467); and the relative
value of the narratives, together with the minor documents,
is discussed in the same series (VII. 379–387).

The Gentleman of Elvas, unlike Ranjel, does not put himself forward, but was so modest that only once does he refer
to himself while on the march through Florida, and that was
on the occasion of the death of some relatives while at Aminoya. Seemingly he did not take an active part at the front
or in the advances, but was always with the main army.

The Narrative of the Gentleman of Elvas was first published at Evora, Portugal, in 1557. It was reprinted at Lisbon in 1844 by the Royal Academy, and again in 1875. The
first French edition appeared in 1685, and an English translation from this edition was published in 1686. The first English version, by Hakluyt, entitled *Virginia richly valued by*

the Description of the Mainland of Florida, appeared in 1609, and a reprint entitled *The worthye and famous Historie of the Travailles, Discovery, and Conquest of Terra Florida,* in 1611. A reprint from the latter, edited by William B. Rye, was published by the Hakluyt Society in 1851. The version of 1611 is included in Force's *Tracts,* Volume IV., 1846, and in French's *Historical Collections of Louisiana,* Part 2. The English translation by Buckingham Smith, which was published by the Bradford Club in 1866, in a volume entitled *The Career of Hernando de Soto in the Conquest of Florida,* is the latest and most authentic version. It is this which is followed in the present volume. A reprint of Smith's translation, edited by Professor Edward G. Bourne, was published in 1904.

T. HAYES LEWIS.

THE NARRATIVE OF THE EXPEDITION OF HERNANDO DE SOTO, BY THE GENTLEMAN OF ELVAS

True relation of the vicissitudes that attended the Governor Don Hernando de Soto and some nobles of Portugal in the discovery of the Province of Florida now just given by a Fidalgo of Elvas. Viewed by the Lord Inquisitor.[1]

Fernando da Silveira, Senhor da Serzedas, great Poet and very Illustrious, respecting the Material of this Book, and in Praise of the Author.

EPIGRAM

He who would see the New World,
The Golden Pole,[2] the second,
Other seas, other lands,
Achievements great, and wars,
And such things attempted
As alarm and give pleasure,
Strike terror and lend delight; —
Read of the author this pleasing story,
Where nothing fabulous is told,
All worthy of being esteemed,
Read, considered, used.

[1] From the title page of the original.

[2] We inhabit the Northern Arctic Pole, and that people inhabit the Southern Antarctic Pole. Golden Pole is used because the region is rich. (Footnote in the original.)

ANDRÉ DE BURGOS [1] TO THE PRUDENT READER.

ARISTOTLE writes that all, or at least most men, are given or prone to look at and listen to novelties, especially when they are of foreign or remote countries. These things, he says, enliven the heavy while they give recreation to delicate and subtile minds, that propensity moving men not only to see and hear, but, if possible, to take part in occurrences. This desire exists in the Lusitanians more than in any other people, — for two reasons: the one, because they are very ingenious and warlike; the other, because they are by nature great navigators, having discovered more land, with wider sailing, than all the nations of the earth beside. So, it appearing to me that I could do some little service to those who should read this book, I resolved to imprint it, assured, beyond its being in the Portuguese, that it is composed by a native, and likewise because citizens of Elvas took part in the discovery, as the narrative will itself disclose. What he has written I undoubtingly credit: he tells no tales, nor speaks of fabulous things; and we may believe that the author — having no interest in the matter — would not swerve from truth. We have his assurance besides, that all he has set down passed before him. Should the language, by chance, appear to you careless, lay not the fault on me; I imprint and do not write. God be your protector.

DISCOVERY OF FLORIDA

Relation of the toils and hardships that attended Don Hernando de Soto, governor of Florida, in the conquest of that country; in which is set forth who he was, and also who were others with him; containing some account of the peculiarities and diversities of the country, of all that they saw and of what befell them.

[1] The printer.

Chapter 1

Who Soto was, and how he came to get the government
of Florida.

Hernando de Soto was the son of an esquire of Xeréz de
Badajóz, and went to the Indias of the Ocean Sea, belonging
to Castile, at the time Pedrárias Dávila was the Governor.
He had nothing more than blade and buckler: for his courage and good qualities Pedrárias appointed him to be captain
of a troop of horse, and he went by his order with Hernando
Pizarro to conquer Peru.[1] According to the report of many
persons who were there, he distinguished himself over all the
captains and principal personages present, not only at the
seizure of Atabalípa, lord of Peru, and in carrying the City of
Cuzco, but at all other places wheresoever he went and found
resistance. Hence, apart from his share in the treasure of
Atabalípa, he got a good amount, bringing together in time,
from portions falling to his lot, one hundred and eighty thousand cruzados, which he brought with him to Spain. Of this
the Emperor borrowed a part, which was paid; six hundred
thousand reales [2] in duties on the silks of Granada, and the
rest at the Casa de Contratacion.[3]

In Seville, Soto employed a superintendent of household,
an usher, pages, equerry, chamberlain, footmen, and all the
other servants requisite for the establishment of a gentleman.
Thence he went to Court, and while there was accompanied
by Juan de Añasco of Seville, Luis Moscoso de Alvarado, Nuño
de Tobár, and Juan Rodriguez Lobillo. All, except Añasco,
came with him from Peru; and each brought fourteen or fifteen thousand cruzados. They went well and costly apparelled; and Soto, although by nature not profuse, as it was the
first time he was to show himself at Court, spent largely, and
went about closely attended by those I have named, by his
dependents, and by many others who there came about him

---

[1] In 1531.
[2] Span. *real*, the eighth of a silver dollar.
[3] The India House, or Board of Trade, at Seville.

He married Doña Ysabel de Bobadilla, daughter of Pedrárias Dávila, Count of Puñonrostro. The Emperor made him Governor of the Island of Cuba and Adelantado of Florida, with title of Marquis to a certain part of the territory he should conquer.

Chapter 2

How Cabeça de Vaca arrived at Court, and gave account of the country of Florida; and of the persons who assembled at Seville to accompany Don Hernando de Soto.

After Don Hernando had obtained the concession, a fidalgo[1] arrived at Court from the Indias, Cabeça de Vaca by name, who had been in Florida with Narvaez; and he stated how he with four others had escaped, taking the way to New Spain; that the Governor had been lost in the sea, and the rest were all dead. He brought with him a written relation of adventures, which said in some places: Here I have seen this; and the rest which I saw I leave to confer of with His Majesty: generally, however, he described the poverty of the country, and spoke of the hardships he had undergone. Some of his kinsfolk, desirous of going to the Indias, strongly urged him to tell them whether he had seen any rich country in Florida or not; but he told them that he could not do so; because he and another (by name Orantes,[2] who had remained in New Spain with the purpose of returning into Florida) had sworn not to divulge certain things which they had seen, lest some one might beg the government in advance of them, for which he had come to Spain; nevertheless, he gave them to understand that it was the richest country in the world.

Don Hernando de Soto was desirous that Cabeça de Vaca should go with him, and made him favorable proposals; but after they had come upon terms they disagreed, because the Adelantado would not give the money requisite to pay for a ship that the other had bought. Baltasar de Gallegos and Cristóbal de Espindola told Cabeça de Vaca, their kinsman

---

[1] Gentleman.   [2] Dorantes.

that as they had made up their minds to go to Florida, in consequence of what he had told them, they besought him to
counsel them; to which he replied, that the reason he did not
go was because he hoped to receive another government, being
reluctant to march under the standard of another; that he
had himself come to solicit the conquest of Florida, and though
he found it had already been granted to Don Hernando de
Soto, yet, on account of his oath, he could not divulge what
they desired to know; nevertheless, he would advise them to
sell their estates and go — that in so doing they would act
wisely.

As soon as Cabeça de Vaca had an opportunity he spoke
with the Emperor; and gave him an account of all that he
had gone through with, seen, and could by any means ascertain. Of this relation, made by word of mouth, the Marquis
of Astorga was informed. He determined at once to send his
brother, Don Antonio Osorio; and with him Francisco and
Garcia Osorio, two of his kinsmen, also made ready to go.
Don Antonio disposed of sixty thousand reales income that he
received of the Church, and Francisco of a village of vassals
he owned in Campos. They joined the Adelantado at Seville,
as did also Nuño de Tobár, Luis de Moscoso, and Juan Rodriguez Lobillo. Moscoso took two brothers; there went likewise Don Carlos, who had married the Governor's niece, and
he carried her with him. From Badajóz went Pedro Calderon,
and three kinsmen of the Adelantado: Arias Tinoco, Alonso
Romo, and Diego Tinoco.

As Luis de Moscoso passed through Elvas,[1] André de Vasconcelos spoke with him, and requested him to speak to Don
Hernando de Soto in his behalf; and he gave him warrants,
issued by the Marquis of Vilareal, conferring on him the cap-
taincy of Ceuta, that he might show them; which when the
Adelantado saw, and had informed himself of who he was, he
wrote to him that he would favor him in and through all,
and would give him a command in Florida. From Elvas
went André de Vasconcelos, Fernan Pegado, Antonio Mar-

---

[1] In eastern Portugal, near the Spanish border.

tinez Segurado, Men Royz Pereyra, Joam Cordeiro, Estevan
Pegado, Bento Fernandez, Alvaro Fernandez; and from
Salamanca, Jaen, Valencia, Albuquerque, and other parts
of Spain, assembled many persons of noble extraction in
Seville; so much so that many men of good condition, who
had sold their lands, remained behind in Sanlúcar for want
of shipping, when for known countries and rich it was usual
to lack men: and the cause of this was what Cabeça de Vaca
had told the Emperor, and given persons to understand who
conversed with him respecting that country. He went for
Governor to Rio de la Plata, but his kinsmen followed Soto.

Baltasar de Gallegos received the appointment of chief
castellan, and took with him his wife. He sold houses, vineyards, a rent of wheat, and ninety geiras of olive-field in the
Xarafe of Seville. There went also many other persons of
mark. The offices, being desired of many, were sought through
powerful influence: the place of factor was held by Antonio
de Biedma, that of comptroller by Juan de Añasco, and that
of treasurer by Juan Gaytan, nephew of the Cardinal of
Ciguenza.

Chapter 3

*How the Portuguese went to Seville and thence to Sanlúcar;
and how the captains were appointed over the ships,
and the people distributed among them.*

The Portuguese left Elvas the 15th day of January, and
came to Seville on the vespers of Saint Sebastian.[1] They went
to the residence of the Governor; and entering the court, over
which were some galleries in which he stood, he came down
and met them at the foot of the stairs, whence they returned
with him; and he ordered chairs to be brought, in which they
might be seated. André de Vasconcelos told him who he was,
and who the others were; that they had all come to go with
him, and aid in his enterprise. The Adelantado thanked him,

[1] January 20.

and appeared well pleased with their coming and proffer. The table being already laid, he invited them to sit down; and while at dinner, he directed his major-domo to find lodgings for them near his house.

From Seville the Governor went to Sanlúcar, with all the people that were to go. He commanded a muster to be made, to which the Portuguese turned out in polished armor, and the Castilians very showily, in silk over silk, pinked and slashed. As such luxury did not appear to him becoming on such occasion, he ordered a review to be called for the next day, when every man should appear with his arms; to which the Portuguese came as at first; and the Governor set them in order near the standard borne by his ensign. The greater number of the Castilians were in very sorry and rusty shirts of mail; all wore steel caps or helmets, but had very poor lances. Some of them sought to get among the Portuguese. Those that Soto liked and accepted of were passed, counted, and enlisted; six hundred men in all followed him to Florida. He had bought seven ships; and the necessary subsistence was already on board. He appointed captains, delivering to each of them his ship, with a roll of the people he was to take with him.

Chapter 4

How the Adelantado with his people left Spain, going to the Canary Islands, and afterward arrived in the Antillas.

In the month of April, of the year 1538 of the Christian era, the Adelantado delivered the vessels to their several captains, took for himself a new ship, fast of sail, and gave another to André de Vasconcelos, in which the Portuguese were to go. He passed over the bar of Sanlúcar on Sunday, the morning of Saint Lazarus, with great festivity, commanding the trumpets to be sounded and many charges of artillery to be fired. With a favorable wind he sailed four days, when it lulled, the calms continuing for eight days, with such rolling sea that the ships made no headway.

The fifteenth day after our departure we came to Gomera,

one of the Canaries, on Easter Sunday, in the morning. The Governor of the Island was apparelled all in white, cloak, jerkin, hose, shoes, and cap, so that he looked like a governor of Gypsies. He received the Adelantado with much pleasure, lodging him well and the rest with him gratuitously. To Doña Ysabel he gave a natural daughter of his to be her waiting-maid. For our money we got abundant provision of bread, wine, and meats, bringing off with us what was needful for the ships. Sunday following, eight days after arrival, we took our departure.

On Pentecost we came into the harbor of the city of Santiago, in Cuba of the Antillas. Directly a gentleman of the town sent to the seaside a splendid roan horse, well caparisoned, for the Governor to mount, and a mule for his wife; and all the horsemen and footmen in town at the time came out to receive him at the landing. He was well lodged, attentively visited and served by all the citizens. Quarters were furnished to every one without cost. Those who wished to go into the country were divided among the farm-houses, into squads of four and six persons, according to the several ability of the owners, who provided them with food.

Chapter 5

Of the inhabitants there are in the city of Santiago and other towns of the island,—the character of the soil and of the fruit.

The city of Santiago consists of about eighty spacious and well-contrived dwellings. Some are built of stone and lime, covered with tiles: the greater part have the sides of board and the roofs of dried grass. There are extensive country seats, and on them many trees, which differ from those of Spain. The fig-tree bears fruit as big as the fist, yellow within and of little flavor: another tree with a delicious fruit, called anane, is of the shape and size of a small pine-apple, the skin of which being taken off, the pulp appears like a piece of curd. On the farms about in the country are other larger pines, of very agreeable and high flavor, produced on low trees that

look like the aloe. Another tree yields a fruit called mamei,
the size of a peach, by the islanders more esteemed than any
other in the country. The guayaba is in the form of a filbert,
and is the size of a fig. There is a tree, which is a stalk without any branch, the height of a lance, each leaf the length of
a javelin, the fruit of the size and form of a cucumber, the
bunch having twenty or thirty of them, with which the tree
goes on bending down more and more as they grow: they
are called plantanos in that country, are of good flavor, and
will ripen after they are gathered, although they are better
when they mature on the tree. The stalks yield fruit but
once, when they are cut down, and others, which spring up
at the butt, bear in the coming year. There is another fruit
called batata, the subsistence of a multitude of people, principally slaves, and now grows in the island of Terceira, belonging to this kingdom of Portugal. It is produced in the
earth, and looks like the ynhame, with nearly the taste of
chestnut. The bread of the country is made from a root that
looks like the batata, the stalk of which is like alder. The
ground for planting is prepared in hillocks; into each are laid
four or five stalks, and a year and a half after they have been
set the crop is fit to be dug. Should any one, mistaking the
root for batata, eat any of it, he is in imminent danger; as
experience has shown, in the case of a soldier, who died instantly from swallowing a very little. The roots being peeled
and crushed, they are squeezed in a sort of press; the juice
that flows has an offensive smell; the bread is of little taste
and less nourishment. The fruit from Spain are figs and
oranges, which are produced the year round, the soil being
very rich and fertile.

There are numerous cattle and horses in the country, which
find fresh grass at all seasons. From the many wild cows and
hogs, the inhabitants everywhere are abundantly supplied
with meat. Out of the towns are many fruits wild over the
country; and, as it sometimes happens, when a Christian
misses his way and is lost for fifteen or twenty days, because
of the many paths through the thick woods made by the herds

traversing to and fro, he will live on fruit and on wild cabbage, there being many and large palm-trees everywhere which
yield nothing else available beside.

The island of Cuba is three hundred leagues long from east
to southeast, and in places thirty, in others forty leagues from
north to south. There are six towns of Christians, which are
Santiago, Baracoa, the Báyamo, Puerto Principe, Sancti Spiritus, and Havana. They each have between thirty and forty
householders, except Santiago and Havana, which have some
seventy or eighty dwellings apiece. The towns have all a
chaplain to hear confession, and a church in which to say
mass. In Santiago is a monastery of the order of Saint Francis; it has few friars, though well supported by tithes, as the
country is rich. The Church of Santiago is endowed, has a
cura, a prebend, and many priests, as it is the church of the
city which is the metropolis.

Although the earth contains much gold, there are few
slaves to seek it, many having destroyed themselves because
of the hard usage they receive from the Christians in the mines.
The overseer of Vasco Porcallo, a resident of the island, having understood that his slaves intended to hang themselves,
went with a cudgel in his hand and waited for them in the
place at which they were to meet, where he told them that
they could do nothing, nor think of any thing, that he did
not know beforehand; that he had come to hang himself with
them, to the end that if he gave them a bad life in this world,
a worse would he give them in that to come. This caused
them to alter their purpose and return to obedience.

Chapter 6

How the Governor sent Doña Ysabel with the ships from Santiago
  to Havana, while he with some of the men went thither
  by land.

The Governor sent Don Carlos with the ships, in company
with Doña Ysabel, to tarry for him at Havana, a port in the
eastern end of the island, one hundred and eighty leagues from

Santiago. He and those that remained, having bought horses, set out on their journey, and at the end of twenty-five leagues came to Báyamo, the first town. They were lodged, as they arrived, in parties of four and six, where their food was given to them; and nothing was paid for any other thing than maize for the beasts; because the Governor at each town assessed tax on the tribute paid, and the labor done, by the Indians.

A deep river runs near Báyamo, larger than the Guadiana, called Tanto. The monstrous alligators do harm in it sometimes to the Indians and animals in the crossing. In all the country there are no wolves, foxes, bears, lions, nor tigers: there are dogs in the woods, which have run wild from the houses, that feed upon the swine: there are snakes, the size of a man's thigh, and even bigger; but they are very sluggish and do no kind of injury. From that town to Puerto Principe there are fifty leagues. The roads throughout the island are made by cutting out the undergrowth, which if neglected to be gone over, though only for a single year, the shrubs spring up in such manner that the ways disappear; and so numerous likewise are the paths made by cattle, that no one can travel without an Indian of the country for a guide, there being everywhere high and thick woods.

From Puerto Principe the Governor went by sea in a canoe to the estate of Vasco Porcallo, near the coast, to get news of Doña Ysabel, who, at the time, although not then known, was in a situation of distress, the ships having parted company, two of them being driven in sight of the coast of Florida, and all on board were suffering for lack of water and subsistence. The storm over, and the vessels come together, not knowing where they had been tossed, Cape San Antonio was described, an uninhabited part of the island, where they got water; and at the end of forty days from the time of leaving Santiago, they arrived at Havana. The Governor presently received the news and hastened to meet Doña Ysabel. The troops that went by land, one hundred and fifty mounted men in number, not to be burdensome upon the islanders, were divided into

two squadrons, and marched to Sancti Spiritus, sixty leagues
from Puerto Principe. The victuals they carried was the
caçabe [1] bread I have spoken of, the nature of which is such
that it directly dissolves from moisture; whence it happened
that some ate meat and no bread for many days. They took
dogs with them, and a man of the country, who hunted as
they journeyed, and who killed the hogs at night found further necessary for provision where they stopped; so that they
had abundant supply, both of beef and pork. They found
immense annoyance from mosquitos, particularly in a lake
called Bog of Pia, which they had much ado in crossing between mid-day and dark, it being more than half a league
over, full half a bow-shot of the distance swimming, and all
the rest of the way the water waist deep, having clams on
the bottom that sorely cut the feet, for not a boot nor shoe
sole was left entire at half way. The clothing and saddles
were floated over in baskets of palm-leaf. In this time the
insects came in great numbers and settled on the person where
exposed, their bite raising lumps that smarted keenly, a single
blow with the hand sufficing to kill so many that the blood
would run over the arms and body. There was little rest
at night, as happened also afterwards at like seasons and
places.

They came to Sancti Spiritus, a town of thirty houses, near
which passes a little river. The grounds are very fertile and
pleasant, abundant in good oranges, citrons, and native fruit.
Here one half the people were lodged; the other half went on
twenty-five leagues farther, to a town of fifteen or twenty
householders, called Trinidad. There is a hospital for the
poor, the only one in the island. They say the town was once
the largest of any; and that before the Christians came into
the country a ship sailing along the coast had in her a very
sick man, who begged to be set on shore, which the captain
directly ordered, and the vessel kept on her way. The inhabitants, finding him where he had been left, on that shore
which had never yet been hunted up by Christians carried

[1] Cassava.

him home, and took care of him until he was well. The chief of the town gave him a daughter; and being at war with the country round about, through the prowess and exertion of the Christian he subdued and reduced to his control all the people of Cuba. A long time after, when Diego Velasquez went to conquer the island, whence he made the discovery of New Spain, this man, then among the natives, brought them, by his management, to obedience, and put them under the rule of that Governor.

From Trinidad they travelled a distance of eighty leagues without a town, and arrived at Havana in the end of March. They found the Governor there, and the rest of the people who had come with him from Spain. He sent Juan de Añasco in a caravel, with two pinnaces and fifty men, to explore the harbor in Florida, who brought back two Indians taken on the coast. In consequence, as much because of the necessity of having them for guides and interpreters, as because they said, by signs, that there was much gold in Florida, the Governor and all the company were greatly rejoiced, and longed for the hour of departure — that land appearing to them to be the richest of any which until then had been discovered.

Chapter 7

How we left Havana and came to Florida, and what other matters took place.

Before our departure, the Governor deprived Nuño de Tobár of the rank of captain-general, and conferred it on a resident of Cuba, Vasco Porcallo de Figueroa, which caused the vessels to be well provisioned, he giving a great many hogs and loads of caçabe bread. That was done because Nuño de Tobár had made love to Doña Ysabel's waiting-maid, daughter of the Governor of Gomera; and though he had lost his place, yet, to return to Soto's favor, for she was with child by him, he took her to wife and went to Florida. Doña Ysabel remained, and with her the wife of Don Carlos, of Baltasar de

Gallegos, and of Nuño de Tobár. The Governor left, as his
lieutenant over the island, Juan de Rojas, a fidalgo of
Havana.

On Sunday, the 18th day of May, in the year 1539, the
Adelantado sailed from Havana with a fleet of nine vessels,
five of them ships, two caravels, two pinnaces; and he ran
seven days with favorable weather. On the 25th of the month,
being the festival of Espiritu Santo,[1] the land was seen, and
anchor cast a league from shore, because of the shoals. On
Friday, the 30th, the army landed in Florida, two leagues
from the town[2] of an Indian chief named Ucita. Two hundred
and thirteen horses were set on shore, to unburden the ships,
that they should draw the less water; the seamen only remained on board, who going up every day a little with the
tide, the end of eight days brought them near to the
town.

So soon as the people were come to land, the camp was
pitched on the sea-side, nigh the bay, which goes up close to
the town. Presently the captain-general, Vasco Porcallo, taking seven horsemen with him, beat up the country half a league
about, and discovered six Indians, who tried to resist him
with arrows, the weapons they are accustomed to use. The
horsemen killed two, and the four others escaped, the country
being obstructed by bushes and ponds, in which the horses
bogged and fell, with their riders, of weakness from the voyage. At night the Governor, with a hundred men in the pinnaces, came upon a deserted town; for, so soon as the Christians appeared in sight of land, they were descried, and all
along on the coast many smokes were seen to rise, which the
Indians make to warn one another. The next day, Luis de
Moscoso, master of the camp, set the men in order. The
horsemen he put in three squadrons — the vanguard, battal-
ion, and rearward; and thus they marched that day and the
next, compassing great creeks which run up from the bay;

[1] Whitsunday.
[2] Ucita or Oçita. This first town was on the point at the mouth of Char-
lotte Harbor, Florida.

and on the first of June, being Trinity Sunday, they arrived at the town of Ucita,[1] where the Governor tarried. The town was of seven or eight houses, built of timber, and covered with palm-leaves. The chief's house stood near the beach, upon a very high mount made by hand for defence; at the other end of the town was a temple, on the top of which perched a wooden fowl with gilded eyes, and within were found some pearls of small value, injured by fire, such as the Indians pierce for beads, much esteeming them, and string to wear about the neck and wrists. The Governor lodged in the house of the chief, and with him Vasco Porcallo and Luis de Moscoso; in other houses, midway in the town, was lodged the chief castellan, Baltasar de Gallegos, where were set apart the provisions brought in the vessels. The rest of the dwellings, with the temple, were thrown down, and every mess of three or four soldiers made a cabin, wherein they lodged. The ground about was very fenny, and encumbered with dense thicket and high trees. The Governor ordered the woods to be felled the distance of a crossbow-shot around the place, that the horses might run, and the Christians have the advantage, should the Indians make an attack at night. In the paths, and at proper points, sentinels of foot-soldiers were set in couples, who watched by turns; the horsemen, going the rounds, were ready to support them should there be an alarm.

The Governor made four captains of horsemen and two of footmen: those of the horse were André de Vasconcelos, Pedro Calderon of Badajóz, and the two Cardeñosas his kinsmen (Arias Tinoco and Alfonso Romo), also natives of Badajóz; those of the foot were Francisco Maldonado of Salamanca, and Juan Rodriguez Lobillo. While we were in this town of Ucita, the Indians which Juan de Añasco had taken on that coast, and were with the Governor as guides and interpreters, through the carelessness of two men who had charge of them, got away one night. For this the Governor felt very sorry, as did every one else; for some excursions had already been made, and no

---

[1] The name of this town was Hirriga, according to the Inca, and it seems to have been located on the northeast arm of the harbor.

Indians could be taken, the country being of very high and thick woods, and in many places marshy.

Chapter 8

Of some inroads that were made, and how a Christian was found who had been a long time in the possession of a Cacique.

From the town of Ucita the Governor sent the chief castellan, Baltasar de Gallegos, into the country, with forty horsemen and eighty footmen, to procure an Indian if possible. In another direction he also sent, for the same purpose, Captain Juan Rodriguez Lobillo, with fifty infantry: the greater part were of sword and buckler; the remainder were crossbow and gun men. The command of Lobillo marched over a swampy land, where horses could not travel; and, half a league from camp, came upon some huts near a river. The people in them plunged into the water; nevertheless, four women were secured; and twenty warriors, who attacked our people, so pressed us that we were forced to retire into camp.

The Indians are exceedingly ready with their weapons, and so warlike and nimble, that they have no fear of footmen; for if these charge them they flee, and when they turn their backs they are presently upon them. They avoid nothing more easily than the flight of an arrow. They never remain quiet, but are continually running, traversing from place to place, so that neither crossbow nor arquebuse can be aimed at them. Before a Christian can make a single shot with either, an Indian will discharge three or four arrows; and he seldom misses of his object. Where the arrow meets with no armor, it pierces as deeply as the shaft from a crossbow. Their bows are very perfect; the arrows are made of certain canes, like reeds, very heavy, and so stiff that one of them, when sharpened, will pass through a target. Some are pointed with the bone of a fish, sharp and like a chisel; others with some stone like a point of diamond: of such the greater number, when they strike upon armor, break at the place the parts are put together; those of cane split, and will enter a shirt of mail, doing more injury than when armed.

Juan Rodriguez Lobillo got back to camp with six men wounded, of whom one died, and he brought with him the four women taken in the huts, or cabins. When Baltasar de Gallegos came into the open field, he discovered ten or eleven Indians, among whom was a Christian, naked and sun-burnt, his arms tattooed after their manner, and he in no respect differing from them. As soon as the horsemen came in sight, they ran upon the Indians, who fled, hiding themselves in a thicket, though not before two or three of them were overtaken and wounded. The Christian, seeing a horseman coming upon him with a lance, began to cry out: "Do not kill me, cavalier; I am a Christian! Do not slay these people; they have given me my life!" Directly he called to the Indians, putting them out of fear, when they left the wood and came to him. The horsemen took up the Christian and Indians behind them on their beasts, and, greatly rejoicing, got back to the Governor at nightfall. When he and the rest who had remained in camp heard the news, they were no less pleased than the others.

Chapter 9

How the Christian came to the land of Florida, who he was, and of what passed at his interview with the Governor.

The name of the Christian was Juan Ortiz, a native of Seville, and of noble parentage. He had been twelve years among the Indians, having gone into the country with Pánphilo de Narvaez, and returned in the ships to the island of Cuba, where the wife of the Governor remained; whence, by her command, he went back to Florida, with some twenty or thirty others, in a pinnace; and coming to the port in sight of the town, they saw a cane sticking upright in the ground, with a split in the top, holding a letter, which they supposed the Governor had left there, to give information of himself before marching into the interior. They asked it, to be given to them, of four or five Indians walking along the beach, who, by signs, bade them come to land for it, which Ortiz and another did, though contrary to the wishes of the others. No sooner had they got on shore, when many natives came out of the houses, and, drawing near, held them in such way that they could not escape. One, who would have defended himself, they slew on the spot; the other they seized by the hands, and took him to Ucita, their chief. The people in the pinnace, unwilling to land, kept along the coast and returned to Cuba.

By command of Ucita, Juan Ortiz was bound hand and foot to four stakes, and laid upon scaffolding, beneath which a fire was kindled, that he might be burned; but a daughter of the chief entreated that he might be spared. Though one Christian, she said, might do no good, certainly he could do no harm, and it would be an honor to have one for a captive; to which the father acceded, directing the injuries to be healed. When Ortiz got well, he was put to watching a temple, that the wolves, in the night-time, might not carry off the dead there, which charge he took in hand, having commended himself to God. One night they snatched away from him the body of a little child, son of a principal man; and, going after them, he threw a dart at the wolf that was escaping, which, feeling itself wounded, let go its hold, and went off to die; and he returned, without knowing what he had done in the dark. In the morning, finding the body of the little boy gone, he became very sober; and Ucita, when he heard what had happened, determined he should be killed; but having sent on the trail which Ortiz pointed out as that the wolves had made, the body of the child was found, and a little farther on a dead wolf; at which circumstance the chief became well pleased with the Christian, and satisfied with the guard he had kept, ever after taking much notice of him.

Three years having gone by since he had fallen into the hands of this chief, there came another, named Mocoço,[1] living

---

[1] The town of Mocoço was located west of Miakka River (Macaco of the old maps), which enters the northwest arm of the harbor.

two days' journey distant from that port, and burnt the town, when Ucita fled to one he had in another seaport, whereby Ortiz lost his occupation, and with it the favor of his master. The Indians are worshippers of the Devil, and it is their custom to make sacrifices of the blood and bodies of their people, or of those of any other they can come by; and they affirm, too, that when he would have them make an offering, he speaks, telling them that he is athirst, and that they must sacrifice to him. The girl who had delivered Ortiz from the fire, told him how her father had the mind to sacrifice him the next day, and that he must flee to Mococo, who she knew would receive him with regard, as she had heard that he had asked for him, and said he would like to see him: and as he knew not the way, she went half a league out of town with him at dark, to put him on the road, returning early so as not to be missed.

Ortiz travelled all night, and in the morning came to a river, the boundary of the territory of Mococo, where he discovered two men fishing. As this people were at war with those of Ucita, and their languages different, he did not know how he should be able to tell them who he was, and why he came, or make other explanation, that they might not kill him as one of the enemy. It was not, however, until he had come up to where their arms were placed that he was discovered, when they fled towards the town; and though he called out to them to wait, that he would do them no injury, they only ran the faster for not understanding him. As they arrived, shouting, many Indians came out of the town, and began surrounding, in order to shoot him with their arrows, when he, finding himself pressed, took shelter behind trees, crying aloud that he was a Christian fled from Ucita, come to visit and serve Mococo. At the moment, it pleased God that an Indian should come up, who, speaking the language, understood him and quieted the others, telling them what was said. Three or four ran to carry the news, when the cacique, much gratified, came a quarter of a league on the way to receive him. He caused the Christian immediately to swear to him, according to the custom of his country, that he would not leave him for any other master; and, in return, he promised to show him much honor, and if at any time Christians should come to that land, he would let him go freely, and give him his permission to return to them, pledging his oath to this after the Indian usage.

Three years from that time, some people fishing out at sea, three leagues from land, brought news of having seen ships; when Mocoço, calling Ortiz, gave him permission to depart, who, taking leave, made all haste possible to the shore, where, finding no vessels, he supposed the story to be only a device of the cacique to discover his inclination. In this way he remained with him nine years, having little hope of ever seeing Christians more; but no sooner had the arrival of the Governor in Florida taken place, when it was known to Mocoço, who directly told Ortiz that Christians were in the town of Ucita. The captive, thinking himself jested with, as he had supposed himself to be before, said that his thoughts no longer dwelt on his people, and that his only wish now was to serve him. Still the cacique assured him that it was even as he stated, and gave him leave to go, telling him that if he did not, and the Christians should depart, he must not blame him, for he had fulfilled his promise.

Great was the joy of Ortiz at this news, though still doubtful of its truth; however, he thanked Mocoço, and went his way. A dozen principal Indians were sent to accompany him; and on their way to the port, they met Baltasar de Gallegos, in the manner that has been related. Arrived at the camp, the Governor ordered that apparel be given to him, good armor, and a fine horse. When asked if he knew of any country where there was either gold or silver, he said that he had not been ten leagues in any direction from where he lived; but that thirty leagues distant was a chief named Paracoxi, to whom Mocoço, Ucita, and all they that dwelt along the coast paid tribute, and that he perhaps had knowledge of some good country, as his land was better than theirs, being more fertile, abounding in maize. Hearing this, the Governor was

well pleased, and said he only desired to find subsistence, that
he might be enabled to go inland with safety; for that Florida
was so wide, in some part or other of it, there could not fail
to be a rich country. The cacique of Mocoço came to the
port, and calling on the Governor, he thus spoke:

MOST HIGH AND POWERFUL CHIEF:

Though less able, I believe, to serve you than the least of these
under your control, but with the wish to do more than even the
greatest of them can accomplish, I appear before you in the full
confidence of receiving your favor, as much so as though I deserved
it, not in requital of the trifling service I rendered in setting free
the Christian while he was in my power, which I did, not for the
sake of my honor and of my promise, but because I hold that great
men should be liberal. As much as in your bodily perfections you
exceed all, and in your command over fine men are you superior
to others, so in your nature are you equal to the full enjoyment of
earthly things. The favor I hope for, great Lord, is that you will
hold me to be your own, calling on me freely to do whatever may
be your wish.

The Governor answered him, that although it were true, in
freeing and sending him the Christian, he had done no more
than to keep his word and preserve his honor, nevertheless
he thanked him for an act so valuable, that there was no other
for him that could be compared to it, and that, holding him
henceforth to be a brother, he should in all, and through all,
favor him. Then a shirt and some other articles of clothing
were directed to be given to the chief, who, thankfully receiving them, took leave and went to his town.

Chapter 10

*How the Governor, having sent the ships to Cuba, marched
inland, leaving one hundred men at the port.*

From the port of Espiritu Santo, where the Governor was,
he sent the chief castellan, with fifty cavalry and thirty or
forty infantry, to the province of Paracoxi, to observe the

character of the country, to inquire of that farther on, and to let him hear by message of what he should discover; he also sent the vessels to Cuba, that, at an appointed time, they might return with provisions. As the principal object of Vasco Porcallo de Figueroa in coming to Florida had been to get slaves for his plantation and mines, finding, after some incursions, that no seizures could be made, because of dense forest and extensive bogs, he determined to go back to Cuba; and in consequence of that resolution, there grew up such a difference between him and Soto, that neither of them treated nor spoke to the other kindly. Still, with words of courtesy, he asked permission of him to return, and took his leave.

Baltasar de Gallegos having arrived at Paracoxi, thirty Indians came to him on the part of the absent cacique, one of whom said: "King Paracoxi, lord of this province, whose vassals we are, sends us to ask of you what it is you seek in his country, and in what he can serve you;" to which the chief castellan replied, that he much thanked the cacique for his proffer, and bade them tell him to return to his town, where they would talk together of a peace and friendship he greatly desired to establish. They went off, and came again the next day, reporting that as their lord could not appear, being very unwell, they had come in his stead to see what might be wanted. They were asked if they had knowledge or information of any country where gold and silver might be found in plenty; to which they answered yes; that towards the sunset was a province called Cale, the inhabitants of which were at war with those of territories where the greater portion of the year was summer, and where there was so much gold, that when the people came to make war upon those of Cale, they wore golden hats like casques.

As the cacique had not come, Gallegos, reflecting, suspected the message designed for delay, that he might put himself in a condition of safety; and fearing that, if those men were suffered to depart, they might never return, he ordered them to be chained together, and sent the news to camp by eight men on horseback. The Governor, hearing what had passed, showed great pleasure, as did the rest who were with him, believing what the Indians said might be true. He left thirty cavalry and seventy infantry at the port, with provisions for two years, under command of Captain Calderon, marching with the others inland to Paracoxi; thence, having united with the force already there, he passed through a small town named Acela, and came to another called Tocaste,[1] whence he advanced with fifty of foot and thirty horse towards Cale;[2] and having gone through an untenanted town, some natives were seen in a lake, to whom having spoken by an interpreter, they came out and gave him a guide. From there he went to a river of powerful current, in the midst of which was a tree, whereon they made a bridge. Over this the people passed in safety, the horses being crossed swimming to a hawser, by which they were drawn to the other bank, the first that entered the water having been drowned for the want of one.

The Governor sent two men on horseback, with word to those in the rear that they should advance rapidly, for that the way was becoming toilsome and the provisions were short. He came to Cale and found the town abandoned; but he seized three spies, and tarried there until the people should arrive, they travelling hungry and on bad roads, the country being very thin of maize, low, very wet, pondy, and thickly covered with trees.[3] Where there were inhabitants, some watercresses could be found, which they who arrived first would gather, and, cooking them in water with salt, eat them without other thing; and they who could get none, would seize the stalks of maize and eat them, the ear, being young, as yet containing no grain. Having come to the river, which the Governor had passed, they got cabbage from the low palmetto growing there, like that of Andalusia. There they were met

---

[1] Tocaste was on an island in the marsh at the first crossing of "the great marsh," so graphically described by the Inca.

[2] This was the river or marsh of Cale, and the Inca's second crossing of the great marsh.

[3] They had now reached the higher country, which begins in the southern part of Polk County.

by the messengers, who, reporting a great deal of maize in Cale, gave much satisfaction.

While the people should be coming up, the Governor ordered all the ripe grain in the fields, enough for three months, to be secured. In gathering it three Christians were slain. One of two Indians who were made prisoners stated that seven days' journey distant was a large province, abounding in maize, called Apalache. Presently, with fifty cavalry and sixty infantry, he set out from Cale, leaving Luis de Moscoso, the master of the camp,[1] in command, with directions not to move until he should be ordered. Up to that time, no one had been able to get servants who should make his bread; and the method being to beat out the maize in log mortars with a one-handed pestle of wood, some also sifting the flour afterward through their shirts of mail, the process was found so laborious, that many, rather than crush the grain, preferred to eat it parched and sodden. The mass was baked in clay dishes, set over fire, in the manner that I have described as done in Cuba.

Chapter 11

How the Governor arrived at Caliquen, and thence, taking the cacique with him, came to Napetaca, where the Indians, attempting to rescue him, had many of their number killed and captured.

On the eleventh day of August, in the year 1539, the Governor left Cale, and arrived to sleep at a small town called Ytara, and the next day at another called Potano, and the third at Utinama, and then at another named Malapaz. This place was so called because one, representing himself to be its cacique, came peacefully, saying that he wished to serve the Governor with his people, and asked that he would cause the twenty-eight men and women, prisoners taken the night before, to be set at liberty; that provisions should be brought, and that he would furnish a guide for the country in advance of

[1] An officer somewhat like an adjutant-general.

us; whereupon, the Governor having ordered the prisoners to be let loose, and the Indian put under guard, the next day in the morning came many natives close to a scrub surrounding the town, near which the prisoner asked to be taken, that he might speak and satisfy them, as they would obey in whatever he commanded; but no sooner had he found himself close to them, than he boldly started away, and fled so swiftly that no one could overtake him, going off with the rest into the woods. The Governor ordered a bloodhound, already fleshed upon him, to be let loose, which, passing by many, seized upon the faithless cacique, and held him until the Christians had come up.

From this town the people went to sleep at that of Cholupaha, which, for its abundance of maize, received the name of Villafarta; thence, crossing a river before it, by a bridge they had made of wood, the Christians marched two days through an uninhabited country.

On the seventeenth day of August they arrived at Caliquen, where they heard of the province of Apalache, of Narvaez having been there and having embarked, because no road was to be found over which to go forward, and of there being no other town, and that water was on all sides. Every mind was depressed at this information, and all counselled the Governor to go back to the port, that they might not be lost, as Narvaez had been, and to leave the land of Florida; that, should they go further, they might not be able to get back, as the little maize that was yet left the Indians would secure: to which Soto replied, that he would never return until he had seen with his own eyes what was asserted, things that to him appeared incredible. Then he ordered us to be in readiness for the saddle, sending word to Luis de Moscoso to advance from Cale, that he waited for him; and, as in the judgment of the master of the camp, and of many others, they should have to return from Apalache, they buried in Cale some iron implements with other things. They reached Caliquen through much suffering; for the land over which the Governor had marched lay wasted and was without maize.

All the people having come up, a bridge was ordered to be made over a river that passed near the town, whereon we crossed, the tenth day of September, taking with us the cacique. When three days on our journey, some Indians arrived to visit their lord; and every day they came out to the road, playing upon flutes, a token among them that they come in peace. They stated that further on there was a cacique named Uzachil, kinsman of the chief of Caliquen, their lord, who waited the arrival of the Governor, prepared to do great services; and they besought him to set their cacique free, which he feared to do, lest they should go off without giving him any guides; so he got rid of them from day to day with specious excuses.

We marched five days, passing through some small towns, and arrived at Napetaca on the fifteenth day of September, where we found fourteen or fifteen Indians who begged for the release of the cacique of Caliquen, to whom the Governor declared that their lord was no prisoner, his attendance being wished only as far as Uzachil. Having learned from Juan Ortiz, to whom a native had made it known, that the Indians had determined to assemble and fall upon the Christians, for the recovery of their chief, the Governor, on the day for which the attack was concerted, commanded his men to be in readiness, the cavalry to be armed and on horseback, each one so disposed of in his lodge as not to be seen of the Indians, that they might come to the town without reserve. Four hundred warriors, with bows and arrows, appeared in sight of the camp; and, going into a thicket, they sent two of their number to demand the cacique: the Governor, with six men on foot, taking the chief by the hand, conversing with him the while to assure the Indians, went towards the place where they were, when, finding the moment propitious, he ordered a trumpet to be sounded: directly, they who were in the houses, foot as well as horse, set upon the natives, who, assailed unexpectedly, thought only of their safety. Of two horses killed, one was that of the Governor, who was mounted instantly on another. From thirty to forty natives fell by the lance; the rest escaped into two very large ponds, situated some way apart, wherein they swam about; and, being surrounded by the Christians, they were shot at with crossbow and arquebuse, although to no purpose, because of the long distance they were off.

At night, one of the lakes was ordered to be guarded, the people not being sufficient to encircle both. The Indians, in attempting to escape in the dark, would come swimming noiselessly to the shore, with a leaf of water-lily on the head, that they might pass unobserved; when those mounted, at sight of any ruffle on the surface, would dash into the water up to the breasts of the horses, and the natives would again retire. In such way passed the night, neither party taking any rest. Juan Ortiz told them that, as escape was impossible, they would do well to give up; which they did, driven by extreme chillness of the water; and one after another, as cold overpowered, called out to him, asking not to be killed — that he was coming straightway to put himself in the hands of the Governor. At four o'clock in the morning they had all surrendered, save twelve of the principal men, who, as of more distinction and more valiant than the rest, preferred to die rather than yield: then the Indians of Paracoxi, who were going about unshackled, went in after them, swimming, and pulled them out by the hair. They were all put in chains, and, on the day following, were divided among the Christians for their service.

While captives, these men determined to rebel, and gave the lead to an interpreter, one reputed brave, that when the Governor might come near to speak with him, he should strangle him; but no sooner was the occasion presented, and before his hands could be thrown about the neck of Soto, his purpose was discovered, and he received so heavy a blow from him in the nostrils, that they gushed with blood. The Indians all rose together. He who could only catch up a pestle from a mortar, as well as he who could grasp a weapon, equally exerted himself to kill his master, or the first one he met; and he whose fortune it was to light on a lance, or a sword, handled it in a manner as though he had been accustomed to use it all his days. One

Indian, in the public yard of the town, with blade in hand, fought like a bull in the arena, until the halberdiers of the Governor, arriving, put an end to him. Another got up, with a lance, into a maize crib, made of cane, called by Indians bar-bacoa, and defended the entrance with the uproar of ten men, until he was stricken down with a battle-axe. They who were subdued may have been in all two hundred men: some of the youngest the Governor gave to those who had good chains and were vigilant; all the rest were ordered to execution, and, being bound to a post in the middle of the town yard, they were shot to death with arrows by the people of Paracoxi.

Chapter 12

How the Governor arrived at Palache, and was informed that there was much gold inland.

On the twenty-third day of September the Governor left Napetaca, and went to rest at a river, where two Indians brought him a deer from the cacique of Uzachil; and the next day, having passed through a large town called Hapaluya, he slept at Uzachil. He found no person there; for the inhab-itants, informed of the deaths at Napetaca, dared not remain. In the town was found their food, much maize, beans, and pumpkins, on which the Christians lived. The maize is like coarse millet; the pumpkins are better and more savory than those of Spain.

Two captains having been sent in opposite directions, in quest of Indians, a hundred men and women were taken, one or two of whom were chosen out for the Governor, as was always customary for officers to do after successful inroads, dividing the others among themselves and companions. They were led off in chains, with collars about the neck, to carry luggage and grind corn, doing the labor proper to servants. Some-times it happened that, going with them for wood or maize, they would kill the Christian, and flee, with the chain on, which others would file at night with a splinter of stone, in the place

of iron, at which work, when caught, they were punished, as
a warning to others, and that they might not do the like.
The women and youths, when removed a hundred leagues
from their country, no longer cared, and were taken along
loose, doing the work, and in a very little time learning the
Spanish language.

From Uzachil the Governor went towards Apalache, and at
the end of two days' travel arrived at a town called Axille.
After that, the Indians having no knowledge of the Christians,
they were come upon unawares, the greater part escaping,
nevertheless, because there were woods near town. The next
day, the first of October, the Governor took his departure in
the morning, and ordered a bridge to be made over a river
which he had to cross. The depth there, for a stone's throw,
was over the head, and afterward the water came to the waist,
for the distance of a crossbow-shot, where was a growth of
tall and dense forest, into which the Indians came, to ascertain
if they could assail the men at work and prevent a passage;
but they were dispersed by the arrival of crossbowmen, and
some timbers being thrown in, the men gained the opposite
side and secured the way. On the fourth day of the week,
Wednesday of St. Francis,[1] the Governor crossed over and
reached Uitachuco, a town subject to Apalache, where he slept.
He found it burning, the Indians having set it on fire.

Thenceforward the country was well inhabited, producing
much corn, the way leading by many habitations like villages.
Sunday, the twenty-fifth of October,[2] he arrived at the town
of Uzela,[3] and on Monday at Anhayca Apalache, where the
lord of all that country and province resided. The camp-master, whose duty it is to divide and lodge the men, quartered
them about the town, at the distance of half a league to a

---

[1] St. Francis's day is the fourth of the month (October), but it was not
Wednesday in 1539. Ranjel says that the crossing was finished on Friday,
October 3.

[2] This should be Sunday, October 5. October 25, 1539, came on Saturday.

[3] Calahuchi, according to Ranjel. The modern name may be Chattahuchi.

league apart. There were other towns which had much maize, pumpkins, beans, and dried plums of the country, whence were brought together at Anhayca Apalache what appeared to be sufficient provision for the winter. These *ameixas* [1] are better than those of Spain, and come from trees that grow in the fields without being planted.

Informed that the sea was eight leagues distant, the Governor directly sent a captain thither, with cavalry and infantry, who found a town called Ochete, eight leagues on the way; and, coming to the coast, he saw where a great tree had been felled, the trunk split up into stakes, and with the limbs made into mangers. He found also the skulls of horses. With these discoveries he returned, and what was said of Narvaez was believed to be certain, that he had there made boats, [2] in which he left the country, and was lost in them at sea. Presently Juan de Añasco made ready to go to the port of Espiritu Santo, taking thirty cavalry, with orders from the Governor to Calderon, who had remained there, that he should abandon the town, and bring all the people to Apalache.

In Uzachill, and other towns on the way, Añasco found many people who had already become careless; still, to avoid detention, no captures were made, as it was not well to give the Indians sufficient time to come together. He went through the towns at night, stopping at a distance from the population for three or four hours, to rest, and at the end of ten days arrived at the port. He despatched two caravels to Cuba, in which he sent to Doña Ysabel twenty women brought by him from Ytara and Potano, near Cale; and, taking with him the foot-soldiers in the brigantines, from point to point along the coast by sea, he went towards Palache. Calderon with the cavalry, and some crossbowmen of foot, went by land. The Indians at several places beset him, and wounded some of the men. On his arrival, the Governor ordered planks and spikes

---

[1] This word means plums, but when applied to the American fruit, it has reference to the persimmon.

[2] The bay where Narvaez built his brigantines was known to the Spaniards as Bahia de Caballos, or Horse Bay. The modern name is Bay Ocklockonee.

to be taken to the coast for building a piragua, into which thirty men entered well armed from the bay, going to and coming from sea, waiting the arrival of the brigantines, and sometimes fighting with the natives, who went up and down the estuary in canoes. On Saturday, the twenty-ninth of November, in a high wind, an Indian passed through the sentries undiscovered, and set fire to the town, two portions of which, in consequence, were instantly consumed.

On Sunday, the twenty-eighth of December, Juan de Añasco arrived; and the Governor directed Francisco Maldonado, captain of infantry, to run the coast to the westward with fifty men, and look for an entrance; proposing to go himself in that direction by land on discoveries. The same day, eight men rode two leagues about the town in pursuit of Indians, who had become so bold that they would venture up within two crossbow-shot of the camp to kill our people. Two were discovered engaged in picking beans, and might have escaped, but a woman being present, the wife of one of them, they stood to fight. Before they could be killed, three horses were wounded, one of which died in a few days. Calderon going along the coast near by, the Indians came out against him from a wood, driving him from his course, and capturing from many of his company a part of their indispensable subsistence.

Three or four days having elapsed beyond the time set for the going and return of Maldonado, the Governor resolved that, should he not appear at the end of eight days, he would go thence and wait no longer; when the captain arrived, bringing with him an Indian from a Province called Ochus, sixty leagues from Apalache, and the news of having found a sheltered port with a good depth of water. The Governor was highly pleased, hoping to find a good country ahead; and he sent Maldonado to Havana for provisions, with which to meet him at that port of his discovery, to which he would himself come by land; but should he not reach there that summer, then he directed him to go back to Havana and return there the next season to await him, as he would make it his express object to march in quest of Ochus.

Francisco Maldonado went, and Juan de Guzman remained instead, captain of his infantry. Of the Indians taken in Napetuca, the treasurer, Juan Gaytan, brought a youth with him, who stated that he did not belong to that country, but to one afar in the direction of the sun's rising, from which he had been a long time absent visiting other lands; that its name was Yupaha, and was governed by a woman, the town she lived in being of astonishing size, and many neighboring lords her tributaries, some of whom gave her clothing, others gold in quantity. He showed how the metal was taken from the earth, melted, and refined, exactly as though he had seen it all done, or else the Devil had taught him how it was; so that they who knew aught of such matters declared it impossible that he could give that account without having been an eye-witness; and they who beheld the signs he made, credited all that was understood as certain.

Chapter 13

How the Governor went from Apalache in quest of Yupaha, and what befell him.

On Wednesday, the third of March, in the year 1540, the Governor left Anhaica Apalache to seek Yupaha. He had ordered his men to go provided with maize for a march through sixty leagues of desert. The cavalry carried their grain on the horses, and the infantry theirs on the back; because the Indians they brought with them for service, being naked and in chains, had perished in great part during the winter. On the fourth day of the journey they arrived at a deep river,[1] where a piragua was made; and, in consequence of the violence of the current, a cable of chains was extended from shore to shore, along which the boat passed, and the horses were drawn over, swimming thereto, by means of a windlass to the other side.

A day and a half afterwards, they arrived at a town by the

[1] Probably Flint River.

name of Capachiqui, and on Friday, the eleventh,[1] the inhabitants were found to have gone off. The following day, five Christians, going in the rear of the camp to search for mortars, in which the natives beat maize, went to some houses surrounded by a thicket, where many Indians lurked as spies, an equal number of whom, separating from the rest, set upon our men, one of whom fled back, crying out to arms. When they who could first answer to the call reached the spot, they found one of the Christians killed, and the three others badly wounded, the Indians fleeing into a sheet of water, full of woods, into which the horses could not go. The Governor left Capachiqui, passing through a desert; and on Wednesday, the twenty-first[2] of the month, came to Toalli.

The houses of this town were different from those behind, which were covered with dry grass; thenceforward they were roofed with cane, after the fashion of tile. They are kept very clean: some have their sides so made of clay as to look like tapia.[3] Throughout the cold country every Indian has a winter house, plastered inside and out, with a very small door, which is closed at dark, and a fire being made within, it remains heated like an oven, so that clothing is not needed during the night-time. He has likewise a house for summer, and near it a kitchen, where fire is made and bread baked. Maize is kept in a barbacoa, which is a house with wooden sides, like a room, raised aloft on four posts, and has a floor of cane. The difference between the houses of the masters, or principal men, and those of the common people is that, besides being larger than the others, they have deep balconies on the front side, with cane seats, like benches; and about are many barbacoas, in which they bring together the tribute their people give them of maize, skins of deer, and blankets of the country. These are like shawls, some of them made from the inner bark of

[1] This should be Thursday the eleventh, which was the day on which they arrived at the first town in Capachiqui. Capachiqui was the second town in that province, according to Ranjel.

[2] Wednesday was the twenty-fourth, but they arrived at Toalli early on the morning of the twenty-third, according to Ranjel.

[3] Mud walls.

trees, and others of a grass resembling nettle, which, by treading out, becomes like flax. The women use them for covering,
wearing one about the body from the waist downward, and
another over the shoulder, with the right arm left free, after
the manner of the Gypsies: the men wear but one, which they
carry over the shoulder in the same way, the loins being covered with a *bragueiro* of deer-skin, after the fashion of the
woollen breech-cloth that was once the custom of Spain. The
skins are well dressed, the color being given to them that is
wished, and in such perfection, that, when of vermilion, they
look like very fine red broadcloth; and when black, the sort
in use for shoes, they are of the purest. The same hues are
given to blankets.

The Governor left Toalli on the twenty-fourth day of
March, and arrived on Thursday, in the evening, at a little
stream [1] where a small bridge was made, and the people passed
to the opposite side. Benito Fernandes, a Portuguese, fell off
from it, and was drowned. So soon as the Governor had
crossed, he found a town, a short way on, by the name of
Achese, the people of which, having had no knowledge of the
Christians, plunged into a river; nevertheless, some men and
women were taken, among whom was found one who understood the youth, the guide to Yupaha, which rather confirmed
what he stated, as they had come through regions speaking
different languages, some of which he did not understand.
By one of the Indians taken there, the Governor sent to call
the cacique from the farther side of the river, who, having
come to him, thus spoke:

VERY HIGH, POWERFUL, AND GOOD MASTER:

The things that seldom happen bring astonishment. Think,
then, what must be the effect on me and mine, of the sight of you
and your people, whom we have at no time seen, astride the fierce
brutes, your horses, entering with such speed and fury into my

---

[1] Before arriving at this stream they crossed a very broad river, according to Ranjel, which Biedma says was the first river flowing to the east.
This was the Ocmulgee River.

country, that we had no tidings of your coming — things so altogether new, as to strike awe and terror to our hearts, which it was not nature to resist, so that we should receive you with the sobriety due to so kingly and famous a lord. Trusting to your greatness and personal qualities, I hope no fault will be found in me, and that I shall rather receive favors, of which one is that with my person, my country, and my vassals, you will do as with your own things; and another, that you tell me who you are, whence you come, whither you go, and what it is you seek, that I may the better serve you.

The Governor responded, that he greatly thanked him for his good-will, as much so as though he had given him a great treasure. He told him that he was the child of the Sun, coming from its abode, and that he was going about the country, seeking for the greatest prince there, and the richest province. The cacique stated that farther on was a great lord, whose territory was called Ocute. He gave him a guide, who understood the language, to conduct him thither; and the Governor commanded his subjects to be released. A high cross, made of wood, was set up in the middle of the town-yard; and, as time did not allow more to be done, the Indians were instructed that it was put there to commemorate the suffering of Christ, who was God and man; that he had created the skies and the earth, and had suffered for the salvation of all, and therefore, that they should revere that sign; and they showed by their manner that they would do so.

The Governor set out on the first day of April, and advanced through the country of the chief, along up a river, the shores of which were very populous. On the fourth he went through the town of Altamaca,[1] and on the tenth arrived at Ocute. The cacique sent him a present, by two thousand Indians, of many rabbits and partridges, maize bread, many dogs, and two turkeys. On account of the scarcity of meat, the dogs were as much esteemed by the Christians as though they had been fat sheep. There was such want of meat and salt that

---

[1] Altamaha, according to Ranjel. Before arriving at this place they crossed a great river which was either the Oconee or the Altamaha River.

oftentimes, in many places, a sick man had nothing for his nourishment, and was wasting away to bone, of some ail that elsewhere might have found a remedy; and would die of pure debility, saying: "Now, if I had but a slice of meat, or only a few lumps of salt, I should not thus die."

The Indians never lacked meat. With arrows they get abundance of deer, turkeys, rabbits, and other wild animals, being very skilful in killing game, which the Christians were not; and even if they had been, there was not the opportunity for it, they being on the march the greater part of their time; nor did they, besides, ever dare to straggle off. Such was the craving for meat, that when the six hundred men who followed Soto arrived at a town, and found there twenty or thirty dogs, he who could get sight of one and kill him, thought he had done no little; and he who proved himself so active, if his captain knew of it, and he forgot to send him a quarter, would show his displeasure, and make him feel it in the watches, or in any matter of labor that came along, with which he could bear upon him.

On Monday, the twelfth of April, the Governor took his departure, the cacique of Ocute giving him four hundred tamemes, the Indians that carry burdens. He passed through a town, the lord of which was called Cofaqui, and came to the province of another, named Patofa, who, being at peace with the chief of Ocute and other neighboring lords, had heard of the Governor for a long time, and desired to see him. He went to call on him, and made this speech:

POWERFUL LORD:

Not without reason, now, will I ask that some light mishap befall me, in return for so great good fortune, and deem my lot a happy one; since I have come to what I most wished in life, to behold and have the opportunity in some way to serve you. Thus the tongue casts the shadow of the thought; but I, nevertheless, am as unable to produce the perfect image of my feelings as to control the appearances of my contentment. By what circumstance has this your land, which I govern, deserved to be seen by one so superior and excellent that all on earth should obey and

serve him [Soto] as a prince? And those who here inhabit being
so insignificant, how can they forget, in receiving this vast enjoyment, that, in the order of things, will follow upon it some great
adversity? If we are held worthy of being yours, we can never
be other than favored, nor less than protected in whatsoever is
reasonable and just; for they that fail of deserving either, with
the name of men can only be considered brutes. From the depth
of my heart, and with the respect due to such a chief, I make mine
offer; and pray that, in return for so sincere good-will, you dispose of me, my country, and my vassals.

The Governor answered that his offers and good-will,
shown in works, would greatly please him, and that he should
ever bear them in memory to honor and favor him as he would
a brother. From this province of Patofa, back to the first
cacique we found at peace, a distance of fifty leagues, the
country is abundant, picturesque, and luxuriant, well watered,
and having good river margins; thence to the harbor of Espiritu Santo, where we first arrived, the land of Florida, which
may be three hundred leagues in length, a little more or less,
is light, the greater part of it of pine-trees, and low, having
many ponds; and in places are high and dense forests, into
which the Indians that were hostile betook themselves, where
they could not be found; nor could horses enter there, which,
to the Christians, was the loss of the food they carried away,
and made it troublesome to get guides.

Chapter 14

*How the Governor left the province of Patofa, marching into a
desert country, where he, with his people, became exposed to great peril and underwent severe privation.*

In the town of Patofa, the youth, whom the Governor
brought with him for guide and interpreter, began to froth
at the mouth, and threw himself on the ground as if he were
possessed of the Devil. An exorcism being said over him,
the fit went off. He stated that four days' journey from there,

towards the sunrise, was the province he spoke of: the Indians at Patofa said that they knew of no dwellings in that direction, but that towards the northwest there was a province called Coça, a plentiful country having very large towns. The cacique told the Governor that if he desired to go thither he would give him a guide and Indians to carry burdens, and if he would go in the direction pointed out by the youth, he would furnish him with everything necessary for that also.

With words of love, and tendering each other services, they parted, the Governor receiving seven hundred tamemes. He took maize for the consumption of four days, and marched by a road that, gradually becoming less, on the sixth day disappeared. Led by the youth, they forded two rivers,[1] each the breadth of two shots of a crossbow, the water rising to the stirrups of the saddles, and passing in a current so powerful, that it became necessary for those on horseback to stand one before another, that they on foot, walking near, might cross along above them: then came to another[2] of a more violent current, and larger, which was got over with more difficulty, the horses swimming for a lance's length at the coming out, into a pine-grove. The Governor menaced the youth, motioning that he would throw him to the dogs for having lied to him in saying that it was four days' journey, whereas they had travelled nine, each day of seven or eight leagues; and that the men and horses had become very thin, because of the sharp economy practised with the maize. The youth declared that he knew not where he was. Fortunately for him, at the time, there was not another whom Juan Ortiz understood, or he would have been cast to the dogs.

The Governor, leaving the camp among the pine-trees, marched that day, with some cavalry and infantry, five or six leagues, looking for a path, and came back at night very cast down, not having found any sign of inhabitants. The next day there was a variety of opinion about the course proper to take, whether to return or do otherwise. The country through

---

[1] The Great Ohoopee and Cannouchee rivers.
[2] The Ogeechee River.

which they had come remained wasted and without maize;
the grain they had so far brought with them was spent; the
beasts, like the men, were become very lean; and it was held
very doubtful whether relief was anywhere to be found: moreover, it was the opinion that they might be beaten by any
Indians whatsoever who should venture to attack them, so
that continuing thus, whether by hunger or in strife, they must
inevitably be overcome. The Governor determined to send
thence in all directions on horseback, in quest of habitations;
and the next day he despatched four captains to as many points,
with eight of cavalry to each. They came back at night leading their beasts by the bridle, unable to carry their masters, or
driven before them with sticks, having found no road, nor any
sign of a settlement. He sent other four again the next day,
with eight of cavalry apiece, men who could swim, that they
might cross any ponds and rivers in the way, the horses being
chosen of the best that were; Baltasar de Gallegos ascending
by the river, Juan de Añasco going down it, Alfonso Romo and
Juan Rodriguez Lobillo striking into the country.

The Governor had brought thirteen sows to Florida, which
had increased to three hundred swine; and the maize having
failed for three or four days, he ordered to be killed daily,
for each man, half a pound of pork, on which small allowance,
and some boiled herbs, the people with much difficulty lived.
There being no food to give to the Indians of Patofa, they were
dismissed, though they still wished to keep with the Christians
in their extremity, and showed great regret at going back before leaving them in a peopled country. Juan de Añasco
came in on Sunday, in the afternoon, bringing with him a
woman and a youth he had taken, with the report that he
had found a small town twelve or thirteen leagues off; at
which the Governor and his people were as much delighted
as though they had been raised from death to life.

On Monday, the twenty-sixth of April, the Governor set
out for Aymay, a town to which the Christians gave the name
of Socorro. At the foot of a tree, in the camp, they buried a
paper, and in the bark, with a hatchet, they cut these words:

"Dig here; at the root of this pine you will find a letter;" and this was so fixed that the captains, who had gone in quest of an inhabited country, should learn what the Governor had done and the direction he had taken. There was no other road than the one Juan de Añasco had made moving along through the woods.

On Monday the Governor arrived at the town, with those the best mounted, all riding the hardest possible; some sleeping two leagues off, others three and four, each as he was able to travel and his strength held out. A barbacoa was found full of parched meal and some maize, which were distributed by allowance. Four Indians were taken, not one of whom would say anything else than that he knew of no other town. The Governor ordered one of them to be burned; and thereupon another said, that two days' journey from there was a province called Cutifachiqui.[1]

On Wednesday the three captains came up: they had found the letter and followed on after the rest. From the command of Juan Rodriguez two men remained behind, their horses having given out, for which the Governor reprimanded him severely, and sent him to bring them. While they should be coming on he set out for Cutifachiqui, capturing three Indians in the road, who stated that the mistress of that country had already information of the Christians, and was waiting for them in a town. He sent to her by one of them, offering his friendship and announcing his approach. Directly as the Governor arrived, four canoes came towards him, in one of which was a kinswoman of the Cacica, who, coming near, addressed him in these words:

EXCELLENT LORD:

My sister sends me to salute you, and to say, that the reason why she has not come in person is, that she has thought to serve

---

[1] From the wording of the Ranjel narrative, Aymay was on the east side of the Savannah River and Cutifachiqui on the west side. The latter town was not at Silver Bluff, South Carolina, as commonly thought, but further down the river. Cofitachequi (as Ranjel spells it) is proper Creek, and means Dog-wood Town.

you better by remaining to give orders on the other shore; and that, in a short time, her canoes will all be here, in readiness to conduct you thither, where you may take your repose and be obeyed.

The Governor thanked her, and she returned to cross the river. After a little time the Cacica came out of the town, seated in a chair, which some principal men having borne to the bank, she entered a canoe. Over the stern was spread an awning, and in the bottom lay extended a mat where were two cushions, one above the other, upon which she sate; and she was accompanied by her chief men, in other canoes, with Indians. She approached the spot where the Governor was, and, being arrived, thus addressed him:

EXCELLENT LORD:
Be this coming to these your shores most happy. My ability can in no way equal my wishes, nor my services become the merits of so great a prince; nevertheless, good wishes are to be valued more than all the treasures of the earth without them. With sincerest and purest good-will I tender you my person, my lands, my people, and make you these small gifts.

The Cacica presented much clothing of the country, from the shawls and skins that came in the other boats; and drawing from over her head a large string of pearls, she threw them about his neck, exchanging with him many gracious words of friendship and courtesy. She directed that canoes should come to the spot, whence the Governor and his people passed to the opposite side of the river. So soon as he was lodged in the town, a great many turkeys were sent to him. The country was delightful and fertile, having good interval lands upon the streams; the forest was open, with abundance of walnut and mulberry trees. The sea was stated to be distant two days' travel. About the place, from half a league to a league off, were large vacant towns, grown up in grass, that appeared as if no people had lived in them for a long time. The Indians said that, two years before, there had been a pest in the land, and the inhabitants had moved away to other towns. In the barbacoas were large quantities of clothing, shawls of thread, made from the bark of trees, and others of feathers, white, gray, vermilion, and yellow, rich and proper for winter. There were also many well-dressed deer-skins, of colors drawn over with designs, of which had been made shoes, stockings, and hose. The Cacica, observing that the Christians valued the pearls, told the Governor that, if he should order some sepulchres that were in the town to be searched, he would find many; and if he chose to send to those that were in the uninhabited towns, he might load all his horses with them. They examined those in the town, and found three hundred and fifty pounds' weight of pearls, and figures of babies and birds made of them.

The inhabitants are brown of skin, well formed and proportioned. They are more civilized than any people seen in all the territories of Florida, wearing clothes and shoes. This country, according to what the Indians stated, had been very populous. It appeared that the youth who was the guide had heard of it; and what was told him he declared to have seen, and magnified such parts as he chose, to suit his pleasure. He told the Governor that they had begun to enter upon the country he had spoken to him about, which, because of its appearance, with his being able to understand the language of the people, gained for him some credit. He wished to become a Christian, and asked to be baptized, which was done, he receiving the name of Pedro; and the Governor commanded the chain to be struck off that he had carried until then.

In the town were found a dirk and beads that had belonged to Christians, who, the Indians said, had many years before been in the port, distant two days' journey. He that had been there was the Governor-licentiate Ayllon, who came to conquer the land, and, on arriving at the port, died, when there followed divisions and murders among the chief personages, in quarrels as to who should command; and thence, without knowing any thing of the country, they went back to Spain.

To all it appeared well to make a settlement there, the point being a favorable one, to which could come all the ships from New Spain, Peru, Sancta Marta, and Tierra-Firme, going to

Spain; because it is in the way thither, is a good country, and one fit in which to raise supplies; but Soto, as it was his object to find another treasure like that of Atabalípa, lord of Peru, would not be content with good lands nor pearls, even though many of them were worth their weight in gold (and if the country were divided among Christians, more precious should those be the Indians would procure than these they have, being bored with heat, which causes them to lose their hue): so he answered them who urged him to make a settlement, that in all the country together there was not support for his troops a single month; that it was necessary to return to Ochus, where Maldonado was to wait; and should a richer country not be found, they could always return to that who would, and in their absence the Indians would plant their fields and be better provided with maize. The natives were asked if they had knowledge of any great lord farther on, to which they answered, that twelve days' travel thence was a province called Chiaha, subject to a chief of Coça.

The Governor then resolved at once to go in quest of that country, and being an inflexible man, and dry of word, who, although he liked to know what the others all thought and had to say, after he once said a thing he did not like to be opposed, and as he ever acted as he thought best, all bent to his will; for though it seemed an error to leave that country, when another might have been found about it, on which all the people could have been sustained until the crops had been made and the grain gathered, there were none who would say a thing to him after it became known that he had made up his mind.

Chapter 15

How the Governor went from Cutifachiqui in quest of Coça, and what occurred to him on the journey.

On the third day of May,[1] the Governor set out from Cutifachiqui; and, it being discovered that the wish of the Cacica was to leave the Christians, if she could, giving them

[1] This should be May 13, according to Ranjel.

neither guides nor tamemes, because of the outrages committed
upon the inhabitants, there never failing to be men of low degree among the many, who will put the lives of themselves
and others in jeopardy for some mean interest, the Governor
ordered that she should be placed under guard and took her
with him. This treatment, which was not a proper return
for the hospitable welcome he had received, makes true the
adage, For well doing, etc. ; and thus she was carried away
on foot with her female slaves.

This brought us service in all the places that were passed,
she ordering the Indians to come and take the loads from town to
town. We travelled through her territories a hundred leagues,
in which, according to what we saw, she was greatly obeyed,
whatsoever she ordered being performed with diligence and
efficacy. Pedro, the guide, said she was not the suzeraine,
but her niece, who had come to that town by her command to
punish capitally some principal Indians who had seized upon
the tribute; but to this no credit was given, because of the
falsehoods in which he had been taken, though all was put up
with, from the necessity of having some one whereby to understand what the Indians said.

In seven days the Governor arrived at the province of
Chalaque,[1] the country poorest off for maize of any that was
seen in Florida, where the inhabitants subsisted on the roots
of plants that they dig in the wilds, and on the animals they
destroy there with their arrows. They are very domestic
people, are slight of form, and go naked. One lord brought the
Governor two deer-skins as a great gift. Turkeys were abundant; in one town they presented seven hundred, and in others
brought him what they had and could procure. He was detained in going from this province to that of Xualla[2] five days,

---

[1] In two days, according to Ranjel.

[2] This town is the Choualla of the Inca and the old Cherokee town of
Qualla, which was located above the junction of the Tuckaseegee and Oconna-
Luftee Rivers, in Swain County, North Carolina. From Cofitachequi the
army took a northerly course, probably following the old Indian and traders'
trail to old Fort Prince George, in Jackson County, South Carolina, and from
there to Xualla.

where they found little grain, but remained two days, because of the weariness of the men and the leanness of the horses.

From Ocute to Cutifachiqui are one hundred and thirty leagues, of which eighty are desert; from Cutifa to Xualla are two hundred and fifty of mountainous country; thence to Guaxule, the way is over very rough and lofty ridges.

One day while on this journey, the Cacica of Cutifachi, whom the Governor brought with him, as has been stated, to the end of taking her to Guaxule, the farthest limit of her territories, conducted by her slaves, she left the road, with an excuse of going into a thicket, where, deceiving them, she so concealed herself that for all their search she could not be found. She took with her a cane box, like a trunk, called petaca, full of unbored pearls, of which those who had the most knowledge of their value said they were very precious. They were carried for her by one of the women; and the Governor, not to give offence, permitted it so, thinking that in Guaxulle he would beg them of her when he should give her leave to depart; but she took them with her, going to Xualla, with three slaves who had fled from the camp. A horseman, named Alimamos, who remained behind, sick of a fever, wandering out of the way, got lost; and he labored with the slaves to make them leave their evil design. Two of them did so, and came on with him to the camp. They overtook the Governor, after a journey of fifty leagues, in a province called Chiaha; and he reported that the Cacica remained in Xualla, with a slave of André de Vasconcelos, who would not come with him, and that it was very sure they lived together as man and wife, and were to go together to Cutifachiqui.

At the end of five days the Governor arrived at Guaxulle.[1] The Christians being seen to go after dogs, for their flesh, which the Indians do not eat, they gave them three hundred of those animals. Little maize was found there, or anywhere upon that route. The Governor sent a native with a message to the

[1] The second day after leaving Xualla they camped at the junction of two rivers, according to Ranjel. This was probably at the junction of the Little Tennessee and Oconna-Luftee rivers.

cacique of Chiaha, begging that he would order some maize to be brought together at his town, that he might sojourn there some time. He left Guaxulle, and after two days' travel arrived at Canasagua, where twenty men came out from the town on the road, each laden with a basket of mulberries. This fruit is abundant and good, from Cutifachiqui to this place, and thence onward in other provinces, as are the walnut and the plum (persimmon); the trees growing about over the country, without planting or pruning, of the size and luxuriance they would have were they cultivated in orchards, by hoeing and irrigation. Leaving Canasagua, he marched five days through a desert.

Two leagues before he came to Chiaha, fifteen men met the Governor, bearing loads of maize, with word from the cacique that he waited for him, having twenty barbacoas full; that, moreover, himself, his lands, and his vassals, were subject to his orders. On the fifth day of July [1] the Governor entered Chiaha.[2] The cacique received him with great pleasure, and, resigning to him his dwellings for his residence, thus addressed him: —

POWERFUL AND EXCELLENT MASTER:

Fortunate am I that you will make use of my services. Nothing could happen that would give me so great contentment, or which I should value more. From Guaxule you sent to have maize for you in readiness to last two months: you have in this town twenty barbacoas full of the choicest and the best to be found in all this country. If the reception I give is not worthy of so great a prince, consider my youth, which will relieve me of blame, and receive my good-will, which, with true loyalty and pure, shall ever be shown in all things that concern your welfare.

The Governor answered him, that his gifts and his kindness pleased him greatly, and that he should ever consider him to be his brother.

There was abundance of lard in calabashes, drawn like

---

[1] It should be June 5, according to Ranjel.

[2] Chiaha was evidently on the island at the junction of the Little Tennessee and Tennessee Rivers, in Loudon County, Tennessee.

olive oil, which the inhabitants said was the fat of bear. There
was likewise found much oil of walnuts, which, like the lard,
was clear and of good taste; and also a honey-comb, which the
Christians had never seen before, nor saw afterwards, nor honey,
nor bees, in all the country.

The town was isolated, between two arms of a river, and
seated near one of them. Above it, at the distance of two crossbow-shot, the water divided, and united again a league below.
The vale between, from side to side, was the width in places of
a crossbow-shot, and in others of two. The branches were very
wide, and both were fordable: along their shores were very
rich meadow-lands, having many maize-fields.

As the Indians remained at home, no houses were taken
save those of the chief, in which the Governor lodged; the
people lived out, wherever there happened to be shelter, each
man having his tree. In this manner the army lay, the men
out of order and far apart. The Governor passed it over, as
the Indians were peaceful, and the weather very calm: the
people would have suffered greatly had they been required
to do differently. The horses arrived so worn out, that they
could not bear their riders from weakness; for they had come
all the way with only a little maize to live on, travelling, hungry and tired, even from beyond the desert of Ocute; so, as
the greater part of them were unfit to be mounted, even in
the necessary case of battle, they were turned out at night to
graze, about a quarter of a league from the camp. The Christians were greatly exposed, so much so that if at that time the
Indians had set upon them, they would have been in bad way
to defend themselves.

The duration of the sojourn was thirty days, in which time,
the soil being covered with verdure, the horses fattened. At
the departure, in consequence of the importunity of some who
wanted more than was in reason, the Governor asked thirty
women of the chief for slaves, who replied that he would confer
with his principal men; when one night, before giving an answer, all went off from the town with their women and children.
The next day, he having made up his mind to go in search of

them, the cacique arrived, and, approaching, thus addressed him: —

POWERFUL LORD:

Because of my shame, and out of fear of you, discovering that my subjects, contrary to my wishes, had chosen to absent themselves, I left without your permission; but, finding the error of my way, I have returned like a true vassal, to put myself in your power, that you may do with my person as shall seem best to you. My people will not obey me, nor do any thing that an uncle of mine does not command: he governs this country, in my place, until I shall be of mature age. If you would pursue and punish them for disobedience, I will be your guide, since my fate at present forbids me doing more.

The Governor then, with thirty mounted men and as many footmen, went in search of the people. Passing by the towns of some of the chiefs who had gone off, he cut down and destroyed the great maize-fields; and going along up the stream where the natives were, on an islet, to which the cavalry could not go, he sent word to them, by an Indian, that they should put away all their fears, and, returning to their abodes, give him tamemes, as had been done all the way along, since he did not wish to have women, finding how very dear they were to them. The Indians judged it well to come and make their excuses to him, so they all went back to the town.

A cacique of Acoste, who came to see the Governor, after tendering his services, and they had exchanged compliments and proffers of friendship, was asked if he had any information of a rich land; he answered yes: that towards the north there was a province called Chisca, and that a forge was there for copper, or other metal of that color, though brighter, having a much finer hue, and was to appearances much better, but was not so much used, for being softer; which was the statement that had been given in Cutifachiqui, where we had seen some chopping-knives that were said to have a mixture of gold. As the country on the way was thinly peopled, and it was said there were mountains over which the beasts could not go, the

Governor would not march directly thither, but judged that, keeping in an inhabited territory, the men and animals would be in better condition, while he would be more exactly informed of what there was, until he should turn to it through the ridges and a region which he could more easily travel. He sent two Christians to the country of Chisca, by Indians who spoke the language, that they might view it, and were told that he would await their return at Chiaha for what they should have to say.

Chapter 16

How the Governor left Chiaha, and, having run a hazard of falling by the hands of the Indians, at Acoste, escaped by his address: what occurred to him on the route, and how he came to Coça.

When the Governor had determined to move from Chiaha towards Coste,[1] he sent for the cacique to come before him, and with kind words took his leave, receiving some slaves as a gift, which pleased him. In seven days the journey was concluded. On the second day of July, the camp being pitched among the trees, two crossbow-shot distant from the town, he went with eight men of his guard toward where the cacique was, who received him evidently with great friendship. While they were conversing, some infantry went into the town after maize, and, not satisfied with what they got, they rummaged and searched the houses, taking what they would; at which conduct the owners began to rise and arm; some of them, with clubs in their hands, going at five or six men who had given offence, beat them to their satisfaction. The Governor, discovering that they were all bent upon some mischief, and himself among them with but few Christians about him, turned to escape from the difficulty by a stratagem much against his nature, clear and reliable as it was, and the more unwillingly as it grieved him that an Indian should presume, either with or

[1] This place was located on one of the islands in the Tennessee River, just above Chattanooga.

without cause, to offer any indignity to a Christian: he seized
a stave and took part with the assailants against his own people,
which while it gave confidence, directly he sent a message
secretly to the camp, that armed men should approach where
he was; then taking the chief by the hand, speaking to him
with kind words, drew him with some principal men away from
the town, out into an open road in sight of the encampment,
where cautiously the Christians issued and by degrees surrounded them.   In this manner they were conducted within
the tents; and when near his marquee the Governor ordered
them to be put under guard.   He told them that they could
not go thence without giving him a guide and Indians for carrying loads, nor until the sick men had arrived whom he had
ordered to come down by the river in canoes from Chiaha,
and so likewise those he had sent to the province of Chisca.
He feared that both the one and the other had been killed by
the Indians.   In three days they that went to Chisca got back,
and related that they had been taken through a country so
scant of maize, and with such high mountains, that it was impossible the army should march in that direction; and finding
the distance was becoming long, and that they should be back
late, upon consultation they agreed to return, coming from
a poor little town where there was nothing of value, bringing
a cow-hide as delicate as a calf-skin the people had given them,
the hair being like the soft wool on the cross of the merino
with the common sheep.

The cacique having furnished the guide and tamemes,
by permission of the Governor he went his way.   The Christians left Coste the ninth day of July, and slept that night at
Tali.[1]   The cacique had come from the town to meet the
Governor on the road, and made him this speech: —

EXCELLENT GREAT PRINCE:

Worthy are you of being served and obeyed by all the princes
of the world, for by the face can one judge far of the inner qualities.

---

[1] Tali was located in the bend of the Tennessee River, just below Chattanooga.   Here they left the river.

Who you are I knew, and also of your power, before your coming here. I wish not to draw attention to the lowliness in which I stand before you, to make my poor services acceptable and agreeable, since, where the strength fails, the will should instead be praised and taken. Hence, I dare to ask that you will only consider and attend to what you will command me to do here in your country.

The Governor answered, that his good-will and offer pleased him as much as though he had tendered him all the treasures of the earth: that he would always be treated by him as a true brother, favored and esteemed. The cacique ordered provision to be brought for two days' use, the time the Governor should be present; and on his departure, gave him the use of two men and four women, who were wanted to carry burdens.

They travelled six days, passing by many towns subject to the cacique of Coça; and, as they entered those territories, numerous messengers came from him on the road every day to the Governor, some going, others coming, until they arrived at Coça,[1] on Friday, the sixteenth of July. The cacique came out to receive him at the distance of two crossbow-shot from the town, borne in a litter on the shoulders of his principal men, seated on a cushion, and covered with a mantle of marten-skins, of the size and shape of a woman's shawl: on his head he wore a diadem of plumes, and he was surrounded by many attendants playing upon flutes and singing. Coming to where the Governor was, he made his obeisance, and followed it by these words: —

POWERFUL LORD, SUPERIOR TO EVERY OTHER OF THE EARTH:

Although I come but now to meet you, it is a long time since I have received you in my heart. That was done the first day I heard of you, with so great desire to serve, please, and give you contentment, that this, which I express, is nothing in comparison with that which is within me. Of this you may be sure, that to have received the dominion of the world would not have interested me so greatly as the sight of you, nor would I have held it for so great a felicity. Do not look for me to offer you that which is your

---

[1] Coça may not have been the Coosa of the last century, which was located some two miles north of Childersburg, in Talladega County, Alabama.

own — this person, these lands, these vassals. My only desire is
to employ myself in commanding these people, that, with all diligence and befitting respect, they conduct you hence to the town
in festivity of voices and with flutes, where you will be lodged and
waited upon by me and them, where all I possess you will do with
as with your own, and in thus doing you will confer favor.

The Governor gave him thanks, and with mutual satisfaction they walked on toward the place conferring, the
Indians giving up their habitations by order of their cacique,
and in which the General and his men took lodging.   In the
barbacoas was a great quantity of maize and beans: the country, thickly settled in numerous and large towns, with fields
between, extending from one to another, was pleasant, and
had a rich soil with fair river margins.   In the woods were many
plums (persimmons), as well those of Spain as of the country;
and wild grapes on vines growing up into the trees, near the
streams; likewise a kind that grew on low vines elsewhere, the
berry being large and sweet, but, for want of hoeing and dressing, had large stones.

It was the practice to keep watch over the caciques that
none should absent themselves, they being taken along by the
Governor until coming out of their territories; for by thus having them the inhabitants would await their arrival in the towns,
give a guide, and men to carry the loads, who before leaving
their country would have liberty to return to their homes, as
sometimes would the tamemes, so soon as they came to the
domain of any chief where others could be got.   The people of
Coça, seeing their lord was detained, took it amiss, and, going
off, hid themselves in the scrub, as well those of the town of the
cacique as those of the towns of the principal men his vassals.
The Governor despatched four captains in as many directions to
search for them: many men and women were taken who were
put in chains. Seeing how much harm they received, and
how little they gained by going off, they came in, declaring
that they desired to serve in all that was possible.   Of the
prisoners, some of the chiefs, whom the cacique interceded for,
were let go; of the rest, each one took away with him as slaves

those he had in chains, none returning to their country save
some whose fortune it was to escape, laboring diligently to file
off their irons at night; or, while on the march, could slip out
of the way, observing the carelessness of those who had them in
charge, sometimes taking off with them in their chains the burdens and the clothing with which they were laden.

Chapter 17

Of how the Governor went from Coça to Tascaluça.

The Governor rested in Coça twenty-five days. On
Friday, the twentieth of August, he set out in quest of a province called Tascaluça, taking with him the cacique of Coça.
The first day he went through Tallimuchase, a great town
without inhabitants, halting to sleep half a league beyond,
near a river-bank. The following day he came to Ytaua, a
town subject to Coça. He was detained six days, because of
a river near by that was then swollen: so soon as it could be
crossed he took up his march, and went towards Ullibahali.
Ten or twelve chiefs came to him on the road, from the cacique
of that province, tendering his service, bearing bows and
arrows and wearing bunches of feathers.

The Governor having arrived at the town with a dozen
cavalry and several of his guard, he left them at the distance
of a crossbow-shot and entered the town. He found all the
Indians with their weapons, and, according to their ways, it
appeared to him in readiness for action: he understood afterwards that they had determined to wrest the cacique of Coça
from his power, should that chief have called on them. The
place was enclosed, and near by ran a small stream. The
fence, which was like that seen afterwards to other towns,
was of large timber sunk deep and firmly into the earth, having
many long poles the size of the arm, placed crosswise to nearly
the height of a lance, with embrasures, and coated with mud
inside and out, having loop-holes for archery.[1] The Gov-

---

[1] Ranjel applies a similar description to an old town on the road, three
days' march from Toasi or Tuasi.

ernor ordered all his men to enter the town. The cacique, who at the moment was at a town on the opposite shore, was sent for, and he came at once. After some words between him and the Governor, proffering mutual service, he gave the tamemes that were requisite and thirty women as slaves. Mançano, a native of Salamanca, of noble ancestry, having strayed off in search of the grapes, which are good here, and plenty, was lost.

The Christians left, and that day they arrived to sleep at a town subject to the lord of Ullibahali, and the next day they came to pass the night at the town of Toasi, where the inhabitants gave the Governor thirty women and the tamemes that were wanted. The amount of travel usually performed was five or six leagues a day, passing through settled country; and when through desert, all the haste possible was made, to avoid the want of maize. From Toasi, passing through some towns subject to the lord of the province of Tallise,[1] he journeyed five days, and arrived at the town the eighteenth day of September.

Tallise was large, situated by the side of a great river, other towns and many fields of maize being on the opposite shore, the country on both sides having the greatest abundance of grain. The inhabitants had gone off. The Governor sent to call the cacique, who, having arrived, after an interchange of kind words and good promises, lent him forty men. A chief came to the Governor in behalf of the cacique of Tastaluça,[2] and made the following address:

VERY POWERFUL, VIRTUOUS, AND ESTEEMED LORD:

The grand cacique of Tascaluça, my master, sends me to salute you. He bids me say, that he is told how all, not without reason, are led captive by your perfections and power; that wheresoever lies your path you receive gifts and obedience, which he

---

[1] This is probably not the modern town of that name, which was located above the elbow of the Tallapoosa River, in Tallapoosa County.

[2] Tascaluça is correct Creek (meaning Black Warrior), and Tastaluça, there can be little doubt, is a misspelling; nevertheless we think it better to present all the native names in the spellings of the Portuguese original.

knows are all your due; and that he longs to see you as much as
he could desire for the continuance of life. Thus, he sends me to
offer you his person, his lands, his subjects; to say, that wheresoever it shall please you to go through his territories, you will find
service and obedience, friendship and peace. In requital of this
wish to serve you, he asks that you so far favor him as to say
when you will come; for that the sooner you do so, the greater
will be the obligation, and to him the earlier pleasure.

The Governor received and parted with the messenger
graciously, giving him beads (which by the Indians are not
much esteemed) and other articles, that he should take them
to his lord. He dismissed the cacique of Coça, that he might
return to his country: he of Tallise gave him the tamemes
that were needed; and, having sojourned twenty days, the
Governor set out for Tastaluça. He slept the night at a large
town called Casiste, and the next day, passing through another,
arrived at a village in the province of Tastaluça; and the following night he rested in a wood, two leagues from the town
where the cacique resided, and where he was then present. He
sent the master of the camp, Luis de Moscoso, with fifteen cavalry, to inform him of his approach.

The cacique was at home, in a piazza. Before his dwelling,
on a high place, was spread a mat for him, upon which two
cushions were placed, one above another, to which he went
and sat down, his men placing themselves around, some way
removed, so that an open circle was formed about him, the
Indians of the highest rank being nearest to his person. One
of them shaded him from the sun with a circular umbrella,
spread wide, the size of a target, with a small stem, and having
deer-skin extended over cross-sticks, quartered with red and
white, which at a distance made it look of taffeta, the colors
were so very perfect. It formed the standard of the chief,
which he carried into battle. His appearance was full of dignity: he was tall of person, muscular, lean, and symmetrical.
He was the suzerain of many territories, and of a numerous
people, being equally feared by his vassals and the neighboring nations. The master of the camp, after he had spoken to

him, advanced with his company, their steeds leaping from side to side, and at times towards the chief, when he, with great gravity, and seemingly with indifference, now and then would raise his eyes, and look on as in contempt.

The Governor approached him, but he made no movement to rise; he took him by the hand, and they went together to seat themselves on the bench that was in the piazza. The cacique addressed him these words: —

POWERFUL CHIEF:

Your lordship is very welcome. With the sight of you I receive as great pleasure and comfort as though you were an own brother whom I dearly loved. It is idle to use many words here, as it is not well to speak at length where a few may suffice. The greater the will the more estimable the deed; and acts are the living witnesses of truth. You shall learn how strong and positive is my will, and how disinterested my inclination to serve you. The gifts you did me the favor to send I esteem in all their value, but most because they were yours. See in what you will command me.

The Governor satisfied the chief with a few brief words of kindness. On leaving he determined, for certain reasons, to take him along. The second day on the road he came to a town called Piache;[1] a great river ran near, and the Governor asked for canoes. The Indians said they had none, but that they could have rafts of cane and dried wood, whereon they might readily enough go over, which they diligently set about making, and soon completed. They managed them; and the water being calm, the Governor and his men easily crossed.

From the port of Espiritu Santo to Palache, a march of about a hundred leagues, the course was west; from Apalache to Cutifachiqui, which may be four hundred and thirty leagues, it was northeast; from thence to Xualla, two hundred and fifty leagues, it was towards the north; and thence to Tastaluça, which may be some other two hundred and fifty leagues,

---

[1] From Ranjel's description of this place it is not improbable that Piachi was located on the north side of the Black Warrior River.

one hundred and ninety of them were toward the west, going to the province of Coça, and the sixty southwardly, in going thence to Tastaluça.

After crossing the river of Piache, a Christian having gone to look after a woman gotten away from him, he had been either captured or killed by the natives, and the Governor pressed the chief to tell what had been done; threatening, that should the man not appear, he would never release him. The cacique sent an Indian thence to Mauilla, the town of a chief, his vassal, whither they were going, stating that he sent to give him notice that he should have provisions in readiness and Indians for loads; but which, as afterwards appeared, was a message for him to get together there all the warriors in his country.

The Governor marched three days, the last one of them continually through an inhabited region, arriving on Monday, the eighteenth day of October, at Mauilla.[1] He rode forward in the vanguard, with fifteen cavalry and thirty infantry, when a Christian he had sent with a message to the cacique, three or four days before, with orders not to be gone long, and to discover the temper of the Indians, came out from the town and reported that they appeared to him to be making preparation; for that while he was present many weapons were brought, and many people came into the town, and work had gone on rapidly to strengthen the palisade. Luis de Moscoso said that, since the Indians were so evil disposed, it would be better to stop in the woods; to which the Governor answered, that he was impatient of sleeping out, and that he would lodge in the town.

Arriving near, the chief came out to receive him, with many Indians singing and playing on flutes, and after tendering his services, gave him three cloaks of marten-skins. The Governor entered the town with the caciques, seven or eight men of his guard, and three or four cavalry,[2] who had dismounted to accompany them; and they seated themselves in a piazza. The

---

[1] Mauilla or Mabila may have been located on the prairie north of the Black Warrior and east of the Tombigbee River, in Greene County, Alabama.

[2] "Only forty horsemen," according to Ranjel.

cacique of Tastaluça asked the Governor to allow him to remain there, and not to weary him any more with walking; but, finding that was not to be permitted, he changed his plan, and, under pretext of speaking with some of the chiefs, he got up from where he sate, by the side of the Governor, and entered a house where were many Indians with their bows and arrows. The Governor, finding that he did not return, called to him; to which the cacique answered that he would not come out, nor would he leave that town; that if the Governor wished to go in peace, he should quit at once, and not persist in carrying him away by force from his country and its dependencies.

Chapter 18

How the Indians rose upon the Governor, and what followed upon that rising.

The Governor, in view of the determination and furious answer of the cacique, thought to soothe him with soft words; to which he made no answer, but, with great haughtiness and contempt, withdrew to where Soto could not see nor speak to him. The Governor, that he might send word to the cacique for him to remain in the country at his will, and to be pleased to give him a guide, and persons to carry burdens, that he might see if he could pacify him with gentle words, called to a chief who was passing by. The Indian replied, loftily, that he would not listen to him. Baltasar de Gallegos, who was near, seized him by the cloak of marten-skins that he had on, drew it off over his head, and left it in his hands; whereupon, the Indians all beginning to rise, he gave him a stroke with a cutlass, that laid open his back, when they, with loud yells, came out of the houses, discharging their bows.

The Governor, discovering that if he remained there they could not escape, and if he should order his men, who were outside of the town, to come in, the horses might be killed by the Indians from the houses and great injury done, he ran out; but before he could get away he fell two or three times, and

was helped to rise by those with him. He and they were all
badly wounded: within the town five Christians were instantly
killed. Coming forth, he called out to all his men to get
farther off, because there was much harm doing from the palisade. The natives discovering that the Christians were retiring, and some, if not the greater number, at more than a
walk, the Indians followed with great boldness, shooting at
them, or striking down such as they could overtake. Those
in chains having set down their burdens near the fence while
the Christians were retiring, the people of Mauilla lifted the
loads on to their backs, and, bringing them into the town,
took off their irons, putting bows and arms in their hands, with
which to fight. Thus did the foe come into possession of all
the clothing, pearls, and whatsoever else the Christians had
beside, which was what their Indians carried. Since the natives had been at peace as far as to that place, some of us,
putting our arms in the luggage, had gone without any; and
two, who were in the town, had their swords and halberds
taken from them, and put to use.

The Governor, presently as he found himself in the field,
called for a horse, and, with some followers, returned and lanced
two or three of the Indians; the rest, going back into the town,
shot arrows from the palisade. Those who would venture on
their nimbleness came out a stone's throw from behind it, to
fight, retiring from time to time, when they were set upon.

At the time of the affray there was a friar, a clergyman,
a servant of the Governor, and a female slave in the town, who,
having no time in which to get away, took to a house, and there
remained until after the Indians became masters of the place.
They closed the entrance with a lattice door; and there being
a sword among them, which the servant had, he put himself
behind the door, striking at the Indians that would have come
in; while, on the other side, stood the friar and the priest, each
with a club in hand, to strike down the first that should enter.
The Indians, finding that they could not get in by the door,
began to unroof the house: at this moment the cavalry were
all arrived at Mauilla, with the infantry that had been on the

march, when a difference of opinion arose as to whether the
Indians should be attacked, in order to enter the town; for
the result was held doubtful, but finally it was concluded to
make the assault.

Chapter 19

*How the Governor set his men in order of battle and entered the
town of Mauilla.*

So soon as the advance and the rear of the force were come
up, the Governor commanded that all the best armed should
dismount, of which he made four squadrons of footmen. The
Indians, observing how he was going on arranging his men,
urged the cacique to leave, telling him, as was afterwards made
known by some women who were taken in the town, that as he
was but one man, and could fight but as one only, there being
many chiefs present very skilful and experienced in matters of
war, any one of whom was able to command the rest, and as
things in war were so subject to fortune, that it was never certain which side would overcome the other, they wished him to
put his person in safety; for if they should conclude their lives
there, on which they had resolved rather than surrender, he
would remain to govern the land: but for all that they said,
he did not wish to go, until, from being continually urged, with
fifteen or twenty of his own people he went out of the town,
taking with him a scarlet cloak and other articles of the Christians' clothing, being whatever he could carry and that seemed
best to him.

The Governor, informed that the Indians were leaving the
town, commanded the cavalry to surround it; and into each
squadron of foot he put a soldier, with a brand, to set fire to the
houses, that the Indians might have no shelter. His men being
placed in full concert, he ordered an arquebuse to be shot off:
at the signal the four squadrons, at their proper points, commenced a furious onset, and, both sides severely suffering, the
Christians entered the town. The friar, the priest, and the rest
who were with them in the house, were all saved, though at the

cost of the lives of two brave and very able men who went thither
to their rescue. The Indians fought with so great spirit that
they many times drove our people back out of the town. The
struggle lasted so long that many Christians, weary and very
thirsty, went to drink at a pond near by, tinged with the blood
of the killed, and returned to the combat. The Governor, witnessing this, with those who followed him in the returning
charge of the footmen, entered the town on horseback, which
gave opportunity to fire the dwellings; then breaking in upon
the Indians and beating them down, they fled out of the place,
the cavalry and infantry driving them back through the gates,
where, losing the hope of escape, they fought valiantly; and
the Christians getting among them with cutlasses, they found
themselves met on all sides by their strokes, when many, dash-
ing headlong into the flaming houses, were smothered, and,
heaped one upon another, burned to death.

They who perished there were in all two thousand five hundred, a few more or less: of the Christians there fell eighteen,
among whom was Don Carlos, brother-in-law of the Governor;
one Juan de Gamez, a nephew; Men. Rodriguez, a Portuguese;
and Juan Vazquez, of Villanueva de Barcarota, men of condition and courage; the rest were infantry. Of the living, one
hundred and fifty Christians had received seven hundred
wounds from the arrow; and God was pleased that they should
be healed in little time of very dangerous injuries. Twelve
horses died, and seventy were hurt. The clothing the Christians carried with them, the ornaments for saying mass, and
the pearls, were all burned there; they having set the fire
themselves, because they considered the loss less than the injury
they might receive of the Indians from within the houses, where
they had brought the things together.

The Governor learning in Mauilla that Francisco Maldonado
was waiting for him in the port of Ochuse, six days' travel distant, he caused Juan Ortiz to keep the news secret, that he
might not be interrupted in his purpose; because the pearls
he wished to send to Cuba for show, that their fame might
raise the desire of coming to Florida, had been lost, and he

o

feared that, hearing of him without seeing either gold or silver, or other thing of value from that land, it would come to have such reputation that no one would be found to go there when men should be wanted: so he determined to send no news of himself until he should have discovered a rich country.

Chapter 20

How the Governor set out from Mauilla to go to Chicaça, and what befell him.

From the time the Governor arrived in Florida until he went from Mauilla, there died one hundred and two Christians, some of sickness, others by the hand of the Indians. Because of the wounded, he stopped in that place twenty-eight days, all the time remaining out in the fields. The country was a rich soil, and well inhabited: some towns were very large, and were picketed about. The people were numerous everywhere, the dwellings standing a crossbow-shot or two apart.

On Sunday, the eighteenth of November,[1] the sick being found to be getting on well, the Governor left Mauilla, taking with him a supply of maize for two days. He marched five days through a wilderness, arriving in a province called Pafallaya, at the town Taliepataua; and thence he went to another, named Cabusto,[2] near which was a large river, whence the Indians on the farther bank shouted to the Christians that they would kill them should they come over there. He ordered the building of a piragua within the town, that the natives might have no knowledge of it; which being finished in four days, and ready, he directed it to be taken on sleds half a league up stream, and in the morning thirty men entered it, well armed. The Indians discovering what was going on, they who were nearest went to oppose the landing, and did the best they could;

---

[1] This should be the fourteenth, according to Ranjel.

[2] According to Ranjel they crossed a large river at a town called Moçulixa which was located one-half league from Taliepataua, and recrossed the river at Cabusto. Apparently Cabusto was above the Sipsey River and west of the Tombigbee River, while Moçulixa was below the former and east of the latter stream.

but the Christians drawing near, and the piragua being about to reach the shore, they fled into some cane-brakes. The men on horses went up the river to secure a landing-place, to which the Governor passed over, with the others that remained. Some of the towns were well stored with maize and beans.

Thence towards Chicaça the Governor marched five days through a desert, and arrived at a river,[1] on the farther side of which were Indians, who wished to arrest his passage. In two days another piragua was made, and when ready he sent an Indian in it to the cacique, to say, that if he wished his friendship he should quietly wait for him; but they killed the messenger before his eyes, and with loud yells departed. He crossed the river the seventeenth of December, and arrived the same day at Chicaça, a small town of twenty houses.[2] There the people underwent severe cold, for it was already winter, and snow fell: the greater number were then lying in the fields, it being before they had time to put up habitations. The land was thickly inhabited, the people living about over it as they do in Mauilla; and as it was fertile, the greater part being under cultivation, there was plenty of maize. So much grain was brought together as was needed for getting through with the season.

Some Indians were taken, among whom was one the cacique greatly esteemed. The Governor sent an Indian to the cacique to say, that he desired to see him and have his friendship. He came, and offered him the services of his person, territories, and subjects: he said that he would cause two chiefs to visit him in peace. In a few days he returned with them, they bringing their Indians. They presented the Governor one hundred and fifty rabbits, with clothing of the country, such as shawls and skins. The name of the one was Alimamu, of the other Nicalasa.

---

[1] The east side of the Tombigbee River, and probably in the northern part of Monroe County, Mississippi.

[2] This town was located about one mile northwest of Redland, in Pontotoc County, Mississippi.

The cacique of Chicaça came to visit him many times: on some occasions he was sent for, and a horse taken, on which to bring and carry him back. He made complaint that a vassal of his had risen against him, withholding tribute; and he asked for assistance, desiring to seek him in his territory, and give him the chastisement he deserved. The whole was found to be feigned, to the end that, while the Governor should be absent with him, and the force divided, they would attack the parts separately — some the one under him, others the other, that remained in Chicaça. He went to the town where he lived, and came back with two hundred Indians, bearing bows and arrows.

The Governor, taking thirty cavalry and eighty infantry, marched to Saquechuma,[1] the province of the chief whom the cacique said had rebelled. The town was untenanted, and the Indians, for greater dissimulation, set fire to it; but the people with the Governor being very careful and vigilant, as were also those that had been left in Chicaça, no enemy dared to fall upon them. The Governor invited the caciques and some chiefs to dine with him, giving them pork to eat, which they so relished, although not used to it, that every night Indians would come up to some houses where the hogs slept, a crossbow-shot off from the camp, to kill and carry away what they could of them. Three were taken in the act: two the Governor commanded to be slain with arrows, and the remaining one, his hands having first been cut off, was sent to the cacique, who appeared grieved that they had given offence, and glad that they were punished.

This chief was half a league from where the Christians were, in an open country, whither wandered off four of the cavalry: Francisco Osorio, Reynoso, a servant of the Marquis of Astorga, and two servants of the Governor, — the one Ribera, his page, the other Fuentes, his chamberlain. They took some skins and shawls from the Indians, who made great out-

---

[1] This province was located on the lower Tallahatchie River, and the town burned by the Indians, as mentioned by Ranjel, was probably located in Tallahatchie County.

cry in consequence, and abandoned their houses. When the
Governor heard of it, he ordered them to be apprehended, and
condemned Osorio and Fuentes to death, as principals, and all
of them to lose their goods. The friars, the priests, and other
principal personages solicited him to let Osorio live, and moderate the sentence; but he would do so for no one. When about
ordering them to be taken to the town-yard to be beheaded,
some Indians arrived, sent by the chief to complain of them.
Juan Ortiz, at the entreaty of Baltasar de Gallegos and others,
changed their words, telling the Governor, as from the cacique,
that he had understood those Christians had been arrested on
his account; that they were in no fault, having offended him
in nothing, and that if he would do him a favor, to let them go
free: then Ortiz said to the Indians, that the Governor had
the persons in custody, and would visit them with such punishment as should be an example to the rest. The prisoners were
ordered to be released.

So soon as March had come, the Governor, having determined to leave Chicaça, asked two hundred tamemes of the
cacique, who told him that he would confer with his chiefs.
Tuesday, the eighth, he went where the cacique was, to ask
for the carriers, and was told that he would send them the next
day. When the Governor saw the chief, he said to Luis de
Moscoso that the Indians did not appear right to him; that a
very careful watch should be kept that night, to which the
master of the camp paid little attention. At four o'clock in
the morning the Indians fell upon them in four squadrons,
from as many quarters, and directly as they were discovered,
they beat a drum. With loud shouting, they came in such
haste, that they entered the camp at the same moment with
some scouts that had been out; of which, by the time those in
the town were aware, half the houses were in flames. That
night it had been the turn of three horsemen to be of the watch,
— two of them men of low degree, the least value of any in the
camp, and the third a nephew of the Governor, who had been
deemed a brave man until now, when he showed himself as
great a coward as either of the others; for they all fled, and

the Indians, finding no resistance, came up and set fire
to the place. They waited outside of the town for the
Christians, behind the gates, as they should come out of the
doors, having had no opportunity to put on their arms; and
as they ran in all directions, bewildered by the noise, blinded
by the smoke and the brightness of the flame, knowing not
whither they were going, nor were able to find their arms, or
put saddles on their steeds, they saw not the Indians who
shot arrows at them. Those of the horses that could break
their halters got away, and many were burned to death in
the stalls.

The confusion and rout were so great that each man fled
by the way that first opened to him, there being none to oppose
the Indians: but God, who chastiseth his own as he pleaseth,
and in the greatest wants and perils hath them in his hand,
shut the eyes of the Indians, so that they could not discern
what they had done, and believed that the beasts running about
loose were the cavalry gathering to fall upon them. The
Governor, with a soldier named Tapia, alone got mounted,
and, charging upon the Indians, he struck down the first of
them he met with a blow of the lance, but went over with the
saddle, because in the haste it had not been tightly drawn, and
he fell. The men on foot, running to a thicket outside of the
town, came together there: the Indians imagining, as it was
dark, that the horses were cavalry coming upon them, as has
been stated, they fled, leaving only one dead, which was he
the Governor smote.

The town lay in cinders. A woman, with her husband,
having left a house, went back to get some pearls that had remained there; and when she would have come out again the
fire had reached the door, and she could not, neither could her
husband assist her, so she was consumed. Three Christians
came out of the fire in so bad plight, that one of them died
in three days from that time, and the two others for a long while
were carried in their pallets, on poles borne on the shoulders
of Indians, for otherwise they could not have got along. There
died in this affair eleven Christians, and fifty horses. One

hundred of the swine remained, four hundred having been destroyed, from the conflagration of Mauilla.

If, by good luck, any one had been able to save a garment until then, it was there destroyed. Many remained naked, not having had time to catch up their skin dresses. In that place they suffered greatly from cold, the only relief being in large fires, and they passed the night long in turning, without the power to sleep; for as one side of a man would warm, the other would freeze. Some contrived mats of dried grass sewed together, one to be placed below, and the other above them: many who laughed at this expedient were afterwards compelled to do the like. The Christians were left so broken up, that what with the want of the saddles and arms which had been destroyed, had the Indians returned the second night, they might, with little effort, have been overpowered. They removed from that town to the one where the cacique was accustomed to live, because it was in the open field.[1] In eight days' time they had constructed many saddles from the ash, and likewise lances, as good as those made in Biscay.

Chapter 21

How the Indians returned to attack the Christians, and how the Governor went to Alimamu, and they tarried to give him battle in the way.

On Wednesday,[2] the fifteenth day of March, in the year 1541, eight days having passed since the Governor had been living on a plain, half a league from the place where he wintered, after he had set up a forge, and tempered the swords which in Chicaça had been burned, and already had made many targets, saddles, and lances, on Tuesday, at four o'clock in the morning, while it was still dark, there came many Indians, formed in three squadrons, each from a different direc-

---

[1] Chicacilla of the Inca, which was probably located about three and one-half miles north of Chicaça.
[2] This should be Tuesday.

tion, to attack the camp, when those who watched beat to arms. In all haste he drew up his men in three squadrons also, and leaving some for the defence of the camp, he went out to meet them. The Indians were overthrown and put to flight. The ground was plain, and in a condition advantageous to the Christians. It was now daybreak; and but for some disorder, thirty or forty more enemies might have been slain. It was caused by a friar raising great shouts in the camp, without any reason, crying, "To the camp! To the camp!" In consequence the Governor and the rest went thither, and the Indians had time to get away in safety.

From some prisoners taken, the Governor informed himself of the region in advance. On the twenty-fifth day of April he left Chicaça and went to sleep at a small town called Alimamu. Very little maize was found; and as it became necessary to attempt thence to pass a desert, seven days' journey in extent, the next day the Governor ordered that three captains, each with cavalry and foot, should take a different direction, to get provision for the way. Juan de Añasco, the comptroller, went with fifteen horse and forty foot on the course the Governor would have to march, and found a staked fort,[1] where the Indians were awaiting them. Many were armed, walking upon it, with their bodies, legs, and arms painted and ochred, red, black, white, yellow, and vermilion in stripes, so that they appeared to have on stockings and doublet. Some wore feathers, and others horns on the head, the face blackened, and the eyes encircled with vermilion, to heighten their fierce aspect. So soon as they saw the Christians draw nigh they beat drums, and, with loud yells, in great fury came forth to meet them. As to Juan de Añasco and others it appeared well to avoid them and to inform the Governor, they retired over an even ground in sight, the distance of a crossbow-shot from the enclosure, the footmen, the crossbowmen, and targeteers putting themselves before those on horseback, that

---

[1] This fort and ford were on the Tallahatchie River, and probably at or near New Albany, in Union County, Mississippi. From here the army **turned** to the westward.

the beasts might not be wounded by the Indians, who came forth by sevens and eights to discharge their bows at them and retire. In sight of the Christians they made a fire, and, taking an Indian by the head and feet, pretended to give him many blows on the head and cast him into the flames, signifying in this way what they would do with the Christians.

A message being sent with three of the cavalry to the Governor, informing him of this, he came directly. It was his opinion that they should be driven from the place. He said that if this was not done they would be emboldened to make an attack at some other time, when they might do him more harm: those on horseback were commanded to dismount, and, being set in four squadrons, at the signal charged the Indians. They resisted until the Christians came up to the stakes; then, seeing that they could not defend themselves, they fled through that part near which passed a stream, sending back some arrows from the other bank; and because, at the moment, no place was found where the horses might ford, they had time to make their escape. Three Indians were killed and many Christians wounded, of whom, after a few days, fifteen died on the march. Every one thought the Governor committed a great fault in not sending to examine the state of the ground on the opposite shore, and discover the crossing-place before making the attack; because, with the hope the Indians had of escaping unseen in that direction, they fought until they were broken; and it was the cause of their holding out so long to assail the Christians, as they could, with safety to themselves.

Chapter 22

How the Governor went from Quizquiz, and thence to the River Grande.

Three days having gone by since some maize had been sought after, and but little found in comparison with the great want there was of it, the Governor became obliged to move at once, notwithstanding the wounded had need of repose, to where there should be abundance. He accordingly set out for Quizquiz, and marched seven days through a wilderness, having many pondy places, with thick forests, all fordable, however, on horseback, except some basins or lakes that were swum. He arrived at a town of Quizquiz without being descried, and seized all the people before they could come out of their houses. Among them was the mother of the cacique; and the Governor sent word to him, by one of the captives, to come and receive her, with the rest he had taken. The answer he returned was, that if his lordship would order them to be loosed and sent, he would come to visit and do him service.

The Governor, since his men arrived weary, and likewise weak, for want of maize, and the horses were also lean, determined to yield to the requirement and try to have peace; so the mother and the rest were ordered to be set free, and with words of kindness were dismissed. The next day, while he was hoping to see the chief, many Indians came, with bows and arrows, to set upon the Christians, when he commanded that all the armed horsemen should be mounted and in readiness. Finding them prepared, the Indians stopped at the distance of a crossbow-shot from where the Governor was, near a river-bank, where, after remaining quietly half an hour, six chiefs arrived at the camp, stating that they had come to find out what people it might be; for that they had knowledge from their ancestors that they were to be subdued by a white race; they consequently desired to return to the cacique, to tell him that he should come presently to obey and serve the Governor. After presenting six or seven skins and shawls brought with them, they took their leave, and returned with the others who were waiting for them by the shore. The cacique came not, nor sent another message.

There was little maize in the place, and the Governor moved to another town, half a league from the great river,[1] where it was found in sufficiency. He went to look at the river, and saw that near it there was much timber of which piraguas might be made, and a good situation in which the camp might

---

[1] The Mississippi.

be placed. He directly moved, built houses, and settled on a plain a crossbow-shot from the water, bringing together there all the maize of the towns behind, that at once they might go to work and cut down trees for sawing out planks to build barges. The Indians soon came from up the stream, jumped on shore, and told the Governor that they were the vassals of a great lord, named Aquixo, who was the suzerain of many towns and people on the other shore; and they made known from him, that he would come the day after, with all his people, to hear what his lordship would command him.

The next day the cacique arrived, with two hundred canoes filled with men, having weapons. They were painted with ochre, wearing great bunches of white and other plumes of many colors, having feathered shields in their hands, with which they sheltered the oarsmen on either side, the warriors standing erect from bow to stern, holding bows and arrows. The barge in which the cacique came had an awning at the poop, under which he sate; and the like had the barges of the other chiefs; and there, from under the canopy, where the chief man was, the course was directed and orders issued to the rest. All came down together, and arrived within a stone's cast of the ravine, whence the cacique said to the Governor, who was walking along the river-bank, with others who bore him company, that he had come to visit, serve, and obey him; for he had heard that he was the greatest of lords, the most powerful on all the earth, and that he must see what he would have him do. The Governor expressed his pleasure, and besought him to land, that they might the better confer; but the chief gave no reply, ordering three barges to draw near, wherein was great quantity of fish, and loaves like bricks, made of the pulp of plums (persimmons), which Soto receiving, gave him thanks and again entreated him to land.

Making the gift had been a pretext, to discover if any harm might be done; but, finding the Governor and his people on their guard, the cacique began to draw off from the shore, when the crossbowmen who were in readiness, with loud cries shot at the Indians, and struck down five or six of them. They retired with great order, not one leaving the oar, even though the one next to him might have fallen, and covering themselves, they withdrew. Afterwards they came many times and landed; when approached, they would go back to their barges. These were fine-looking men, very large and well formed; and what with the awnings, the plumes, and the shields, the pennons, and the number of people in the fleet, it appeared like a famous armada of galleys.

During the thirty days that were passed there, four piraguas were built, into three of which, one morning, three hours before daybreak, the Governor ordered twelve cavalry to enter, four in each, men in whom he had confidence that they would gain the land notwithstanding the Indians, and secure the passage, or die: he also sent some crossbowmen of foot with them, and in the other piragua, oarsmen, to take them to the opposite shore. He ordered Juan de Guzman to cross with the infantry, of which he had remained captain in the place of Francisco Maldonado; and because the current was stiff, they went up along the side of the river a quarter of a league, and in passing over they were carried down, so as to land opposite the camp; but, before arriving there, at twice the distance of a stone's cast, the horsemen rode out from the piraguas to an open area of hard and even ground, which they all reached without accident.

So soon as they had come to shore the piraguas returned; and when the sun was up two hours high, the people had all got over.[1] The distance was near half a league: a man standing on the shore could not be told, whether he were a man or something else, from the other side. The stream was swift, and very deep; the water, always flowing turbidly, brought along from above many trees and much timber, driven onward by its force. There were many fish of several sorts, the greater part differing from those of the fresh waters of Spain, as will be told hereafter.

---

[1] The crossing was made either at Council Bend or Walnut Bend, in Tunica County, Mississippi, in a straight line some twenty-five to thirty-eight miles below Memphis.

Chapter 23

How the Governor went from Aquixo to Casqui, and thence to Pacaha; and how this country differs from the other.

The Rio Grande being crossed, the Governor marched a league and a half, to a large town of Aquixo, which was abandoned before his arrival.   Over a plain thirty Indians were seen to draw nigh, sent by the cacique to discover what the Christians intended to do, but who fled directly as they saw them. The cavalry pursued, killed ten, and captured fifteen.   As the town toward which the Governor marched was near the river, he sent a captain, with the force he thought sufficient, to take the piraguas up the stream.   As they frequently wound about through the country, having to go round the bays that swell out of the river, the Indians had opportunity to attack those in the piraguas, placing them in great peril, being shot at with bows from the ravines, while they dared not leave the shore, because of the swiftness of the current; so that, as soon as the Governor got to the town, he directly sent crossbowmen to them down the stream, for their protection.   When the piraguas arrived, he ordered them to be taken to pieces, and the spikes kept for making others, when they should be needed.

The Governor slept at the town one night, and the day following he went in quest of a province called Pacaha, which he had been informed was nigh Chisca, where the Indians said there was gold.   He passed through large towns in Aquixo, which the people had left for fear of the Christians.   From some Indians that were taken, he heard that three days' journey thence resided a great cacique, called Casqui.   He came to a small river, over which a bridge was made, whereby he crossed.[1]   All that day, until sunset, he marched through water, in places coming to the knees; in others, as high as the waist.   They were greatly rejoiced on reaching the dry land; because it had appeared to them that they should travel about, lost, all night in the water.   At mid-day they came to

---

[1] This was Fifteen-Mile Bayou, and the crossing-place was probably near the southeast corner of St. Francis County, Arkansas.

the first town of Casqui, where they found the Indians off
their guard, never having heard of them. Many men and
women were taken, much clothing, blankets, and skins; such
they likewise took in another town in sight of the first, half a
league off in the field, whither the horsemen had run.

This land is higher, drier, and more level than any other
along the river that had been seen until then. In the fields
were many walnut-trees, bearing tender-shelled nuts in the
shape of acorns, many being found stored in the houses. The
tree did not differ in any thing from that of Spain, nor from
the one seen before, except the leaf was smaller. There were
many mulberry-trees, and trees of plums (persimmons), having
fruit of vermilion hue, like one of Spain, while others were
gray, differing, but far better. All the trees, the year round,
were as green as if they stood in orchards, and the woods were
open.

The Governor marched two days through the country of
Casqui, before coming to the town[1] where the cacique was,
the greater part of the way lying through fields thickly set
with great towns, two or three of them to be seen from one.
He sent word by an Indian to the cacique, that he was coming
to obtain his friendship and to consider him as a brother; to
which he received for answer, that he would be welcomed;
that he would be received with special good-will, and all that
his lordship required of him should be done; and the chief
sent him on the road a present of skins, shawls, and fish.
After these gifts were made, all the towns into which the
Governor came were found occupied; and the inhabitants
awaited him in peace, offering him skins, shawls, and fish.

Accompanied by many persons, the cacique came half a
league on the road from the town where he dwelt to receive
the Governor, and, drawing nigh to him, thus spoke:

VERY HIGH, POWERFUL, AND RENOWNED MASTER:

I greet your coming. So soon as I had notice of you, your
power and perfections, although you entered my territory captur-

---

[1] This place was probably located near the mouth of Tyronza River.

ing and killing the dwellers upon it, who are my vassals, I determined to conform my wishes to your will, and hold as right all
that you might do, believing that it should be so for a good reason,
providing against some future event, to you perceptible but from
me concealed; since an evil may well be permitted to avoid another greater, that good can arise, which I trust will be so; for
from so excellent a prince, no bad motive is to be suspected. My
ability is so small to serve you, according to your great merit, that
though you should consider even my abundant will and humility
in proffering you all manner of services, I must still deserve little
in your sight. If this ability can with reason be valued, I pray
you receive it, and with it my country and my vassals, of me and
them disposing at your pleasure; for though you were lord of the
earth, with no more good-will would you be received, served, and
obeyed.

The Governor responded appropriately in a few words
which satisfied the chief. Directly they fell to making each
other great proffers, using much courtesy, the cacique inviting
the Governor to go and take lodging in his houses. He
excused himself, the better to preserve peace, saying that he
wished to lie in the field; and, because the heat was excessive,
he pitched the camp among some trees, quarter of a league
from the town. The cacique went to his town, and returned
with many Indians singing, who, when they had come to
where the Governor was, all prostrated themselves. Among
them were two blind men. The cacique made an address, of
which, as it was long, I will give the substance in a few words.
He said, that inasmuch as the Governor was son of the Sun,
he begged him to restore sight to those Indians: whereupon
the blind men arose, and they very earnestly entreated him
to do so. Soto answered them, that in the heavens above
there was One who had the power to make them whole, and do
whatever they could ask of Him, whose servant he was; that
this great Lord made the sky and the earth, and man after
His image; that He had suffered on the tree of the true cross
to save the human race, and risen from the grave on the third
day, — what of man there was of Him dying, what of divinity
being immortal; and that, having ascended into heaven, He

was there with open arms to receive all that would be con-
verted to Him.   He then directed a lofty cross of wood to be
made and set up in the highest part of the town, declaring to
the cacique that the Christians worshipped that, in the form
and memory of the one on which Christ suffered.   He placed
himself with his people before it, on their knees, which the
Indians did likewise; and he told them that from that time
thenceforth they should thus worship the Lord, of whom he
had spoken to them, that was in the skies, asking Him for
whatsoever they stood in need of.

The chief being asked what was the distance to Pacaha,
he answered that it was one day's journey, and said that on
the extreme of his territory there was a lake, like an estuary,
that entered into the Rio Grande, to which he would send persons in advance to build a bridge, whereby they might pass
over it.   The night of the day the Governor left, he slept at
a town of Casqui; and the next day he passed in sight of two
other towns, and arrived at the lake, which was half a crossbow-shot over, of great depth and swiftness of current.[1]
The Indians had just got the bridge done as he came up.   It
was built of wood, in the manner of timber thrown across
from tree to tree; on one side there being a rail of poles, higher
than the rest, as a support for those who should pass.   The
cacique of Casqui having come with his people, the Governor
sent word by an Indian to the cacique of Pacaha, that though
he might be at enmity with him of Casqui, and that chief be
present, he should receive neither injury nor insult, provided
that he attended in peace and desired his friendship, for as a
brother would he treat him.   The Indian went as he was bid,
and returned, stating that the cacique took no notice of the
message, but that he fled out of the town, from the back part,
with all his people.   Then the Governor entered there, and with
the cavalry charged in the direction the Indians were running,
and at another town, a quarter of a league off, many were
taken.   As fast as they were captured, the horsemen delivered them to the Indians of Casqui, who, from being their

[1] Tyronza River.

enemies, brought them with great heed and pleasure to the town where the Christians were, greatly regretting that they had not the liberty to kill them. Many shawls, deer-skins, lion and bear-skins, and many cat-skins were found in the town. Numbers who had been a long time badly covered, there clothed themselves. Of the shawls they made mantles and cassocks; some made gowns and lined them with cat-skins, as they also did the cassocks. Of the deer-skins were made jerkins, shirts, stockings, and shoes: and from the bear-skins they made very good cloaks, such as no water could get through. They found shields of raw cowhide out of which armor was made for the horses.

Chapter 24

Of how the cacique of Pacaha came in peace, and he of Casqui having absented himself, returned to excuse his conduct; and how the Governor made friendship between the chiefs.

On Wednesday, the nineteenth day of June, the Governor entered Pacaha,[1] and took quarters in the town where the cacique was accustomed to reside. It was enclosed and very large. In the towers and the palisade were many loopholes. There was much dry maize, and the new was in great quantity, throughout the fields. At the distance of half a league to a league off were large towns, all of them surrounded with stockades.

Where the Governor stayed was a great lake, near to the enclosure; and the water entered a ditch that well-nigh went round the town. From the River Grande to the lake was a canal, through which the fish came into it, and where the chief kept them for his eating and pastime. With nets that were found in the place, as many were taken as need required; and however much might be the casting, there was never any lack of them. In the many other lakes about were also many fish,

---

[1] It was on Wednesday, June 29, that they entered Pacaha. This place was probably located in the vicinity of Osceola, Mississippi County, Arkansas, but not further northward.

P

though the flesh was soft, and none of it so good as that which came from the river. The greater number differ from those in the fresh water of Spain. There was a fish called bagre, the third part of which was head, with gills from end to end, and along the sides were great spines, like very sharp awls. Those of this sort that lived in the lake were as big as pike; in the river were some that weighed from one hundred to one hundred and fifty pounds. Many were taken with the hook. There was one in the shape of barbel; another like bream, with the head of a hake, having a color between red and brown, and was the most esteemed. There was likewise a kind called peel-fish, the snout a cubit in length, the upper lip being shaped like a shovel. Another fish was like a shad. Except the bagres and the peel, they were all of scale. There was one, called pereo, the Indians sometimes brought, the size of a hog, and had rows of teeth above and below.

The cacique of Casqui many times sent large presents of fish, shawls, and skins. Having told the Governor that he would deliver into his hands the cacique of Pacaha, he went to Casqui, and ordered many canoes to ascend the river, while he should march by land, taking many of his warriors. The Governor, with forty cavalry and sixty infantry, was conducted by him up stream; and the Indians who were in the canoes discovered the cacique of Pacaha on an islet between two arms of the river. Five Christians entered a canoe, of whom was Don Antonio Osorio, to go in advance and see what number of people the cacique had with him. There were five or six thousand souls, of whom, directly as they saw the people, taking the Indians who went in the canoes to be Christians also, the cacique and as many as could get into three canoes that were there, fled to the opposite bank; the greater part of the rest, in terror and confusion, plunging into the river to swim, many, mostly women and infants, got drowned. Then the Governor, who was on land, without knowing what was passing with Don Antonio and those who accompanied him, ordered the Christians, in all haste, to enter the canoes with the Indians of Casqui, and they directly join-

ing Don Antonio on the islet, many men and women were
taken, and much clothing.

Many clothes, which the Indians had in cane hurdles and
on rafts to carry over, floated down stream, the people of Casqui filling their canoes with them; and, in fear that the Christians might take these away, their chief went off with them
down the river to his territory, without taking leave. At this
the Governor became indignant, and directly returning to
Pacaha, two leagues on the road, he overran the country of
Casqui, capturing twenty or thirty of its men. The horses
being tired, and there remaining no time that day to go farther, he went on to Pacaha, with the intention of marching
in three or four days upon Casqui, directly letting loose a
man of Pacaha, sending word by him to its chief, that should
he wish his friendship he should come to him, and together they
would go to carry war upon Casqui: and immediately there
arrived many people of Pacaha, bringing as the chief an Indian, who was exposed by a prisoner, brother of the cacique.
The Governor told them that their lord must come; that he
well knew that Indian was not he; for that nothing could be
done without its being known to him before they so much as
thought of it. The cacique came the next day, followed by
many Indians, with a large gift of fish, skins, and shawls. He
made a speech, that all were glad to hear, and concluded by
saying, that although his lordship had causelessly inflicted injury on his country and his subjects, he did not any the less cease
to be his, and was always at his command. The Governor
ordered his brother to be let go, and some principal men he held
captives. That day a messenger arrived from Casqui, saying
that his master would come early on the morrow to excuse
the error he had committed in going away without his licence;
to which the Governor bade him say, in return, to the cacique,
that if he did not come himself in person he would go after
him, and inflict the punishment he deserved.

The chief of Casqui came the next day, and after presenting many shawls, skins, and fish, he gave the Governor a
daughter, saying that his greatest desire was to unite his

blood with that of so great a lord as he was, begging that he would take her to wife. He made a long and discreet oration, full of praise of Soto; and concluded by asking his forgiveness, for the love of that cross he had left, for having gone off without his permission; that he had done so because of the shame he felt for what his people had done without his consent. The Governor said that he had taken a good sponsor; that he had himself determined, if the cacique had not come to apologize, to go after him and burn his towns, kill him and his people, and lay waste his country. To this the chief replied:

MASTER:

I and mine belong to you; and my territory is yours, so that you will destroy it, if you will, as your own, and your people you will slay. All that falls from your hand I shall receive as from my lord's, and as merited chastisement. Know, that the service you have done me in leaving that cross has been signal, and more than I have deserved; for, you know, of great droughts the maize in our fields was perishing, and no sooner had I and mine thrown ourselves on our knees before it, asking for water, than the want was supplied.

The Governor made friendship between the chiefs of Casqui and Pacaha, and placed them at the table, that they should eat with him. They had a difficulty as to who should sit at his right hand, which the Governor quieted by telling them that among the Christians the one seat was as good as the other; that they should so consider it, and while with him no one should understand otherwise, each taking the seat he first came to. Thence he sent thirty horsemen and fifty footmen to the province of Caluça,[1] to see if in that direction they could turn back towards Chisca, where the Indians said there was a foundry of gold and copper. They travelled seven days through desert, and returned in great extremity, eating green

---

[1] It was from Chicaça that the expedition was sent. This province was probably located in the northeastern part of Mississippi, extending from Baldwyn, Prentiss County, to the Tennessee River, in Tishomingo County.

plums (persimmons) and maize-stalks, which they had found in a poor town of seven or eight houses. The Indians stated that thence towards the north, the country, being very cold, was very thinly populated; that cattle were in such plenty, no maize-field could be protected from them, and the inhabitants lived upon the meat. Seeing that the country was so poorly off for maize that there could be no support, the Governor asked the Indians in what direction there were most inhabitants; and they said that they had knowledge of a large province and a country of great abundance, called Quiguate, that lay in the southern direction.

Chapter 25

How the Governor went from Pacaha to Aquiguate and to Coligoa, and came to Cayas.

The Governor rested in Pacaha forty days, during which time the two caciques made him presents of fish, shawls, and skins, in great quantity, each striving to outdo the other in the magnitude of the gifts. At the time of his departure, the chief of Pacaha bestowed on him two of his sisters, telling him that they were tokens of love, for his remembrance, to be his wives. The name of one was Macanoche, that of the other Mochila. They were symmetrical, tall, and full: Macanoche bore a pleasant expression; in her manners and features appeared the lady; the other was robust. The cacique of Casqui ordered the bridge to be repaired; and the Governor, returning through his territory, lodged in the field near his town. He brought there much fish, exchanged two women for as many shirts with two of the Christians, and furnished a guide and tamemes. The Governor marched to one of his towns, and slept, and the next night came to another that was near a river,[1] where he ordered him to bring canoes, that he might cross over. There taking his leave, the chief went back.

[1] St. Francis River.

The Governor travelled towards Aquiguate,[1] and on the fourth day of August came to the residence of the cacique, who, although he had sent him a present, on the road, of many shawls and skins, abandoned the place through fear on his arrival. That town was the largest seen in Florida: one-half of it was occupied by the Governor and his people; and, after a few days, discovering that the Indians were dealing in falsehoods, he ordered the other part to be burned, that it might not afford them cover should they attack him at night, nor be an embarrassment to his cavalry in a movement to repel them. An Indian having come, attended by a multitude, declaring himself to be the cacique, the Governor delivered him over to be looked after by his body-guard. Many of the Indians went off, and returned with shawls and skins; but, finding small opportunity for carrying out their evil plan, one day the pretended cacique, walking out of the house with the Governor, ran away with such swiftness that not one of the Christians could overtake him; and plunging into the river, at the distance of a crossbow-shot from the town, he made for the other shore, where many Indians, giving loud shouts, began to make use of their arrows. The Governor directly crossed over to attack them with horse and foot; but they dared not await him: following them up, he came to a town that was abandoned, before which there was a lake [2] the horses could not pass over, and on the other side were many females. The footmen having crossed, capturing many of them, took much clothing. Returning to the camp early in the night, the sentinels seized a spy, who assenting to the request to lead to where the cacique was, the Governor directly set out with twenty cavalry and fifty infantry in quest of him. After travelling a day and a half, they found him in a thick wood; and a soldier, ignorant of who he was, having struck him on the head with a cutlass, he called out not to

---

[1] This place was on the west side of the St. Francis River, in the northern part of Lee County or the southern part of St. Francis County, Arkansas.

[2] This may have been Lake Michigamia of the French maps, which ceased to exist after the New Madrid earthquakes.

kill him, that he was the chief; so he was captured, and with him one hundred and forty of his people.

The Governor, returning to Quiguate, directed him to tell his people to come and serve the Christians; but, after waiting some days, in the hope of their arrival, and finding that they did not come, he sent two captains, each on an opposite side of the river, with infantry and cavalry, whereby many of both sexes were made prisoners. The Indians, seeing the harm that they received for their rebellious conduct, waited on the Governor to take his commands, coming and going often, bringing with them presents of fish. The cacique and two of his wives being at their liberty in the quarters of the Governor, which were guarded by his halberdiers, he asked them what part of the country was most inhabited; to which they replied, that to the south, or down the river, where were large towns, and the caciques governed wide territories, with numerous people; and that to the northwest was a province, near some mountains, called Coligoa. He, with the others, deemed it well to go thither first; saying that the mountains, perhaps, would make a difference in the soil, and that silver and gold might afterward follow.

The country of Aquiguate, like that of Casqui and Pacaha, was level and fertile, having rich river margins, on which the Indians made extensive fields. From Tascaluça to the River Grande may be three hundred leagues; a region very low, having many lakes: from Pacaha to Quiguate there may be one hundred and ten leagues. There he left the cacique in his own town; and an Indian guided them through an immense pathless thicket of desert for seven days, where they slept continually in ponds and shallow puddles.[1] Fish were so plentiful in them that they were killed with blows of cudgels; and as the Indians travelled in chains, they disturbed the mud at the bottom, by which the fish, becoming stupefied, would swim to the surface, when as many were taken as were desired.

The inhabitants of Coligoa had never heard of the Chris-

---

[1] They crossed four swamps, according to Ranjel, which were the L'Anguille River, Big Creek. Bayou de Vue, and Cache River.

tians, and when these got so near their town as to be seen,
they fled up stream along a river that passed near by there;
some throwing themselves into the water, whence they were
taken by their pursuers, who, on either bank, captured many
of both sexes, and the cacique with the rest. Three days from
that time came many Indians, by his order, with offerings of
shawls, deer-skins, and two cowhides: they stated that at the
distance of five or six leagues towards the north were many
cattle, where the country, being cold, was thinly inhabited;
and that, to the best of their knowledge, the province that was
better provisioned than any other, and more populous, was
one to the south, called Cayas.

About forty leagues from Quiguate stood Coligoa,[1] at the
foot of a mountain, in the vale of a river of medium size, like
the Caya, a stream that passes through Estremadura. The
soil was rich, yielding maize in such profusion that the old
was thrown out of store to make room for the new grain.
Beans and pumpkins were likewise in great plenty: both were
larger and better than those of Spain: the pumpkins, when
roasted, have nearly the taste of chestnuts. The cacique continued behind in his own town, having given a guide for the
way to Cayas.

We travelled five days, and came to the province of Palisema.[2] The house of the cacique was canopied with colored
deer-skins, having designs drawn on them, and the ground
was likewise covered in the same manner, as if with carpets.
He had left it in that state for the use of the Governor, a token
of peace, and of a desire for friendship, though still he did not
dare to await his coming. The Governor, finding that he had
gone away, sent a captain with horse and foot to look after
him; and though many persons were seen, because of the
roughness of the country, only a few men and boys were

---

[1] Coligoa was in the valley of Little Red River, and before arriving there,
they crossed White River below the mouth of Little Red River, in Woodruff
County, Arkansas.

[2] According to Ranjel, before arriving at this place they passed through
Calpista, where there was a flowing salt spring. This spring was on the bank
of Little Red River, in Cleburne County.

secured. The houses were few and scattered: only a little maize was found.

Directly the Governor set forward and came to Tatalicoya,[1] whence he took the cacique, who guided him to Cayas, a distance of four days' journey from that town. When he arrived and saw the scattered houses, he thought, from the information he had received of the great populousness of the country, that the cacique was lying to him — that it was not the province; and he menaced him, bidding him tell where he was. The chief, as likewise the other Indians taken near by, declared that to be in Cayas,[2] the best town in all the province; and that although the houses were far apart, the country occupied being extensive, it had numerous people and many maize-fields. The town was called Tanico.[3] The camp was placed in the best part of it, nigh a river. On the day of arrival, the Governor, with some mounted men, went a league farther, but found no one, and only some skins, which the cacique had put on the road to be taken, a sign of peace, by the usage of the country.

Chapter 26

How the Governor went to visit the province of Tulla, and what happened to him.

The Governor tarried a month in the province of Cayas. In this time the horses fattened and throve more than they had done at other places in a longer time, in consequence of the large quantity of maize there. The blade of it, I think, is the best fodder that grows. The beasts drank so copiously from the very warm and brackish lake, that they came having their bellies swollen with the leaf when they were brought back from watering. Till they reached that spot the Christians

---

[1] After leaving Tatalicoya they came to a great river, according to Ranjel. This was White River.

[2] This province was in the region of northwestern Arkansas and the Indian Territory.

[3] Tanico was located on the east side of Grand or Neosho River, in the Indian Territory.

had wanted salt: they now made a quantity and took it with them. The Indians carry it into other parts, to exchange for skins and shawls.

The salt is made along by a river, which, when the water goes down, leaves it upon the sand. As they cannot gather the salt without a large mixture of sand, it is thrown together into certain baskets they have for the purpose, made large at the mouth and small at the bottom. These are set in the air on a ridge-pole; and water being thrown on, vessels are placed under them wherein it may fall; then, being strained and placed on the fire, it is boiled away, leaving salt at the bottom.

The lands on the shores of the river were fields, and maize was in plenty. The Indians dared not cross the river to where we were. Some appearing, were called to by the soldiers who saw them, and having come over were conducted by them before the Governor. On being asked for the cacique, they said that he was peaceful but afraid to show himself. The Governor directly sent them back to tell him to come, and, if he desired his friendship, to bring an interpreter and a guide for the travel before them; that if he did not do so he would go in pursuit, when it would be the worse for him. The Governor waited three days, and finding that the cacique did not come, he went in pursuit and brought him there a captive, with one hundred and fifty of his people. He asked him if he had knowledge of any great cacique, and in what direction the country was most inhabited. The Indian stated, that the largest population about there was that of a province lying to the southward, thence a day and a half's travel, called Tulla; that he could give him a guide, but no interpreter; that the tongue of that country was different from his, and that he and his ancestors had ever been at war with its chiefs, so that they neither conversed together nor understood each other.

Then the Governor, with cavalry and fifty infantry, directly set out for Tulla, to see if it were such a land as he might pass through with his troops. So soon as it became known

that he had reached there, the inhabitants were summoned;
and as they gathered by fifteen and twenty at a time, they
would come to attack the Christians. Finding that they were
sharply handled, and that in running the horses would overtake them, they got upon the house-tops, where they endeavored to defend themselves with their bows and arrows. When
beaten off from one roof, they would get up on to another;
and while the Christians were going after some, others would
attack them from an opposite direction. The struggle lasted
so long that the steeds, becoming tired, could not be made
to run. One horse was killed and others were wounded. Of
the Indians fifteen were slain, and forty women and boys
made prisoners; for to no one who could draw a bow and could
be reached was his life spared him.

The Governor determined at once to go back, before the
inhabitants should have time to come together. That afternoon, he set out, and travelling into the night, he slept on the
road to avoid Tulla, and arrived the next day at Cayas. Three
days later he marched to Tulla, bringing with him the cacique,
among whose Indians he was unable to find one who spoke
the language of that place. He was three days on the way,
and at his arrival found the town abandoned, the inhabitants
not venturing to remain for him. But no sooner did they
know that he was in the town, than, at four o'clock on the
morning of the first night, they came upon him in two squadrons, from different directions, with bows and arrows and with
long staves like pikes. So soon as they were felt, both cavalry
and infantry turned out. Some Christians and some horses
were injured. Many of the Indians were killed.

Of those made captive, the Governor sent six to the cacique,
their right hands and their noses cut off, with the message,
that, if he did not come to him to apologize and render obedience, he would go in pursuit, and to him, and as many of his
as he might find, would he do as he had done to those he sent.
He allowed him three days in which to appear, making himself understood by signs, in the best manner possible, for want
of an interpreter. At the end of that time an Indian, bearing

a back-load of cow-skins from the cacique, arrived, weeping with great sobs, and coming to where the Governor was, threw himself at his feet. Soto raised him up, and the man made a speech, but there was none to understand him. The Governor, by signs, told him to return and say to the cacique, that he must send him some one who could speak with the people of Cayas. Three Indians came the next day with loads of cow-skins, and three days afterward came twenty others. Among them was one who understood those of Cayas. After a long oration from him, of apologies for the cacique and in praise of the Governor, he concluded by saying, that he with the others had come, in behalf of the chief, to inquire what his lordship would command, for that he was ready to serve him.

At hearing these words the Governor and the rest were all rejoiced; for in no way could they go on without a guide. He ordered the man to be safely kept, and told the Indians who came with him to go back to the cacique and say, that he forgave him the past and greatly thanked him for the interpreter and the presents; that he should be pleased to see him, and to come the next day, that they might talk together. He came at the end of three days, and with him eighty Indians. As he and his men entered the camp they wept, — the token of obedience and the repentance of a past error, according to the usage of that country. He brought a present of many cow-skins, which were found very useful; the country being cold, they were taken for bed-covers, as they were very soft and the wool like that of sheep.[1] Near by, to the northward, are many cattle. The Christians did not see them, nor go where they were, because it was a country thinly populated, having little maize. The cacique of Tulla made an address to the Governor, in which he apologized and offered him his country, his vassals, and his person. The speech of this cacique — like those of the other chiefs, and all the messengers in their behalf who came before the Governor — no orator could more elegantly phrase.

[1] Buffalo skins are meant.

Chapter 27

How the Governor went from Tulla to Autiamque, where he passed the winter.

The Governor informed himself of the country in every direction. He ascertained that toward the west there was a thin population, and to the southeast were great towns, principally in a province, abundant of maize, called Autiamque, at the distance of about eighty leagues, ten days' journey from Tulla. The winter was already come. The cold, rain, and snow did not permit the people to travel for two or three months in the year, and the Governor feared to remain among that sparse population, lest his force could not be subsisted for that length of time. Moreover, the Indians said that near Autiamque was a great water, which, from their account, appeared to him to be an arm of the sea. Hence, he determined to winter in that province, and in the following summer to go to the sea-side, where he would build two brigantines, — one to send to Cuba, the other to New Spain, that the arrival of either might bear tidings of him. Three years had elapsed since he had been heard of by Doña Ysabel, or by any person in a civilized community. Two hundred and fifty men of his were dead, likewise one hundred and fifty horses. He desired to recruit from Cuba of man and beast, calculating, out of his property there, to refit and again go back to advance, to discover and to conquer farther on towards the west, where he had not reached, and whither Cabeça de Vaca had wandered.

Having dismissed the caciques of Tulla and Cayas, the Governor took up his course, marching five days over very sharp mountains,[1] and arrived in a peopled district called Quipana. Not a native could be captured, because of the roughness of the country, and the town was among ridges. At night an ambuscade was set, in which two men were taken, who said that Autiamque was six days' journey distant, and that there was another province toward the south, eight days'

---

[1] The Boston Mountains.

travel off, called Guahate, very abundant in maize and very populous. However, as Autiamque was nearer, and most of the Indians spoke of it, the Governor continued on his journey thither.[1]

At the end of three days he came to a town called Anoixi. Having sent a captain in advance, with thirty horse and fifty foot, they came suddenly upon the inhabitants, taking many of both sexes. On the second day afterwards, the Governor arrived at another town, called Catamaya, and slept in the adjacent fields. Two Indians coming to him from the cacique, with the pretext of a message, in order to ascertain his business, he told them to say to their master, that he wished to speak with him; but they came no more, nor was other word returned. The next day the Christians went to the town, which was without people, and having taken what maize they needed, that night they reached a wood to rest, and the day following arrived at Autiamque.[2]

They found in store much maize, also beans, walnuts, and dried plums (persimmons) in large quantities. Some Indians were taken while gathering up their clothing, having already carried away their wives. The country was level and very populous. The Governor lodged in the best portion of the town, and ordered a fence immediately to be put up about the encampment, away from the houses, that the Indians without might do no injury with fire. Measuring off the ground by pacing, he allotted to each his part to build, according to the Indians he possessed; and the timber being soon brought by them, in three days it was finished, made of very high trees sunk deep in the ground, and traversed by many pieces.

Near by passed a river of Cayas, the shores of it well peopled, both above and below the town. Indians appeared on the part of the cacique with a present of shawls and skins,

---

[1] According to Ranjel they entered the plains on the second day after leaving Quipana. Before doing so, they crossed the Arkansas River, probably at the old ford, located some fifteen miles above Fort Smith.

[2] This town was located within thirty miles east of Fort Smith, and on the south side of the Arkansas River.

and a lame chief, the lord of a town called Tietiquaquo,[1] subject to the cacique of Autiamque, came frequently to visit the
Governor, and brought him gifts of the things he possessed.
The cacique sent to the Governor to inquire what length of
time he would remain in his territory; and hearing that he was
to be there more than three days, he sent no more messages
nor Indians, but treated with the lame chief to rise in revolt.
Numerous inroads were made, in which many persons of both
sexes were taken, and among the rest that chief, whom the
Governor, having reprehended and admonished, set at liberty,
in consideration of the presents he had made, giving him two
Indians to bear him away on their shoulders.

The cacique of Autiamque, desiring to drive the strangers
out of his territory, ordered spies to be set about them. An
Indian, coming at night to the entrance of the palisade, was
noticed by a soldier on guard, who, putting himself behind
the door as he entered, struck him down with a cutlass. When
taken before the Governor, he was asked why he came, but
fell dead without utterance. The next night the Governor
sent a soldier to beat the alarm, and cry out that he saw
Indians, in order to ascertain how fast the men would hasten
to the call. This was done also in other places, at times when
it appeared to him they were careless, that he might reprove
those who were late in coming; so that for danger, as well as
for doing his duty, each one on such occasion would strive
to be the first.

The Christians stayed three months in Autiamque, enjoying the greatest plenty of maize, beans, walnuts, and dried
plums (persimmons); also rabbits, which they had never had
ingenuity enough to ensnare until the Indians there taught
them. The contrivance is a strong spring, that lifts the animal off its feet, a noose being made of a stiff cord to run about
the neck, passing through rings of cane, that it may not be
gnawed. Many of them were taken in the maize-fields, usually when it was freezing or snowing. The Christians were

---

[1] This place was located in the province of Chaguate.

there a month in snow, when they did not go out of town, save to a wood, at the distance of two crossbow-shots, to which, whenever fuel was wanted, a road was opened, the Governor and others, on horseback, going to and returning from it many times, when the fuel was brought from there by those on foot. In this time many rabbits were killed with arrows by the Indians, who were now allowed to go at large in their shackles. The animal is of two sorts; one of them like that of Spain, the other of the color, form, and size of the great hare, though longer even, and having bigger loins.

Chapter 28

How the Governor went from Autiamque to Nilco, and thence to Guachoya.

On Monday, the sixth day of March, of the year 1542 of the Christian era, the Governor set out from Autiamque to seek Nilco, which the Indians said was nigh the River Grande, with the purpose, by going to the sea, to recruit his forces. He had not over three hundred efficient men, nor more than forty horses. Some of the beasts were lame, and useful only in making out the show of a troop of cavalry; and, from the lack of iron, they had all gone a year without shoes, though, from the circumstance of travelling in a smooth country, they had little need of them.

Juan Ortiz died in Autiamque, a loss the Governor greatly regretted; for, without an interpreter, not knowing whither he was travelling, Soto feared to enter the country, lest he might get lost. Thenceforth a lad, taken in Cutifachiqui, who had learned somewhat of the language of the Christians, served as the interpreter. The death was so great a hindrance to our going, whether on discovery or out of the country, that to learn of the Indians what would have been rendered in four words, it became necessary now to have the whole day: and oftener than otherwise the very opposite was understood of what was asked; so that many times it happened the road that we travelled one day, or sometimes two or three days,

would have to be returned over, wandering up and down,
lost in thickets.

The Governor went to a province called Ayays,[1] arriving
at a town near the river that passed by Cayas, and by Autiamque, from which he had been ten days in coming. He ordered a piragua to be built, in which he crossed;[2] and, having
arrived on the other shore, there set in such weather that
marching was impossible for four days, because of snow. When
that ceased to fall, he travelled three days through desert, a
region so low, so full of lakes and bad passages, that at one
time, for the whole day, the travel lay through water up to
the knees at places, in others to the stirrups; and occasionally,
for the distance of a few paces, there was swimming. And he
came to Tutelpinco,[3] a town untenanted, and found to be
without maize, seated near a lake that flowed copiously into
the river with a violent current. Five Christians, in charge
of a captain, in attempting to cross, by order of the Governor,
were upset; when some seized hold of the canoe they had
employed, others of trees that grew in the water, while one, a
worthy man, Francisco Bastian, a native of Villanueva de
Barcarota, became drowned. The Governor travelled all one
day along the margin of the lake, seeking for a ford, but could
discover none, nor any way to get over.

Returning to Tutelpinco at night, the Governor found two
friendly natives, who were willing to show him the crossing,
and the road he was to take. From the reeds and timber of
the houses, rafts and causeways were made, on which the
river was crossed. After three days' marching, at Tianto, in
the territory of Nilco, thirty Indians were taken, among whom
were two chiefs of the town. A captain, with infantry and
cavalry, was directly despatched to Nilco, that the inhabitants
might not have time to carry off their provisions. In going

---

[1] This province should not be confounded with the province of Aays,
which was located to the southward of Red River, in Texas.

[2] This crossing-place was to the northward of Pine Bluff, and probably
in Jefferson County.

[3] This place was on Big Bayou Meto, near the southeast corner of town
6, range 5, east, in Jefferson County.

through three or four large towns, at the one where the cacique resided, two leagues from where the Governor stayed,
many Indians were found to be in readiness, with bows and
arrows, who, surrounding the place, appeared to invite an
onset; but so soon as they saw the Christians drawing nigh
to them without faltering, they approached the dwelling of
the cacique, setting fire to it, and, by a pond near the town,
through which the horses could not go, they fled.

The following day, Wednesday, the twenty-ninth of March,
the Governor arrived at Nilco,[1] making his quarters, and those
of his people, in the town of the cacique, which was in an
open field, that for a quarter of a league over was all inhabited; and at the distance of from half a league to a league off
were many other large towns, in which was a good quantity
of maize, beans, walnuts, and dried plums (persimmons). This
was the most populous of any country that was seen in Florida,
and the most abundant in maize, excepting Coça and Apalache.
An Indian, attended by a party, arrived at the camp, and,
presenting the Governor with a cloak of marten-skins and a
string of pearls, he received some margaridetas (a kind of
bead much esteemed in Peru) and other trinkets, with which
he was well pleased. At leaving, he promised to be back in
two days, but did not return. In the night-time, however,
the Indians came in canoes, and carrying away all the maize
they could take, set up their huts on the other side of the
river, among the thickest bushes. The Governor, finding that
the Indians did not arrive within the time promised, ordered
an ambuscade to be placed at some cribs, near the lake, to
which the Indians came for maize. Two of them were taken,
who told him that the person who had come to visit him was
not the cacique, but one sent by him, pretending to be he, in
order to observe what might be the vigilance of the Christians,
and whether it was their purpose to remain in that country, or
to go farther. Directly a captain, with men on horseback and
foot, were sent over to the other shore; but, as their crossing

---

[1] Nilco was located a few miles southeast of Arkansas Post, on section 30,
town 8, south, range 2, west, in Desha County, where there is a large mound.

was observed, only ten or a dozen Indians, of both sexes, could be taken; and with these the Christians returned to camp.

This river, passing by Anilco, is the same that flows by Cayas and Autiamque, and falls into the River Grande, which flows by Pacaha and Aquixo, near the province of Guachoya, the lord of which ascended in canoes to carry war upon him of Nilco. In his behalf a messenger came to the Governor, saying that the cacique was his servant, desiring to be so considered, and that in two days from that time he would come to make his salutation. He arrived in season, accompanied by some of his principal men, and with great proffers and courtesy, he presented many shawls and deer-skins. The Governor gave him some articles of barter, showing him much attention, and inquired what towns there might be on the river below. He replied that he knew of none other than his own; that opposite was the province of a cacique called Quigaltam; then, taking his leave, returned to his town.

The Governor determined to go to Guachoya within a few days, to learn if the sea were near, or if there were any inhabited territory nigh it, where he might find subsistence whilst those brigantines were building, that he desired to send to a country of Christians. As he crossed the River of Nilco, there came up Indians in canoes from Guachoya, who, when they saw him, thinking that he was in their pursuit, to do them harm, they returned down the river, and informed the cacique, when he took away from the town whatsoever his people could carry, and passed over with them, all that night, to the other bank of the River Grande. The Governor sent a captain with fifty men, in six canoes, down the river to Guachoya;[1] while he, with the rest, marched by land, arriving there on Sunday, the seventeenth day of April.[2] He took up his quarters in the town of the cacique, which was palisaded, seated a cross-

---

[1] Guachoya was in the vicinity of Arkansas City, in Desha County, and possibly at or near the large mound one mile to the northward.

[2] Sunday was the sixteenth of April.

bow-shot from the stream, that is there called the River Tam-
aliseu, Tapatu at Nilco, Mico at Coça, and at its entrance is
known as The River.

Chapter 29

*The message sent to Quigaltam, and the answer brought back
to the Governor, and what occurred the while.*

So soon as the Governor arrived in Guachoya, he ordered
Juan de Añasco, with as many people as could go in the canoes,
to ascend the river; for while they were coming from Anilco
they saw some cabins newly built on the opposite shore. The
comptroller went, and brought back the boats laden with
maize, beans, dried plums (persimmons), and the pulp of them
made into many loaves. The same day an Indian arrived
from Guachoya, and said that the cacique would come on the
morrow. The next day, many canoes were seen ascending
the river; and the people in them remained for an hour on
the opposite side of the River Grande, in consultation, as to
whether they should come to us or not; but finally they concluded to come, and crossed the river, among them being the
cacique of Guachoya with many Indians, bringing much fish,
many dogs, skins, and blankets. So soon as they had landed,
they went to the lodging of the Governor in the town, and
having presented him with the offerings, the cacique thus
spoke:

POTENT AND EXCELLENT MASTER:
I entreat you to forgive me the error I committed in going
away from this town, and not waiting to greet and to obey you;
since the occasion should have been for me, and is, one of pride;
but I dreaded what I should not have feared, and did consequently
what was out of reason; for error comes of haste, and I left without
proper thought. So soon as I had reflected, I resolved not to follow the inclination of the foolish, which is to persist in his course,
but to take that of the discreet and the wise: thus have I changed
my purpose, coming to see in what it is you will bid me serve you,
within the farthermost limits of my control.

The Governor received him with much pleasure, thanking him for the proffers and gift. Being asked if he had any information of the sea, he said, none, nor of any other inhabited country below on that side of the river, except a town two leagues distant, belonging to a chief subject to him; nor on the other shore, save three leagues down, the province of Quigaltam, the lord of which was the greatest of that country. The Governor, suspecting that the cacique spoke untruthfully, to rid his towns of him, sent Juan de Añasco with eight of cavalry down the river, to discover what population might be there, and get what knowledge there was of the sea. He was gone eight days, and stated, when he got back, that in all that time he could not travel more than fourteen or fifteen leagues, on account of the great bogs that came out of the river, the canebrakes and thick scrubs there were along the margin, and that he had found no inhabited spot.

The Governor sank into a deep despondency at sight of the difficulties that presented themselves to his reaching the sea; and, what was worse, from the way in which the men and horses were diminishing in numbers, he could not sustain himself in the country without succor. Of that reflection he pined: but, before he took to his pallet, he sent a messenger to the cacique of Quigaltam, to say that he was the child of the Sun, and whence he came all obeyed him, rendering their tribute; that he besought him to value his friendship, and to come where he was; that he would be rejoiced to see him; and in token of love and his obedience, he must bring him something from his country that was in most esteem there. By the same Indian, the chief returned this answer:

As to what you say of your being the son of the Sun, if you will cause him to dry up the great river, I will believe you: as to the rest, it is not my custom to visit any one, but rather all, of whom I have ever heard, have come to visit me, to serve and obey me, and pay me tribute, either voluntarily or by force. If you desire to see me, come where I am; if for peace, I will receive you with special good-will; if for war, I will await you in my town; but neither for you, nor for any man, will I set back one foot.

When the messenger returned, the Governor was already low, being very ill of fevers. He grieved that he was not in a state to cross the river at once, and go in quest of the cacique, to see if he could not abate that pride; though the stream was already flowing very powerfully, was nearly half a league broad, sixteen fathoms in depth, rushing by in furious torrent, and on either shore were many Indians; nor was his power any longer so great that he might disregard advantages, relying on his strength alone.

Every day the Indians of Guachoya brought fish, until they came to be in such plenty that the town was covered with them.

The Governor having been told by the cacique, that on a certain night, the chief of Quigaltam would come to give him battle, he suspected it to be a fiction of his devising to get him out of his country, and he ordered him to be put under guard, and from that night forth the watch to be well kept. When asked why the chief did not come, he said that he had, but that, finding the Governor in readiness, he dared not adventure; and he greatly importuned him to send the captains over the river, offering to supply many men to go upon Quigaltam; to which the Governor said, that so soon as he got well he would himself go to seek that cacique. Observing how many Indians came every day to the town, and how populous was that country, the Governor fearing that they would plot together, and practise on him some perfidy, he permitted the gates in use, and some gaps in the palisade that had not yet been closed up, to remain open, that the Indians might not suppose he stood in fear, ordering the cavalry to be distributed there; and the night long they made the round, from each squadron going mounted men in couples to visit the scouts, outside the town, at points in the roads, and to the crossbowmen that guarded the canoes in the river.

That the Indians might stand in terror of them, the Governor determined to send a captain to Nilco, which the people of Guachoya had told him was inhabited, and, treating the inhabitants there severely, neither town would dare to attack

him: so he commanded Captain Nuño de Tobar to march
thither with fifteen horsemen, and Captain Juan de Guzman,
with his company of foot, to ascend the river by water in
canoes. The cacique of Guachoya ordered canoes to be brought,
and many warriors to come, who went with the Christians.
Two leagues from Nilco, the cavalry, having first arrived,
waited for the foot, and thence together they crossed the river
in the night. At dawn, in sight of the town, they came upon
a scout, who, directly as he saw the Christians, set up loud
yells, and fled to carry the news to those in the place. Nuño
de Tobar, and those with him, hastened on so rapidly, that
they were upon the inhabitants before they could all get out
of town. The ground was open field; the part of it covered
by the houses, which might be a quarter of a league in extent,
contained five or six thousand souls. Coming out of them,
the Indians ran from one to another habitation, numbers collecting in all parts, so that there was not a man on horseback
who did not find himself amidst many; and when the captain
ordered that the life of no male should be spared, the surprise
was such, that there was not a man among them in readiness
to draw a bow. The cries of the women and children were such
as to deafen those who pursued them. About one hundred
men were slain; many were allowed to get away badly
wounded, that they might strike terror into those who were
absent.

Some persons were so cruel and butcher-like that they
killed all before them, young and old, not one having resisted
little nor much; while those who felt it their duty to be wherever there might be resistance, and were esteemed brave,
broke through the crowds of Indians, bearing down many
with their stirrups and the breasts of their horses, giving some
a thrust and letting them go, but encountering a child or a
woman would take and deliver it over to the footmen. To
the ferocious and bloodthirsty, God permitted that their sin
should rise up against them in the presence of all — when
there was occasion for fighting showing extreme cowardice,
and in the end paying for it with their lives.

Eighty women and children were captured at Nilco, and much clothing. The Indians of Guachoya, before arriving at the town, had come to a stop, and from without watched the success of the Christians over the inhabitants; and when they saw that these were scattered, that the cavalry were following and lancing them, they went to the houses for plunder, filling the canoes with clothing; and lest the Christians might take away what they got, they returned to Guachoya, where they came greatly astonished at what they had seen done to the people of Nilco, which they, in great fear, recounted circumstantially to their cacique.

Chapter 30

The death of the Adelantado, Don Hernando de Soto, and how Luys Moscoso de Alvarado was chosen Governor.

The Governor, conscious that the hour approached in which he should depart this life, commanded that all the King's officers should be called before him, the captains and the principal personages, to whom he made a speech. He said that he was about to go into the presence of God, to give account of all his past life; and since He had been pleased to take him away at such a time, and when he could recognize the moment of his death, he, His most unworthy servant, rendered Him hearty thanks. He confessed his deep obligations to them all, whether present or absent, for their great qualities, their love and loyalty to his person, well tried in the sufferance of hardship, which he ever wished to honor, and had designed to reward, when the Almighty should be pleased to give him repose from labor with greater prosperity to his fortune. He begged that they would pray for him, that through mercy he might be pardoned his sins, and his soul be received in glory: he asked that they would relieve him of the charge he held over them, as well of the indebtedness he was under to them all, as to forgive him any wrongs they might have received at his hands. To prevent any divisions that might arise, as to who should command, he asked that they would be pleased to elect a principal and able person to be governor, one with whom they should all be satisfied, and, being chosen, they would swear before him to obey: that this would greatly satisfy him, abate somewhat the pains he suffered, and moderate the anxiety of leaving them in a country, they knew not where.

Baltasar de Gallegos responded in behalf of all, consoling him with remarks on the shortness of the life of this world, attended as it was by so many toils and afflictions, saying that whom God earliest called away, He showed particular favor; with many other things appropriate to such an occasion: And finally, since it pleased the Almighty to take him to Himself, amid the deep sorrow they not unreasonably felt, it was necessary and becoming in him, as in them, to conform to the Divine Will: that as respected the election of a governor, which he ordered, whomsoever his Excellency should name to the command, him would they obey. Thereupon the Governor nominated Luys Moscoso de Alvarado to be his captain-general; when by all those present was he straightway chosen and sworn Governor.

The next day, the twenty-first of May, departed this life the magnanimous, the virtuous, the intrepid captain, Don Hernando de Soto, Governor of Cuba and Adelantado of Florida. He was advanced by fortune, in the way she is wont to lead others, that he might fall the greater depth: he died in a land, and at a time, that could afford him little comfort in his illness, when the danger of being no more heard from stared his companions in the face, each one himself having need of sympathy, which was the cause why they neither gave him their companionship nor visited him, as otherwise they would have done.

Luys de Moscoso determined to conceal what had happened from the Indians; for Soto had given them to understand that the Christians were immortal; besides, they held him to be vigilant, sagacious, brave; and, although they were at peace, should they know him to be dead, they, being of their nature inconstant, might venture on making an attack; and they were credulous of all that he had told them, for he made them believe that some things which went on among them privately, he had discovered without their being able to see how, or by what means; and that the figure which appeared in a mirror he showed, told him whatsoever they might be about, or desired to do; whence neither by word nor deed did they dare undertake any thing to his injury.

So soon as the death had taken place, Luys de Moscoso directed the body to be put secretly into a house, where it remained three days; and thence it was taken at night, by his order, to a gate of the town, and buried within. The Indians, who had seen him ill, finding him no longer, suspected the reason; and passing by where he lay, they observed the ground loose, and, looking about, talked among themselves. This coming to the knowledge of Luys de Moscoso, he ordered the corpse to be taken up at night, and among the shawls that enshrouded it having cast abundance of sand, it was taken out in a canoe and committed to the middle of the stream. The cacique of Guachoya asked for him, saying: "What has been done with my brother and lord, the Governor?" Luys de Moscoso told him that he had ascended into the skies, as he had done on many other occasions; but as he would have to be detained there some time, he had left him in his stead. The chief, thinking within himself that he was dead, ordered two well-proportioned young men to be brought, saying, that it was the usage of the country, when any lord died, to kill some persons, who should accompany and serve him on the way, on which account they were brought; and he told him to command their heads to be struck off, that they might go accordingly to attend his friend and master. Luys de Moscoso replied to him, that the Governor was not dead, but only gone into the heavens, having taken with him of his soldiers sufficient number for his need, and be besought him to let those Indians go, and from that time forward not to follow so evil a practice. They were presently ordered to be let loose, that they might return to their houses; but one of them refused to leave, alleging that he did not wish to remain in the power of one who, without cause, condemned him to die, and that he who had saved his life he desired to serve as long as he should live.

Luys de Moscoso ordered the property of the Governor to be sold at public outcry. It consisted of two male and three female slaves, three horses, and seven hundred swine. For each slave, or horse, was given two or three thousand cruzados, to be paid at the first melting of gold or silver, or division of vassals and territory, with the obligation that should there be nothing found in the country, the payment should be made at the end of a year, those having no property to pledge to give their bond. A hog bought in the same way, trusted, two hundred cruzados. Those who had left anything at home bought more sparingly, and took less than others. From that time forward most of the people owned and raised hogs; they lived on pork, observed Fridays and Saturdays, and the vespers of holidays, which they had not done before; for, at times, they had passed two or three months without tasting any meat, and on the day they got any, it had been their custom to eat it.

Chapter 31

How the Governor Luys de Moscoso left Guachoya and went to Chaguete, and from thence to Aguacay.

Some were glad of the death of Don Hernando de Soto, holding it certain that Luys de Moscoso, who was given to leading a gay life, preferred to see himself at ease in a land of Christians, rather than continue the toils of war, discovering and subduing, which the people had come to hate, finding the little recompense that followed. The Governor ordered that the captains and principal personages should come together, to consult and determine upon what they would do; and, informed of the population there was on all sides, he found that towards the west the country was most inhabited, and that descending the stream, after passing Quigaltam, it was desert and had little subsistence. He besought them all to give him their opinion in writing, signed with their names, that, having the views of every one, he might determine whether to follow down the river or enter the land.

To every one it appeared well to march westwardly, because in that direction was New Spain, the voyage by sea being held more hazardous and of doubtful accomplishment, as a vessel of sufficient strength to weather a storm could not be built, nor was there captain nor pilot, needle nor chart, nor was it known how distant might be the sea; neither had they any tidings of it, or if the river did not take some great turn through the land, or might not have some fall over rocks where they might be lost. Some, who had seen the sea-card, found that by the shore, from the place where they were to New Spain, there should be about five hundred leagues; and they said that by land, though they might have to go round about sometimes, in looking for a peopled country, unless some great impassable wilderness should intervene, they could not be hindered from going forward that summer; and, finding provision for support in some peopled country where they might stop, the following summer they should arrive in a land of Christians; and that, going by land, it might be they should discover some rich country which would avail them. Moscoso, although it was his desire to get out of the land of Florida in the shortest time, seeing the difficulties that lay before him in a voyage by sea, determined to undertake that which should appear to be the best to all.

Monday, the fifth of June, the Governor left Guachoya, receiving a guide from the cacique who remained in his town. They passed through a province called Catalte; and, going through a desert six days' journey in extent, on the twentieth of the month they came to Chaguate.[1] The cacique of the province had been to visit the Governor, Don Hernando de Soto, at Autiamque, where he took him presents of shawls, skins, and salt. The day before Luys de Moscoso arrived, a sick Christian becoming missed, whom the Indians were suspected to have killed, he sent word to the cacique to look for

---

[1] This province was probably on Saline River, in Saline County. From here they turned to the south-southeast.

and return him — that in so doing he would continue to be his
friend; if otherwise, the cacique should not hide from him
anywhere, nor he nor his, and that he would leave his country
in ashes. The chief directly came, and, bringing the Christian, with a large gift of shawls and skins, he made this speech:

Excellent Master:

I would not deserve that opinion you have of me for all the
wealth of the world. Who impelled me to visit and serve that excellent lord, the Governor, your father, in Autiamque, which you
should have remembered, where I offered myself, with all loyalty,
truth, and love, to serve and obey his lifetime: or what could have
been my purpose, having received favors of him, and without either
of you having done me any injury, that I should be moved to do
that which I should not? Believe me, no outrage, nor worldly
interest, could have been equal to making me act thus, or could
have so blinded me. Since, however, in this life, the natural course
is, after one pleasure should succeed many pains, fortune has been
pleased with your indignation to moderate the joy I felt in my
heart at your coming, and have failed where I aimed to hit, in
pleasing this Christian, who remained behind lost, treating him in
a manner of which he shall himself speak, thinking that in this I
should do you service, and intending to come with and deliver him
to you at Chaguate, serving you in all things, to the extent possible
in my power. If for this I deserve punishment from your hand, I
shall receive it, as coming from my master's, as though it were favor.

The Governor answered, that because he had not found him
in Chaguete he was incensed, supposing that he had kept away,
as others had done; but that, as he now knew his loyalty and
love, he would ever consider him a brother, and would favor
him in all matters. The cacique went with him to the town
where he resided, the distance of a day's journey. They passed
through a small town where was a lake, and the Indians made
salt: the Christians made some on the day they rested there,
from water that rose near by from springs in pools. The Governor was six days in Chaguete, where he informed himself of
the people there were to the west. He heard that three days'
journey distant, was a province called Aguacay.

On leaving Chaguete, a Christian remained behind, named Francisco de Guzman, bastard son of a gentleman of Seville, who, in fear of being made to pay for gaming debts in the person of an Indian girl, his concubine, he took her away with him; and the Governor, having marched two days before he was missed, sent word to the cacique to seek for and send him to Aguacay, whither he was marching, but the chief never did. Before arriving at this province, they received five Indians, coming with a gift of skins, fish, and roasted venison, sent on the part of the cacique. The Governor reached his town on Wednesday, the fourth day of July,[1] and finding it unoccupied, lodged there. He remained in it a while, making some inroads, in which many Indians of both sexes were captured. There they heard of the South Sea. Much salt was got out of the sand, gathered in a vein of earth like slate, and was made as they make it in Cayas.

Chapter 32

How the Governor went from Aguacay to Naguatex, and what happened to him.

The day the Governor left Aguacay he went to sleep near a small town, subject to the lord of that province. He set the encampment very nigh a salt lake,[2] and that afternoon some salt was made. He marched the next day, and slept between two mountains, in an open grove; the next after, he arrived at a small town called Pato; and on the fourth day of his departure from Aguacay he came to the first inhabited place, in a province called Amaye. There they took an Indian, who said that thence to Naguatex was a day and a half's journey, all the way lying through an inhabited region.

Having passed out of Amaye, on Saturday, the twentieth of July,[3] between that place and Naguatex, at mid-day, along

---

[1] The fourth of July was Tuesday.

[2] This town and lake were on the west side of Quachita River, about two miles south of Arkadelphia, in Clark County.

[3] The twentieth of July was Thursday.

a clump of luxuriant woods,[1] the camp was seated.   From thence Indians being seen, who had come to espy them, those on horseback went in their pursuit, killed six, and captured two. The prisoners being asked by the Governor why they had come, they said, to discover the numbers he had, and their condition, having been sent by their lord, the chief of Naguatex; and that he, with other caciques, who came in his company and his cause, had determined on giving him battle that day.

While thus conferring, many Indians advanced, formed in two squadrons, who, so soon as they saw that they were descried, giving whoops, they assailed the Christians with great fury, each on a different quarter; but finding how firm was the resistance, they turned, and fleeing, many lost their lives; the greater part of the cavalry pursuing them, forgetful of the camp, when those that remained were attacked by other two squadrons, that had lain in concealment, who, in their turn, having been withstood, paid the penalty that the first had done.

When the Christians came together, after the Indians fled, they heard loud shouting, at the distance of a crossbow-shot from where they were; and the Governor sent twelve cavalry to see what might be the cause.   Six Christians were found amidst numerous Indians, two, that were mounted, defending four on foot, with great difficulty; and they, as well as those who went to their succor, finally ended by killing many.   They had got lost from those who followed after the first squadrons, and, in returning to the camp, fell among them with whom they were found fighting.   One Indian, brought back alive, being asked by the Governor who they were that had come to give him battle, said the cacique of Naguatex, the one of Maye, and another of a province called Hacanac, lord of great territories and numerous vassals, he of Naguatex being in command.   The Governor, having ordered his right arm to be cut off, and his nose, sent him to the cacique, with word that he would march the next day into his territory to destroy it, and that if he wished to dispute his entrance to await him.

[1] Probably on Prairie de Roane, near Hope.

The Governor stopped there that night, and the following day he came to the habitations of Naguatex, which were much scattered, and having asked for the town of the cacique, he was told that it stood on the opposite side of a river near by.   He marched thitherward; and coming to the river,[1] on the other bank he saw many Indians awaiting him, set in order to defend the passage; but, as he did not know whether it might be forded or not, nor whereabouts it could be crossed, and having some wounded men and horses, he determined to repose for some time in the town where he was, until they should be healed.

In consequence of the great heats that prevailed, he pitched his camp a quarter of a league from the river, in a fine open grove of high trees, near a brook, close to the town. Some Indians taken there, having been asked if the river was fordable, said yes, at times it was, in certain places; on the tenth day he sent two captains, each with fifteen cavalry, one up and the other down the stream, with guides to show where they might get over, to see what towns were to be found on the opposite side.   They were both opposed by the Indians, who defended the passages the best they could; but these being taken notwithstanding, on the other shore they found many habitations, with much subsistence; and having seen this, the detachments went back to the camp.

Chapter 33

How the cacique of Naguatex came to visit the Governor, and how the Governor went thence, and arrived at Nondacao.

From Naguatex, where the Governor was, he sent a message to the cacique, that, should he come to serve and obey him, he would pardon the past; and if he did not, he would go to look after him, and would inflict the chastisement he deserved for what he had done.   At the end of two days the Indian got back, bringing word that to-morrow the cacique would come.

[1] Little River, in Hempstead County.

The day before his arrival, the chief sent many Indians in advance of him, among whom were some principal men, to discover in what mood the Governor was, and determine whether he would himself come or not. They went back directly as they had announced his approach, the cacique arriving in a couple of hours afterward, well attended by his people. They came one before another, in double file, leaving an opening through the midst, where he walked. They arrived in the Governor's presence weeping, after the usage of Tula (thence to the eastward not very distant), when the chief, making his proper obeisance, thus spoke:

VERY HIGH AND POWERFUL LORD, WHOM ALL THE EARTH SHOULD SERVE AND OBEY:

I venture to appear before you, after having been guilty of so great and bad an act, that, for only having thought of it, I merit punishment. Trusting in your greatness, although I do not deserve pardon, yet for your own dignity you will show me mercy, having regard to my inferiority in comparison with you, forgetting my weakness, which to my sorrow, and for my greater good, I have come to know.

I believe that you and yours must be immortal; that you are master of the things of nature; since you subject them all, and they obey you, even the very hearts of men. Witnessing the slaughter and destruction of my men in battle, which came of my ignorance, and the counsel of a brother of mine, who fell in the action, from my heart did I repent the error that I committed, and directly I desired to serve and obey you: wherefore have I come, that you may chastise and command me as your own.

The Governor replied, that the past would be forgiven; and that, should he thenceforward do his duty, he would be his friend, favoring him in all matters.

At the end of four days Luys de Moscoso set forward, and arrived at a river he could not pass,[1] it ran so full, which to him appeared wonderful at the time, more than a month having gone by since there had been rain. The Indians said, that it

---

[1] Red River.

often increased in that manner, without there being rain anywhere, in all the country. It was supposed to be caused by the
sea entering in; but he learned that the water always flowed
from above, and that the Indians nowhere had any information
of the sea.

The Governor returned back to where he had been the last
days; and, at the end of eight more, understanding that the
river might then be crossed, he left, and passed over to the
other bank,[1] where he found houses, but no people.   He
lodged out in the fields, and sent word to the cacique to come
where he was, and to give him a guide to go on with. After
some days, finding that the cacique did not come, nor send any
one, he despatched two captains, each of them in a different
direction, to set fire to the towns, and seize the people that
might be found. They burned much provision, and captured
many Indians. The cacique, seeing the damage his territories
were receiving, sent five principal men to Moscoso, with three
guides, who understood the language farther on, whither he
would go.

Directly the Governor set out from Naguatex, arriving, on
the third day, at a hamlet of four or five houses, belonging to
the cacique of the poor province named Nissohone, a thinly
peopled country, having little maize. Two days' journey on
the way, the Indians who guided the Governor, in place of
taking him to the west, would lead him to the east, and at times
they went through heavy thickets, out of the road: in consequence, he ordered that they should be hanged upon a tree.
A woman, taken in Nissohone, served as the guide, who went
back to find the road.

In two days' time the Governor came to another miserable
country, called Lacane. An Indian was taken, who said the
land of Nondacao was very populous, the houses much scattered, as in mountainous regions, and there was plenty of
maize. The cacique came with his Indians, weeping, as those
of Naguatex had done, which is, according to their custom,

---

[1] This ford was located about three miles east of the line between Texas
and Arkansas, in the latter state, and is known as White Oak Shoals.

significant of obedience; and he made a present of much fish,
offering to do whatsoever might be required of him. He took
his departure, leaving a guide for the province of Soacatino.

Chapter 34

How the Governor marched from Nondacao to Soacatino and
Guasco, passing through a wilderness, whence, for want
of a guide and interpreter, he retired to Nilco.

The Governor set out from Nondacao for Soacatino, and
on the fifth day came to a province called Aays.[1] The inhabitants had never heard of the Christians. So soon as they
observed them entering the territory the people were called out,
who, as fast as they could get together, came by fifties and
hundreds on the road, to give battle. While some encountered
us, others fell upon our rear; and when we followed up those,
these pursued us. The attack continued during the greater
part of the day, until we arrived at their town. Some men
were injured, and some horses, but nothing so as to hinder
travel, there being not one dangerous wound among all. The
Indians suffered great slaughter.

The day on which the Governor departed, the guide told
him he had heard it said in Nondacao, that the Indians of
Soacatino had seen other Christians; at which we were all
delighted, thinking it might be true, and that they could have
come by the way of New Spain; for if it were so, finding nothing
in Florida of value, we should be able to go out of it, there being
fear we might perish in some wilderness. The Governor, having been led for two days out of the way, ordered that the Indian be put to the torture, when he confessed that his master,
the cacique of Nondacao, had ordered him to take them in
that manner, we being his enemies, and he, as his vassal, was
bound to obey him. He was commanded to be cast to the dogs,

---

[1] This was apparently to the southward of Gainesville, Texas, the town
being located just west of the "Lower Cross Timbers," on the prairie.

and another Indian guided us to Soacatino,[1] where we came the following day.

The country was very poor, and the want of maize was greatly felt. The natives being asked if they had any knowledge of other Christians, said they had heard that near there, towards the south, such men were moving about. For twenty days the march was through a very thinly peopled country, where great privation and toil were endured; the little maize there was, the Indians having buried in the scrub, where the Christians, at the close of the day's march, when they were well weary, went trailing, to seek for what they needed of it to eat.

Arrived at a province called Guasco,[2] they found maize, with which they loaded the horses and the Indians; thence they went to another settlement, called Naquiscoça, the inhabitants of which said that they had no knowledge of any other Christians. The Governor ordered them put to torture, when they stated that farther on, in the territories of another chief, called Naçacahoz,[3] the Christians had arrived, and gone back toward the west, whence they came. He reached there in two days, and took some women, among whom was one who said that she had seen Christians, and, having been in their hands, had made her escape from them. The Governor sent a captain with fifteen cavalry to where she said they were seen, to discover if there were any marks of horses, or signs of any Christians having been there; and after travelling three or four leagues, she who was the guide declared that all she had said was false; and so it was deemed of everything else the Indians had told of having seen Christians in Florida.

As the region thereabout was scarce of maize, and no information could be got of any inhabited country to the west,

---

[1] This place was apparently located in the "Upper Cross Timbers." The Spaniards here turned to the southward.

[2] Waco. The town was evidently located on the Brazos River, near old Fort Belknap, in Young County, Texas.

[3] These two provinces were to the southeast of Guasco, in the Brazos valley.

the Governor went back to Guasco. The residents stated, that ten days' journey from there, toward the sunset, was a river called Daycao,[1] whither they sometimes went to drive and kill deer, and whence they had seen persons on the other bank, but without knowing what people they were. The Christians took as much maize as they could find, to carry with them; and journeying ten days through a wilderness,[2] they arrived at the river of which the Indians had spoken. Ten horsemen sent in advance by the Governor had crossed; and, following a road leading up from the bank, they came upon an encampment of Indians living in very small huts, who, directly as they saw the Christians, took to flight, leaving what they had, indications only of poverty and misery. So wretched was the country, that what was found everywhere, put together, was not half an alqueire of maize.[3] Taking two natives, they went back to the river, where the Governor waited; and on coming to question the captives, to ascertain what towns there might be to the west, no Indian was found in the camp who knew their language.

The Governor commanded the captains and principal personages to be called together that he might determine now by their opinions what was best to do. The majority declared it their judgment to return to the River Grande of Guachoya, because in Anilco and thereabout was much maize; that during the winter they would build brigantines, and the following spring go down the river in them in quest of the sea, where having arrived, they would follow the coast thence along to New Spain, — an enterprise which, although it appeared to be one difficult to accomplish, yet from their experience it offered the only course to be pursued. They could not travel by land, for want of an interpreter; and they considered the country

[1] Probably the Double Mountain fork of Brazos River. The crossing was probably made at the south angle of the river, in the northwestern part of Fisher County, Texas.

[2] A continuous forest extends from old Fort Belknap to the eastern slope of the "Staked Plains," and is the only one through which they could have marched for ten days to the westward.

[3] *I.e.*, less than a peck.

farther on, beyond the River Daycao, on which they were, to
be that which Cabeça de Vaca had said in his narrative should
have to be traversed, where the Indians wandered like Arabs,
having no settled place of residence, living on prickly pears,
the roots of plants, and game; and that if this should be so,
and they, entering upon that tract, found no provision for sustenance during winter, they must inevitably perish, it being
already the beginning of October; and if they remained any
longer where they were, what with rains and snow, they should
neither be able to fall back, nor, in a land so poor as that, to
subsist.

The Governor, who longed to be again where he could get his
full measure of sleep, rather than govern and go conquering a
country so beset for him with hardships, directly returned,
getting back from whence he came.

Chapter 35

*How the Christians returned to Nilco, and thence went to Minoya,
    where they prepared to build vessels in which to leave
    Florida.*

When what had been determined on was proclaimed in the
camp, many were greatly disheartened. They considered the
voyage by sea to be very hazardous, because of their poor subsistence, and as perilous as was the journey by land, whereon
they had looked to find a rich country, before coming to the soil
of Christians. This was according to what Cabeça de Vaca
told the Emperor, that after seeing cotton cloth, would be found
gold, silver, and stones of much value, and they were not yet
come to where he had wandered; for before arriving there, he
had always travelled along the coast, and they were marching
far within the land; hence by keeping toward the west they
must unavoidably come to where he had been, as he said that
he had gone about in a certain region a long time, and marched
northward into the interior. Now, in Guasco, they had already
found some turquoises, and shawls of cotton, which the Indians
gave them to understand, by signs, were brought from the

direction of the sunset; so that they who should take that
course must approach the country of Christians.

There was likewise much other discontent. Many grieved
to go back, and would rather have continued to run the peril
of their lives than leave Florida poor. They were not equal,
however, to changing what was resolved on, as the persons of
importance agreed with the Governor. There was one, nevertheless, who said afterwards that he would willingly pluck
out an eye, to put out another for Luys de Moscoso, so greatly
would he grieve to see him prosper; with such bitterness did
he inveigh against him and some of his friends, which he would
not have dared to do, only he knew that in a couple of days
from that time the government would have to be relinquished.

From Daycao, where they were, to the Rio Grande, was a
distance of one hundred and fifty leagues, which they had
marched, toward that place, always westwardly; and, as they
returned over the way, with great difficulty could they find
maize to eat; for, wheresoever they had passed, the country
lay devastated, and the little that was left, the Indians had now
hidden. The towns they had burned in Naguatex, of which
they had repented, they found already rebuilt, and the houses
full of maize. That country is populous and abundant. Pottery is made there of clay, little differing from that of Estremoz
or Montemor.

To Chaguete, by command of the cacique, the Indians came
in peace, and said, that the Christian who had remained there
would not come. The Governor wrote to him, sending ink
and paper, that he might answer. The purport of the letter
stated his determination to leave Florida, reminded him of his
being a Christian, and that he was unwilling to leave him
among heathen; that he would pardon the error he had committed in going to the Indians, should he return; and that if
they should wish to detain him, to let the Governor know by
writing. The Indian who took the letter came back, bringing
no other response than the name and rubric of the person
written on the back, to signify that he was alive. The Governor
sent twelve mounted men after him; but, having his watchers,

he so hid himself that he could not be found. For want of maize the Governor could not tarry longer to look for him; so he left Chaguete, crossed the river at Aays,[1] and following it down, he discovered a town which they had not seen before, called Chilano.

They came to Nilco, where the Governor found so little maize, that there was not enough to last while they made the vessels; for during seed-time, while the Christians were in Guachoya, the Indians, in fear of them, had not dared to come and plant the grounds; and no other land about there was known to have maize, that being the most fertile region of the vicinity, and where they had the most hope of finding sustenance. Everybody was confounded.

Many thought it bad counsel to have come back from the Daycao, and not to have taken the risk of continuing in the way they were going by land; as it seemed impossible they should escape by sea, unless a miracle might be wrought for them; for there was neither pilot nor sea-chart; they knew not where the river entered the sea, nor of the sea could they get any information; they had nothing out of which to make sails, nor for rope a sufficiency of enequen (a grass growing there, which is like hemp), and what they did find was saved for calk; nor was there wherewith to pitch them. Neither could they build vessels of such strength that any accident might not put them in jeopardy of life; and they greatly feared that what befell Narvaez, who was lost on the coast, might happen to them also. But the most of all they feared was the want of maize; for without that they could not support themselves, or do anything they would. All were in great dismay.

The Christians chose to commend themselves to God for relief, and beseech Him to point them out a way by which they might be saved. By His Goodness He was pleased that the people of Anilco should come peacefully, and state that two days' journey thence, near the River Grande, were two towns of which the Christians had not heard, in a fertile country

---

[1] This name should be Ayays, — the old crossing-place on the Arkansas River, above Pine Bluff.

named Aminoya; but whether it then contained maize or not, they were unable to tell, as they were at war with those places; they would nevertheless be greatly pleased to go and destroy them, with the aid of the Christians. The Governor sent a captain thither, with horsemen and footmen, and the Indians of Anilco. Arriving at Aminoya,[1] he found two large towns in a level, open field, half a league apart, in sight of each other, where he captured many persons, and found a large quantity of maize. He took lodging in one of the towns, and directly sent a message to the Governor concerning what he had found, with which all were well content. They set out from Anilco in the beginning of December, and on that march, as well as before coming there from Chilano, they underwent great exposure; for they passed through much water, and rain fell many times, bringing a north wind, with severe cold, so that when in the field they had the water both above and below them; and if at the end of a day's journey they found dry ground to lie upon, they had occasion to be thankful. In these hardships nearly all the Indians in service died, and also many Christians, after coming to Aminoya; the greater number being sick of severe and dangerous diseases, marked with inclination to lethargy. André de Vasconcelos died there, and two Portuguese brothers of Elvas, near of kin to him, by the name of Soti.

The Christians chose for their quarters what appeared to be the best town: it was stockaded, and stood a quarter of a league distant from the Rio Grande. The maize that lay in the other town was brought there, and when together the quantity was estimated to be six thousand fanegas.[2] For the building of ships better timber was found than had been seen elsewhere in all Florida; on which account, all rendered many thanks to God for so signal mercy, encouraging the hope in them, that they should be successful in their wish to reach a shore of Christians.

[1] The town was located above the mouth of the Arkansas River, in Desha County, Arkansas.

[2] The fanega of Lisbon was somewhat more than a pint.

Chapter 36

How seven brigantines were built, and the Christians took their departure from Aminoya.

So soon as the Christians arrived in Aminoya, the Governor commanded the chains to be collected which every one brought along for Indians, the iron in shot, and what was in the camp. He ordered a furnace to be set up for making spikes, and likewise timber to be cut down for the brigantines. A Portuguese, of Ceuta, had learned to saw lumber while a captive in Fez; and saws had been brought for that purpose, with which he taught others, who assisted him. A Genoese, whom God had been pleased to spare (as without him we could not have gone away, there being not another person who knew how to construct vessels), built the brigantines with the help of four or five Biscayan carpenters, who hewed the plank and ribs for him; and two calkers, one a Genoese, the other a Sardinian, closed them up with the oakum, got from a plant like hemp, called enequen, of which I have before spoken; but from its scarcity the flax of the country was likewise used, as well as the ravellings of shawls. The cooper sickened to the point of death, and there was not another workman; but God was pleased to give him health, and notwithstanding he was very thin, and unfit to labor, fifteen days before the vessels sailed, he had made for each of them two of the half-hogsheads sailors call quartos, four of them holding a pipe of water.

The Indians of a province called Tagoanate, two days' journey up the river, likewise those of Anilco and Guachoya, and other neighboring people, seeing the vessels were building, thought, as their places of concealment were by the water's side, that it was the purpose to come in quest of them; and because the Governor had asked for shawls, as necessary out of which to make sails, they came often, and brought many, as likewise a great deal of fish.

Of a verity, it did appear that God chose to favor the

Christians in their extreme need, disposing the Indians to bring the garments; otherwise, there had been no way but to go and fetch them. Then the town where they were, as soon as the winter should set in, would become so surrounded by water, and isolated, that no one could travel from it by land farther than a league, or a league and a half, when the horses could no longer be used. Without them we were unable to contend, the Indians being so numerous; besides, man to man on foot, whether in the water or on dry ground, they were superior, being more skilful and active, and the conditions of the country more favorable to the practice of their warfare.

They also brought us ropes; and the cables needed were made from the bark of the mulberry-trees. Anchors were made of stirrups, for which others of wood were substituted. In March, more than a month having passed since rain fell, the river became so enlarged that it reached Nilco, nine leagues off; and the Indians said, that on the opposite side it also extended an equal distance over the country.

The ground whereon the town stood was higher, and where the going was best, the water reached to the stirrups. Rafts were made of trees, upon which were placed many boughs, whereon the horses stood; and in the houses were like arrangements; yet, even this not proving sufficient, the people ascended into the lofts; and when they went out of the houses it was in canoes, or, if on horseback, they went in places where the earth was highest.

Such was our situation for two months, in which time the river did not fall, and no work could be done. The natives, coming in canoes, did not cease to visit the brigantines. The Governor, fearing they would attack him in that time, ordered one of those coming to the town to be secretly seized, and kept until the rest were gone; which being done, he directed that the prisoner should be tortured, in order to draw out from him any plotting of treason that might exist. The captive said, that the caciques of Nilco, Guachoya, Taguanate, and others, in all some twenty, had determined to come upon him, with a great body of people. Three days before they should do so, the better to veil their evil purpose and perfidy, they were to send a present of fish; and on the day itself, another present was to be sent in advance of them, by some Indians, who, with others in the conspiracy, that were serving, should set fire to the houses, after getting possession of the lances placed near the doors of the dwellings, when the caciques, with all their people, being concealed in the thicket nigh the town, on seeing the flame, should hasten to make an end of them.

The Governor ordered the Indian to be put in a chain; and on the day that was stated, thirty men having come with fish, he commanded their right hands to be cut off, sending word by them to the cacique of Guachoya, whose they were, that he and his might come when they pleased, he desired nothing better, but they should learn that they could not think of a thing that he did not know their thought before them. At this they were all greatly terrified; the caciques of Nilco and Taguanate came to make excuses, and a few days after came the cacique of Guachoya, with a principal Indian, his vassal, stating that he had certain information of an agreement between the caciques of Nilco and Taguanate to come and give the Christians battle.

So soon as some Indians arrived from Nilco, the Governor questioned them, and they confirming what was said, he delivered them at once to the principal Indian of Guachoya, who took them out of the town and killed them. The next day came others from Taguanate, who likewise having confessed, the Governor commanded that their right hands and their noses should be cut off, and he sent them to the cacique. With this procedure the people of Guachoya were well satisfied, and often came with presents of shawls and fish, and of hogs, which were the breeding of some sows lost there the year before. Having persuaded the Governor to send people to Taguanate, so soon as the waters fell, they brought canoes, in which infantry went down [up] the river, and a captain proceeded by land with cavalry; and having guided them until they came to

Taguanate,[1] the Christians assaulted the town, took many
men and women, and shawls, which, with what they had
already, sufficed for their want.

In the month of June the brigantines were finished, and the
Indians having stated that the river rose but once in the year,
which was with the melting of snow, that had already passed,
it being now summer, and a long time since rain had fallen,
God was pleased that the water should come up to the town,
where the vessels were, whence they floated into the river;
for had they been taken over ground, there would have been
danger of tearing open the bottoms, thereby entirely wrecking
them, the planks being thin, and the spikes made short for the
lack of iron.

In the time that the Christians were there, the people of
Aminoya came to offer their service, being compelled by hunger
to beg some ears of that corn which had been taken from them.
As the country was fertile, they were accustomed to subsist
on maize; and as all that they possessed had been seized, and
the population was numerous, they could not exist. Those
who came to the town were weak, and so lean that they had not
flesh on their bones, and many died near by, of clear hunger and
debility. The Governor ordered, under pain of heavy punish-
ments, that maize should not be given to them; still, when it
was seen that they were willing to work, and that the hogs had
a plenty, the men, pitying their misery and destitution, would
share their grain with them; so that when the time arrived for
departure, there was not enough left to answer for what was
needed. That which remained was put into the brigantines and
the great canoes, which were tied together in couples. Twenty-
two horses were taken on board, being the best there were in
the camp; the flesh of the rest was jerked, as was also that of
the hogs that remained. On the second day of July, of the
year one thousand five hundred and forty-three, we took our
departure from Aminoya.

[1] This province was on White River, and the town was probably in
the southern part of Monroe County, Arkansas, possibly at Indian
Bay.

Chapter 37

How the Christians, on their voyage, were attacked in the river,
by the Indians of Quigualtam, and what happened.

The day before the Christians left Aminoya, it was determined to dismiss the men and women that were serving, with
the exception of some hundred slaves, more or less, put on
board by the Governor, and by those he favored. As there
were many persons of condition, whom he could not refuse
what he allowed to others, he made use of an artifice, saying,
that while they should be going down the river they might
have the use of them; but on coming to the sea they would have
to be left, because of the necessity for water, and there were
but few casks; while he secretly told his friends to take the
slaves, that they would carry them to New Spain. All those
to whom he bore ill-will, the greater number, not suspecting
his concealment from them, which after a while appeared,
thought it inhuman for so short service, in return for so much
as the natives had done, to take them away, to be left captives
out of their territories, in the hands of other Indians, abandoning five hundred males and females, among whom were many
boys and girls who understood and spoke Spanish. The most
of them wept, which caused great compassion, as they were
all Christians of their own free will, and were now to remain
lost.

In seven brigantines went three hundred and twenty-two
Spaniards from Aminoya. The vessels were of good build,
except that the planks were thin, on account of the shortness
of the spikes; and they were not pitched, nor had they decks
to shed the water that might enter them, but planks were placed
instead, upon which the mariners might run to fasten the sails,
and the people accommodate themselves above and below.

The Governor appointed his captains, giving to each of them
his brigantine, taking their word and oath to obey him until
they should come to the land of Christians. He chose for
himself the brigantine he liked best. On the day of his depar-

ture they passed by Guachoya, where the Indians, in canoes, were waiting for them in the river, having made a great arbor on the shore, to which they invited him, but he made excuse, and passed along. They accompanied him until arriving where an arm of the river extends to the right,[1] near which they said was Quigualtam; and they importuned him to go and make war upon it, offering their assistance. As they told him there were three days' journey down the river to that province, suspecting they had arranged some perfidy, he dismissed them there; then, submitting himself to where lay the full strength of the stream, went his voyage, driven on rapidly by the power of the current and aid of oars.

On the first day they came to land in a clump of trees, by the left bank, and at dark they retired to the vessels. The following day they came to a town, where they went on shore, but the occupants dared not tarry for them. A woman who was captured, being questioned, said the town was that of a chief named Huhasene, a subject of Quigualtam, who, with a great many people, was waiting for them. Mounted men went down the river, and finding some houses, in which was much maize, immediately the rest followed. They tarried there a day, in which they shelled and got ready as much maize as was needed. In this time many Indians came up the river in canoes; and, on the opposite side, in front, somewhat carelessly put themselves in order of battle. The Governor sent after them the crossbowmen he had with him, in two canoes, and as many other persons as they could hold, when the Indians fled; but, seeing the Spaniards were unable to overtake them, returning, they took courage, and, coming nearer, menaced them with loud yells. So soon as the Christians retired, they were followed by some in canoes, and others on land, along the river; and, getting before them, arrived at a town near the river's bluff,[2] where they united, as if to make a stand.   Into

---

[1] This was a channel connecting the Mississippi River with Bayou Macon, and was located in the northern part of Chicot County, Arkansas.

[2] From the time and distance travelled, this place was at the Vicksburg Bluffs.

each canoe, for every brigantine was towing one at the stern for its service, directly entered some men, who, causing the Indians to take flight, burned the town. Soon after, on the same day, they went on shore in a large open field, where the Indians dared not await their arrival.

The next day a hundred canoes came together, having from sixty to seventy persons in them, those of the principal men having awnings, and themselves wearing white and colored plumes, for distinction. They came within two crossbow-shot of the brigantines, and sent a message in a small canoe, by three Indians, to the intent of learning the character of the vessels, and the weapons that we use. Arriving at the brigantine of the Governor, one of the messengers got in, and said that he had been sent by the cacique of Quigaltam, their lord, to commend him, and to make known that whatever the Indians of Guachoya had spoken of him was falsely said, they being his enemies; that the chief was his servant, and wished to be so considered. The Governor told him that he believed all that he had stated to be true; to say so to him, and that he greatly esteemed him for his friendship.

With this the messengers went to where the others, in the canoes, were waiting for them; and thence they all came down yelling, and approached the Spaniards with threats. The Governor sent Juan de Guzman, captain of foot, in the canoes, with twenty-five men in armor, to drive them out of the way. So soon as they were seen coming, the Indians, formed in two parts, remained quietly until they were come up with, when, closing, they took Juan de Guzman, and those who came ahead with him, in their midst, and, with great fury, closed hand to hand with them. Their canoes were larger than his, and many leaped into the water — some to support them, others to lay hold of the canoes of the Spaniards, to cause them to capsize, which was presently accomplished, the Christians falling into the water, and, by the weight of their armor, going to the bottom; or when one by swimming, or clinging to a canoe, could sustain himself, they with paddles and clubs, striking him on the head, would send him below.

When those in the brigantines who witnessed the defeat desired to render succor, the force of the stream would not allow them to return. One brigantine, which was that nighest to the canoes, saved four men, who were all of those that went after the Indians who escaped. Eleven lost their lives; among whom was Juan de Guzman and a son of Don Carlos, named Juan de Vargas. The greater number of the others were also men of consideration and of courage. Those who escaped by swimming said, that they saw the Indians get into the stern of one of their canoes with Juan de Guzman, but whether he was carried away dead or alive, no one could state.

Chapter 38

How the Christians were pursued by the Indians.

The natives, finding they had gained a victory, took so great encouragement that they proceeded to attack the brigantines, which they had not dared to before. They first came up with one in the rear-guard, commanded by Calderon, and at the first volley of arrows twenty-five men were wounded. There were only four on board in armor, who went to the side of the vessel for its defence. Those unprotected, finding how they were getting hurt, left the oars, placing themselves below under the cover; and the brigantine, beginning to swing about, was going where the current of water chanced to take her, when one of the men in armor, seeing this, without waiting the captain's order, made one of the infantry take the oar and steer, while he stood before to cover him with his shield. The Indians afterwards came no nearer than bow-shot, whence they could assail without being assaulted, or receiving injury, there being in each brigantine only a single crossbow much out of order; so that the Christians had little else to do than to stand as objects to be shot at, watching for the shafts. The natives, having left this brigantine, went to another, against which they fought for half an hour: and one after another, in this way they ran through with them all.

The Christians had mats with them to lie upon of two thick-

s

nesses, very close and strong, so that no arrow could pierce them, and these, when safety required, were hung up; and the Indians, finding that these could not be traversed, directed their shafts upward, which, exhausted, fell on board, inflicting some wounds. Not satisfied with this, they strove to get at the men with the horses; but the brigantines were brought about the canoes in which they were, to give them protection, and in this position conducted them along. The Christians, finding themselves thus severely tried, and so worn out that they could bear up no longer, determined to continue their journey in the dark, thinking that they should be left alone on getting through the region of Quigualtam. While they proceeded and were least watchful, supposing themselves to be left, they would be roused with deafening yells near by; and thus were they annoyed through the night and until noon, when they got into another country, to the people of which they were recommended for a like treatment, and received it.

Those Indians having gone back to their country, these followed the Christians in fifty canoes, fighting them all one day and night. They sprang on board a brigantine of the rearguard, by the canoe that floated at the stern, whence they took out an Indian woman, and wounded from thence some men in the brigantines. The men with the horses in the canoes, becoming weary with rowing day and night, at times got left behind, when the Indians would directly set upon them, and those in the brigantines would wait until they should come up: so that in consequence of the slow way that was made, because of the beasts, the Governor determined to go on shore and slaughter them. So soon as any befitting ground for it was seen, a landing was made, the animals were butchered, and the meat cured and brought on board. Four or five horses having been let go alive, the Indians, after the Spaniards had embarked, went up to them, to whom being unused, they were alarmed, running up and down, neighing in such a way that the Indians took fright, plunging into the water; and thence entering their canoes, they went after the brigantines, shooting at the people without mercy, following them that evening and the night en-

suing, until ten o'clock the next day, when they returned up-
stream.

From a small town near the bank, there came out seven
canoes that pursued the Christians a short distance, shooting at
them; but finding, as they were few, that little harm was done,
they went back. From that time forth the voyage, until near
the end, was unattended by any misadventure; the Christians
in seventeen days going down a distance of two hundred and
fifty leagues,[1] a little more or less, by the river. When near
the sea, it becomes divided into two arms, each of which may
be a league and a half broad.

Chapter 39

*How the Christians came to the sea, what occurred then, and what
befell them on the voyage.*

Half a league before coming to the sea, the Christians cast
anchor, in order to take rest for a time, as they were weary
from rowing. They were disheartened also, many days having
gone by since they had eaten other thing than maize, parched
and then boiled, given out in daily rations of a casque by
strike to a mess of three.

While riding at anchor, seven canoes of natives came to
attack those we had brought in the canoes along with us. The
Governor ordered men to enter ours in armor, to go after the
Indians and drive them away. There also came some by land,
through thicket and bog, with staves, having very sharp heads
of fish-bone, who fought valiantly those of us who went out
to meet them. Such as were in the canoes, awaited with their
arrows the approach of those sent against them; and presently,
on the engaging of these, as well as those on land, they wounded
some on our side in both contests. When we on shore drew
nigh to them they would turn their backs, running like fleet
steeds before infantry, making some turns without ever getting
much beyond the flight of an arrow, and, returning again, they

---

[1] The Inca gives the distance as being seven hundred and fifty leagues
The real distance was about seven hundred and twenty miles.

would shoot without receiving any injury from us, who, though
we had some bows, were not skilled to use them; while the Indians on the water, finding their pursuers unable to do them
harm, though straining at the oars to overtake them, leisurely
kept within a circle, their canoes pausing and returning, as in a
skirmish. The men discovered that the more successful their
efforts to approach, the greater was their own injury; so,
when they succeeded simply in driving them off, they went
back to the brigantines.

After remaining two days, the Christians went to where
that branch of the river enters the sea; and having sounded
there, they found forty fathoms depth of water. Pausing then,
the Governor required that each should give his opinion respecting the voyage, whether they should sail to New Spain
direct, by the high sea, or go thither keeping along from shore
to shore. There were different opinions upon this, in which
Juan de Añasco, who was very presumptuous, valuing himself
much upon his knowledge of navigation, with other matters
of the sea of which he had little experience, influenced the
Governor; and his opinion, like that of some others, was, that
it would be much better to put out to sea, and cross the Gulf
by a passage three-fourths less far, than going from shore to
shore, which was very circuitous, because of the bend made by
the land.   He said that he had seen the sea-chart; that whence
they were the coast ran west to the River of Palmas, and thence
south to New Spain; consequently, that keeping in sight of
land, there would be wide compassing, with long detention,
and risk of being overtaken by the winter before coming to the
country of Christians; while, with a fair wind, in ten or twelve
days' time they should arrive there, by keeping a straight
course.

The majority were not of that way of thinking, and said
there was more safety in going along the coast, though it
might take longer; the vessels being frail, and without decks,
a light storm might suffice to wreck them; and in consequence
of the little room they had for water, if calm or head wind
should occur, or adverse weather, they would also run great

hazard; but even were the vessels so substantial that they might venture in them, there being neither pilot nor sea-card to show the way, it was not wise to traverse the sea. This, the opinion of the greater number, was approved; and it was decided to go along from one to another shore.

When they were about to depart, the brigantine of the Governor parted her cable, the anchor attached to it remaining in the river; and, notwithstanding she was near the shore, the depth was so great that, although it was industriously sought for by divers, it could not be found. This gave much anxiety to the Governor and the others on board. With a stone for crushing maize, and the bridles that remained, belonging to some of the fidalgos and gentlemen who rode, they made a weight that took the place of the anchor.

On the eighteenth day of July the vessels got under way, with fair weather, and wind favorable for the voyage. The Governor, with Juan de Añasco, put to sea in their brigantines, and were followed by all the rest, who, at two or three leagues out, having come up with the two, the captains asked the Governor why he did not keep the land; and told him that if he meant to leave it he should say so, though he ought not to do that without having the consent of the rest, otherwise they would not follow his lead, but each would do as he thought best. The Governor replied that he would do nothing without consulting them; he desired to get away from the shore to sail the better, and with the greater safety at night; that in the morning, when time served, he would return. With a favorable wind they sailed all that day in fresh water, the next night, and the day following until vespers, at which they were greatly amazed; for they were very distant from the shore, and so great was the strength of the current of the river, the coast so shallow and gentle, that the fresh water entered far into the sea.[1]

That afternoon, on the starboard bow, they saw some kays,

---

[1] At that time the Atchafalaya probably formed the lower course of Red River, the latter not having cut through to the Mississippi, and it was its current that they encountered.

whither they went, and where they reposed at night. There Juan de Añasco, with his reasoning, concluded by getting all to consent, and deem it good, that they should go to sea, declaring, as he had before said, that it would be a great gain, and shorten their voyage. They navigated two days, and when they desired to get back in sight of land they could not, because the wind came off from it: and on the fourth day, finding that the water was giving out, fearing extremity and peril, they all complained of Juan de Añasco, and of the Governor, who had listened to his advice: and all the captains declared they would run no farther out, and that the Governor might go as he chose.

It pleased God that the wind should change a little; and, at the end of four days from the time of their having gone out to sea, by strength of arm they arrived, in want of fresh water, in sight of the coast, and with great labor gained it on an open beach. That afternoon, the wind came round from the south, which on that coast is a side wind, and so stiff that it threw the brigantines on to the land, the anchors bending in their slenderness, and dragging. The Governor ordered all to leap into the water, on the larboard side, to hold them, and when each wave had passed they would launch the brigantines to seaward, sustaining them in this manner until the wind went down.

Chapter 40

How the brigantines lost sight of each other in a storm, and afterwards came together at a kay.

The tempest having passed off from the beach where the brigantines were riding, the people went on shore. With mattocks they dug holes there, into which the water having flowed, they thence filled their pipkins. The next day they left; and sailing two days, they entered a basin, like a cove, which afforded shelter against a high wind that blew from the south. There they tarried, unable to leave, until the fourth day, when the sea subsided and they went out by rowing. They sailed until near evening; the wind then freshened, driving them in such manner upon the land, that they regretted having left the harbor; for no sooner was it nightfall than the storm began to rise on the sea, and with its approach the wind gradually increased. The brigantines separated. The two that were farthest out entered an arm of the sea, a couple of leagues beyond the place where the others found themselves at dark. The five that were astern remained from half a league to a league apart, along an exposed beach, upon which the winds and waves were casting them, without one vessel's knowing the fate of another. The anchors having yielded, the vessels were dragging them: the oars, at each of which seven and eight were pulling seaward, could not hold the vessels; the rest of the men, leaping into the water, with the utmost diligence, after the wave had passed that drove them to the shore, would launch the brigantine; while those on board, before another wave could come, baled out with bowls the water that came in upon them.

While thus engaged, in great fear of being lost, from midnight forward they suffered the intolerable torment of a myriad of mosquitos. The flesh is directly inflamed from their sting, as though it had received venom. Towards morning the wind lulled, and the sea went down; but the insects continued none the less. The sails, which were white, appeared black with them at daylight; while the men could not pull at the oars without assistance to drive away the insects. Fear having passed off with the danger of the storm, the people observing the swollen condition of each other's faces, and the marks of the blows they had given and received to rid them of the mosquitos, they could but laugh. The vessels came together in a creek, where lay the two brigantines that preceded them. Finding a scum the sea casts up, called copee, which is like pitch, and used instead on shipping, where that is not to be had, they payed the bottoms of their vessels with it.

After remaining two days they resumed their voyage; and having run likewise two days, they entered an arm of the sea and landed. Spending there a couple of days, they left; six men on the last day having gone up the bay in a canoe without finding its head   ⎽ne brigantines went out in a head-wind blowing from the south, which being light, and the people having a strong desire to hasten the voyage, they pulled out by strength of arm to sea with great toil, and making little headway for two days, they entered by an arm of the sea behind an islet which it encircles, where followed such bad weather, that they were not unmindful to give thanks for that good shelter. Fish abounded there. They were taken in nets and with the line. A man having thrown out a cord made fast to his arm, a fish caught at the hook and drew him into the water up to the neck, when, remembering a knife that he had providentially kept, he cut himself loose.

At the close of the fourteenth day of their stay, the Almighty having thought proper to send fair weather, the Christians very devoutly formed a procession for the return of thanks, in which, moving along the beach, they supplicated Him that He would take them to a land in which they might better do Him service.

Chapter 41

How the Christians arrived at the river Panico.

Wheresoever the people dug along the shore they found fresh water. The jars being filled, and the procession concluded, they embarked; and, going ever in sight of land, they navigated for six days. Juan de Añasco said it would be well to stand directly out to sea; for that he had seen the card, and remembered that, from Rio de Palmas onward, the coast ran south, and up to that time they had gone westwardly. According to his opinion, by the reckoning he kept, the river could not be distant from where they were.

That night they ran out, and in the morning they saw palm-trees rising above the water, the coast trending southwardly; and from midday forward great mountains appeared, which had nowhere been seen until then; for to that place, from the port of Espiritu Santo, where they had entered Florida, was a low, level shore, not discoverable at sea until very

near. From what they observed, they thought that during
the night they had passed the Rio de Palmas, sixty leagues
distant from Panico, in New Spain. So they consulted
together.

Some were of opinion that it would not be well to sail in
the dark, lest they should overrun the Rio de Panico; others,
that they could not be so near as to run by it that night, and
that it would not be well to lose a favorable wind; so they
agreed to spread half the sails and keep on their way. Two
of the brigantines, which ran with all sail up, at daylight passed
the river without seeing it: of the five that remained behind,
the first that arrived was the one Calderon commanded, from
which, when a quarter of a league off, and before the entrance
had been discovered, the water was observed to be thick and
found to be fresh. Coming opposite the river, they saw where
the waves broke upon a shoal, at the entrance into the sea;
and, not any one knowing the place, they were in doubt whether
they should go in there or pass by; but finally, having agreed
to enter, they approached the shore without getting into the
current, and went in the port, where no sooner had they come,
than they saw Indians of both sexes in the apparel of Spain.
Asking in what country they were, they received the answer
in their own language, that it was the Rio de Panico,[1] and
that the town of the Christians was fifteen leagues inland.
The pleasure that all received at this news cannot be sufficiently
expressed: they felt as though a life had been newly given them.
Many, leaping on shore, kissed the ground; and all, on bended
knees, with hands raised above them, and their eyes to heaven,
remained untiring in giving thanks to God.

Those who were coming astern, when they saw that Calderon
with his brigantine had anchored in the river, directly steered
to enter the port. The other two, which had gone by, tried
to run to sea, that they might put about and join the rest,
but could not, the wind being adverse and the sea fretful; so,
fearing that they might be lost, they came nigh the land and

[1] Or Pánuco. A Mexican river which flows into the Gulf about a hundred and fifty miles north of Vera Cruz.

cast anchor. A storm came up, and finding that they could not sustain themselves there, much less at sea, they determined to run on shore; and as the brigantines were small, drawing but little water, and the beach sandy, the force of the wind on the sails carried them up dry, without injury to any one.

If those who gained the haven at that time were made happy, these were oppressed by a double weight of gloom, not knowing what had happened to their companions, nor in what country they were, fearing likewise that it might be one of a hostile people. They had come upon the coast two leagues below the port. So soon as they found themselves clear of the sea, each took on the back what he could carry of his things, and, travelling inland, they found Indians, who told whence they were, and changed what was sorrow into joy. The Christians rendered many thanks to God for having rescued them from those numberless perils.

Chapter 42

How the Christians came to Panico, and of their reception by the inhabitants.

From the time the Christians left the River Grande, to come by sea from Florida to the River of Panico, were fifty-two days. On the tenth day of September, of the year 1543, they entered the Panico, going up with the brigantines. In the many windings taken by the stream, the light wind was often unfavorable, and the vessels in many places made slow headway, having to be towed with much labor against a strong current; so that, after having sailed four days, the people, discovering themselves greatly retarded in the desire to get among Christians, and of taking part in the divine offices, which for a long season had not been listened to by them, they gave up the brigantines to the sailors, and went on by land to Panico.

Just as the Christians arrived at the town, in their clothing of deer-skin, dressed and dyed black, consisting of frock, hose, and shoes, they all went directly to the church, to pray and return thanks for their miraculous preservation. The towns-people, having already been informed of their coming by the Indians, and now knowing of the arrival, invited some to their houses, and entertained them for acquaintance sake, or for having heard of them, or because they came from the same parts of country with themselves. The alcalde-mayor took the Governor home with him: the rest, as they came up, he directed to be lodged by sixes and tens, according to the means of individuals, who provided their guests with abundance of fowls and maizen-bread, and with the fruits of the country, which are like those of Cuba, already described.

The town of Panico might contain some seventy house-keepers. The dwellings were chiefly of stone and mortar; some were of poles, and all of them thatched with grass. The country is poor. No gold or silver is to be found. Residents have the fullest supply both of food and servants. The most wealthy have not an income above five hundred cruzados annually, which is tribute paid by their Indian vassals, in cotton clothing, fowls, and maize.

Of the persons who got back from Florida, there landed at that port three hundred and eleven Christians. The alcalde-mayor directly sent a townsman by post to inform the Viceroy, who resided in Mexico, of the arrival of three hundred of the men who had gone with Don Hernando de Soto in the discovery and conquest of Florida; and, for their being in the service of the King, that he would make provision for their support. Don Antonio de Mendoza [1] was greatly amazed at this news, as were all others of that city; for the people having entered far into Florida, they had been considered lost, nothing being heard from them in a long while; and it appeared to him to be a thing impossible, that without a fortress to which they might betake themselves, or support of any sort, they should have sustained themselves for such a length of time among the heathen. He immediately gave an order, directing that subsistence should be given them where-

---

[1] The viceroy.

soever it might be needed, and the Indians found requisite for carrying their burdens; and, should there be refusal, to take by force, without incurring any penalty, whatsoever should be necessary. The mandate was so well obeyed, that on the road, before the people had arrived at the towns, the inhabitants went out to receive them, bringing fowls and provisions.

Chapter 43

The favor the people found in the Viceroy and residents of Mexico.

From Panico to the great city of Mestitam (Mexico), there are sixty leagues, and as many leagues from each to the port of Vera Cruz, which is where the embarkations take place for Spain, and where those who go hence to New Spain arrive. These three towns, equidistant, are inhabited by Spaniards, and form a triangle: Vera Cruz on the south, Panico on the east, and Mexico, which is inland, on the west. The country is so populous, that the Indian towns farthest apart are not more than half a league to a league from each other.

Some of the people who came from Florida remained in Panico, reposing a month, others fifteen days, or such time as each pleased; for no one turned a grudging face to his guest, but, on the contrary, gave him of every thing he had, and appeared sad at his leave-taking; which may well enough be believed, for the provision the natives brought in payment of their tribute more than sufficed for consumption, so that there was no one in that town to buy or to sell, and few Spaniards being there, the inhabitants were glad of company. All the clothing in the custody of the alcalde-mayor, paid to him there as the Emperor's tax, he divided among those that would go to receive any.

He who had a coat of mail was happy, since for it a horse might be had in exchange. Some got mounted, and those not able to get beasts, who were the greater number, took up the journey on foot. They were well received by the Indians, and better served than they could have been at their own homes,

particularly in respect of everything to eat; for, if an Indian
was asked for a fowl, he would bring four; and if for any sort
of fruit, though it might be a league off, some one would run to
fetch it; and were a Christian ill, the people would carry him,
in a chair, from their own to the next town. Wheresoever
they came, the cacique of the place, through an Indian who
bears a rod of justice in his hand they call tapile (which is
equivalent to saying meirinho), ordered provisions to be
brought, and men for the loads of such things as there were,
and the others necessary to carry the invalids.

The Viceroy sent a Portuguese to them, twenty leagues
from Mexico, with quantity of confections, raisins, pome-
granates, and other matters proper for the sick, should they
need them; and, in advance, ordered that all should be clothed
at the royal charge. The news of their approach being known
to the citizens, they went out on the highway to receive them,
and with great courtesy entreated for their companionship as
favor, each one taking to his house as many as he dared, giving
them for raiment all the best he could, the least well dressed
wearing clothes worth thirty cruzados and upward. Clothing was given to those who chose to go for it to the residence
of the Viceroy, and the persons of condition ate at his board:
at his house was a table for all those of less rank that would eat
there. Directly he informed himself of the quality of each one,
that he might show him the consideration that was his due.
Some of the conquistadores placed them all down to table together, fidalgos and boors, oftentimes seating the servant and
his master shoulder to shoulder; which was done mostly by
artisans and men of mean condition, those better bred asking
who each one was, and making a difference in persons.

Nevertheless, all did the best they could with good will,
telling those they had under their roofs that they could bring
no impoverishment, nor should they hesitate to receive whatsoever they offered; since they had found themselves in like
condition when others had assisted them, such being the fortunes of the country. God reward them: and those whom
He saw fit should escape, coming out of Florida to tread the

soil of Christians, be He pleased that they live to serve Him; and to the dead, and to all those who believe in Him, and confess that in Him is their faith, grant, through His compassion, the glory of paradise. Amen.

Chapter 44

Which sets forth some of the diversities and peculiarities of Florida; and the fruit, birds, and beasts of the country.

From the port of Espiritu Santo, where the Christians went on shore, to the province of Ocute, which may be a distance of four hundred leagues, a little more or less, the country is very level, having many ponds, dense thickets, and, in places, tall pine-trees: the soil is light, and there is not in it a mountain nor a hill.

The land of Ocute is more strong and fertile than the rest, the forest more open; and it has very good fields along the margins of the rivers. From there to Cutifachiqui are about one hundred and thirty leagues, of which eighty leagues are of desert and pine forests, through which run great rivers. From Cutifachiqui to Xuala there may be two hundred and fifty leagues, and all a country of mountains: the places themselves are on high level ground, and have good fields upon the streams.

Thence onward, through Chiaha, Coça, and Talise, the country of which is flat, dry, and strong, yielding abundance of maize, to Tascaluça, may be two hundred and fifty leagues; and thence to Rio Grande, a distance of about three hundred leagues, the land is low, abounding in lakes. The country afterward is higher, more open, and more populous than any other in Florida; and along the River Grande, from Aquixo to Pacaha and Coligoa, a distance of one hundred and fifty leagues, the land is level, the forest open, and in places the fields very fertile and inviting.

From Coligoa to Autiamque may be two hundred and fifty leagues of mountainous country; thence to Guacay may be two hundred and thirty leagues of level ground; and the region

to Daycao, a distance of one hundred and twenty leagues, is
continuously of mountainous lands.

From the port of Espiritu Santo to Apalache they marched
west and northeast; from Cutifachiqui to Xuala, north; to
Coça, westwardly; and thence to Tascaluça and the River
Grande, as far as the provinces of Quizquiz and Aquixo, to
the westward; from thence to Pacaha northwardly, to Tula
westwardly, to Autiamque southwardly, as far as the province
of Guachoya and Daycao.

The bread that is eaten all through Florida is made of maize,
which is like coarse millet; and in all the islands and Indias
belonging to Castile, beginning with the Antillas, grows this
grain.   There are in the country many walnuts likewise, and
plums (persimmons), mulberries, and grapes.   The maize is
planted and picked in, each person having his own field; fruit
is common for all, because it grows abundantly in the woods,
without any necessity of setting out trees or pruning them.
Where there are mountains the chestnut is found, the fruit
of which is somewhat smaller than the one of Spain.   Westward of the Rio Grande the walnut differs from that which is
found before coming there, being of tenderer shell, and in form
like an acorn; while that behind, from the river back to the
port of Espiritu Santo, is generally rather hard, the tree and the
nut being in their appearance like those of Spain.   There is
everywhere in the country a fruit, the produce of a plant like
ligoacam, that is propagated by the Indians, having the appearance of the royal pear, with an agreeable smell and taste; and
likewise another plant, to be seen in the fields, bearing a fruit
like strawberry, near to the ground, and is very agreeable.   The
plums (persimmons) are of two sorts, vermilion and gray, of
the form and size of walnuts, having three or four stones in
them.   They are better than any plums that are raised in
Spain, and make much better prunes.   The grapes appear only
to need dressing; for, although large, they have great stones;
the other fruits are all in great perfection, and are less un-
healthy than those of Spain.

There are many lions and bears in Florida, wolves, deer,

jackals, cats, and rabbits; numerous wild fowl, as large as pea-fowl; small partridges, like those of Africa, and cranes, ducks, pigeons, thrushes, and sparrows. There are blackbirds larger than sparrows and smaller than stares; hawks, goshawks, falcons, and all the birds of rapine to be found in Spain.

The Indians are well proportioned: those of the level country are taller and better shaped of form than those of the mountains; those of the interior enjoy a greater abundance of maize and clothing than those of the coast, where the land is poor and thin, and the people along it more warlike.

The direction from the port of Espiritu Santo to Apalache, and thence to Rio de las Palmas, is from east to west; from that river towards New Spain, it is southwardly; the sea-coast being gentle, having many shoals and high sand-hills.

Deo Gratias.

This Relation of the Discovery of Florida was printed in the house of Andree de Burgos, Printer and Cavalleiro of the house of the Senhor Cardinal Iffante.[1]

It was finished the tenth day of February, of the year one thousand five hundred and fifty-seven, in the noble and ever loyal city of Evora.

[1] Henry, cardinal archbishop of Evora, uncle of King John III., great uncle of King Sebastian, and himself King of Portugal from 1578 to 1580.

THE NARRATIVE OF THE EXPEDITION OF CORONADO, BY PEDRO DE CASTAÑEDA

INTRODUCTION

From the time of the appearance in Mexico, in 1536, of Alvar Nuñez Cabeza de Vaca of the ill-fated Narvaez expedition of nine years before, with definite news of the hitherto unknown north, there had been a strong desire to explore that region, but nothing of importance was accomplished until 1539. In that year Fray Marcos of Nice, the Father Provincial of the Franciscan order in New Spain, with Estévan, the negro companion of Cabeza de Vaca, as a guide, penetrated the country to the northwest as far as the Seven Cities of Cibola, the villages of the ancestors of the present Zuñi Indians in western New Mexico. Estévan, preceding Fray Marcos by a few days and accompanied by natives whom he gathered en route, reached Hawikuh, the southernmost of the seven towns, where he and all but three of his Indian followers were killed. The survivors of this massacre fled back to Fray Marcos, whose life was now threatened by those who had lost their kindred at the hands of the Zuñis; but the friar, fearful that the world would lose the knowledge of his discoveries, appeased the wrath of his Indians by dividing among them the goods he had brought and induced them to continue until he reached a mesa from which was gained a view of the village in which Estévan had met his fate. Here Fray Marcos erected a cross, took possession of the region in the name of Spain, and hastened back to Mexico "with more fear than victuals."

The glowing accounts which the friar gave of what he had seen, and particularly of what he believed the Indians intended to communicate to him, resulted in another expedition in the following year (1540). This was planned by the Viceroy Don Antonio de Mendoza, and the command was given to Francisco Vazquez de Coronado.

The elaborate expedition of Coronado is the subject of the narrative of a private soldier in his army, Pedro de Castañeda, a native of Nájera, in the province of Logroño, in the upper valley of the Ebro, in Old Castile. Of the narrator little is known beyond the fact that he was one of the colonists who settled at San Miguel Culiacan, founded by Nuño de Guzman in 1531, where he doubtless lived when Coronado's force reached that point in its northward journey, and where, more than twenty years later, he wrote his account of the expedition and its achievements. The dates of Castañeda's birth and death are not known, but he was born probably between 1510 and 1518. In 1554, according to a document published in the *Coleccion de Documentos Inéditos del Archivo de Indias* (XIV. 206), his wife, María de Acosta, with her four sons and four daughters, filed a claim against the treasury of New Spain for payment for the service the husband and father had rendered in behalf of the King.

As a rhetorician and geographer Castañeda was not a paragon, as he himself confesses; but although his narration leaves the impression that its author was somewhat at odds with the world, it bears every evidence of honesty and a sincere desire to tell all he knew of the most remarkable expedition that ever traversed American soil — even of exploits in which the writer did not directly participate. Castañeda's narration is by far the most important of the several documents bearing on the expedition, and in some respects is one of the most noteworthy contributions to early American history.

The accompanying translation, by Mr. George Parker Winship of the John Carter Brown Library, was first published, together with other documents pertaining to the expedition, in the *Fourteenth Annual Report of the Bureau of Ethnology* (Washington, 1896), now out of print. Barring a few corrections, most of which were communicated to the present writer by Mr. Winship in 1899, the translation is here printed as it first appeared.

Mr. Winship's translation of Castañeda, together with the letters and the other narratives pertaining to the expedition, was reprinted, with an introduction, under the title *The Journey of Coronado, 1540-1542, from the City of Mexico to the Grand Cañon of the Colorado and the Buffalo Plains of Texas, Kansas, and Nebraska,* as a volume of the "Trail Makers" series (New York, 1904).

The original manuscript of Castañeda is not known to exist, the Winship translation being that of a manuscript copy made at Seville in 1596. This copy, which is now in the Lenox branch of the New York Public Library, was first translated into French by Henri Ternaux-Compans, who found it in the Uguina collection in Paris and published it in Volume IX. of his *Voyages* (Paris, 1838).

In addition to Castañeda's narration there are several letters and reports that shed important light on the route traversed by the expedition, the aborigines encountered, and other noteworthy details which the student should consult. These are as follows:

1. The Relation by Fray Marcos of his *entrada* during the preceding year (1539), Coronado following the same route as far as the first of the Seven Cities of Cibola with Marcos as both guide and spiritual adviser. A brief bibliography of this narration is given in a note on p. 290.

2. A letter from the viceroy, Don Antonio de Mendoza, to the King, dated Jacona (Mexico), April 17, 1540, in which is set forth the progress of Coronado's expedition from Culiacan, and containing extracts from a report by Melchior Diaz, who had been sent forward in November, 1539, to explore the route from Culiacan to Chichilticalli, in the valley of the present Gila River, Arizona, for the purpose of verifying the reports of Fray Marcos. This letter appears in the *Documentos Inéditos de Indias,* II. 356, and in English in Winship's memoir in the *Fourteenth Annual Report of the Bureau of Ethnology,* p. 547, as well as in his *Journey of Coronado,* p. 149.

3. An important and extended letter from Coronado to Mendoza, written at Granada (as Coronado called Hawikuh, the first of the Seven Cities of Cibola), August 3, 1540. This letter appears in Italian in Ramusio's *Terzo Volume delle*

Navigationi et Viaggi (ed. 1556), fol. 359, translated by Hakluyt, *Voyages*, IX. 145–169 (ed. 1904); reprinted in *Old South Leaflets*, Gen. Ser., No. 20. A translation from Ramusio into English appears in both of Mr. Winship's works on the expedition. It should perhaps here be mentioned that the Hakluyt translations of the Coronado documents, at least, are so unreliable as to warrant careful use.

4. The *Traslado de las Nuevas*, an anonymous "Copy of the Reports and Descriptions that have been received regarding the Discovery of a City which is called Cibola, situated in the New Country." This important document was written evidently by a member of the expedition while the Spaniards were at Cibola. It appears in Spanish in the *Documentos Inéditos de Indias*, XIX. 529, from which it was translated into English by Mr. Winship and printed in each of his memoirs.

5. The important letter of Coronado to the King, dated Tiguex (the present Bernalillo, New Mexico), October 20, 1541, after the return of the expedition from Quivira. Printed in the *Documentos Inéditos de Indias*, III. 363; XIII. 261; in French in Ternaux-Compans' *Voyages*, IX. 355; translated into English by Mr. Winship and printed in each of his memoirs, as well as in *American History Leaflets*, No. 13.

6. The *Relación Postrera de Síbola, y de mas de Cuatrocientas Leguas Adelante* (the "Latest Account of Cibola, and of more than Four Hundred Leagues Beyond"). This important anonymous account, written apparently in New Mexico in 1541 by one of the Franciscans who accompanied the expedition, was published, both in Spanish and in English, for the first time, in Mr. Winship's *Coronado Expedition* (*Fourteenth Annual Report of the Bureau of Ethnology*, pp. 566–571). In his *Journey of Coronado* only the translation appears (pp. 190–196).

7. The anonymous *Relación del Suceso*, an "Account of what happened on the Journey which Francisco Vazquez made to discover Cibola." First printed, in Spanish, in Buckingham Smith's *Coleccion de Varios Documentos para la Historia de la Florida* (1857), I. 147; it appears also, under the erroneous

date 1531, in the *Documentos Inéditos de Indias*, XIV. 318, whereas the account was written apparently in 1541 or early in 1542. An English translation appears in each of Mr. Winship's works, and also in *American History Leaflets*, No. 13.

8. "Account given by Captain Juan Jaramillo of the Journey which he made to the New Country, on which Francisco Vazquez Coronado was the General." Next to Castañeda's narration this is the most important document pertaining to the expedition, inasmuch as it contains many references to directions, distances, streams, etc., that are not noted in the other accounts. The Jaramillo narration was written long after the events transpired, and is based on the keen memory of the writer. It is printed in Spanish in Buckingham Smith's *Coleccion*, I. 154, and in the *Documentos Inéditos*, XIV. 304. A French translation is given by Ternaux-Compans, IX. 364, and an English translation in both of Mr. Winship's works.

9. "Account of what Hernando de Alvarado and Friar Juan de Padilla discovered going in Search of the South Sea." A brief account of the journey of Alvarado from Hawikuh (Coronado's Granada) to the Rio Grande pueblos in 1540. Printed in Spanish in Buckingham Smith's *Coleccion*, I. 65, and in the *Documentos Inéditos*, III. 511. An English translation by Mr. Winship is included in each of his works on the expedition, and was printed also in the *Boston Transcript*, October 14, 1893. The title of this document is a misnomer, as Alvarado did not go in search of the Pacific.

10. "Testimony concerning those who went on the Expedition with Francisco Vazquez Coronado." This testimony is printed in the *Documentos Inéditos de Indias*, XIV. 373, and an abridgment, freely translated, is included in Mr. Winship's works.

11. Although the account of the voyage of the fleet under Hernando de Alarcon does not directly concern us, reference should perhaps be made to the sources of information regarding it. These are: Herrera's *Historia General*, dec. VI., lib. IX., cap. XIII. (1601–1615), and in various subsequent editions,

Ramusio's *Navigationi et Viaggi* (1556), III., fol. 363–370; Hakluyt's *Voyages*, IX. 279–318 (1904); Ternaux-Compans' *Voyages*, IX. 299–348; *Coleccion de Documentos Inéditos para la Historia de España*, IV. 218–219.

The Coronado expedition was of far-reaching importance from a geographical point of view, for it combined with the journey of De Soto in giving to the world an insight into the hitherto unknown vast interior of the northern continent and formed the basis of the cartography of that region. It was the means also of making known the sedentary Pueblo tribes of our Southwest and the hunting tribes of the Great Plains, the Grand Cañon of the Colorado and the lower reaches of that stream, and the teeming herds of bison and the absolute dependence on them by the hunting Indians for every want. But alas for the Spaniards, the grand pageant resulted in disappointment for all, and its indefatigable leader ended his days practically forgotten by his country for which he had accomplished so much.

F. W. Hodge.

THE NARRATIVE OF THE EXPEDITION OF CORONADO BY CASTAÑEDA

Account of the Expedition to Cíbola which took place in the year 1540, in which all those settlements, their ceremonies and customs, are described. Written by Pedro de Castañeda, of Najera.[1]

PREFACE

To me it seems very certain, my very noble lord, that it is a worthy ambition for great men to desire to know and wish to preserve for posterity correct information concerning the things that have happened in distant parts, about which little is known. I do not blame those inquisitive persons who, perchance with good intentions, have many times troubled me not a little with their requests that I clear up for them some doubts which they have had about different things that have been commonly related concerning the events and occurrences that took place during the expedition to Cíbola, or the New Land, which the good viceroy — may he be with God in His glory — Don Antonio de Mendoza,[2] ordered and arranged, and on which he sent Francisco Vazquez de Coronado as captain-general. In truth, they have reason for wishing to know the truth, because most people very often make things of which they have heard, and about which they have perchance no knowledge, appear either greater or less than they are. They make nothing of those things that amount to something, and

---

[1] For information concerning the author of this narrative, see the Introduction.

[2] Mendoza was first viceroy of New Spain (Mexico), serving from 1535 to 1550, when he was ordered to Peru as its second viceroy. He reached Lima in September, 1551, and died July 21 of the year following.

those that do not they make so remarkable that they appear to be something impossible to believe. This may very well have been caused by the fact that, as that country was not permanently occupied, there has not been any one who was willing to spend his time in writing about its peculiarities, because all knowledge was lost of that which it was not the pleasure of God — He alone knows the reason — that they should enjoy. In truth, he who wishes to employ himself thus in writing out the things that happened on the expedition, and the things that were seen in those lands, and the ceremonies and customs of the natives, will have matter enough to test his judgment, and I believe that the result can not fail to be an account which, describing only the truth, will be so remarkable that it will seem incredible.

And besides, I think that the twenty years and more since that expedition took place [1] have been the cause of some stories which are related. For example, some make it an uninhabitable country, others have it bordering on Florida, and still others on Greater India, which does not appear to be a slight difference. They are unable to give any basis upon which to found their statements. There are those who tell about some very peculiar animals, who are contradicted by others who were on the expedition, declaring that there was nothing of the sort seen. Others differ as to the limits of the provinces and even in regard to the ceremonies and customs, attributing what pertains to one people to others. All this has had a large part, my very noble lord, in making me wish to give now, although somewhat late, a short general account for all those who pride themselves on this noble curiosity, and to save myself the time taken up by these solicitations. Things enough will certainly be found here which are hard to believe. All or the most of these were seen with my own eyes, and the rest is from reliable information obtained by inquiry of the natives themselves. Understanding as I do that this little work would be nothing in itself, lacking authority, unless it

---

[1] Castañeda is supposed to have been writing at Culiacan, in western Mexico, about 1565.

were favored and protected by a person whose authority
would protect it from the boldness of those who, without reverence, give their murmuring tongues liberty, and knowing as
I do how great are the obligations under which I have always
been, and am, to your grace, I humbly beg to submit this little
work to your protection.   May it be received as from a faithful
retainer and servant.   It will be divided into three parts, that
it may be better understood.   The first will tell of the discovery
and the armament or army that was made ready, and of the
whole journey, with the captains who were there; the second,
of the villages and provinces which were found, and their limits,
and ceremonies and customs, the animals, fruits, and vegetation, and in what parts of the country these are; the third, of
the return of the army and the reasons for abandoning the
country, although these were insufficient, because this is the
best place there is for discoveries — the marrow of the land in
these western parts, as will be seen.   And after this has been
made plain, some remarkable things which were seen will be
described at the end, and the way by which one might more
easily return to discover that better land which we did not
see, since it would be no small advantage to enter the country
through the land which the Marquis of the Valley, Don Fernando Cortes, went in search of under the Western star, and
which cost him no small sea armament.   May it please our
Lord to so favor me that with my slight knowledge and small
abilities I may be able by relating the truth to make my little
work pleasing to the learned and wise readers, when it has been
accepted by your grace.   For my intention is not to gain the
fame of a good composer or rhetorician, but I desire to give a
faithful account and to do this slight service to your grace, who
will, I hope, receive it as from a faithful servant and soldier,
who took part in it.   Although not in a polished style, I write
that which happened — that which I heard, experienced, saw,
and did.

I always notice, and it is a fact, that for the most part when
we have something valuable in our hands, and deal with it
without hindrance, we do not value or prize it so highly as if

we understood how much we should miss it after we had lost it, and the longer we continue to have it the less we value it; but after we have lost it and miss the advantages of it, we have a great pain in the heart, and we are all the time imagining and trying to find ways and means by which to get it back again. It seems to me that this has happened to all or most of those who went on the expedition which, in the year of our Savior Jesus Christ 1540, Francisco Vazquez Coronado led in search of the Seven Cities.[1] Granted that they did not find the riches of which they had been told, they found a place in which to search for them and the beginning of a good country to settle in, so as to go on farther from there. Since they came back from the country which they conquered and abandoned, time has given them a chance to understand the direction and locality in which they were, and the borders of the good country they had in their hands, and their hearts weep for having lost so favorable an opportunity. Just as men see more at the bullfight when they are upon the seats than when they are around in the ring, now when they know and understand the direction and situation in which they were, and see, indeed, that they can not enjoy it nor recover it, now when it is too late they enjoy telling about what they saw, and even of what they realize that they lost, especially those who are now as poor as when they went there. They have never ceased their labors and have spent their time to no advantage. I say this because I have known several of those who came back from there who amuse themselves now by talking of how it would be to go back and proceed to recover that which is lost, while others enjoy trying to find the reason why it was discovered at all. And now I will proceed to relate all that happened from the beginning.

[1] The Seven Cities of Cibola. See p. 287, note 1; p. 300, note 1.

FIRST PART

Chapter 1

Which treats of the way we first came to know about the Seven Cities, and of how Nuño de Guzman made an expedition to discover them.

In the year 1530 Nuño de Guzman, who was President of New Spain,[1] had in his possession an Indian, a native of the valley or valleys of Oxitipar, who was called Tejo by the Spaniards. This Indian said he was the son of a trader who was

[1] Nuño Beltrán de Guzman was appointed governor of Pánuco, Mexico, in 1526, assuming the office in May, 1527. In December he became president of the Audiencia, the administrative and judicial board which governed the province, and in the following year participated in the trial of Cortés, his personal and political enemy, for strangling his wife to death in 1522. Guzman's barbarous cruelty, especially to the natives, whom he enslaved and bartered for his personal gain, resulted in a protest to the crown by Bishop Zumárraga, and in the hope of finding new fields for the gratification of his avarice he raised a large force, including 10,000 Aztecs and Tlascaltecs, and started from Mexico late in 1529 to explore the northwest (later known as Nueva Galicia), notwithstanding Cortés had already penetrated the region.

He conquered the territory through which he passed, laying waste the settlements and fields and inflicting unspeakable punishment on the native inhabitants. Guzman built a chapel at Tonalá, which formed the beginning of the settlement of the present city of Guadalajara, named from his native town in Spain; he also founded the towns of Santiago de Compostela and San Miguel Culiacan, in Tepic and Sinaloa respectively, and started on his return journey late in 1531. Meanwhile a new Audiencia had arrived in New Spain, and Guzman was summoned to appear at the capital. This he refused to do, and when Luis de Castilla was sent by Cortés, the captain-general of the province, to subdue him, Guzman captured him and his force of 100 men by a ruse. In May, 1533, the king commanded him to submit to the provincial authorities; many of his friends and adherents deserted him, and he was stripped of his title as governor of Pánuco. In 1536 (March 17) the licentiate Diego Perez de la Torre was appointed *juez de residencia,* an officer whose duty was to conduct a rigid investigation of the accounts and administration of governmental officials — this time with special reference to Guzman. By Torre's order, Guzman was arrested and confined in jail until 1538, when his case was appealed to Spain; but from this he received no comfort. He was banished to Torrejon de Velasco, where he died in 1544, penniless and despised.

dead, but that when he was a little boy his father had gone into the back country with fine feathers to trade for ornaments, and that when he came back he brought a large amount of gold and silver, of which there is a good deal in that country. He went with him once or twice, and saw some very large villages, which he compared to Mexico and its environs. He had seen seven very large towns which had streets of silver workers. It took forty days to go there from his country, through a wilderness in which nothing grew, except some very small plants about a span high. The way they went was up through the country between the two seas, following the northern direction. Acting on this information, Nuño de Guzman got together nearly 400 Spaniards and 20,000 friendly Indians of New Spain, and, as he happened to be in Mexico, he crossed Tarasca, which is in the province of Michoacan, so as to get into the region which the Indian said was to be crossed toward the North Sea, in this way getting to the country which they were looking for, which was already named "The Seven Cities." He thought, from the forty days of which the Tejo had spoken, that it would be found to be about 200 leagues, and that they would easily be able to cross the country. Omitting several things that occurred on this journey, as soon as they had reached the province of Culiacan, where his government ended, and where the New Kingdom of Galicia is now, they tried to cross the country, but found the difficulties very great, because the mountain chains which are near that sea are so rough that it was impossible, after great labor, to find a passageway in that region. His whole army had to stay in the district of Culiacan for so long on this account that some rich men who were with him, who had possessions in Mexico, changed their minds, and every day became more anxious to return. Besides this, Nuño de Guzman received word that the Marquis of the Valley, Don Fernando Cortes, had come from Spain with his new title,[1] and with great favors and estates, and as Nuño de Guzman had been a great rival of his at the time he was presi-

---

[1] Marqués del Valle de Oaxaca y Capitan General de la Nueva España y de la Costa del Sur. He arrived at Vera Cruz in July, 1529.

dent, and had done much damage to his property and to that of his friends, he feared that Don Fernando Cortes would want to pay him back in the same way, or worse. So he decided to establish the town of Culiacan there and to go back with the other men, without doing anything more. After his return from this expedition, he founded Xalisco, where the city of Compostela is situated, and Tonala, which is called Guada-laxara, and now this is the New Kingdom of Galicia. The guide they had, who was called Tejo, died about this time, and thus the name of these Seven Cities and the search for them remains until now, since they have not been discovered.[1]

Chapter 2

Of how Francisco Vazquez Coronado came to be governor, and the second account which Cabeza de Vaca gave.

Eight years after Nuño de Guzman made this expedition, he was put in prison by a juez de residencia, named the licentiate Diego de la Torre, who came from Spain with sufficient powers to do this. After the death of the judge, who had also managed the government of that country himself, the good Don Antonio de Mendoza, viceroy of New Spain, appointed as governor of that province Francisco Vazquez de Coronado, a gentleman from Salamanca, who had married a lady in the city of Mexico, the daughter of Alonso de Estrada, the treas-urer and at one time governor of Mexico, and the son, most people said, of His Catholic Majesty Don Ferdinand, and many stated it as certain. As I was saying, at the time Francisco Vazquez was appointed governor, he was travelling through New Spain as an official inspector, and in this way he gained the friendship of many worthy men who afterward went on his expedition with him. It happened that just at this time three

[1] The best discussion of the stories of the Seven Caves and the Seven Cities is in A. F. Bandelier's *Contributions to the History of the Southwestern Portion of the United States,* in *Papers of the Archaeological Institute of America,* American Series, V. (Cambridge, 1890).

Spaniards, named Cabeza de Vaca, Dorantes, and Castillo
Maldonado, and a negro [Estévan], who had been lost on the
expedition which Pamfilo de Narvaez led into Florida, reached
Mexico. They came out through Culiacan, having crossed the
country from sea to sea, as anyone who wishes may find out
for himself by an account which this same Cabeza de Vaca
wrote and dedicated to Prince Don Philip, who is now King
of Spain and our sovereign.[1] They gave the good Don Antonio de Mendoza an account of some large and powerful villages, four and five stories high, of which they had heard a
great deal in the countries they had crossed, and other things
very different from what turned out to be the truth. The
noble viceroy communicated this to the new governor, who
gave up the visits he had in hand, on account of this, and
hurried his departure for his government, taking with him the
negro [Estévan] who had come [with Cabeza de Vaca] with the
three friars of the order of Saint Francis, one of whom was
named Friar Marcos of Nice, a regular priest, and another Friar
Daniel, a lay brother, and the other Friar Antonio de Santa
Maria. When he reached the province of Culiacan he sent the
friars just mentioned and the negro, who was named Estevan,
off in search of that country, because Friar Marcos offered to
go and see it, because he had been in Peru at the time Don
Pedro de Alvarado went there overland. It seems that, after
the friars I have mentioned and the negro had started, the
negro did not get on well with the friars, because he took the
women that were given him and collected turquoises, and got
together a stock of everything. Besides, the Indians in those
places through which they went got along with the negro better, because they had seen him before. This was the reason he
was sent on ahead to open up the way and pacify the Indians,
so that when the others came along they had nothing to do except to keep an account of the things for which they were
looking.

[1] See the narrative of Alvar Nuñez Cabeza de Vaca in the present volume.

Chapter 3

Of how they killed the negro Estevan at Cibola, and Friar Marcos
returned in flight.

After Estevan had left the friars, he thought he could get
all the reputation and honor himself, and that if he should discover those settlements with such famous high houses, alone,
he would be considered bold and courageous. So he proceeded
with the people who had followed him, and attempted to cross
the wilderness which lies between the country he had passed
through and Cibola. He was so far ahead of the friars that,
when these reached Chichilticalli, which is on the edge of the
wilderness, he was already at Cibola, which is eighty leagues
beyond. It is 220 leagues from Culiacan to the edge of the
wilderness, and eighty across the desert, which makes 300, or
perhaps ten more or less. As I said, Estevan reached Cibola
loaded with the large quantity of turquoises they had given him
and some beautiful women whom the Indians who followed
him and carried his things were taking with them and had
given him. These had followed him from all the settlements he
had passed, believing that under his protection they could
traverse the whole world without any danger. But as the
people in this country were more intelligent than those who followed Estevan, they lodged him in a little hut they had outside
their village, and the older men and the governors heard his
story and took steps to find out the reason he had come to that
country. For three days they made inquiries about him
and held a council. The account which the negro gave them of
two white men who were following him, sent by a great lord,
who knew about the things in the sky, and how these were coming to instruct them in divine matters, made them think that
he must be a spy or a guide from some nations who wished
to come and conquer them, because it seemed to them unrea-
sonable to say that the people were white in the country from
which he came and that he was sent by them, he being black.
Besides these other reasons, they thought it was hard of him

U

to ask them for turquoises and women, and so they decided to kill him. They did this, but they did not kill any of those who went with him, although they kept some young fellows and let the others, about sixty persons, return freely to their own country. As these, who were badly scared, were returning in flight, they happened to come upon the friars in the desert sixty leagues from Cibola, and told them the sad news, which frightened them so much that they would not even trust these folks who had been with the negro, but opened the packs they were carrying and gave away everything they had except the holy vestments for saying mass. They returned from here by double marches, prepared for anything, without seeing any more of the country except what the Indians told them.[1]

Chapter 4

Of how the noble Don Antonio de Mendoza made an expedition to discover Cibola.

After Francisco Vazquez Coronado had sent Friar Marcos of Nice and his party on the search already related, he was engaged in Culiacan about some business that related to his government, when he heard an account of a province called Topira,[2] which was to the north of the country of Culiacan. He started to explore this region with several of the conquerors and some friendly Indians, but he did not get very far, because the mountain chains which they had to cross were very difficult. He returned without finding the least signs of a good country,

[1] See the account of this journey by Marcos de Niza in *Coleccion de Documentos Inéditos de Indias*, III. 325–351; Ramusio, *Terzo Volume delle Navigationi* (Venice, 1556); Hakluyt, *Voyages*, IX. 125–144 (1904); Ternaux-Compans, *Voyages*, IX. 249–284 (1838); and an English translation by Fanny Bandelier in *The Journey of Alvar Nuñez Cabeza de Vaca* (1905). *Cf.* also A. F. Bandelier, "The Discovery of New Mexico by Fray Marcos de Nizza," in *Magazine of Western History*, IV. 659–670 (Cleveland, 1886).

[2] Bandelier, *Papers of the Archaeological Institute of America*, Am. ser., V. (1890), p. 104, says this was Topia, in Durango, a locality since noted for its rich mines.

and when he got back, he found the friars who had just arrived, and who told such great things about what the negro Estevan had discovered and what they had heard from the Indians, and other things they had heard about the South Sea [1] and islands and other riches, that, without stopping for anything, the governor set off at once for the City of Mexico, taking Friar Marcos with him, to tell the viceroy about it. He made the things seem more important by not talking about them to anyone except his particular friends, under promise of the greatest secrecy, until after he had reached Mexico and seen Don Antonio de Mendoza. Then it began to be noised abroad that the Seven Cities for which Nuño de Guzman had searched had already been discovered, and a beginning was made in collecting an armed force and in bringing together people to go and conquer them. The noble viceroy arranged with the friars of the order of Saint Francis so that Friar Marcos was made father provincial, as a result of which the pulpits of that order were filled with such accounts of marvels and wonders that more than 300 Spaniards and about 800 natives of New Spain collected in a few days. There were so many men of such high quality among the Spaniards, that such a noble body was never collected in the Indies, nor so many men of quality in such a small body, there being 300 men. Francisco Vazquez Coronado, governor of New Galicia, was captain-general, because he had been the author of it all. The good viceroy Don Antonio did this because at this time Francisco Vazquez was his closest and most intimate friend, and because he considered him to be wise, skillful, and intelligent, besides being a gentleman. Had he paid more attention and regard to the position in which he was placed and the charge over which he was placed, and less to the estates he left behind in New Spain, or, at least, more to the honor he had and might secure from having such gentlemen under his command, things would not have turned out as they did. When this narrative is ended, it will be seen that he did not know how to keep his position nor the government that he held.

[1] The Pacific.

Chapter 5

Concerning the captains who went to Cíbola.

When the viceroy, Don Antonio de Mendoza, saw what a noble company had come together, and the spirit and good will with which they had all presented themselves, knowing the worth of these men, he would have liked very well to make every one of them captain of an army; but as the whole number was small he could not do as he would have liked, and so he issued the commissions and captaincies as he saw fit, because it seemed to him that if they were appointed by him, as he was so well obeyed and beloved, nobody would find fault with his arrangements. After everybody had heard who the general was, he made Don Pedro de Tovar ensign-general, a young gentleman who was the son of Don Fernando de Tovar, the guardian and lord high steward of the Queen Doña Juana,[1] our demented mistress — may she be in glory — and Lope de Samaniego, the governor of the arsenal at Mexico,[2] a gentleman fully equal to the charge, army-master. The captains were Don Tristan de Arellano; Don Pedro de Guevara, the son of Don Juan de Guevara and nephew of the Count of Oñate; Don Garcia Lopez de Cardenas; Don Rodrigo Maldonado, brother-in-law of the Duke of the Infantado; Diego Lopez, alderman of Seville, and Diego Gutierres, for the cavalry. All the other gentlemen were placed under the flag of the general, as being distinguished persons, and some of them became captains later, and their appointments were confirmed by order of the viceroy and by the general, Francisco Vazquez. To name some of them whom I happen to remember, there were Francisco de Barrionuevo, a gentleman from Granada; Juan de Saldivar, Francisco de Ovando, Juan Gallego, and Melchior Diaz — a captain who had been mayor of Culiacan, who, al-

---

[1] Daughter of Ferdinand and Isabella, wife of Philip I., and mother of Charles V.

[2] In a letter of the Viceroy Mendoza to the King, April 17, 1540, Samaniego is mentioned as the warden of a fortress.

though he was not a gentleman, merited the position he held. The other gentlemen who were prominent, were Don Alonso Manrique de Lara; Don Lope de Urrea, a gentleman from Aragon; Gomez Suarez de Figueroa, Luis Ramirez de Vargas, Juan de Sotomayor, Francisco Gorbalan, the commissioner Riberos, and other gentlemen, men of high quality, whom I do not now recall. The infantry captain was Pablo de Melgosa of Burgos, and of the artillery, Hernando de Alvarado of the mountain district. As I say, since then I have forgotten the names of many gentlemen. It would be well if I could name some of them, so that it might be clearly seen what cause I had for saying that they had on this expedition the most brilliant company ever collected in the Indies to go in search of new lands. But they were unfortunate in having a captain who left in New Spain estates and a pretty wife, a noble and excellent lady, which were not the least causes for what was to happen.

Chapter 6

Of how all the companies collected in Compostela and set off on the journey in good order.

When the viceroy Don Antonio de Mendoza had fixed and arranged everything as we have related, and the companies and captaincies had been arranged, he advanced a part of their salaries from the chest of His Majesty to those in the army who were in greatest need. And as it seemed to him that it would be rather hard for the friendly Indians in the country if the army should start from Mexico, he ordered them to assemble at the city of Compostela, the chief city in the New Kingdom of Galicia, 110 leagues from Mexico, so that they could begin their journey there with everything in good order. There is nothing to tell about what happened on this trip, since they all finally assembled at Compostela by Shrovetide, in the year (fifteen hundred and) forty-one.[1] After the

---

[1] The correct date is 1540. Castañeda carries the error throughout his narration, although he gives the year correctly in the preface.

whole force had left Mexico, he ordered Don Pedro de Alarcon[1] to set sail with two ships that were in the port of La Natividad on the South Sea coast, and go to the port of Xalisco[2] to take the baggage which the soldiers were unable to carry, and thence to sail along the coast near the army, because he had understood from the reports that they would have to go through the country near the seacoast, and that we could find the harbors by means of the rivers, and that the ships could always get news of the army, which turned out afterward to be false, and so all this stuff was lost, or, rather, those who owned it lost it, as will be told farther on.[3] After the viceroy had completed all his arrangements, he set off for Compostela, accompanied by many noble and rich men. He kept the New Year of (fifteen hundred and) forty-one at Pasquaro, which is the chief place in the bishopric of Michoacan, and from there he crossed the whole of New Spain, taking much pleasure in enjoying the festivals and great receptions which were given him, till he reached Compostela, which is, as I have said, 110 leagues. There he found the whole company assembled, being well treated and entertained by Christobal de Oñate, who had the whole charge of that government[4] for the time being. He had had the management of it and was in command of all that region when Francisco Vazquez was made governor. All were very glad when he arrived, and he made an examination of the company and found all those whom we have mentioned. He assigned the captains to their companies, and after this was done, on the next day, after they had all heard mass, captains and soldiers together, the viceroy made them a very eloquent short speech, telling them of the fidelity they owed to their general and showing them

[1] An error for *Hernando* de Alarcon.

[2] That is, from a point on the Pacific coast in latitude 19° to another in latitude 21° 30′.

[3] See Alarcon's narrative translated by Hakluyt in his *Voyages*, IX. 279–318 (ed. 1904), and also Buckingham Smith, *Coleccion de Varios Documentos para la Historia de la Florida* (1857), p. 1.

[4] The province of Nueva Galicia, explored under Guzman's direction. See p. 285, note 1.

clearly the benefits which this expedition might afford, from
the conversion of those peoples as well as in the profit of those
who should conquer the territory, and the advantage to His
Majesty and the claim which they would thus have on his
favor and aid at all times. After he had finished, they all,
both captains and soldiers, gave him their oaths upon the Gos-
pels in a missal that they would follow their general on this
expedition and would obey him in everything he commanded
them, which they faithfully performed, as will be seen. The
next day after this was done, the army started off with its
colors flying. The viceroy, Don Antonio, went with them for
two days, and there he took leave of them, returning to New
Spain with his friends.

Chapter 7

Of how the army reached Chiametla, and the killing of the army-
master, and the other things that happened up to the
arrival at Culiacan.

After the viceroy Don Antonio left them, the army continued its march. As each one was obliged to transport his
own baggage and all did not know how to fasten the packs, and
as the horses started off fat and plump, they had a good deal of
difficulty and labor during the first few days, and many left
many valuable things, giving them to anyone who wanted them,
in order to get rid of carrying them. In the end necessity,
which is all powerful, made them skillful, so that one could see
many gentlemen become carriers, and anybody who despised
this work was not considered a man. With such labors, which
they then thought severe, the army reached Chiametla, where
it was obliged to delay several days to procure food. During
this time the army-master, Lope de Samaniego, went off with
some soldiers to find food, and at one village, a crossbowman
having entered it indiscreetly in pursuit of the enemies, they
shot him through the eye and it passed through his brain, so
that he died on the spot. They also shot five or six of his companions before Diego Lopez, the alderman from Seville, since

the commander was dead, collected the men and sent word to the general. He put a guard in the village and over the provisions. There was great confusion in the army when this news became known. He was buried here. Several sorties were made, by which food was obtained and several of the natives taken prisoners. They hanged those who seemed to belong to the district where the army-master was killed.

It seems that when the general Francisco Vazquez left Culiacan with Friar Marcos to tell the viceroy Don Antonio de Mendoza the news, as already related, he left orders for Captain Melchior Diaz and Juan de Saldivar to start off with a dozen good men from Culiacan and verify what Friar Marcos had seen and heard. They started and went as far as Chichil-ticalli,[1] which is where the wilderness begins, 220 leagues from Culiacan, and there they turned back, not finding anything important. They reached Chiametla just as the army was ready to leave, and reported to the general. Although it was kept secret, the bad news leaked out, and there were some reports which, although they were exaggerated, did not fail to give an indication of what the facts were. Friar Marcos, noticing that some were feeling disturbed, cleared away these clouds, promising that what they would see should be good, and that he would place the army in a country where their hands would be filled, and in this way he quieted them so that they appeared well satisfied. From there the army marched to Culiacan, making some detours into the country to seize provisions. They were two leagues from the town of Culiacan at Easter vespers, when the inhabitants came out to welcome their governor and begged him not to enter the town till the day after Easter.[2]

[1] For this locality see p. 299, note 1.

[2] Culiacan, or San Miguel Culiacan, as it was named by Guzman, is in central Sinaloa. Castañeda was a resident of this town and evidently joined the expedition there.

Chapter 8

*Of how the army entered the town of Culiacan and the recep-
tion it received, and other things which happened before
the departure.*

When the day after Easter came, the army started in the
morning to go to the town and, as they approached, the inhabitants of the town came out on to an open plain with foot
and horse drawn up in ranks as if for a battle, and having its
seven bronze pieces of artillery in position, making a show of
defending their town. Some of our soldiers were with them.
Our army drew up in the same way and began a skirmish with
them, and after the artillery on both sides had been fired they
were driven back, just as if the town had been taken by force
of arms, which was a pleasant demonstration of welcome, except for the artilleryman who lost a hand by a shot, from
having ordered them to fire before he had finished drawing out
the ramrod. After the town was taken, the army was well
lodged and entertained by the townspeople, who, as they were
all very well-to-do people, took all the gentlemen and people of
quality who were with the army into their own apartments,
although they had lodgings prepared for them all just outside
the town. Some of the townspeople were not ill repaid for
this hospitality, because all had started with fine clothes and
accoutrements, and as they had to carry provisions on their
animals after this, they were obliged to leave their fine stuff,
so that many preferred giving it to their hosts instead of risk-
ing it on the sea by putting it in the ship that had followed the
army along the coast to take the extra baggage, as I have said.
After they arrived and were being entertained in the town, the
general, by order of the viceroy Don Antonio, left Fernandarias de Saabedra, uncle of Hernandarias de Saabedra, count of
Castellar, formerly mayor of Seville, as his lieutenant and captain in this town. The army rested here several days, because
the inhabitants had gathered a good stock of provisions that
year and each one shared his stock very gladly with his guests

from our army. They not only had plenty to eat here, but they also had plenty to take away with them, so that when the departure came they started off with more than six hundred loaded animals, besides the friendly Indians and the servants — more than a thousand persons. After a fortnight had passed, the general started ahead with about fifty horsemen and a few foot soldiers and most of the Indian allies, leaving the army, which was to follow him a fortnight later, with Don Tristan de Arellano in command as his lieutenant.

At this time, before his departure, a pretty sort of thing happened to the general, which I will tell for what it is worth. A young soldier named Trugillo (Truxillo) pretended that he had seen a vision while he was bathing in the river. Feigning that he did not want to, he was brought before the general, whom he gave to understand that the devil had told him that if he would kill the general, he could marry his wife, Doña Beatris, and would receive great wealth and other very fine things. Friar Marcos of Nice preached several sermons on this, laying it all to the fact that the devil was jealous of the good which must result from this journey and so wished to break it up in this way. It did not end here, but the friars who were in the expedition wrote to their monasteries about it, and this was the reason the pulpits of Mexico proclaimed strange rumors about this affair.

The general ordered Truxillo to stay in that town and not to go on the expedition, which was what he was after when he made up that falsehood, judging from what afterward appeared to be the truth. The general started off with the force already described to continue his journey, and the army followed him, as will be related.

Chapter 9

Of how the army started from Culiacan and the arrival of the general at Cibola, and of the army at Señora and of other things that happened.

The general, as has been said, started to continue his journey from the valley of Culiacan somewhat lightly equipped, taking with him the friars, since none of them wished to stay behind with the army. After they had gone three days, a regular friar who could say mass, named Friar Antonio Victoria, broke his leg, and they brought him back from the camp to have it treated. He stayed with the army after this, which was no slight consolation for all. The general and his force crossed the country without trouble, as they found everything peaceful, because the Indians knew Friar Marcos and some of the others who had been with Melchior Diaz when he went with Juan de Saldibar to investigate. After the general had crossed the inhabited region and came to Chichilticalli, where the wilderness begins, and saw nothing favorable, he could not help feeling somewhat downhearted, for, although the reports were very fine about what was ahead, there was nobody who had seen it except the Indians who went with the negro, and these had already been caught in some lies. Besides all this, he was much affected by seeing that the fame of Chichilticalli was summed up in one tumbledown house without any roof, although it appeared to have been a strong place at some former time when it was inhabited, and it was very plain that it had been built by a civilized and warlike race of strangers who had come from a distance. This building was made of red earth.[1] From here they went on through the wilderness, and in fifteen days came to a river about eight leagues from Cibola which they called Red River,[2] because its waters were muddy and reddish. In this river they found mullets like those of Spain. The first Indians from that country were seen here— two of them, who ran away to give the news. During the night following the next day, about two leagues from the village, some Indians in a safe place yelled so that, although the men were ready for anything, some were so excited that they

---

[1] Chichilticalli, or the "Red House," was so named by the Aztec Indians on account of its color. It was doubtless situated on or near the Rio Gila, east of the mouth of the San Pedro, probably not far from the present Solomonsville in southern Arizona.

[2] The Zuñi River, within the present Arizona. Its waters are very muddy in springtime, which is the only time of the year that it flows into the Little Colorado.

put their saddles on hind-side before; but these were the new fellows. When the veterans had mounted and ridden round the camp, the Indians fled. None of them could be caught because they knew the country.

The next day they entered the settled country in good order, and when they saw the first village, which was Cibola, such were the curses that some hurled at Friar Marcos that I pray God may protect him from them.

It is a little, crowded village,[1] looking as if it had been crumpled all up together. There are haciendas in New Spain which make a better appearance at a distance. It is a village of about two hundred warriors, is three and four stories high, with the houses small and having only a few rooms, and without a courtyard. One yard serves for each section.[2] The people of the whole district had collected here, for there are seven villages in the province, and some of the others are even larger and stronger than Cibola. These folks waited for the army, drawn up by divisions in front of the village. When they refused to have peace on the terms the interpreters extended to them, but appeared defiant, the Santiago[3] was given, and they were at once put to flight. The Spaniards then attacked the village, which was taken with not a little difficulty, since they held the narrow and crooked entrance. During the

---

[1] This was the Zuñi Indian pueblo of Hawikuh, one of their seven villages, from which Coronado wrote to the Viceroy Mendoza, dating his letter "from the province of Cevola, and this city of Granada, the 3d of August, 1540." (See Winship's translation in *Fourteenth Report of the Bureau of Ethnology*, pp. 552–563.) Hawikuh, or "Granada," was situated about fifteen miles southwest of the present Zuñi, near the Zuñi River, in New Mexico, and its ruins are still to be seen. This was the pueblo in which Estévan doubtless lost his life the year before, and which was viewed from an adjacent height by Fray Marcos. Hawikuh was the seat of a mission established by the Franciscans in 1629; it was abandoned in 1670 after having been raided by the Apaches and its priest killed. The name "Cibola," now and later applied to Hawikuh, is believed to be a Spanish form of *Shiwina*, the Zuñi name for their tribal range. *Cibolo* later became the term by which the Spaniards of Mexico designated the bison.

[2] The houses were built in terrace fashion, one above the other, the roof of one tier forming a sort of front yard for the tier of houses next above it.

[3] The war cry or "loud invocation addressed to Saint James before engaging in battle with the Infidels."— Captain John Stevens's *Dictionary*.

attack they knocked the general down with a large stone, and would have killed him but for Don Garcia Lopez de Cardenas and Hernando de Alvarado, who threw themselves above him and drew him away, receiving the blows of the stones, which were not few. But the first fury of the Spaniards could not be resisted, and in less than an hour they entered the village and captured it. They discovered food there, which was the thing they were most in need of. After this the whole province was at peace.

The army which had stayed with Don Tristan de Arellano started to follow their general, all loaded with provisions, with lances on their shoulders, and all on foot, so as to have the horses loaded. With no slight labor from day to day, they reached a province which Cabeza de Vaca had named Hearts (Corazones), because the people here offered him many hearts of animals.[1] He founded a town here and named it San Hieronimo de los Corazones (Saint Jerome of the Hearts). After it had been started, it was seen that it could not be kept up here, and so it was afterward transferred to a valley which had been called Señora. The Spaniards call it Señora,[2] and so it will be known by this name.

From here a force went down the river to the seacoast to find the harbor and to find out about the ships. Don Rodrigo Maldonado, who was captain of those who went in search of the ships, did not find them, but he brought back with him an Indian so large and tall that the best man in the army reached only to his chest.[3] It was said that other Indians were even taller on that coast. After the rains ceased the army went on to where the town of Señora was afterward located,[4] because

[1] See Cabeza de Vaca's narrative in the present volume. The place was at or near the present Ures, on the Rio Sonora in Sonora, Mexico.

[2] Whence the name of the present state of Sonora.

[3] Evidently a Seri Indian. The Seri are a wild tribe speaking an independent language and occupying the island of Tiburon and the adjacent Sonora coast of the Gulf of California. They are noted for their stature. For an account of this people, see McGee in *Seventeenth Report of the Bureau of American Ethnology*, pt. 1 (1898).

[4] Believed to be in the present Sonora valley, where it opens out into a broader plain a number of miles above Ures.

there were provisions in that region, so that they were able to wait there for orders from the general.

About the middle of the month of October,[1] Captains Melchior Diaz and Juan Gallego came from Cibola, Juan Gallego [2] on his way to New Spain and Melchior Diaz to stay in the new town of Hearts, in command of the men who remained there. He was to go along the coast in search of the ships.

Chapter 10

Of how the army started from the town of Señora, leaving it inhabited, and how it reached Cibola, and of what happened to Captain Melchior Diaz on his expedition in search of the ships and how he discovered the Tison (Firebrand) River.

After Melchior Diaz and Juan Gallego had arrived in the town of Señora, it was announced that the army was to depart for Cibola; that Melchior Diaz was to remain in charge of that town with eighty men; that Juan Gallego was going to New Spain with messages for the viceroy, and that Friar Marcos was going back with him, because he did not think it was safe for him to stay in Cibola, seeing that his report had turned out to be entirely false, because the kingdoms that he had told about had not been found, nor the populous cities, nor the wealth of gold, nor the precious stones which he had reported, nor the fine clothes, nor other things that had been proclaimed from the pulpits. When this had been announced, those who were to remain were selected and the rest loaded their provisions and set off in good order about the middle of September on the way to Cibola, following their general.

[1] This should be September.

[2] It is not without interest to record here the finding, in 1886, in western Kansas, of a sword-blade, greatly corroded, but still bearing sufficient trace of the name " Juan Gallego " to enable its determination, as well as the inscription " *No me saques sin razon   No me embaines sin honor.*" See W. E. Ritchey in *Mail and Breeze*, Topeka, Kansas, July 26, 1902.

Don Tristan de Arellano stayed in this new town with the
weakest men, and from this time on there was nothing but
mutinies and strife, because after the army had gone Captain
Melchior Diaz took twenty-five of the most efficient men,
leaving in his place one Diego de Alcaraz, a man unfitted to
have people under his command.   He took guides and went
toward the north and west in search of the seacoast.   After
going about 150 leagues, they came to a province of exceedingly tall and strong men — like giants.   They are naked and
live in large straw cabins built underground like smoke-houses,
with only the straw roof above ground.   They enter these at one
end and come out at the other.   More than a hundred persons,
old and young, sleep in one cabin.   When they carry anything,
they can take a load of more than three or four hundred weight
on their heads.   Once when our men wished to fetch a log for the
fire, and six men were unable to carry it, one of these Indians
is reported to have come and raised it in his arms, put it on his
head alone, and carried it very easily.   They eat bread cooked
in the ashes, as big as the large two-pound loaves of Castile.
On account of the great cold, they carry a firebrand (*tison*)
in the hand when they go from one place to another, with which
they warm the other hand and the body as well, and in this
way they keep shifting it every now and then.[1]   On this account the large river which is in that country was called Rio
del Tison (Firebrand River).   It is a very great river and is
more than two leagues wide at its mouth; here it is half a
league across.   Here the captain heard that there had been
ships at a point three days down toward the sea.   When he
reached the place where the ships had been, which was more
than fifteen leagues up the river from the mouth of the harbor,
they found written on a tree: "Alarcon reached this place;
there are letters at the foot of this tree."   He dug up the
letters and learned from them how long Alarcon had waited
for news of the army and that he had gone back with the ships

---

[1] These were evidently the Cocopa, a Yuman tribe, whose descendants
still inhabit the lower Rio Colorado, which is the Rio del Tison of this narrative   The Cocopa now number perhaps 800.

to New Spain, because he was unable to proceed farther, since
this sea was a bay, which was formed by the Isle of the Marquis, which is called California, and it was explained that California was not an island, but a point of the mainland forming
the other side of that gulf.[1]

After he had seen this, the captain turned back to go up the
river, without going down to the sea, to find a ford by which
to cross to the other side, so as to follow the other bank.   After
they had gone five or six days, it seemed to them as if they could
cross on rafts.   For this purpose they called together a large
number of the natives, who were waiting for a favorable opportunity to make an attack on our men, and when they saw that
the strangers wanted to cross, they helped make the rafts with
all zeal and diligence, so as to catch them in this way on the
water and drown them or else so divide them that they could
not help one another.   While the rafts were being made, a soldier who had been out around the camp saw a large number of
armed men go across to a mountain, where they were waiting
till the soldiers should cross the river.   He reported this, and
an Indian was quietly shut up, in order to find out the truth,
and when they tortured him he told all the arrangements that
had been made.   These were, that when our men were crossing and part of them had got over and part were on the river
and part were waiting to cross, those who were on the rafts
should drown those they were taking across and the rest of
their force should make an attack on both sides of the river.
If they had had as much discretion and courage as they had
strength and power, the attempt would have succeeded.[2]

When he knew their plan, the captain had the Indian who
had confessed the affair killed secretly, and that night he was
thrown into the river with a weight, so that the Indians would
not suspect that they were found out.   The next day they

---

[1] It had been supposed that Lower California, the "Isle of the Marquis"
(Cortés), was an island, yet notwithstanding its determination as a peninsula
it appeared as an island on maps of a much later period.

[2] The rafts, or *balsas*, referred to, were made by tying together a large
number of reeds.   The vessel was wide at the middle and pointed at the
ends, and was very buoyant.

noticed that our men suspected them, and so they made an attack, shooting showers of arrows, but when the horses began to catch up with them and the lances wounded them without mercy and the musketeers likewise made good shots, they had to leave the plain and take to the mountain, until not a man of them was to be seen. The force then came back and crossed all right, the Indian allies and the Spaniards going across on the rafts and the horses swimming alongside the rafts, where we will leave them to continue their journey.

To relate how the army that was on its way to Cibola got on: Everything went along in good shape, since the general had left everything peaceful, because he wished the people in that region to be contented and without fear and willing to do what they were ordered. In a province called Vacapan there was a large quantity of prickly pears, of which the natives make a great deal of preserves.[1] They gave this preserve away freely, and as the men of the army ate much of it, they all fell sick with a headache and fever, so that the natives might have done much harm to the force if they had wished. This lasted regularly twenty-four hours. After this they continued their march until they reached Chichilticalli. The men in the advance guard saw a flock of sheep one day after leaving this place. I myself saw and followed them. They had extremely large bodies and long wool; their horns were very thick and large, and when they run they throw back their heads and put their horns on the ridge of their back. They are used to the rough country, so that we could not catch them and had to leave them.[2]

Three days after we entered the wilderness we found a horn

---

[1] Vacapan was apparently an Opata pueblo, or rather two pueblos, on a branch of the Rio Yaqui, which the Spaniards passed through shortly before reaching Corazones (Ures) on the Rio Sonora. The preserved cactus fruit is regarded highly by all the Indians of the general region even to-day, and in season they subsist largely upon it. The saguara (*Cereus giganteus*), or great columnar cactus, furnishes the chief supply.

[2] The well-known Rocky Mountain sheep. As late as twenty years ago some of the mountain ranges of southeastern Arizona, especially the Catalina Mountains, were noted for this animal.

on the bank of a river that flows in the bottom of a very steep, deep gully, which the general had noticed and left there for his army to see, for it was six feet long and as thick at the base as a man's thigh. It seemed to be more like the horn of a goat than of any other animal. It was something worth seeing. The army proceeded and was about a day's march from Cibola when a very cold tornado came up in the afternoon, followed by a great fall of snow, which was a bad combination for the carriers. The army went on till it reached some caves in a rocky ridge, late in the evening. The Indian allies, who were from New Spain, and for the most part from warm countries, were in great danger. They felt the coldness of that day so much that it was hard work the next day taking care of them, for they suffered much pain and had to be carried on the horses, the soldiers walking. After this labor the army reached Cibola, where their general was waiting for them, with their quarters all ready, and here they were reunited, except some captains and men who had gone off to discover other provinces.

Chapter 11

Of how Don Pedro de Tovar discovered Tusayan or Tutahaco [1] and Don Garcia Lopez de Cardenas saw the Firebrand River, and the other things that had happened.

While the things already described were taking place, Cibola being at peace, the general, Francisco Vazquez, found out from the people of the province about the provinces that lay around it, and got them to tell their friends and neighbors that Christians had come into the country, whose only desire was to be their friends, and to find out about good lands to live in, and for them to come to see the strangers and talk with them. They did this, since they know how to communicate with one another in these regions, and they informed him about a province with seven villages of the same sort as theirs, although somewhat different. They had nothing to do with these peo-

[1] Compare Chapter 13. These two groups of pueblos were not the same.

ple. This province is called Tusayan. It is twenty-five leagues
from Cibola. The villages are high and the people are warlike.
The general had sent Don Pedro de Tovar to these villages
with seventeen horsemen and three or four foot-soldiers.[1]
Juan de Padilla, a Franciscan friar, who had been a fighting
man in his youth, went with them. When they reached the
region, they entered the country so quietly that nobody
observed them, because there were no settlements or farms
between one village and another and the people do not leave
the villages except to go to their farms, especially at this time,
when they had heard that Cibola had been captured by very
fierce people, who travelled on animals which ate people. This
information was generally believed by those who had never seen
horses, although it was so strange as to cause much wonder.
Our men arrived after nightfall and were able to conceal themselves under the edge of the village, where they heard the
natives talking in their houses. But in the morning they were
discovered and drew up in regular order, while the natives came
out to meet them, with bows, and shields, and wooden clubs,
drawn up in lines without any confusion. The interpreter was
given a chance to speak to them and give them due warning, for
they were very intelligent people, but nevertheless they drew
lines and insisted that our men should not go across these
lines toward their village.[2] While they were talking, some men
acted as if they would cross the lines, and one of the natives
lost control of himself and struck a horse a blow on the cheek
of the bridle with his club. Friar Juan, fretted by the time
that was being wasted in talking with them, said to the cap-

---

[1] Castañeda speaks as a member of the "army," not of the advance guard.
See the preceding chapter.

[2] These lines were drawn in corn meal and must not be crossed. To this
day similar lines of meal are made across a trail when certain ceremonies
are being performed. The Spaniards were now at the pueblo of Awatobi, the
first village of the Hopi (Moqui) people of Tusayan, in northeastern Arizona,
reached in coming from the southward. It was destroyed by the other Hopi
villagers in 1700, because the Awatobi people favored the re-establishment
of the Spanish mission that had been destroyed in the great Pueblo revolt
of 1680.

tain: "To tell the truth, I do not know why we came here."
When the men heard this, they gave the Santiago so suddenly
that they ran down many Indians and the others fled to the
town in confusion. Some indeed did not have a chance to do
this, so quickly did the people in the village come out with
presents, asking for peace. The captain ordered his force to
collect, and, as the natives did not do any more harm, he and
those who were with him found a place to establish their head-
quarters near the village. They had dismounted here when
the natives came peacefully, saying that they had come to
give in the submission of the whole province and that they
wanted him to be friends with them and to accept the presents
which they gave him. This was some cotton cloth, although
not much, because they do not make it in that district.[1]
They also gave him some dressed skins and cornmeal, and
pine nuts [2] and corn and birds of the country. Afterward
they presented some turquoises,[3] but not many. The people
of the whole district came together that day and submitted
themselves, and they allowed him to enter their villages freely
to visit, buy, sell, and barter with them.

It is governed like Cibola, by an assembly of the oldest
men. They have their governors and generals. This was
where they obtained the information about a large river, and
that several days down the river there were some people
with very large bodies.[4]

As Don Pedro de Tovar was not commissioned to go farther,
he returned from there and gave this information to the general,
who dispatched Don Garcia Lopez de Cardenas with about

[1] Castañeda, speaking from hearsay with respect to the Tovar expedition,
errs in this statement, as the Hopi were the principal cotton growers and
weavers of all the Pueblos. Later Spanish accounts all agree on this point.
Indeed, even now the Hopi cotton kilts, sashes, and ceremonial robes are
bartered throughout the Pueblo region.

[2] Piñon nuts.

[3] Obtained by trade with the Rio Grande Pueblos, who mined them in the
Cerillos, southeast of Santa Fé, New Mexico. It is from the same deposits
that much of the "matrix turquoise" of our present-day commerce is derived.

[4] See the reference to the Cocopa Indians met by Melchior Diaz, in
Chapter 10.

twelve companions to go to see this river. He was well received when he reached Tusayan and was entertained by the natives, who gave him guides for his journey. They started from here loaded with provisions, for they had to go through a desert country before reaching the inhabited region, which the Indians said was more than twenty days' journey. After they had gone twenty days they came to the banks of the river, which seemed to be more than three or four leagues in an air line across to the other bank of the stream which flowed between them.[1] This country was elevated and full of low twisted pines, very cold, and lying open toward the north, so that, this being the warm season, no one could live there on account of the cold. They spent three days on this bank looking for a passage down to the river, which looked from above as if the water was six feet across, although the Indians said it was half a league wide. It was impossible to descend, for after these three days Captain Melgosa and one Juan Galeras and another companion, who were the three lightest and most agile men, made an attempt to go down at the least difficult place, and went down until those who were above were unable to keep sight of them. They returned about four o'clock in the afternoon, not having succeeded in reaching the bottom on account of the great difficulties which they found, because what seemed to be easy from above was not so, but instead very hard and difficult. They said that they had been down about a third of the way and that the river seemed very large from the place which they reached, and that from what they saw they thought the Indians had given the width correctly. Those who stayed above had estimated that some huge rocks on the sides of the cliffs seemed to be about as tall as a man, but those who went down swore that when they reached these rocks they were bigger than the great tower of Seville.[2] They did not go farther up the river, because they could not get water. Before this they

---

[1] The Grand Cañon of the Colorado, now visited and described by white men for the first time.

[2] The Giralda, or celebrated bell-tower of the Cathedral of Seville, which is 275 feet high.

had had to go a league or two inland every day late in the evening in order to find water, and the guides said that if they should go four days farther it would not be possible to go on, because there was no water within three or four days, for when they travel across this region themselves they take with them women loaded with water in gourds, and bury the gourds of water along the way, to use when they return, and besides this, they travel in one day over what it takes us two days to accomplish.

This was the Tison (Firebrand) River, much nearer its source than where Melchior Diaz and his company crossed it. These were the same kind of Indians, judging from what was afterward learned. They came back from this point and the expedition did not have any other result. On the way they saw some water falling over a rock and learned from the guides that some bunches of crystals which were hanging there were salt. They went and gathered a quantity of this and brought it back to Cibola, dividing it among those who were there. They gave the general a written account of what they had seen, because one Pedro de Sotomayor had gone with Don Garcia Lopez [de Cardenas] as chronicler for the army. The villages of that province [of Tusayan] remained peaceful, since they were never visited again, nor was any attempt made to find other peoples in that direction.

Chapter 12

Of how people came from Cicuye to Cibola to see the Christians, and how Hernando de Alvarado went to see the cows.

While they were making these discoveries, some Indians came to Cibola from a village which was seventy leagues east of this province, called Cicuye. Among them was a captain who was called Bigotes (Whiskers) by our men, because he wore a long mustache. He was a tall, well-built young fellow, with a fine figure. He told the general that they had come in response to the notice which had been given, to offer themselves as friends, and that if we wanted to go through their country they would consider us as their friends. They brought a present of tanned hides and shields and head-pieces, which were very gladly received, and the general gave them some glass dishes and a number of pearls and little bells which they prized highly, because these were things they had never seen. They described some cows which, from a picture that one of them had painted on his skin, seemed to be cows, although from the hides this did not seem possible, because the hair was woolly and snarled so that we could not tell what sort of skins they had. The general ordered Hernando de Alvarado to take twenty companions and go with them, and gave him a commission for eighty days, after which he should return to give an account of what he had found.[1]

Captain Alvarado started on this journey and in five days reached a village which was on a rock called Acuco [2] having a population of about two hundred men. These people were robbers, feared by the whole country round about. The village was very strong, because it was up on a rock out of reach, having steep sides in every direction, and so high that it was a very good musket that could throw a ball as high. There was only one entrance by a stairway built by hand, which began at the top of a slope which is around the foot of the rock.[3] There was a broad stairway for about two hundred steps, then a stretch of about one hundred narrower steps, and at the top they had to go up about three times as high as a man by means of holes in the rock, in which they put the points of their feet,

---

[1] The report of Alvarado, translated by George Parker Winship, is published in the *Fourteenth Annual Report of the Bureau of Ethnology* (Washington, 1896).

[2] This is the pueblo of Acoma, about fifty miles east of Zuñi. It occupies the summit of the same rocky mesa, 357 feet high, that it did in Coronado's time. The name here given is doubtless an attempt to give the Zuñi designation, *Hákukia*, from *Ako*, the name by which it is known to the Acoma people. The present population is 650. Acoma has the distinction of being the oldest continuously occupied settlement in the United States.

[3] The slope referred to is an immense sand-dune. The horse trail did not exist in Coronado's time, having been built by Fray Juan Ramirez, who established a mission at Acoma in 1629.

holding on at the same time by their hands. There was a wall of large and small stones at the top, which they could roll down without showing themselves, so that no army could possibly be strong enough to capture the village. On the top they had room to sow and store a large amount of corn, and cisterns to collect snow and water.[1] These people came down to the plain ready to fight, and would not listen to any arguments. They drew lines on the ground and determined to prevent our men from crossing these, but when they saw that they would have to fight they offered to make peace before any harm had been done. They went through their forms of making peace, which is to touch the horses and take their sweat and rub themselves with it, and to make crosses with the fingers of the hands. But to make the most secure peace they put their hands across each other, and they keep this peace inviolably. They made a present of a large number of [turkey-] cocks with very big wattles, much bread, tanned deerskins, pine [piñon] nuts, flour [cornmeal], and corn.

From here they went to a province called Triguex,[2] three days distant. The people all came out peacefully, seeing that Whiskers was with them. These men are feared throughout all those provinces. Alvarado sent messengers back from here to advise the general to come and winter in this country. The general was not a little relieved to hear that the country was growing better. Five days from here he came to Cicuye,[3] a very strong village four stories high. The people came out from the village with signs of joy to welcome Hernando de Alvarado and their captain, and brought them into the town with drums and pipes something like flutes, of which they have a great many. They made many presents of cloth and turquoises, of which there are quantities in that region.[4] The Spaniards enjoyed themselves here for several days and talked with an Indian slave, a native of the country

---

[1] The Acomas still obtain their water supply from this source.
[2] Tiguex.   See p. 317, note.
[3] Pecos.   See p. 329, note 2.
[4] See p. 308, note 3.

toward Florida, which is the region Don Fernando de
Soto discovered. This fellow said that there were large
settlements in the farther part of that country. Hernando de Alvarado took him to guide them to the cows; but
he told them so many and such great things about the wealth
of gold and silver in his country that they did not care about
looking for cows, but returned after they had seen some few,
to report the rich news to the general. They called the Indian "Turk," because he looked like one. Meanwhile the general
had sent Don Garcia Lopez de Cardenas to Tiguex with men to
get lodgings ready for the army, which had arrived from Señora
about this time, before taking them there for the winter; and
when Hernando de Alvarado reached Tiguex, on his way back
from Cicuye, he found Don Garcia Lopez de Cardenas there,
and so there was no need for him to go farther. As it was
necessary that the natives should give the Spaniards lodging
places, the people in one village had to abandon it and go to
others belonging to their friends, and they took with them nothing but themselves and the clothes they had on. Information
was obtained here about many towns up toward the north, and
I believe that it would have been much better to follow this
direction than that of the Turk, who was the cause of all the
misfortunes which followed.

Chapter 13

*Of how the general went toward Tutahaco with a few men and
left the army with Don Tristan, who took it to Tiguex.*

Everything already related had happened when Don Tristan de Arellano reached Cibola from Señora. Soon after he
arrived, the general, who had received notice of a province containing eight villages, took thirty of the men who were most fully
rested and went to see it, going from there directly to Tiguex
with the skilled guides who conducted him. He left orders for
Don Tristan de Arellano to proceed to Tiguex by the direct
road, after the men had rested twenty days. On this journey,

between one day when they left the camping place and mid-day
of the third day, when they saw some snow-covered mountains, toward which they went in search of water, neither the
Spaniards nor the horses nor the servants drank anything.
They were able to stand it because of the severe cold, although
with great difficulty. In eight days they reached Tutahaco,[1]
where they learned that there were other towns down the river.
These people were peaceful. The villages are terraced, like
those at Tiguex, and of the same style. The general went up
the river from here, visiting the whole province, until he reached
Tiguex, where he found Hernando de Alvarado and the Turk.
He felt no slight joy at such good news, because the Turk said
that in his country there was a river in the level country which
was two leagues wide, in which there were fishes as big as horses,
and large numbers of very big canoes, with more than twenty
rowers on a side, and that they carried sails, and that their
lords sat on the poop under awnings, and on the prow they had
a great golden eagle. He said also that the lord of that country
took his afternoon nap under a great tree on which were hung
a great number of little gold bells, which put him to sleep as
they swung in the air. He said also that everyone had their
ordinary dishes made of wrought plate, and the jugs and bowls
were of gold. He called gold *acochis*. For the present he was
believed, on account of the ease with which he told it and because they showed him metal ornaments and he recognized
them and said they were not gold, and he knew gold and silver
very well and did not care anything about other metals.[2]

---

[1] This name has always been a problem to students of the expedition, and
various attempts have been made to determine its application. Jaramillo,
one of Coronado's captains, applies the name to Acoma, and indeed its final
syllables are the same as the native name of Acoma. In the heading to
Chapter 11 Castañeda erroneously makes Tutahaco synonymous with
Tusayan. The description indicates that the Tigua village of Isleta and
others in its vicinity on the Rio Grande in the sixteenth century were intended.

[2] This Eldorado is seemingly a combination of falsehood and misinterpre-
tation. The Turk's only means of communication were signs; and we shall
see later on that he deliberately deceived the Spaniards for the purpose of
leading them astray. The name *acochis* here given is an aid in the identification of the mysterious province of Quivira. See p. 337, note 1.

The general sent Hernando de Alvarado back to Cicuye to demand some gold bracelets which this Turk said they had taken from him at the time they captured him. Alvarado went, and was received as a friend at the village, and when he demanded the bracelets they said they knew nothing at all about them, saying the Turk was deceiving him and was lying. Captain Alvarado, seeing that there were no other means, got the captain Whiskers and the governor to come to his tent, and when they had come he put them in chains. The villagers prepared to fight, and let fly their arrows, denouncing Hernando de Alvarado, and saying that he was a man who had no respect for peace and friendship. Hernando de Alvarado started back to Tiguex, where the general kept them prisoners more than six months. This began the want of confidence in the word of the Spaniards whenever there was talk of peace from this time on, as will be seen by what happened afterward.

Chapter 14

Of how the army went from Cibola to Tiguex and what happened to them on the way, on account of the snow.

We have already said that when the general started from Cibola, he left orders for Don Tristan de Arellano to start twenty days later. He did so as soon as he saw that the men were well rested and provided with food and eager to start off to find their general. He set off with his force toward Tiguex, and the first day they made their camp in the best, largest, and finest village of that (Cibola) province.[1] This is the only village that has houses with seven stories. In this village certain houses are used as fortresses; they are higher than the others and set up above them like towers, and there are embrasures and loopholes in them for defending the roofs of the different

---

[1] This was Matsaki, at the northwestern base of Thunder Mountain, about three miles east of the present Zuñi and eighteen miles northeast of Hawikuh, where the advance force had encamped. The ruins may still be seen, but no standing walls are visible.

stories, because, like the other villages, they do not have streets, and the flat roofs are all of a height and are used in common. The roofs have to be reached first, and these upper houses are the means of defending them. It began to snow on us there, and the force took refuge under the wings of the village, which extend out like balconies, with wooden pillars beneath, because they generally use ladders to go up to those balconies, since they do not have any doors below.[1]

The army continued its march from here after it stopped snowing, and as the season had already advanced into December, during the ten days that the army was delayed, it did not fail to snow during the evenings and nearly every night, so that they had to clear away a large amount of snow when they came to where they wanted to make a camp. The road could not be seen, but the guides managed to find it, as they knew the country. There are junipers and pines all over the country, which they used in making large brushwood fires, the smoke and heat of which melted the snow from two to four yards all around the fire. It was a dry snow, so that although it fell on the baggage, and covered it for half a man's height, it did not hurt it. It fell all night long, covering the baggage and the soldiers and their beds, piling up in the air, so that if anyone had suddenly come upon the army nothing would have been seen but mountains of snow. The horses stood half buried in it. It kept those who were underneath warm instead of cold. The army passed by the great rock of Acuco,[2] and the natives, who were peaceful, entertained our men well, giving them provisions and birds, although there are not many people here, as I have said. Many of the gentlemen went up to the top to see it, and they had great difficulty in going up the steps in the rock, because they were not used to them, for the natives go up

---

[1] The first-story rooms were entered by means of hatchways through the roof. As the necessity for defence no longer exists, the rooms of the lower stories of Zuñi houses are provided with doors and windows.

[2] The army passed from Cibola by way of the present farming village of Pescado, Inscription Rock or El Morro (thirty miles east of Zuñi), and over the Zuñi Mountains to Acoma. Alvarado followed an almost impassable trail eastward from Hawikuh, across a great lava flow, to reach Acoma.

and down so easily that they carry loads and the women carry water, and they do not seem even to touch their hands, although our men had to pass their weapons up from one to another.

From here they went on to Tiguex, where they were well received and taken care of, and the great good news of the Turk gave no little joy and helped lighten their hard labors, although when the army arrived we found the whole country or province in revolt, for reasons which were not slight in themselves, as will be shown, and our men had also burnt a village the day before the army arrived, and returned to the camp.

Chapter 15

Of why Tiguex revolted, and how they were punished, without being to blame for it.

It has been related how the general reached Tiguex,[1] where he found Don Garcia Lopez de Cardenas and Hernando de Alvarado, and how he sent the latter back to Cicuye, where he took the captain Whiskers and the governor of the village, who was an old man, prisoners. The people of Tiguex did not feel well about this seizure. In addition to this, the general wished to obtain some clothing to divide among his soldiers, and for this purpose he summoned one of the chief Indians of Tiguex, with whom he had already had much inter-course and with whom he was on good terms, who was called Juan Aleman by our men, after a Juan Aleman who lived in Mexico, whom he was said to resemble. The general told him that he must furnish about three hundred or more pieces of cloth, which he needed to give his people. He said that he

---

[1] Tiguex (pronounced Tee-guaysh′) is the name of a group of Pueblo tribes, now consisting of Isleta, Sandia, Taos, and Picuris, speaking the Tigua language, as it is now designated. Their principal village in Coronado's time was also called Tiguex by the Spaniards; this was the Puaray of forty years later (1583), the first time the native name was recorded. It was situated at the site of Bernalillo, on the Rio Grande, and was inhabited up to the time of the Pueblo rebellion of 1680, when it contained two hundred Tiguas and Spaniards.

was not able to do this, but that it pertained to the governors;
and that besides this, they would have to consult together and
divide it among the villages, and that it was necessary to make
the demand of each town separately. The general did this,
and ordered certain of the gentlemen who were with him to go
and make the demand; and as there were twelve villages, some
of them went on one side of the river and some on the other.
As they were in very great need, they did not give the natives
a chance to consult about it, but when they came to a village
they demanded what they had to give, so that they could proceed at once. Thus these people could do nothing except take
off their own cloaks and give them to make up the number demanded of them. And some of the soldiers who were in these
parties, when the collectors gave them some blankets or cloaks
which were not such as they wanted, if they saw any Indian
with a better one on, they exchanged with him without more
ado, not stopping to find out the rank of the man they were
stripping, which caused not a little hard feeling.

Besides what I have just said, one whom I will not name, out
of regard for him, left the village where the camp was and went
to another village about a league distant, and seeing a pretty
woman there he called her husband down to hold his horse by
the bridle while he went up; and as the village was entered by
the upper story, the Indian supposed he was going to some
other part of it. While he was there the Indian heard some
slight noise, and then the Spaniard came down, took his horse,
and went away. The Indian went up and learned that he had
violated, or tried to violate, his wife, and so he came with the
important men of the town to complain that a man had violated
his wife, and he told how it happened. When the general
made all the soldiers and the persons who were with him come
together, the Indian did not recognize the man, either because
he had changed his clothes or for whatever other reason there
may have been, but he said that he could tell the horse, because
he had held his bridle, and so he was taken to the stables, and
found the horse, and said that the master of the horse must be
the man. He denied doing it, seeing that he had not been

recognized, and it may be that the Indian was mistaken in the horse; anyway, he went off without getting any satisfaction. The next day one of the Indians, who was guarding the horses of the army, came running in, saying that a companion of his had been killed, and that the Indians of the country were driving off the horses toward their villages. The Spaniards tried to collect the horses again, but many were lost, besides seven of the general's mules.[1]

The next day Don Garcia Lopez de Cardenas went to see the villages and talk with the natives. He found the villages closed by palisades and a great noise inside, the horses being chased as in a bull fight and shot with arrows. They were all ready for fighting. Nothing could be done, because they would not come down on to the plain and the villages are so strong that the Spaniards could not dislodge them. The general then ordered Don Garcia Lopez de Cardenas to go and surround one village with all the rest of the force. This village was the one where the greatest injury had been done and where the affair with the Indian woman occurred. Several captains who had gone on in advance with the general, Juan de Saldivar and Barrionuevo and Diego Lopez and Melgosa, took the Indians so much by surprise that they gained the upper story, with great danger, for they wounded many of our men from within the houses. Our men were on top of the houses in great danger for a day and a night and part of the next day, and they made some good shots with their crossbows and muskets. The horsemen on the plain with many of the Indian allies from New Spain smoked them out from the cellars [2] into which they had broken, so that they begged for peace. Pablo de Melgosa and Diego Lopez, the alderman from Seville, were left on the roof and answered the Indians with the same signs they were making for peace, which was to make a cross. They then put down

---

[1] Antonio de Espejo learned of this occurrence at "Puala" (Puaray) when the place was visited by him in 1583 (see *Documentos Inéditos de Indias*, XV. 175).

[2] The pueblos are not provided with cellars. The underground ceremonial chambers, or *kivas*, are doubtless here meant.

their arms and received pardon. They were taken to the tent
of Don Garcia, who, according to what he said, did not know
about the peace and thought that they had given themselves
up of their own accord because they had been conquered. As
he had been ordered by the general not to take them alive, but
to make an example of them so that the other natives would
fear the Spaniards, he ordered two hundred stakes to be prepared at once to burn them alive. Nobody told him about
the peace that had been granted them, for the soldiers knew
as little as he, and those who should have told him about it
remained silent, not thinking that it was any of their business.
Then when the enemies saw that the Spaniards were binding
them and beginning to roast them, about a hundred men who
were in the tent began to struggle and defend themselves with
what there was there and with the stakes they could seize.
Our men who were on foot attacked the tent on all sides, so
that there was great confusion around it, and then the horsemen chased those who escaped. As the country was level,
not a man of them remained alive, unless it was some who remained hidden in the village and escaped that night to spread
throughout the country the news that the strangers did not
respect the peace they had made, which afterward proved a
great misfortune. After this was over, it began to snow, and
they abandoned the village and returned to the camp just as
the army came from Cibola.

Chapter 16

*Of how they besieged Tiguex and took it and of what happened
during the siege.*

As I have already related, it began to snow in that country just after they captured the village, and it snowed so
much that for the next two months [1] it was impossible to do
anything except to go along the roads to advise them to make

[1] The altitude of Bernalillo is 5260 feet, and snowstorms are sometimes
severe.

peace and tell them that they would be pardoned and might
consider themselves safe, to which they replied that they did
not trust those who did not know how to keep good faith
after they had once given it, and that the Spaniards should
remember that they were keeping Whiskers prisoner and
that they did not keep their word when they burned those
who surrendered in the village. Don Garcia Lopez de
Cardenas was one of those who went to give this notice.
He started out with about thirty companions and went to
the village of Tiguex to talk with Juan Aleman. Although
they were hostile, they talked with him and said that if he
wished to talk with them he must dismount and they would
come out and talk with him about a peace, and that if he would
send away the horsemen and make his men keep away, Juan
Aleman and another captain would come out of the village and
meet him. Everything was done as they required, and then
when they approached they said that they had no arms and
that he must take his off. Don Garcia Lopez did this in order
to give them confidence, on account of his great desire to get
them to make peace. When he met them, Juan Aleman approached and embraced him vigorously, while the other two
who had come with him drew two mallets [1] which they had
hidden behind their backs and gave him two such blows over
his helmet that they almost knocked him senseless. Two of
the soldiers on horseback had been unwilling to go very far off,
even when he ordered them, and so they were near by and rode
up so quickly that they rescued him from their hands, although
they were unable to catch the enemies because the meeting was
so near the village that of the great shower of arrows which were
shot at them one arrow hit a horse and went through his nose.
The horsemen all rode up together and hurriedly carried off
their captain, without being able to harm the enemy, while
many of our men were dangerously wounded. They then
withdrew, leaving a number of men to continue the attack.
Don Garcia Lopez de Cardenas went on with a part of the force
to another village about half a league distant, because almost

---

[1] Wooden war-clubs.

all the people in this region had collected into these two villages. As they paid no attention to the demands made on them except by shooting arrows from the upper stories with loud yells, and would not hear of peace, he returned to his companions whom he had left to keep up the attack on Tiguex. A large number of those in the village came out and our men rode off slowly, pretending to flee, so that they drew the enemy on to the plain, and then turned on them and caught several of their leaders. The rest collected on the roofs of the village and the captain returned to his camp.

After this affair the general ordered the army to go and surround the village. He set out with his men in good order, one day, with several scaling ladders. When he reached the village, he encamped his force near by, and then began the siege; but as the enemy had had several days to provide themselves with stores, they threw down such quantities of rocks upon our men that many of them were laid out, and they wounded nearly a hundred with arrows, several of whom afterward died on account of the bad treatment by an unskillful surgeon who was with the army. The siege lasted fifty days, during which time several assaults were made. The lack of water was what troubled the Indians most. They dug a very deep well inside the village, but were not able to get water, and while they were making it, it fell in and killed thirty persons. Two hundred of the besieged died in the fights. One day when there was a hard fight, they killed Francisco de Obando, a captain who had been army-master all the time that Don Garcia Lopez de Cardenas was away making the discoveries already described, and also Francisco Pobares, a fine gentleman. Our men were unable to prevent them from carrying Francisco de Obando inside the village, which was regretted not a little, because he was a distinguished person, besides being honored on his own account, affable and much beloved, which was noticeable. One day, before the capture was completed, they asked to speak to us, and said that, since they knew we would not harm the women and children, they wished to surrender their women and sons, because they were using up their water. It was impossible to persuade them to make peace, as they said that the Spaniards would not keep an agreement made with them. So they gave up about a hundred persons, women and boys, who did not want to leave them. Don Lope de Urrea rode up in front of the town without his helmet and received the boys and girls in his arms, and when all of these had been surrendered, Don Lope begged them to make peace, giving them the strongest promises for their safety. They told him to go away, as they did not wish to trust themselves to people who had no regard for friendship or their own word which they had pledged. As he seemed unwilling to go away, one of them put an arrow in his bow ready to shoot, and threatened to shoot him with it unless he went off, and they warned him to put on his helmet, but he was unwilling to do so, saying that they would not hurt him as long as he stayed there. When the Indian saw that he did not want to go away, he shot and planted his arrow between the fore feet of the horse, and then put another arrow in his bow and repeated that if he did not go away he would really shoot him. Don Lope put on his helmet and slowly rode back to where the horsemen were, without receiving any harm from them. When they saw that he was really in safety, they began to shoot arrows in showers, with loud yells and cries. The general did not want to make an assault that day, in order to see if they could be brought in some way to make peace, which they would not consider.

Fifteen days later they decided to leave the village one night, and did so, taking the women in their midst. They started about the fourth watch, in the very early morning, on the side where the cavalry was. The alarm was given by those in the camp of Don Rodrigo Maldonado. The enemy attacked them and killed one Spaniard and a horse and wounded others, but they were driven back with great slaughter until they came to the river,[1] where the water flowed swiftly and very cold. They threw themselves into this, and as the men had come quickly from the whole camp to assist the cavalry,

[1] The Rio Grande, which is near by.

there were few who escaped being killed or wounded. Some
men from the camp went across the river next day and found
many of them who had been overcome by the great cold.
They brought these back, cured them, and made servants of
them. This ended that siege, and the town was captured, although there were a few who remained in one part of the town
and were captured a few days later.

Two captains, Don Diego de Guevara and Juan de Saldivar,
had captured the other large village after a siege. Having
started out very early one morning to make an ambuscade in
which to catch some warriors who used to come out every
morning to try to frighten our camp, the spies, who had been
placed where they could see when they were coming, saw the
people come out and proceed toward the country. The soldiers
left the ambuscade and went to the village and saw the people
fleeing. They pursued and killed large numbers of them.
At the same time those in the camp were ordered to go over
the town, and they plundered it, making prisoners of all the
people who were found in it, amounting to about a hundred
women and children. This siege ended the last of March, in
the year '42 [1541]. Other things had happened in the meantime, which would have been noticed, but that it would have
cut the thread. I have omitted them, but will relate them now,
so that it will be possible to understand what follows.

Chapter 17

*Of how messengers reached the army from the valley of Señora,
and how Captain Melchior Diaz died on the expedition
to the Firebrand River.*

We have already related how Captain Melchior Diaz crossed
the Firebrand River [Rio Colorado] on rafts, in order to continue
his discoveries farther in that direction. About the time the
siege ended, messengers reached the army from the city of San
Hieronimo with letters from Diego de Alarcon,[1] who had re-

[1] Should be Alcaraz. See Chapter 10.

mained there in the place of Melchior Diaz. These contained
the news that Melchior Diaz had died while he was conducting
his search, and that the force had returned without finding any
of the things they were after. It all happened in this fashion:

After they had crossed the river they continued their
search for the coast, which here turned back toward the
south,[1] or between south and east, because that arm of the sea
enters the land due north, and this river, which brings its
waters down from the north, flowing toward the south, enters
the head of the gulf.[2] Continuing in the direction they had
been going, they came to some sandbanks of hot ashes which
it was impossible to cross without being drowned as in the
sea. The ground they were standing on trembled like a sheet
of paper, so that it seemed as if there were lakes underneath
them. It seemed wonderful and like something infernal, for
the ashes to bubble up here in several places. After they had
gone away from this place, on account of the danger they
seemed to be in and of the lack of water, one day a greyhound
belonging to one of the soldiers chased some sheep which they
were taking along for food. When the captain noticed this,
he threw his lance at the dog while his horse was running, so
that it stuck up in the ground, and not being able to stop his
horse he went over the lance so that it nailed him through
the thighs and the iron came out behind, rupturing his blad-
der. After this the soldiers turned back with their captain,
having to fight every day with the Indians, who had remained hostile. He lived about twenty days, during which
they proceeded with great difficulty on account of the necessity of carrying him. They returned in good order without
losing a man, until he died, and after that they were relieved
of the greatest difficulty. When they reached Señora, Alcaraz
despatched the messengers already referred to, so that the
general might know of this and also that some of the soldiers

---

[1] That is, the west coast of the Gulf of California.

[2] During 1905 the waters of the Rio Colorado were diverted westward
below Yuma and are now (1906) flowing into the Salton Sink, or Imperial
Valley, in southern California, forming an immense lake.

were ill-disposed and had caused several mutinies, and that he had sentenced two of them to the gallows, but they had afterward escaped from the prison.

When the general learned this, he sent Don Pedro de Tovar to that city to sift out some of the men. He was accompanied by messengers whom the general sent to Don Antonio de Mendoza the viceroy, with an account of what had occurred and with the good news given by the Turk. When Don Pedro de Tovar arrived there, he found that the natives of that province had killed a soldier with a poisoned arrow, which had made only a very little wound in one hand.[1] Several soldiers went to the place where this happened to see about it, and they were not very well received. Don Pedro de Tovar sent Diego de Alcaraz with a force to seize the chiefs and lords of a village in what they call the Valley of Knaves (*de los Vellacos*), which is in the hills. After getting there and getting these men prisoners, Diego de Alcaraz decided to let them go in exchange for some thread and cloth and other things which the soldiers needed. Finding themselves free, they renewed the war and attacked them, and as they were strong and had poison, they killed several Spaniards and wounded others so that they died on the way back. They retired toward the town, and if they had not had Indian allies from the country of the Hearts, it would have gone worse with them. They got back to the town, leaving seventeen soldiers dead from the poison. They would die in agony from only a small wound, the bodies breaking out with an insupportable pestilential stench. When Don Pedro de Tovar saw the harm done, and as it seemed to them that they could not safely stay in that city, he moved forty leagues toward Cibola into the valley of Suya,[2] where we will leave them, in order to relate what happened to the general and his army after the siege of Tiguex.

---

[1] Doubtless the Opatas, whose poisoned arrows are often alluded to by later Spanish writers. See, for example, the *Rudo Ensayo* (ca. 1762), (San Augustin, 1863); also Guiteras's translation in *Records of the American Catholic Historical Society*, V. No. 2 (Philadelphia, June, 1894).

[2] The upper part of the Rio San Pedro (which rises in northern Sonora), according to recent studies by Mr. James Newton Baskett.

Chapter 18

*Of how the general managed to leave the country in peace so as
to go in search of Quivira, where the Turk said there
was the most wealth.*

During the siege of Tiguex the general decided to go to
Cicuye and take the governor with him, in order to give him
his liberty and to promise them that he would give Whiskers
his liberty and leave him in the village, as soon as he should
start for Quivira.   He was received peacefully when he reached
Cicuye, and entered the village with several soldiers.   They
received their governor with much joy and gratitude.   After
looking over the village and speaking with the natives he
returned to his army, leaving Cicuye at peace, in the hope of
getting back their captain Whiskers.

After the siege was ended, as we have already related, he
sent a captain to Chia,[1] a fine village with many people, which
had sent to offer its submission.   It was four leagues distant
to the west of the river.[2]   They found it peaceful and gave it
four bronze cannon, which were in poor condition, to take
care of.   Six gentlemen also went to Quirix, a province with
seven villages.[3]   At the first village, which had about a hundred inhabitants, the natives fled, not daring to wait for our
men; but they headed them off by a short cut, riding at full
speed, and then they returned to their houses in the village

[1] The present Sia, a small pueblo on the Rio Jemez.   In 1583 Sia was one
of a group of five pueblos which Antonio de Espejo called Cunames or Puna-
mes.   It suffered severely by the Pueblo revolt a century later, and is now
reduced to about a hundred people who have great difficulty in gaining a
livelihood, owing to lack of water for irrigation.

[2] That is, the Rio Grande.

[3] The "province" occupied by the Queres or Keresan Indians, consisting
of the pueblos of Cochiti, San Felipe, and Santo Domingo, of to-day — all
on the Rio Grande.   Sia and Santa Ana are and were also Queres villages in
Coronado's time, but as these were not on the Rio Grande, they may not
have been included in Castañeda's group.   When Espejo visited the Queres
in 1583, they occupied only five pueblos on the Rio Grande; now only the
three above mentioned are inhabited.

in perfect safety, and then told the other villagers about it and reassured them. In this way the entire region was reassured, little by little, by the time the ice in the river was broken up and it became possible to ford the river and so to continue the journey. The twelve villages of Tiguex, however, were not repopulated at all during the time the army was there, in spite of every promise of security that could possibly be given to them.

And when the river, which for almost four months had been frozen over so that they crossed the ice on horseback, had thawed out, orders were given for the start for Quivira,[1] where the Turk said there was some gold and silver, although not so much as in Arche [2] and the Guaes.[3] There were already some in the army who suspected the Turk, because a Spaniard named Servantes, who had charge of him during the siege, solemnly swore that he had seen the Turk talking with the devil in a pitcher of water, and also that while he had him under lock so that no one could speak to him, the Turk had asked him what Christians had been killed by the people at Tiguex. He told him "nobody," and then the Turk answered: "You lie; five Christians are dead, including a captain." And as Cervantes knew that he told the truth, he confessed it so as to find out who had told him about it, and the Turk said he knew it all by himself and that he did not need to have anyone tell him in order to know it. And it was on account of this that he watched him and saw him speaking to the devil in the pitcher, as I have said.

While all this was going on, preparations were being made to start from Tiguex. At this time people came from Cibola to see the general, and he charged them to take good care of the Spaniards who were coming from Señora with Don Pedro de Tovar. He gave them letters to give to Don Pedro, informing

---

[1] See p. 337, note 1.

[2] Evidently the Harahey of other chroniclers, which has been identified with the Pawnee country of southern Nebraska.

[3] Possibly the Kansa or Kaw tribe, after whom the state of Kansas is named.

him what he ought to do and how he should go to find the
army, and that he would find letters under the crosses which
the army would put up along the way.　The army left Tiguex
on the fifth of May [1] and returned to Cicuye, which, as I have
said, is twenty-five marches, which means leagues, from there,
taking Whiskers with them.[2]　Arrived there, he gave them
their captain, who already went about freely with a guard.
The village was very glad to see him, and the people were
peaceful and offered food.　The governor and Whiskers gave
the general a young fellow called Xabe, a native of Quivira,
who could give them information about the country.　This
fellow said that there was gold and silver, but not so much of
it as the Turk had said.　The Turk, however, continued to
declare that it was as he had said.　He went as a guide, and
thus the army started off from here.

Chapter 19

*Of how they started in search of Quivira and of what happened
on the way.*

The army started from Cicuye, leaving the village at peace
and, as it seemed, contented, and under obligations to main-
tain the friendship because their governor and captain had
been restored to them.　Proceeding toward the plains, which are
all on the other side of the mountains, after four days' journey
they came to a river with a large, deep current, which flowed
from toward Cicuyc, and they named this the Cicuyc river.
They had to stop here to make a bridge so as to cross it.[3]　It

---

[1] In his letter to the King, dated Tiguex October 20, 1541, Coronado says
that he started April 23.　See Winship's translation in *Fourteenth Report
of the Bureau of Ethnology* (1896), p. 580.

[2] Cicuye is Pecos, as above mentioned.　The direction is north of east and
the distance forty miles in an air line, or fifteen Spanish judicial leagues.
By rail, which follows almost exactly the old trail, the distance is sixty-five
miles, or almost precisely twenty-five leagues.

[3] The Rio Pecos.　The bridge was doubtless built across the stream
somewhere near Puerto de Luna.　The Ms. here reads Cicuyc for Cicuye.

was finished in four days, by much diligence and rapid work, and as soon as it was done the whole army and the animals crossed. After ten days more they came to some settlements of people who lived like Arabs and who are called Querechos [1] in that region. They had seen the cows [2] for two days. These folks live in tents made of the tanned skins of the cows. They travel around near the cows, killing them for food. They did nothing unusual when they saw our army, except to come out of their tents to look at us, after which they came to talk with the advance guard, and asked who we were. The general talked with them, but as they had already talked with the Turk, who was with the advance guard, they agreed with what he had said. That they were very intelligent is evident from the fact that although they conversed by means of signs they made themselves understood so well that there was no need of an interpreter. [3] They said that there was a very large river over toward where the sun came from, and that one could go along this river through an inhabited region for ninety days without a break from settlement to settlement. They said that the first of these settlements was called Haxa, [4] and that the river was more than a league wide and that there were many canoes on it. [5] These folks started off from here next day with a lot of dogs which dragged their possessions. For two days, during which the army marched in the same direction as that in which they had come from the settlements — that is, between north and east, but more toward the north — they saw other roaming Querechos and such great numbers of cows that it already seemed something incredible.

[1] The name by which the eastern Apaches, or Apaches Vaqueros of later times, were known to the Pecos Indians. The first Querechos were met near the eastern boundary of New Mexico.

[2] Wherever "cows" are mentioned, bison are of course meant. Herds of these animals ranged as far as the Pecos, which was known as the Rio de las Vacas later in the century.

[3] All the Indians of the great plains were expert in the sign language, as their spoken languages were many and diverse.

[4] The place has not been identified with certainty.

[5] This river, if it existed at all, was in all probability the lower Arkansas or the Mississippi, hundreds of miles away.

These people gave a great deal of information about settlements, all toward the east from where we were.   Here Don
Garcia broke his arm and a Spaniard got lost who went off
hunting so far that he was unable to return to the camp, because the country is very level.   The Turk said it was one or
two days to Haya (Haxa).[1]   The general sent Captain Diego
Lopez with ten companions lightly equipped and a guide to
go at full speed toward the sunrise for two days and discover
Haxa, and then return to meet the army, which set out in the
same direction next day.   They came across so many animals
that those who were on the advance guard killed a large number of bulls.   As these fled they trampled one another in their
haste until they came to a ravine.   So many of the animals
fell into this that they filled it up, and the rest went across on
top of them.   The men who were chasing them on horseback
fell in among the animals without noticing where they were
going.   Three of the horses that fell in among the cows, all
saddled and bridled, were lost sight of completely.

As it seemed to the general that Diego Lopez ought to be
on his way back, he sent six of his companions to follow up
the banks of the little river, and as many more down the banks,
to look for traces of the horses at the trails to and from the
river.   It was impossible to find tracks in this country, because the grass straightened up again as soon as it was trodden
down.   They were found by some Indians from the army who
had gone to look for fruit.   These got track of them a good
league off, and soon came up with them.   They followed the
river down to the camp, and told the general that in the
twenty leagues they had been over they had seen nothing but
cows and the sky.   There was another native of Quivira with
the army, a painted Indian named Ysopete.   This Indian had
always declared that the Turk was lying, and on account of

---

[1] The Turk was evidently lying, at least so far as the distance was concerned.   The Texas Indians were not canoeists.   The army was now in the
western part of the staked plains of Texas, but had changed its course from
northeasterly to south of east.   The country is greatly broken by the cañons
of the streams which take their rise in these parts.

this the army paid no attention to him, and even now, although he said that the Querechos had consulted with him, Ysopete was not believed.

The general sent Don Rodrigo Maldonado, with his company, forward from here. He travelled four days and reached a large ravine like those of Colima, in the bottom of which he found a large settlement of people. Cabeza de Vaca and Dorantes had passed through this place,[1] so that they presented Don Rodrigo with a pile of tanned skins and other things, and a tent as big as a house, which he directed them to keep until the army came up. He sent some of his companions to guide the army to that place, so that they should not get lost, although he had been making piles of stones and cow-dung for the army to follow. This was the way in which the army was guided by the advance guard.

When the general came up with the army and saw the great quantity of skins, he thought he would divide them among the men, and placed guards so that they could look at them. But when the men arrived and saw that the general was sending some of his companions with orders for the guards to give them some of the skins, and that these were going to select the best, they were angry because they were not going to be divided evenly, and made a rush, and in less than a quarter of an hour nothing was left but the empty ground.

The natives who happened to see this also took a hand in it. The women and some others were left crying, because they thought that the strangers were not going to take anything, but would bless them as Cabeza de Vaca and Dorantes had done when they passed through here. They found an Indian girl here who was as white as a Castilian lady,[2] except that she had her chin painted like a Moorish woman. In general they all paint themselves in this way here, and they decorate their eyes.

---

[1] See Cabeza de Vaca's narration in this volume, p. 97.
[2] Probably an albino is here referred to.

Chapter 20

Of how great stones fell in the camp, and how they discovered another ravine, where the army was divided into two parts.

While the army was resting in this ravine, as we have related, a tempest came up one afternoon with a very high wind and hail, and in a very short space of time a great quantity of hailstones, as big as bowls, or bigger, fell as thick as raindrops, so that in places they covered the ground two or three spans or more deep. And one hit the horse — or I should say, there was not a horse that did not break away, except two or three which the negroes protected by holding large sea nets over them, with the helmets and shields which all the rest wore; and some of them dashed up on to the sides of the ravine so that they got them down with great difficulty. If this had struck them while they were upon the plain, the army would have been in great danger of being left without its horses, as there were many which they were not able to cover. The hail broke many tents, and battered many helmets, and wounded many of the horses, and broke all the crockery of the army, and the gourds, which was no small loss, because they do not have any crockery in this region. They do not make gourds, nor sow corn, nor eat bread, but instead raw meat — or only half cooked — and fruit.[1]

From here the general sent out to explore the country, and they found another settlement four days from there [2] . . . . The country was well inhabited, and they had plenty of kidney beans and prunes like those of Castile, and tall vineyards. These village settlements extended for three days. This was called Cona. Some Teyas,[3] as these people are called, went with

[1] Castañeda here refers to the buffalo-hunting Indians in contrast to the Pueblo tribes which the Spaniards had left.

[2] "*A manera de alixares.*" The margin reads *Alexeres*, a word meaning "threshing floor."

[3] These were evidently the Indians later called Tejas, or Texas, from which the state took its name. The name was indiscriminately applied by various later writers, but always to one of the Caddoan tribes or group of tribes.

the army from here and travelled as far as the end of the other settlements with their packs of dogs and women and children, and then they gave them guides to proceed to a large ravine where the army was. They did not let these guides speak with the Turk, and did not receive the same statements from these as they had from the others. These said that Quivira was toward the north, and that we should not find any good road thither. After this they began to believe Ysopete. The ravine which the army had now reached was a league wide from one side to the other, with a little bit of a river at the bottom, and there were many groves of mulberry trees near it, and rosebushes with the same sort of fruit that they have in France. They made verjuice from the unripe grapes at this ravine, although there were ripe ones. There were walnuts and the same kind of fowls as in New Spain, and large quantities of prunes like those of Castile. During this journey a Teya was seen to shoot a bull right through both shoulders with an arrow, which would be a good shot for a musket. These people are very intelligent; the women are well made and modest. They cover their whole body. They wear shoes and buskins made of tanned skin. The women wear cloaks over their small under petticoats, with sleeves gathered up at the shoulders, all of skin, and some wore something like little *sanbenitos* [1] with a fringe, which reached half-way down the thigh over the petticoat.

The army rested several days in this ravine and explored the country. Up to this point they had made thirty-seven days' marches, travelling six or seven leagues a day.[2] It had been the duty of one man to measure and count his steps.

---

[1] "We were brought into the Church, every one with a S. Benito upon his backe, which is a halfe a yard of yellow cloth, with a hole to put in a mans head in the middest, and cast over a mans head: both flaps hang one before, and another behinde, and in the middest of every flap, a S. Andrewes crosse, made of red cloth, sowed on upon the same, and that is called S. Benito."— Robert Tomson, "Voyage into Nova Hispania," 1555, in Hakluyt, *Voyages*, IX. 348 (1904).

[2] The league is equivalent to 2.63 English miles. This Spanish judicial league is still used in Mexico.

They found that it was 250 leagues to the settlements.[1] When
the general Francisco Vazquez realized this, and saw that
they had been deceived by the Turk heretofore, and as the
provisions were giving out and there was no country around
here where they could procure more, he called the captains
and ensigns together to decide on what they thought ought
to be done. They all agreed that the general should go in
search of Quivira with thirty horsemen and half a dozen foot-
soldiers, and that Don Tristan de Arellano should go back to
Tiguex with all the army. When the men in the army learned
of this decision, they begged their general not to leave them
to conduct the further search, but declared that they all
wanted to die with him and did not want to go back. This
did not do any good, although the general agreed to send
messengers to them within eight days saying whether it was
best for them to follow him or not, and with this he set off
with the guides he had and with Ysopete. The Turk was
taken along in chains.

Chapter 21

*Of how the army returned to Tiguex and the general reached
Quivira.*

The general started from the ravine with the guides that
the Teyas had given him. He appointed the alderman Diego
Lopez his army-master, and took with him the men who
seemed to him to be most efficient, and the best horses. The
army still had some hope that the general would send for
them, and sent two horsemen, lightly equipped and riding
post, to repeat their petition.

The general arrived — I mean, the guides ran away during the first few days and Diego Lopez had to return to the
army for guides, bringing orders for the army to return to
Tiguex to find food and wait there for the general. The Teyas,
as before, willingly furnished him with new guides. The army

[1] The Tiguex villages on the Rio Grande are often referred to as the region
where the settlements were.

waited for its messengers and spent a fortnight here, preparing
jerked beef to take with them. It was estimated that during
this fortnight they killed 500 bulls. The number of these
that were there without any cows was something incredible.
Many fellows were lost at this time who went out hunting and
did not get back to the army for two or three days, wandering
about the country as if they were crazy, in one direction or
another, not knowing how to get back where they started
from, although this ravine extended in either direction so that
they could find it. Every night they took account of who
was missing, fired guns and blew trumpets and beat drums
and built great fires, but yet some of them went off so far and
wandered about so much that all this did not give them any
help, although it helped others. The only way was to go back
where they had killed an animal and start from there in one
direction and another until they struck the ravine or fell in
with somebody who could put them on the right road. It is
worth noting that the country there is so level that at midday,
after one has wandered about in one direction and another in
pursuit of game, the only thing to do is to stay near the game
quietly until sunset, so as to see where it goes down, and even
then they have to be men who are practised to do it. Those
who are not, had to trust themselves to others.[1]

The general followed his guides until he reached Quivira,
which took forty-eight days' marching, on account of the great
detour they had made toward Florida.[2] He was received
peacefully on account of the guides whom he had. They
asked the Turk why he had lied and had guided them so far
out of their way. He said that his country was in that direction and that, besides this, the people at Cicuye had asked
him to lead them off on to the plains and lose them, so that
the horses would die when their provisions gave out, and they

---

[1] The point of separation of the army was in all probability the upper
waters of the Rio Colorado in Texas. See the narration of Cabeza de Vaca,
p. 97, note 2.

[2] That is, toward the southeast. At a somewhat later period Florida
included everything from the peninsula northward.

would be so weak if they ever returned that they could be killed without any trouble, and thus they could take revenge for what had been done to them. This was the reason why he had led them astray, supposing that they did not know how to hunt or to live without corn, while as for the gold, he did not know where there was any of it. He said this like one who had given up hope and who found that he was being persecuted, since they had begun to believe Ysopete, who had guided them better than he had, and fearing lest those who were there might give some advice by which some harm would come to him. They garroted him, which pleased Ysopete very much, because he had always said that Ysopete was a rascal and that he did not know what he was talking about and had always hindered his talking with anybody. Neither gold nor silver nor any trace of either was found among these people. Their lord wore a copper plate on his neck and prized it highly.[1]

[1] For additional details respecting the route pursued by Coronado after the main army was sent back, consult the narrative of Jaramillo, the *Relacion del Suceso*, and other documents pertaining to the expedition, in Winship's *Coronado Expedition* (1896) and *Journey of Coronado* (1904), and in connection therewith a discussion of the route by F. W. Hodge, in J. V. Brower's *Memoirs of Explorations in the Basin of the Mississippi*, II. (St. Paul, 1899). Continuing due north from the upper waters of the Rio Colorado of Texas, Coronado's immediate force in thirty days' march, according to the *Relacion del Suceso* (or "more than thirty days' march, although not long marches," according to Jaramillo), reached the river of St. Peter and St. Paul the last of June, 1541. This was the "river of Quivira" of the *Relacion del Suceso*, the present Arkansas River in Kansas, which was crossed at its southern bend, just east of the present Dodge City. The party continued thence northeast, downstream, and in thirty leagues, or six or seven days' march, reached the first of the Quivira settlements. This was at or near the present Great Bend, Kansas, before reaching the site of which the Turk was "made an example of." That the inhabitants of Quivira were the Wichita Indians there can be no reasonable doubt. The Quivira people lived in grass or straw lodges, according to the Spaniards, a fact that was true of the Wichitas only of all the northern plains tribes. The habitations of their congeners and northern neighbors, the Pawnee (who may be regarded as the inhabitants of the province of Harahey), were earth lodges. The word *acochis*, mentioned by Castañeda as the Quivira term for "gold," is merely the Spanish adaptation of *hakwichis*, which signifies "metal," for of gold our Indians knew nothing until after the advent of the white man. After

z

The messengers whom the army had sent to the general returned, as I said, and then, as they brought no news except what the alderman had delivered, the army left the ravine and returned to the Teyas, where they took guides who led them back by a more direct road. They readily furnished these, because these people are always roaming over this country in pursuit of the animals and so know it thoroughly. They keep their road in this way: In the morning they notice where the sun rises and observe the direction they are going to take, and then shoot an arrow in this direction. Before reaching this they shoot another over it, and in this way they go all day toward the water where they are to end the day. In this way they covered in twenty-five days what had taken them thirty-seven days going, besides stopping to hunt cows on the way. They found many salt lakes on this road, and there was a great quantity of salt. There were thick pieces of it on top of the water bigger than tables, as thick as four or five fingers. Two or three spans down under water there was salt which tasted better than that in the floating pieces, because this was rather bitter. It was crystalline. All over these plains there were large numbers of animals like squirrels [1] and a great number of their holes. On its return the army reached the Cicuye river more than thirty leagues below there — I mean below the bridge they had made when they crossed it, and they followed it up to that place.[2] In general, its banks are covered with a sort of rose bushes, the fruit of which tastes like muscatel grapes. They grow on little twigs about as high up as a man. It has the parsley leaf. There were unripe grapes and currants (?) and wild marjoram. The guides said this river joined that of Tiguex more than twenty days from here,

exploring Quivira for twenty-five leagues, Coronado sent "captains and men in many directions," but they failed to find that of which they went in search. There is no reason to suppose that Coronado's party went beyond the limits of the present state of Kansas.

[1] Prairie-dogs.

[2] This would make the point at which the army reached Pecos River about eighty miles below Puerto de Luna, or not far from the present town of Roswell.

and that its course turned toward the east. It is believed that
it flows into the mighty river of the Holy Spirit (Espiritu
Santo), which the men with Don Hernando de Soto discovered
in Florida.[1] A painted Indian woman ran away from Juan
de Saldibar and hid in the ravines about this time, because
she recognized the country of Tiguex where she had been a
slave. She fell into the hands of some Spaniards who had
entered the country from Florida to explore it in this direction.[2] After I got back to New Spain I heard them say that
the Indian told them that she had run away from other men
like them nine days, and that she gave the names of some
captains; from which we ought to believe that we were not
far from the region they discovered, although they said they
were more than 200 leagues inland. I believe the land at
that point is more than 600 leagues across from sea to sea.

As I said, the army followed the river up as far as Cicuye,
which it found ready for war and unwilling to make any advances toward peace or to give any food to the army. From
there they went on to Tiguex where several villages had been
reinhabited, but the people were afraid and left them again.

Chapter 22

*Of how the general returned from Quivira and of other expedi-
tions toward the North.*

After Don Tristan de Arellano reached Tiguex, about the
middle of July, in the year '42,[3] he had provisions collected
for the coming winter. Captain Francisco de Barrionuevo
was sent up the river toward the north with several men. He
saw two provinces, one of which was called Hemes [4] and had

---

[1] Castañeda is writing about twenty years later. De Soto's army was
exploring the eastern country as Coronado was traversing the buffalo
plains. The Espiritu Santo is the Mississippi.

[2] See the Gentleman of Elvas in the second part of the present volume.

[3] As usual Castañeda gives a date a year later than the actual one.

[4] The pueblos occupied by the Jemez people. Only one of these now exists; this is on the Rio Jemez, a western tributary of the Rio Grande, which
enters the latter stream above Bernalillo, New Mexico. See p. 359, note 2.

seven villages, and the other Yuqueyunque.[1] The inhabitants
of Hemes came out peaceably and furnished provisions. At
Yuqueyunque the whole nation left two very fine villages
which they had on either side of the river entirely vacant, and
went into the mountains, where they had four very strong villages in a rough country, where it was impossible for horses to
go.[2] In the two villages there was a great deal of food and some
very beautiful glazed earthenware with many figures and different shapes.[3] Here they also found many bowls full of a
carefully selected shining metal with which they glazed the
earthenware. This shows that mines of silver would be found
in that country if they should hunt for them.

There was a large and powerful river, I mean village, which
was called Braba, twenty leagues farther up the river, which
our men called Valladolid.[4] The river flowed through the
middle of it. The natives crossed it by wooden bridges, made

[1] This was Yukiwingge, on the site of the present small village of Chamita,
at the mouth of the Rio Chama, opposite San Juan pueblo. The other one
of the two villages was doubtless San Juan. Both of these were occupied
by Tewa Indians. At Yukiwingge was established, in 1598, by Juan de
Oñate, the colonizer of New Mexico, the settlement of San Gabriel de los
Españoles, which was occupied until the spring of 1605, when the seat of the
provincial government was moved to Santa Fé, founded for the purpose in
that year. See p. 359, note 4.

[2] These may have been the pueblos, now in ruins, in and north of the
Pajarito Park, one of which, called Puye, gives evidence of occupancy in
post-Spanish times.

[3] It is not known definitely whether actually glazed pottery or merely
the black, highly polished earthenware characteristic of the Tewa Indians of
the neighborhood is here meant. The ancient Pueblos manufactured a ware
with decoration in what appears to be a salt glaze. Specimens of this have
been gathered in the Pajarito Park, at Zuñi, among the Hopi of Arizona, and
from ancient ruins around Acoma, but the art seems to have been lost.
There is abundant evidence that this form of decoration was prehistoric.
The finding of the "shining metal" (called antimony in Pt. 2, chap. 4)
would seem to indicate that the polished rather than the glazed ware was
here meant.

[4] This was the pueblo of Taos, which stood near the site of the present
village of the same name, on both sides of the little stream (Taos River).
The present Taos has 425 inhabitants. The swift and deep river without
the ford, here referred to, must have been the Rio Grande in the neighborhood of Taos, rather than the Rio de Taos, which is insignificant except in
seasons of freshet. Castañeda was evidently not one of Barrionuevo's party.

of very long, large, squared pines. At this village they saw
the largest and finest hot rooms or estufas that there were in
the entire country, for they had a dozen pillars, each one of
which was twice as large around as one could reach and twice
as tall as a man. Hernando de Alvarado visited this village
when he discovered Cicuye. The country is very high and
very cold.[1] The river is deep and very swift, without any ford.
Captain Barrionuevo returned from here, leaving the province
at peace.

Another captain went down the river in search of the settlements which the people at Tutahaco had said were several
days distant from there. This captain went down eighty
leagues and found four large villages which he left at peace.[2]
He proceeded until he found that the river sank into the earth,
like the Guadiana in Estremadura.[3] He did not go on to where
the Indians said that it came out much larger, because his
commission did not extend for more than eighty leagues' march.
After this captain got back, as the time had arrived which the
captain had set for his return from Quivira, and as he had not
come back, Don Tristan selected forty companions and, leaving the army to Francisco de Barrionuevo, he started with them
in search of the general. When he reached Cicuye the people
came out of the village to fight, which detained him there four
days, while he punished them, which he did by firing some
volleys into the village. These killed several men, so that
they did not come out against the army, since two of their
principal men had been killed on the first day. Just then
word was brought that the general was coming, and so Don

---

[1] The altitude of Taos is 6983 feet ; of Taos Peak, 13,145 feet.

[2] Seemingly the Piros villages on the Rio Grande south of Isleta. They
are now extinct, having been finally abandoned during the revolt in 1680,
the inhabitants fleeing with Governor Otermin to El Paso. Senecu and Socorro (taking their names from former villages) were afterward established
below El Paso, where the few survivors of the Piros, almost entirely Mexicanized, still reside.

[3] This rendering, doubtless correct, is due to Ternaux. The Guadiana,
however, reappears above ground some time before it begins to mark the
boundary of the Spanish province of Estremadura. The Castañeda family
had its seat in quite the other end of the peninsula. (Winship.)

Tristan had to stay there on this account also, to keep the road open. Everybody welcomed the general on his arrival, with great joy. The Indian Xabe, who was the young fellow who had been given to the general at Cicuye when he started off in search of Quivira, was with Don Tristan de Arellano and when he learned that the general was coming he acted as if he was greatly pleased, and said, "Now when the general comes, you will see that there are gold and silver in Quivira, although not so much as the Turk said." When the general arrived, and Xabe saw that they had not found anything, he was sad and silent, and kept declaring that there was some. He made many believe that it was so, because the general had not dared to enter into the country on account of its being thickly settled and his force not very strong, and that he had returned to lead his army there after the rains, because it had begun to rain there already, as it was early in August when he left. It took him forty days to return, travelling lightly equipped. The Turk had said when they left Tiguex that they ought not to load the horses with too much provisions, which would tire them so that they could not afterward carry the gold and silver, from which it is very evident that he was deceiving them.

The general reached Cicuye with his force and at once set off for Tiguex, leaving the village more quiet, for they had met him peaceably and had talked with him. When he reached Tiguex, he made his plans to pass the winter there, so as to return with the whole army, because it was said that he brought information regarding large settlements and very large rivers, and that the country was very much like that of Spain in the fruits and vegetation and seasons. They were not ready to believe that there was no gold there, but instead had suspicions that there was some farther back in the country, because, although this was denied, they knew what the thing was and had a name for it among themselves — *acochis*.[1] With this we end this first part, and now we will give an account of the provinces.

[1] See p. 337, note 1.

SECOND PART

*Which treats of the high villages and provinces and of their
habits and customs, as collected by Pedro de Castañeda,
native of the city of Najara.*

Laus Deo

It does not seem to me that the reader will be satisfied with
having seen and understood what I have already related about
the expedition, although that has made it easy to see the difference between the report which told about vast treasures,
and the places where nothing like this was either found or
known. It is to be noted that in place of settlements great
deserts were found, and instead of populous cities villages of
200 inhabitants and only 800 or 1000 people in the largest.
I do not know whether this will furnish grounds for pondering
and considering the uncertainty of this life. To please these,
I wish to give a detailed account of all the inhabited region
seen and discovered by this expedition, and some of their
ceremonies and habits, in accordance with what we came to
know about them, and the limits within which each province
falls, so that hereafter it may be possible to understand in
what direction Florida lies and in what direction Greater India;
and this land of New Spain is part of the mainland with Peru,
and with greater India or China as well, there not being any
strait between to separate them. On the other hand, the
country is so wide that there is room for these vast deserts
which lie between the two seas, for the coast of the North
sea beyond Florida stretches toward the Bacallaos [1] and then
turns toward Norway, while that of the South sea turns toward
the west, making another bend down toward the south almost
like a bow and stretches away toward India, leaving room for
the lands that border on the mountains on both sides to stretch
out in such a way as to have between them these great plains
which are full of cattle and many other animals of different

[1] The Newfoundland region.

sorts, since they are not inhabited, as I will relate farther on. There is every sort of game and fowl there, but no snakes, for they are free from these. I will leave the account of the return of the army to New Spain until I have shown what slight occasion there was for this. We will begin our account with the city of Culiacan, and point out the differences between the one country and the other, on account of which one ought to be settled by Spaniards and the other not. It should be the reverse, however, with Christians, since there are intelligent men in one, and in the other wild animals and worse than beasts.

Chapter 1

Of the province of Culiacan and of its habits and customs.

Culiacan is the last place in the New Kingdom of Galicia, and was the first settlement made by Nuño de Guzman when he conquered this kingdom.[1] It is 210 leagues west of Mexico.[2] In this province there are three chief languages, besides other related dialects. The first is that of the Tahus, who are the best and most intelligent race. They are now the most settled and have received the most light from the faith. They worship idols and make presents to the devil of their goods and riches, consisting of cloth and turquoises. They do not eat human flesh nor sacrifice it. They are accustomed to keep very large snakes, which they venerate. Among them there are men dressed like women who marry other men and serve as their wives. At a great festival they consecrate the women who wish to live unmarried, with much singing and dancing, at which all the chiefs of the locality gather and dance naked, and after all have danced with her they put her in a hut that has been decorated for this event and the chiefs

---

[1] See p. 285, note 1.

[2] Castañeda, like many other early Spanish chroniclers, is careless in his directions. It will be observed that he frequently says west, east, etc., when he means westwardly, eastwardly. This has led one writer on the Coronado expedition seriously astray. Culiacan is decidedly *northwest* of Mexico City.

adorn her with clothes and bracelets of fine turquoises, and then the chiefs go in one by one to lie with her, and all the others who wish, follow them. From this time on these women can not refuse anyone who pays them a certain amount agreed on for this. Even if they take husbands, this does not exempt them from obliging anyone who pays them. The greatest festivals are on market days. The custom is for the husbands to buy the women whom they marry, of their fathers and relatives at a high price, and then to take them to a chief, who is considered to be a priest, to deflower them and see if she is a virgin; and if she is not, they have to return the whole price, and he can keep her for his wife or not, or let her be consecrated, as he chooses. At these times they all get drunk.

The second language is that of the Pacaxes, the people who live in the country between the plains and the mountains. These people are more barbarous. Some of them who live near the mountains eat human flesh. They are great sodomites, and have many wives, even when these are sisters. They worship painted and sculptured stones, and are much given to witchcraft and sorcery.

The third language is that of the Acaxes, who are in possession of a large part of the hilly country and all of the mountains. They go hunting for men just as they hunt animals. They all eat human flesh, and he who has the most human bones and skulls hung up around his house is most feared and respected. They live in settlements and in very rough country, avoiding the plains. In passing from one settlement to another, there is always a ravine in the way which they can not cross, although they can talk together across it. At the slightest call 500 men collect, and on any pretext kill and eat one another. Thus it has been very hard to subdue these people, on account of the roughness of the country, which is very great.

Many rich silver mines have been found in this country. They do not run deep, but soon give out. The gulf of the sea [1]

[1] The Gulf of California.

begins on the coast of this province, entering the land 250 leagues toward the north and ending at the mouth of the Fire-brand (Tizon) River. This country forms its eastern limit, and California [1] the western. From what I have been told by men who had navigated it, it is thirty leagues across from point to point, because they lose sight of this country when they see the other. They say the gulf is over 150 leagues broad (or deep), from shore to shore. The coast makes a turn toward the south at the Firebrand River, bending down to California, which turns toward the west, forming that penin-sula which was formerly held to be an island, because it was a low sandy country. It is inhabited by brutish, bestial, naked people who eat their own offal. The men and women couple like animals, the female openly getting down on all fours.[2]

Chapter 2

Of the province of Petlatlan and all the inhabited country as far as Chichilticalli.

Petlatlan is a settlement of houses covered with a sort of mats made of plants. These are collected into villages, extending along a river from the mountains to the sea.[3] The people are of the same race and habits as the Culuacanian Tahues. There is much sodomy among them. In the moun-tain district there is a large population and more settlements. These people have a somewhat different language from the Tahues, although they understand each other. It is called Petlatlan because the houses are made of petates or palm-leaf mats. Houses of this sort are found for more than 240 leagues in this region, to the beginning of the Cibola wilder-

[1] Lower California is of course meant.

[2] For an account of the Indians of Lower California in the eighteenth cen-tury, see the translation of Father Jacob Baegert's narrative, by Charles Rau, in the *Report of the Smithsonian Institution* for 1863 and 1864.

[3] The Rio Petlatlan is the present Rio Sinaloa. The name Sinaloa is synonymous in application with Cahita, a group of tribes including the present Yaqui and Mayo.

ness.[1] The nature of the country changes here very greatly, because from this point on there are no trees except the pine, nor are there any fruits except a few tunas,[2] mesquites, and pitahayas.[3]

Petlatlan is twenty leagues from Culiacan, and it is 130 leagues from here to the valley of Señora. There are many rivers between the two, with settlements of the same sort of people — for example, Sinoloa, Boyomo, Teocomo, Yaquimi, and other smaller ones. There is also the Corazones (Hearts), which is in our possession, down the valley of Señora.[4]

Señora is a river and valley thickly settled by able-bodied people. The women wear petticoats of tanned deerskin, and little san benitos reaching half way down the body.[5] The chiefs of the villages go up on some little heights they have made for this purpose, like public criers, and there make proclamations for the space of an hour, regulating those things they have to attend to. They have some little huts for shrines, all over the outside of which they stick many arrows, like a hedgehog. They do this when they are eager for war. All about this province toward the mountains there is a large population in separate little provinces containing ten or twelve villages. Seven or eight of them, of which I know the names, are Comupatrico, Mochilagua, Arispa,[6] and the Little Valley. There are others which we did not see.

It is forty leagues from Señora to the valley of Suya.[7] The town of San Hieronimo was established in this valley, where there was a rebellion later, and part of the people who had settled there were killed, as will be seen in the third part. There are many villages in the neighborhood of this valley. The people are the same as those in Señora and have the same

[1] That is, as far northward as the Rio Gila.
[2] The fruit of the prickly-pear cactus.
[3] The giant cactus. See p. 305, note 1.
[4] Sonora. See p. 301, notes 1 and 2.
[5] See p. 334, note 1.
[6] This was Arizpe, on the upper waters of the Rio Sonora. Jaramillo calls it Ispa.
[7] See p. 326, note 2.

dress and language, habits, and customs, like all the rest as far as the desert of Chichilticalli. The women paint their chins and eyes like the Moorish women of Barbary. They are great sodomites.[1] They drink wine made of the pitahaya, which is the fruit of a great thistle which opens like the pomegranate. The wine makes them stupid. They make a great quantity of preserves from the tuna; they preserve it in a large amount of its sap without other honey. They make bread of the mesquite, like cheese, which keeps good for a whole year. There are native melons in this country so large that a person can carry only one of them. They cut these into slices and dry them in the sun. They are good to eat, and taste like figs, and are better than dried meat; they are very good and sweet, keeping for a whole year when prepared in this way.[2]

In this country there were also tame eagles, which the chiefs esteemed to be something fine.[3] No fowls of any sort were seen in any of these villages except in this valley of Suya, where fowls like those of Castile were found. Nobody could find out how they came to be so far inland, the people being all at war with one another. Between Suya and Chichilticalli there are many sheep and mountain goats with very large bodies and horns. Some Spaniards declare that they have seen flocks of more than a hundred together, which ran so fast that they disappeared very quickly.

At Chichilticalli the country changes its character again and the spiky vegetation ceases. The reason is that the gulf reaches as far up as this place, and the mountain chain changes its direction at the same time that the coast does. Here they

---

[1] These are, from the south northward, the Pimas Bajos or Nevome, Opatas, Papagos, and Pimas. The older Pima women still paint their faces in fine lines and also are tattooed, but the custom is becoming a thing of the past. The Opatas are almost entirely Mexicanized.

[2] These were doubtless cantaloupes The southwestern Indians still slice and dry them in a manner similar to that here described.

[3] The Pueblo Indians, particularly the Zuñi and the Hopi, keep eagles for their feathers, which are highly prized because regarded as sacred and are much used in their ceremonies.

had to cross and pass through the mountains in order to get into the level country.[1]

Chapter 3

Of Chichilticalli and the desert, of Cibola, its customs and habits, and of other things.

Chichilticalli is so called because the friars found a house at this place which was formerly inhabited by people who separated from Cibola. It was made of colored or reddish earth.[2] The house was large and appeared to have been a fortress. It must have been destroyed by the people of the district, who are the most barbarous people that have yet been seen. They live in separate cabins and not in settlements.[3] They live by hunting. The rest of the country is all wilderness, covered with pine forests. There are great quantities of the pine nuts. The pines are two or three times as high as a man before they send out branches. There is a sort of oak with sweet acorns, of which they make cakes like sugar plums with dried coriander seeds. It is very sweet, like sugar. Watercress grows in many springs, and there are rosebushes, and pennyroyal, and wild marjoram.

There are barbels and picones,[4] like those of Spain, in the rivers of this wilderness.[5] Gray lions and leopards were seen.[6]

[1] Probably Dragoon Pass, through the Dragoon and Galiuro Mountains of southeastern Arizona, thence between the Pinaleño and Chiricahua mountains to the plains of San Simon.

[2] This ruin is supposed to have been in the vicinity of the present Solomonsville, Graham County. The name is Aztec (*chichiltic* " red," *calli* "house"). Writers have endeavored to identify it with the celebrated Casa Grande farther to the northwest, but this is inconsistent with the directions recorded in the narratives, and all students of the subject have now abandoned this theory.

[3] These people are not identifiable with certainty. If the Apaches of Arizona, it is the only mention of them and is contrary to all other testimony. The Sobaipuris lived on the upper Rio San Pedro and on the Gila near the mouth of the former stream, until the latter part of the eighteenth century.

[4] Picones are catfish.

[5] The "wilderness," or uninhabited region, extended from the Gila in central Graham County to the crossing of the New Mexico boundary by Zuñi River, where Cibola began.

[6] These are the mountain lion and the wildcat.

The country rises continually from the beginning of the wilderness until Cibola is reached, which is eighty leagues, going north. From Culiacan to the edge of the wilderness the route had kept the north on the left hand.

Cibola [1] is seven villages. The largest is called Maçaque.[2] The houses are ordinarily three or four stories high, but in Maçaque there are houses with four and seven stories. These people are very intelligent. They cover their privy parts and all the immodest parts with cloths made like a sort of table napkin, with fringed edges and a tassel at each corner, which they tie over the hips. They wear long robes of feathers and of the skins of hares, and cotton blankets. The women wear blankets, which they tie or knot over the left shoulder, leaving the right arm out.[3] These serve to cover the body. They wear a neat well-shaped outer garment of skin. They gather their hair over the two ears, making a frame which looks like an old-fashioned headdress.[4]

The country is a valley between ridges resembling rocky mountains. They plant in holes. Maize does not grow high; ears from a stalk three or four to each cane, thick and large, of eight hundred grains, a thing not seen in these parts. There are large numbers of bears in this province, and lions, wildcats, deer, and otter. There are very fine turquoises, although not so many as was reported.[5] They collect the pine nuts [6] each year, and store them up in advance. A man does not have more than one wife. There are estufas or hot rooms [7]

[1] See p. 300, note 1.

[2] See p. 315, note 1.

[3] Identical with the dress of the Zuñi women of to-day. Rabbit-skin robes have been replaced by woollen blankets, like those woven by the Navaho, who learned the art from the Pueblos. The rabbit-skin robes are now manufactured chiefly by the Paiutes, the Pueblos having almost ceased to make them.

[4] This custom has been abandoned except by the Hopi maidens, who still wear their hair in picturesque whorls, one on each side of the head, until married.

[5] See p. 308, note 3. This entire description is characteristic of the present Zuñi country, except that game is not so abundant.

[6] Piñon nuts, which are still gathered in large quantities.

[7] The *kivas*, or ceremonial chambers, of which there are usually several in each pueblo. It is in these that most of the secret rites are performed.

in the villages, which are the courtyards or places where they gather for consultation. They do not have chiefs as in New Spain, but are ruled by a council of the oldest men. They have priests who preach to them, whom they call papas.[1] These are the elders. They go up on the highest roof of the village and preach to the village from there, like public criers, in the morning while the sun is rising, the whole village being silent and sitting in the galleries to listen.[2] They tell them how they are to live, and I believe that they give certain commandments for them to keep, for there is no drunkenness among them nor sodomy nor sacrifices, neither do they eat human flesh nor steal, but they are usually at work. The estufas belong to the whole village.[3] It is a sacrilege for the women to go into the estufas to sleep. They make the cross as a sign of peace. They burn their dead, and throw the implements used in their work into the fire with the bodies.[4]

It is twenty leagues to Tusayan,[5] going northwest. This is a province with seven villages, of the same sort, dress, habits, and ceremonies as at Cibola. There may be as many as 3,000 or 4,000 men in the fourteen villages of these two provinces.[6] It is forty leagues or more to Tiguex, the road trending toward the north. The rock of Acuco, which we described in the first part, is between these.

[1] *Pápa* is a true Zuñi word, signifying "elder brother," as distinguished from *sú-e*, "younger brother." These terms allude both to age and to rank.

[2] All public announcements are still made in this way.

[3] Rather to the religious societies. Some of them belong exclusively to the women.

[4] Excavations made at Halona, one of the Seven Cities of Cibola, yielded only skeletons that had been interred within the houses, beneath the floors. In the Salt River and Gila valleys, southern Arizona, this method was also practised, but in addition remains were cremated and deposited in earthen vessels in mounds near by.

[5] See p. 307, note 1; p. 358, note 3.

[6] This would indicate a population of 10,500 to 14,000, which is doubtless an excessive estimate for the sixteenth century. The present population of Zuñi is 1514 ; of the Hopi villages, about 2000.

Chapter 4

Of how they live at Tiguex, and of the province of Tiguex and its neighborhood.

Tiguex is a province with twelve villages on the banks of a large, mighty river; some villages on one side and some on the other.[1] It is a spacious valley two leagues wide, and a very high, rough, snow-covered mountain chain lies east of it.[2] There are seven villages in the ridges at the foot of this — four on the plain and three situated on the skirts of the mountain.

There are seven villages seven leagues to the north, at Quirix, and the seven villages of the province of Hemes are forty leagues northeast [northwest]. It is forty leagues north or east to Acha,[3] and four leagues southeast[4] to Tutahaco, a province with eight villages. In general, these villages all have the same habits and customs, although some have some things in particular which the others have not. They are governed by the opinions of the elders. They all work together to build the villages, the women being engaged in making the mixture and the walls, while the men bring the wood and put it in place. They have no lime, but they make a mixture of ashes, coals, and dirt which is almost as good as mortar, for when the house is to have four stories, they do not make the walls more than half a yard thick. They gather a great pile of twigs of thyme [sagebrush] and sedge grass and set it afire, and when it is half coals and ashes they throw a quantity of dirt and water on it and mix it all together. They make round balls of this, which they use instead of stones after they are dry, fixing them with the same mixture, which

[1] The Rio Grande, as previously described.
[2] The Sandia Mountains.
[3] The pueblo of Picuris, about twenty miles south of Taos. This is a Tigua village of about 125 inhabitants.
[4] Compare the previous reference to Tutahaco (p. 314). Both the distance and the direction here given seem to be erroneous.

comes to be like a stiff clay. Before they are married the
young men serve the whole village in general, and fetch the
wood that is needed for use, putting it in a pile in the courtyard of the villages, from which the women take it to carry to
their houses.[1]

The young men live in the estufas, which are in the yards
of the village. They are underground, square or round, with
pine pillars. Some were seen with twelve pillars and with four
in the centre as large as two men could stretch around. They
usually had three or four pillars. The floor was made of large,
smooth stones, like the baths which they have in Europe.
They have a hearth made like the binnacle or compass box
of a ship, in which they burn a handful of thyme at a time
to keep up the heat, and they can stay in there just as in a
bath. The top was on a level with the ground. Some that
were seen were large enough for a game of ball. When any
man wishes to marry, it has to be arranged by those who govern. The man has to spin and weave a blanket and place it
before the woman, who covers herself with it and becomes his
wife.[2] The houses belong to the women, the estufas to the men.
If a man repudiates his woman, he has to go to the estufa.
It is forbidden for women to sleep in the estufas, or to enter
these for any purpose except to give their husbands or sons
something to eat. The men spin and weave. The women
bring up the children and prepare the food. The country is so
fertile that they do not have to break up the ground the year
round, but only have to sow the seed, which is presently
covered by the fall of snow, and the ears come up under the
snow. In one year they gather enough for seven. A very
large number of cranes and wild geese and crows and starlings
live on what is sown, and for all this, when they come to sow
for another year, the fields are covered with corn which they
have not been able to finish gathering.

---

[1] This would indicate the existence of a true communal system that does
not prevail at the present time.

[2] See Voth, " Oraibi Marriage Customs," *American Anthropologist*, II. 238
(1900).

2 A

There are a great many native fowl in these provinces, and cocks with great hanging chins.[1] When dead, these keep for sixty days, and longer in winter, without losing their feathers or opening, and without any bad smell, and the same is true of dead men.

The villages are free from nuisances, because they go outside to excrete, and they pass their water into clay vessels, which they empty at a distance from the village.[2] They keep the separate houses where they prepare the food for eating and where they grind the meal, very clean. This is a separate room or closet, where they have a trough with three stones fixed in stiff clay. Three women go in here, each one having a stone, with which one of them breaks the corn, the next grinds it, and the third grinds it again.[3] They take off their shoes, do up their hair, shake their clothes, and cover their heads before they enter the door. A man sits at the door playing on a fife while they grind, moving the stones to the music and singing together. They grind a large quantity at one time, because they make all their bread of meal soaked in warm water, like wafers. They gather a great quantity of brushwood and dry it to use for cooking all through the year. There are no fruits good to eat in the country, except the pine nuts. They have their preachers. Sodomy is not found among them. They do not eat human flesh nor make sacrifices of it. The people are not cruel, for they had Francisco de Ovando in Tiguex about forty days, after he was dead, and when the village was captured, he was found among their dead, whole and without any other wound except the one which killed him, white as snow, without any bad smell. I found out several things about them from one of our Indians, who had been a captive among them for a whole year. I asked him especially

---

[1] The American turkey cocks.

[2] A custom still common at Zuñi and other pueblos. Before the introduction of manufactured dyes the Pueblos used urine as a mordant.

[3] See Mindeleff's " Pueblo Architecture," in the *Eighth Annual Report of the Bureau of Ethnology*, p. 208; also Cushing, " Zuñi Breadstuff," in *The Millstone* (Indianapolis, 1884–1885).

for the reason why the young women in that province went entirely naked, however cold it might be, and he told me that the virgins had to go around this way until they took a husband, and that they covered themselves after they had known man. The men here wear little shirts of tanned deerskin and their long robes over this. In all these provinces they have earthenware glazed with antimony and jars of extraordinary labor and workmanship, which were worth seeing.[1]

Chapter 5

*Of Cicuye and the villages in its neighborhood, and of how some
people came to conquer this country.*

We have already said that the people of Tiguex and of all the provinces on the banks of that river were all alike, having the same ways of living and the same customs. It will not be necessary to say anything particular about them. I wish merely to give an account of Cicuye and some depopulated villages which the army saw on the direct road which it followed thither, and of others that were across the snowy mountains near Tiguex, which also lay in that region above the river.

Cicuye[2] is a village of nearly five hundred warriors, who

[1] A number of memoirs on the pottery of the ancient Pueblos may be consulted in the *Annual Reports* of the Bureau of American Ethnology.

[2] This is Pecos, the largest pueblo of New Mexico in the sixteenth century and for a long time after. Its people belonged to the Tanoan family, although their language was understood only by the Jemez villagers, their nearest kindred. It was the scene of the missionary labors of Fray Luis Descalona, who remained behind when Coronado returned to Mexico in 1542, but he was probably killed before the close of that year. Pecos became the seat of an important Franciscan mission early in the seventeenth century, but it began to decline after the revolt of 1680–1692, and in 1838 the half-dozen survivors removed to Jemez, where one of them still (1906) lives. Cicuye is the Isleta, or Tigua, name for Pecos, while "Pecos" itself is the Keresan, or Queres, appellation, with the Spanish-English plural. The ruins of the town are plainly visible from the Santa Fé Railway. See Bandelier in *Papers of the Archaeological Institute of America*, Amer. ser., I. (1881); Hewett in *American Anthropologist*, n. s., VI. No. 4, 1904.

are feared throughout that country.   It is square, situated on
a rock, with a large court or yard in the middle, containing the
estufas.   The houses are all alike, four stories high.   One can
go over the top of the whole village without there being a street
to hinder.   There are corridors going all around it at the first
two stories, by which one can go around the whole village.
These are like outside balconies, and they are able to protect
themselves under these.   The houses do not have doors below,
but they use ladders, which can be lifted up like a drawbridge,
and so go up to the corridors which are on the inside of the
village.   As the doors of the houses open on the corridor of that
story, the corridor serves as a street.   The houses that open on
the plain are right back of those that open on the court, and in
time of war they go through those behind them.   The village
is enclosed by a low wall of stone.   There is a spring of water
inside, which they are able to divert.[1]   The people of this village
boast that no one has been able to conquer them and that they
conquer whatever villages they wish.   The people and their
customs are like those of the other villages.   Their virgins also
go nude until they take husbands, because they say that if
they do anything wrong then it will be seen, and so they do
not do it.   They do not need to be ashamed because they go
around as they were born.

There is a village, small and strong, between Cicuye and
the province of Quirix, which the Spaniards named Ximena,[2]
and another village almost deserted, only one part of which is
inhabited.[3]   This was a large village, and judging from its
condition and newness it appeared to have been destroyed.
They called this the village of the granaries (*silos*), because large
underground cellars were found here stored with corn.   There
was another large village farther on, entirely destroyed and

[1] The spring was "still trickling out beneath a massive ledge of rocks on
the west sill" when Bandelier (*op. cit.*) sketched it in 1880.

[2] The former Tanos pueblo of Galisteo, a mile and a half northeast of the
present town of the same name.

[3] According to Mota Padilla, *Historia de la Conquista*, 1742 (Mexico,
1870), this was called Coquite.

pulled down, in the yards of which there were many stone balls, as big as twelve-quart bowls, which seemed to have been thrown by engines or catapults, which had destroyed the village. All that I was able to find out about them was that, sixteen years before, some people called Teyas [1] had come to this country in great numbers and had destroyed these villages. They had besieged Cicuye but had not been able to capture it, because it was strong, and when they left the region, they had made peace with the whole country. It seems as if they must have been a powerful people, and that they must have had engines to knock down the villages. The only thing they could tell about the direction these people came from was by pointing toward the north. They usually call these people Teyas or brave men, just as the Mexicans say chichimecas or braves,[2] for the Teyas whom the army saw were brave. These knew the people in the settlements, and were friendly with them, and they (the Teyas of the plains) went there to spend the winter under the wings of the settlements. The inhabitants do not dare to let them come inside, because they can not trust them. Although they are received as friends, and trade with them, they do not stay in the villages over night, but outside under the wings. The villages are guarded by sentinels with trumpets, who call to one another just as in the fortresses of Spain.

There are seven other villages along this route, toward the snowy mountains,[3] one of which has been half destroyed by the people already referred to. These were under the rule of Cicuye. Cicuye is in a little valley between mountain chains and mountains covered with large pine forests. There is a little stream [4] which contains very good trout and otters, and there are very large bears and good falcons hereabouts.

---

[1] These Indians were seen by Coronado during his journey across the plains. See p. 333, note 3.

[2] The name applied in Mexico at the time to any warlike, unsubdued tribe.

[3] The mountains to the north, in which the Rio Pecos has its source.

[4] The Rio Pecos, still noted for trout.

Chapter 6

Which gives the number of villages which were seen in the country of the terraced houses, and their population.

Before I proceed to speak of the plains, with the cows and settlements and tribes there, it seems to me that it will be well for the reader to know how large the settlements were, where the houses with stories, gathered into villages, were seen, and how great an extent of country they occupied.[1]   As I say, Cibola is the first:

Cibola, seven villages.[2]

Tusayan, seven villages.[3]

The rock of Acuco, one.[4]

Tiguex, twelve villages.[5]

Tutahaco, eight villages.[6]

These villages were below the river.[7]

Quirix, seven villages.[8]

In the snowy mountains, seven villages.[9]

Ximena, three villages.[10]

---

[1] Only the pueblos of Acoma and Isleta occupy their sixteenth-century sites, all the other villages having shifted their locations after the great revolt of 1680–1692, when the Spaniards granted specific tracts of land, usually a league square, later confirmed to the Indians by Congress under the provisions of the treaty of Guadalupe Hidalgo.

[2] Zuñi, including the pueblos of Halona, Matsaki, Kiakima, Hawiku, Kyanawe, and two others which have not been identified with certainty.

[3] The Hopi villages, among them being Awatobi (destroyed at the beginning of the eighteenth century), Oraibi, Walpi, Mishongnovi, Shongopovi, and Shupaulovi.   The remaining pueblo has not been determined absolutely. Sichomovi and Hano are comparatively modern.

[4] Acoma.   See p. 311, note 2.

[5] The Tigua pueblos; see p. 312, note 2.

[6] See p. 314, note 1.

[7] Meaning that the provinces of Tiguex and Tutahaco were those farthest down the valley.

[8] The pueblos of the Queres, or Keresan, family.   See p. 327, note 3.

[9] Toward the north, in the direction of Santa Fé.

[10] Ximena itself was Galisteo.   The others were "Coquite" and the "Pueblo de los Silos."   See p. 356, notes 2 and 3.

Cicuye, one village.[1]

Hemes, seven villages.[2]

Aguas Calientes, or Boiling Springs, three villages.[3]

Yuqueyunque, in the mountains, six villages.[4]

Valladolid, called Braba, one village.[5]

Chia, one village.[6]

In all, there are sixty-six villages.[7] Tiguex appears to be in the centre of the villages. Valladolid is the farthest up the river toward the northeast. The four villages down the river are toward the southeast, because the river turns toward the east.[8] It is 130 leagues—ten more or less—from the farthest point that was seen down the river to the farthest point up the river, and all the settlements are within this region. Including those at a distance, there are sixty-six villages in all, as I have said, and in all of them there may be some 20,000 men, which may be taken to be a fair estimate of the population of the villages.[9] There are no houses or other buildings between one

---

[1] Pecos. See p. 355, note 2.

[2] Jemez, including Giusiwá, Amushungkwá, Patoqua, and Astyalakwá. There are many ruins in the vicinity, including those of a large Spanish church at Giusiwá. Evidently some of the Sia villages are here included.

[3] The Jemez villages about the Jemez Hot Springs, above the present Jemez pueblo. Castañeda here duplicates his provinces somewhat, as the Aguas Calientes pueblos were Jemez, Giusiwá being one of the most prominent.

[4] See p. 340, note 1. This group of Tewa villages doubtless included San Juan, Santa Clara, San Ildefonso, Tesuque, Nambe, Pojoaque, and Yukiwingge. Jacona, Cuyamunque, and others were also occupied by the Tewas during this period, no doubt, but these may have been included in Castañeda's province of the Snowy Mountains.

[5] Taos. See p. 340, note 4.

[6] Sia, a Queres pueblo, probably included, with Santa Ana, in his "Quirix" group, above.

[7] Castañeda lists seventy-one, probably having added others without altering the total here given.

[8] The trend of the Rio Grande is really southwestward until after the southern limit of the old Pueblo settlements is passed. Perhaps Castañeda had in mind the southeastward course of the stream farther south "toward Florida," as mentioned later in this paragraph. He is probably here speaking from hearsay, as the exploration downstream was not made by the main body

[9] This would give a total Pueblo population of about 70,000, whereas it could scarcely have much exceeded Castañeda's estimated number of men alone.

village and another, but where we went it is entirely uninhabited. These people, since they are few, and their manners, government, and habits are so different from all the nations that have been seen and discovered in these western regions, must come from that part of Greater India, the coast of which lies to the west of this country, for they could have come down from that country, crossing the mountain chains and following down the river, settling in what seemed to them the best place. As they multiplied, they have kept on making settlements until they lost the river when it buried itself underground, its course being in the direction of Florida. It [the Rio Grande] comes down from the northeast, where they [Coronado's army] could certainly have found signs of villages. He [Coronado] preferred, however, to follow the reports of the Turk, but it would have been better to cross the mountains where this river rises. I believe they would have found traces of riches and would have reached the lands from which these people started, which from its location is on the edge of Greater India, although the region is neither known nor understood, because from the trend of the coast it appears that the land between Norway and China is very far up. The country from sea to sea is very wide, judging from the location of both coasts, as well as from what Captain Villalobos discovered when he went in search of China by the sea to the west,[1] and from what has been discovered on the North Sea concerning the trend of the coast of Florida toward the Bacallaos, up toward Norway.[2]

To return then to the proposition with which I began, I say that the settlements and people already named were all that were seen in a region seventy leagues wide and 130 long, in the

---

[1] Ruy Lopez de Villalobos sailed from Acapulco, Mexico, in command of four vessels, in 1542, discovered the Caroline and Pelew archipelagos and sighted Caesarea Caroli, believed to be Luzon, of the Philippine group. Later he established a colony on an island which he called Antonio or Saragan. Supplies failing, he despatched three of the vessels to Mexico, but these were wrecked. Forced by hunger to flee to Amboina, Villalobos was imprisoned by the Portuguese. One of his men, escaping, carried the news to Mexico in 1549.

[2] "The Spanish text," remarks Mr. Winship, "fully justifies Castañeda's statement that he was not skilled in the arts of rhetoric and geography."

settled country along the river Tiguex.[1] In New Spain there
are not one but many establishments containing a larger number of people. Silver metals[2] were found in many of their
villages, which they use for glazing and painting their earthenware.

Chapter 7

*Which treats of the plains that were crossed, of the cows, and of
the people who inhabit them.*

We have spoken of the settlements of high houses which are
situated in what seems to be the most level and open part of
the mountains, since it is 150 leagues across before entering the
level country between the two mountain chains which I said
were near the North Sea and the South Sea, which might better
be called the Western Sea along this coast. This mountain
series is the one which is near the South Sea. In order to show
that the settlements are in the middle of the mountains, I will
state that it is eighty leagues from Chichilticalli, where we began to cross this country, to Cibola; from Cibola, which is the
first village, to Cicuye, which is the last on the way across, is
seventy leagues; it is thirty leagues from Cicuye to where
the plains begin. It may be we went across in an indirect or
roundabout way, which would make it seem as if there was
more country than if it had been crossed in a direct line,[3] and
it may be more difficult and rougher. This can not be known
certainly, because the mountains change their direction above
the bay at the mouth of the Firebrand (Tizon) River.[4]

Now we will speak of the plains. The country is spacious
and level, and is more than 400 leagues wide in the part between

[1] Castañeda here contradicts himself, as Pecos, Acoma, and the Zuñi and
Tusayan groups of pueblos are not in the valley of the Rio Grande.
[2] Previously called antimony. See p. 355, note 1.
[3] After leaving Cicuye (Pecos) the army marched down the river for four
days, crossed the stream over a bridge that they had built, and then reached
the Staked Plain of Texas by travelling first a northeasterly then a south-
easterly course. See Pt. 1, chap. 19.
[4] The Rio Colorado.

the two mountain ranges — one, that which Francisco Vazquez
Coronado crossed, and the other that which the force under
Don Fernando de Soto crossed, near the North Sea, entering
the country from Florida. No settlements were seen anywhere
on these plains.[1]

In traversing 250 leagues, the other mountain range was not
seen, nor a hill nor a hillock which was three times as high as a
man. Several lakes were found at intervals; they were round
as plates, a stone's throw or more across, some fresh and some
salt.[2] The grass grows tall near these lakes; away from them
it is very short, a span or less. The country is like a bowl,
so that when a man sits down, the horizon surrounds him all
around at the distance of a musket shot. There are no groves
of trees except at the rivers, which flow at the bottom of some
ravines where the trees grow so thick that they were not noticed
until one was right on the edge of them. They are of dead
earth. There are paths down into these, made by the cows
when they go to the water, which is essential throughout these
plains. As I have related in the first part, people follow the
cows, hunting them and tanning the skins to take to the settlements in the winter to sell, since they go there to pass the winter, each company going to those which are nearest, some to
the settlements at Cicuye, others toward Quivira, and others to
the settlements which are situated in the direction of Florida.
These people are called Querechos and Teyas. They described some large settlements, and judging from what was
seen of these people and from the accounts they gave of other
places, there are a good many more of these people than there
are of those at the settlements. They have better figures, are
better warriors, and are more feared. They travel like the
Arabs, with their tents and troops of dogs loaded with poles [3]

[1] That is, if the writer overlooks the settlements (one of them called
Cona) in the ravines of the headwaters of the Texas streams, about the
eastern escarpment of the Staked Plain, previously mentioned.

[2] The salt lakes near the Texas-New Mexico boundary. Further allusion
to these salt lakes is made in Pt. 1, chap. 21.

[3] The well-known travois of the plains tribes. The poles were those used
to support the tents, or tipis, and were usually of cedar.

and having Moorish pack-saddles with girths. When the load
gets disarranged, the dogs howl, calling some one to fix them
right. These people eat raw flesh and drink blood. They do
not eat human flesh.[1] They are a kind people and not cruel.
They are faithful friends. They are able to make themselves
very well understood by means of signs.[2] They dry the flesh
in the sun, cutting it thin like a leaf,[3] and when dry they grind
it like meal to keep it and make a sort of sea soup of it to eat.
A handful thrown into a pot swells up so as to increase very
much. They season it with fat, which they always try to secure
when they kill a cow.[4] They empty a large gut and fill it with
blood, and carry this around the neck to drink when they are
thirsty. When they open the belly of a cow, they squeeze
out the chewed grass and drink the juice that remains behind,
because they say that this contains the essence of the stomach.
They cut the hide open at the back and pull it off at the joints,
using a flint as large as a finger, tied in a little stick, with as
much ease as if working with a good iron tool. They give it an
edge with their own teeth. The quickness with which they
do this is something worth seeing and noting.

There are very great numbers of wolves on these plains,
which go around with the cows. They have white skins. The
deer are pied with white. Their skin is loose, so that when they
are killed it can be pulled off with the hand while warm, coming off like pigskin. The rabbits, which are very numerous,
are so foolish that those on horseback killed them with their
lances. This is when they are mounted among the cows.
They fly from a person on foot.

[1] Some of the tribes of Texas, however, especially the Attacapa and the
Tonkawa, were noted as cannibals.

[2] The sign language was in general use among the tribes of the great plains,
rendered necessary by the diversity of languages. See Mallery, *Introduction
to the Study of Sign Language* (Washington, 1880); Clark, *Indian Sign Language* (1885).

[3] The "jerked beef" of the later frontiersmen.

[4] The *pemmican* of the Indians.

Chapter 8

Of Quivira, of where it is and some information about it.

Quivira is to the west [1] of those ravines, in the midst of the country, somewhat nearer the mountains toward the sea, for the country is level as far as Quivira, and there they began to see some mountain chains. The country is well settled. Judging from what was seen on the borders of it, this country is very similar to that of Spain in the varieties of vegetation and fruits. There are plums like those of Castile, grapes, nuts, mulberries, oats, pennyroyal, wild marjoram, and large quantities of flax, but this does not do them any good, because they do not know how to use it.[2] The people are of almost the same sort and appearance as the Teyas. They have villages like those in New Spain. The houses are round, without a wall, and they have one story like a loft, under the roof, where they sleep and keep their belongings. The roofs are of straw.[3] There are other thickly settled provinces around it containing large numbers of men. A friar named Juan de Padilla remained in this province, together with a Spanish-Portuguese and a negro and a half-blood and some Indians from the province of Capothan,[4] in New Spain. They killed the friar because he wanted to go to the province of the Guas,[5] who were their enemies. The Spaniard escaped by taking flight on a mare, and afterward reached New Spain, coming out by way of Panuco. The Indians from New Spain who accompanied the friar were allowed

---

[1] Castañeda is sometimes confused in his directions. In this instance unless "west" (*poniente*) is a slip of the pen, he evidently forgot that the army travelled for weeks to the north, "by the needle," after journeying for some distance toward sunrise from the ravines of western Texas.

[2] This flora is characteristic of the upper plains generally, and the passage has been quoted by students of the route to show that Quivira lay both in Kansas and in Nebraska.

[3] Note the character of the houses as one of the chief means of determining the inhabitants of Quivira. See p. 337, note 1.

[4] The Jaramillo narrative says Capottan or Capotean.

[5] Possibly the Kaw or Kansa Indians. See Pt. 3, chap. 4.

by the murderers to bury him, and then they followed the
Spaniard and overtook him.   This Spaniard was a Portuguese,
named Campo.[1]

The great river of the Holy Spirit (Espiritu Santo),[2] which
Don Fernando de Soto discovered in the country of Florida,
flows through this country.   It passes through a province
called Arache,[3] according to the reliable accounts which were
obtained here.   The sources were not visited, because, according to what they said, it comes from a very distant country in
the mountains of the South Sea, from the part that sheds its
waters onto the plains.   It flows across all the level country
and breaks through the mountains of the North Sea, and comes
out where the people with Don Fernando de Soto navigated it.
This is more than 300 leagues from where it enters the sea.[4]   On
account of this, and also because it has large tributaries, it is
so mighty when it enters the sea that they lost sight of the
land before the water ceased to be fresh.[5]

This country of Quivira was the last that was seen, of which
I am able to give any description or information.   Now it is
proper for me to return and speak of the army, which I left
in Tiguex, resting for the winter, so that it would be able to
proceed or return in search of these settlements of Quivira,
which was not accomplished after all, because it was God's
pleasure that these discoveries should remain for other peoples and that we who had been there should content ourselves
with saying that we were the first who discovered it and obtained any information concerning it, just as Hercules knew

---

[1] Compare Herrera, *Historia General*, dec. vi., lib. ix., cap. xii., Vol. III.,
p. 207 (ed. 1730); Gomara, *Historia General*, cap. ccxiiii. (1553); Mota
Padilla, *Historia de la Conquista*, 1742, p. 167 (1870); and specially Bandelier in *American Catholic Quarterly Review*, XV.   551–565 (Philadelphia,
July, 1890).

[2] The Missouri-Mississippi.

[3] The Harahey of Jaramillo's account — evidently the Pawnee country,
about the Platte River, Nebraska.   The "Relacion del Suceso," *Fourteenth
Report of the Bureau of Ethnology* (Washington, 1896), spells it Harale.

[4] The North and the South seas are the Atlantic and the Pacific oceans
respectively.

[5] See Cabeza de Vaca's narrative in the present volume.

the site where Julius Cæsar was to found Seville or Hispales. May the all-powerful Lord grant that His will be done in everything. It is certain that if this had not been His will Francisco Vazquez [Coronado] would not have returned to New Spain without cause or reason, as he did, and that it would not have been left for those with Don Fernando de Soto to settle such a good country, as they have done, and besides settling it to increase its extent, after obtaining, as they did, information from our army.[1]

THIRD PART

Which describes what happened to Francisco Vazquez Coronado during the winter, and how he gave up the expedition and returned to New Spain.

Laus Deo

Chapter 1

Of how Don Pedro de Tovar came from Señora with some men, and Don Garcia Lopez de Cardenas started back to New Spain.

At the end of the first part of this book, we told how Francisco Vazquez Coronado, when he got back from Quivira, gave orders to winter at Tiguex, in order to return, when the winter was over, with his whole army to discover all the settlements in those regions. Don Pedro de Tovar, who had gone, as we related, to conduct a force from the city of San Hieronimo, arrived in the meantime with the men whom he had brought.

---

[1] Mr. Winship calls attention to Mota Padilla's reasons for the failure of the expedition: "It was most likely the chastisement of God that riches were not found on this expedition, because, when this ought to have been the secondary object of the expedition, and the conversion of all those heathen their first aim, they bartered with fate and struggled after the secondary; and thus the misfortune is not so much that all those labors were without fruit, but the worst is that such a number of souls have remained in their blindness." *Historia de la Conquista*, 1742, p. 166 (repr. 1870).

He had not selected the rebels and seditious men there, but the most experienced ones and the best soldiers — men whom he could trust—wisely considering that he ought to have good men in order to go in search of his general in the country of the Indian called Turk. Although they found the army at Tiguex when they arrived there, this did not please them much, because they had come with great expectations, believing that they would find their general in the rich country of the Indian called Turk. They consoled themselves with the hope of going back there, and lived in anticipation of the pleasure of undertaking this return expedition which the army would soon make to Quivira. Don Pedro de Tovar brought letters from New Spain, both from the viceroy, Don Antonio de Mendoza, and from individuals. Among these was one for Don Garcia Lopez de Cardenas, which informed him of the death of his brother, the heir, and summoned him to Spain to receive the inheritance. On this account he was given permission, and left Tiguex with several other persons who received permission to go and settle their affairs.[1] There were many others who would have liked to go, but did not, in order not to appear fainthearted. During this time the general endeavored to pacify several villages in the neighborhood which were not well disposed, and to make peace with the people at Tiguex. He tried also to procure some of the cloth of the country, because the soldiers were almost naked and poorly clothed, full of lice, which they were unable to get rid of or avoid.

The general, Francisco Vazquez Coronado, had been beloved and obeyed by his captains and soldiers as heartily as any of those who have ever started out in the Indies. Necessity knows no law, and the captains who collected the cloth divided it badly, taking the best for themselves and their friends and soldiers, and leaving the rest for the soldiers, and so there began

[1] According to the *Relacion del Suceso:* "Don Garcia Lopez de Cardenas started off for Mexico, who, besides the fact that his arm was very bad, had permission from the viceroy on account of the death of his brother. Ten or twelve who were sick went with him, and not a man among them all who could fight." Cardenas, it will be recalled, had broken his arm. See Pt. 1, chap. 19.

to be some angry murmuring on account of this. Others also complained because they noticed that some favored ones were spared in the work and in the watches and received better portions of what was divided, both of cloth and food. On this account it is thought that they began to say that there was nothing in the country of Quivira which was worth returning for, which was no slight cause of what afterward happened, as will be seen.

Chapter 2

Of the general's fall, and of how the return to New Spain was ordered.

After the winter[1] was over, the return to Quivira was announced, and the men began to prepare the things needed. Since nothing in this life is at the disposition of men, but all is under the ordination of Almighty God, it was His will that we should not accomplish this, and so it happened that one feast day the general went out on horseback to amuse himself, as usual, riding with the captain Don Rodrigo Maldonado. He was on a powerful horse, and his servants had put on a new girth, which must have been rotten at the time, for it broke during the race and he fell over on the side where Don Rodrigo was, and as his horse passed over him it hit his head with its hoof, which laid him at the point of death, and his recovery was slow and doubtful.

During this time, while he was in his bed, Don Garcia Lopez de Cardenas, who had started to go to New Spain, came back in flight from Suya, because he had found that town deserted and the people and horses and cattle all dead.[2] When he reached Tiguex and learned the sad news that the general was near his end, as already related, they did not dare to tell him until he had recovered, and when he finally got up

[1] Of 1541–1542.
[2] Cardenas had "reached the town of the Spaniards and found it burned and two Spaniards and many Indians and horses dead, and he returned to the river on this account." (*Relacion del Suceso.*)

and learned of it, it affected him so much that he had to go
back to bed again. He may have done this in order to bring
about what he afterward accomplished, as was believed later.
It was while he was in this condition that he recollected what a
scientific friend of his in Salamanca had told him, that he
would become a powerful lord in distant lands, and that he
would have a fall from which he would never be able to recover.
This expectation of death made him desire to return and die
where he had a wife and children. As the physician and surgeon who was doctoring him, and also acted as a talebearer,
suppressed the murmurings that were going about among the
soldiers, he treated secretly and underhandedly with several
gentlemen who agreed with him. They set the soldiers to
talking about going back to New Spain, in little knots and
gatherings, and induced them to hold consultations about it,
and had them send papers to the general, signed by all the
soldiers, through their ensigns, asking for this. They all
entered into it readily, and not much time needed to be spent,
since many desired it already. When they asked him, the
general acted as if he did not want to do it, but all the gentlemen
and captains supported them, giving him their signed opinions,
and as some were in this, they could give it at once, and they
even persuaded others to do the same. Thus they made it
seem as if they ought to return to New Spain, because they
had not found any riches, nor had they discovered any settled
country out of which estates could be formed for all the army.
When he had obtained their signatures, the return to New
Spain was at once announced, and since nothing can ever be
concealed, the double dealing began to be understood, and many
of the gentlemen found that they had been deceived and had
made a mistake. They tried in every way to get their signatures back again from the general, who guarded them so carefully that he did not go out of one room, making his sickness
seem very much worse, and putting guards about his person and
room, and at night about the floor on which he slept. In
spite of all this, they stole his chest, and it is said that they did
not find their signatures in it, because he kept them in his

Q B

mattress; on the other hand, it is said that they did recover them. They asked the general to give them sixty picked men, with whom they would remain and hold the country until the viceroy could send them support, or recall them, or else that the general would leave them the army and pick out sixty men to go back with him. But the soldiers did not want to remain either way, some because they had turned their prow toward New Spain, and others because they saw clearly the trouble that would arise over who should have the command. The gentlemen, I do not know whether because they had sworn fidelity or because they feared that the soldiers would not support them, did what had been decided on, although with an ill-will, and from this time on they did not obey the general as readily as formerly, and they did not show any affection for him. He made much of the soldiers and humored them, with the result that he did what he desired and secured the return of the whole army.

Chapter 3

Of the rebellion at Suya and the reasons the settlers gave for it.

We have already stated in the last chapter that Don Garcia Lopez de Cardenas came back from Suya in flight, having found that country risen in rebellion. He told how and why that town was deserted, which occurred as I will relate. The entirely worthless fellows were all who had been left in that town, the mutinous and seditious men, besides a few who were honored with the charge of public affairs and who were left to govern the others. Thus the bad dispositions of the worthless secured the power, and they held daily meetings and councils and declared that they had been betrayed and were not going to be rescued, since the others had been directed to go through another part of the country, where there was a more convenient route to New Spain, which was not so, because they were still almost on the direct road. This talk led some of them to revolt, and they chose one Pedro de Avila as their captain. They went back to Culiacan, leaving the captain, Diego de Alcaraz, sick in the town of San Hieronimo, with only a small force. He did not have anyone whom he could send after them to compel them to return. They killed a number of people at several villages along the way. Finally they reached Culiacan, where Hernando Arias de Saabedra,[1] who was waiting for Juan Gallego to come back from New Spain with a force, detained them by means of promises, so that Gallego could take them back. Some who feared what might happen to them ran away one night to New Spain. Diego de Alcaraz, who had remained at Suya with a small force, sick, was not able to hold his position, although he would have liked to, on account of the poisonous herb which the natives use.[2] When these noticed how weak the Spaniards were, they did not continue to trade with them as they formerly had done. Veins of gold had already been discovered before this, but they were unable to work these, because the country was at war. The disturbance was so great that they did not cease to keep watch and to be more than usually careful.

The town was situated on a little river.[3] One night they suddenly saw fires which they were not accustomed to, and on this account they doubled the watches, but not having noticed anything during the whole night, they grew careless along toward morning, and the enemy entered the village so silently that they were not seen until they began to kill and plunder. A number of men reached the plain as well as they could, but while they were getting out the captain was mortally wounded. Several Spaniards came back on some horses after they had recovered themselves and attacked the enemy, rescuing some, though only a few. The enemy went off with the booty, leaving three Spaniards killed [4] besides many of the servants and more than twenty horses.

---

[1] Compare the spelling of this name on p. 297.

[2] That is, to poison their arrows.

[3] The San Pedro, in Sonora near the Arizona boundary. The Indians who made this attack may have been the Sobaipuri.

[4] See p. 368, note 2.

The Spaniards who survived started off the same day on foot, not having any horses. They went toward Culiacan, keeping away from the roads, and did not find any food until they reached Corazones where the Indians, like the good friends they have always been, provided them with food. From here they continued to Culiacan, undergoing great hardships. Hernandarias de Saabedra, the mayor, received them and entertained them as well as he could until Juan Gallego arrived with the reinforcements which he was conducting, on his way to find the army. He was not a little troubled at finding that post deserted, when he expected that the army would be in the rich country which had been described by the Indian called Turk, because he looked like one.

Chapter 4

Of how Friar Juan de Padilla and Friar Luis remained in the country and the army prepared to return to Mexico.

When the general, Francisco Vasquez, saw that everything was now quiet, and that his schemes had gone as he wished, he ordered that everything should be ready to start on the return to New Spain by the beginning of the month of April, in the year 1543 [1542].

Seeing this, Friar Juan de Padilla, a regular brother of the lesser order, and another, Friar Luis,[1] a lay brother, told the general that they wanted to remain in that country — Friar Juan de Padilla in Quivira, because his teachings seemed to promise fruit there, and Friar Luis at Cicuye. On this account, as it was Lent at the time, the father made this the subject of his sermon to the companies one Sunday, establishing his proposition on the authority of the Holy Scriptures. He declared his zeal for the conversion of these peoples and his desire to draw them to the faith, and stated that he had received permission to do it, although this was not necessary.

[1] Fray Luis Descalona, or De Escalona, or De Ubeda. For references on these friars, see p. 365, note 1. See also p. 355, note 2.

The general sent a company to escort them as far as Cicuye, where Friar Luis stopped, while Friar Juan went on back to Quivira with the guides who had conducted the general, taking with him the Portuguese, as we related, and the half-blood, and the Indians from New Spain. He was martyred a short time after he arrived there, as we related in the second part, Chapter 8. Thus we may be sure that he died a martyr, because his zeal was holy and earnest.

Friar Luis remained at Cicuye. Nothing more has been heard about him since, but before the army left Tiguex some men who went to take him a number of sheep that were left for him to keep, met him as he was on his way to visit some other villages, which were fifteen or twenty leagues from Cicuye, accompanied by some followers. He felt very hopeful that he was liked at the village and that his teaching would bear fruit, although he complained that the old men were falling away from him. I, for my part, believe that they finally killed him. He was a man of good and holy life, and may Our Lord protect him and grant that he may convert many of those peoples, and end his days in guiding them in the faith. We do not need to believe otherwise, for the people in those parts are pious and not at all cruel. They are friends, or rather, enemies of cruelty, and they remained faithful and loyal friends.[1]

---

[1] Gen. W. W. H. Davis, in his *Spanish Conquest of New Mexico*, p. 231, gives the following extract, translated from an old Spanish MS. at Santa Fé: "When Coronado returned to Mexico, he left behind him, among the Indians of Cibola, the father Fray Francisco Juan de Padilla, the father Fray Juan de la Cruz, and a Portuguese named Andres del Campo. Soon after the Spaniards departed, Padilla and the Portuguese set off in search of the country of the Grand Quivira, where the former understood there were innumerable souls to be saved. After travelling several days, they reached a large settlement in the Quivira country. The Indians came out to receive them in battle array, when the friar, knowing their intentions, told the Portuguese and his attendants to take to flight, while he would await their coming, in order that they might vent their fury on him as they ran. The former took to flight, and, placing themselves on a height within view, saw what happened to the friar. Padilla awaited their coming upon his knees, and when they arrived where he was they immediately put him to death. The same happened to Juan de la Cruz, who was left behind at Cibola, which people killed

After the friars had gone, the general, fearing that they might be injured if people were carried away from that country to New Spain, ordered the soldiers to let any of the natives who were held as servants go free to their villages whenever they might wish. In my opinion, though I am not sure, it would have been better if they had been kept and taught among Christians.

The general was very happy and contented when the time arrived and everything needed for the journey was ready, and the army started from Tiguex on its way back to Cibola. One thing of no small note happened during this part of the trip. The horses were in good condition for their work when they started, fat and sleek, but more than thirty died during the ten days which it took to reach Cibola, and there was not a day in which two or three or more did not die. A large number of them also died afterward before reaching Culiacan, a thing that did not happen during all the rest of the journey.

After the army reached Cibola, it rested before starting across the wilderness, because this was the last of the settlements in that country. The whole country was left well disposed and at peace, and several of our Indian allies remained there.[1]

him. The Portuguese and his attendants made their escape, and ultimately arrived safely in Mexico, where he told what had occurred." In reply to a request for further information regarding this manuscript, General Davis stated that when he revisited Santa Fé, a few years ago, he learned that one of his successors in the post of governor of the territory, having despaired of disposing of the immense mass of old documents and records deposited in his office, by the slow process of using them to kindle fires, had sold the entire lot — an invaluable collection of material bearing on the history of the Southwest and its early European and native inhabitants — as junk. (Winship.) The governor referred to was Rev. William A. Pile, appointed by President Grant and serving in 1869–1870.

[1] When Antonio de Espejo visited Cibola, or Zuñi, in 1583, he found three Indians, natives of Mexico, who had been left by Coronado but who had forgotten their mother tongue. He also found crosses that had been erected by Coronado.

Chapter 5

Of how the army left the settlements and marched to Culiacan,
and of what happened on the way.

Leaving astern, as we might say, the settlements that had
been discovered in the new land, of which, as I have said, the
seven villages of Cibola were the first to be seen and the last
that were left, the army started off, marching across the wilderness. The natives kept following the rear of the army for
two or three days, to pick up any baggage or servants, for
although they were still at peace and had always been loyal
friends, when they saw that we were going to leave the country entirely, they were glad to get some of our people in their
power, although I do not think that they wanted to injure
them, from what I was told by some who were not willing to
go back with them when they teased and asked them to.
Altogether, they carried off several people besides those who
had remained of their own accord, among whom good interpreters could be found to-day. The wilderness was crossed
without opposition, and on the second day before reaching
Chichilticalli Juan Gallego met the army, as he was coming
from New Spain with reenforcements of men and necessary
supplies for the army, expecting that he would find the army
in the country of the Indian called Turk. When Juan Gallego
saw that the army was returning, the first thing he said was
not, "I am glad you are coming back," and he did not like it
any better after he had talked with the general. After he
had reached the army, or rather the quarters, there was quite
a little movement among the gentlemen toward going back
with the new force which had made no slight exertions in coming thus far, having encounters every day with the Indians of
these regions who had risen in revolt, as will be related. There
was talk of making a settlement somewhere in that region until
the viceroy could receive an account of what had occurred.
Those soldiers who had come from the new lands would not
agree to anything except the return to New Spain, so that

nothing came of the proposals made at the consultations, and although there was some opposition, they were finally quieted. Several of the mutineers who had deserted the town of Corazones came with Juan Gallego, who had given them his word as surety for their safety, and even if the general had wanted to punish them, his power was slight, for he had been disobeyed already and was not much respected. He began to be afraid again after this, and made himself sick, and kept a guard. In several places yells were heard and Indians seen, and some of the horses were wounded and killed, before Batuco[1] was reached, where the friendly Indians from Corazones came to meet the army and see the general. They were always friendly and had treated all the Spaniards who passed through their country well, furnishing them with what food they needed, and men, if they needed these. Our men had always treated them well and repaid them for these things. During this journey the juice of the quince was proved to be a good protection against the poison of the natives, because at one place, several days before reaching Señora, the hostile Indians wounded a Spaniard called Mesa, and he did not die, although the wound of the fresh poison is fatal, and there was a delay of over two hours before curing him with the juice. The poison, however, had left its mark upon him. The skin rotted and fell off until it left the bones and sinews bare, with a horrible smell. The wound was in the wrist, and the poison had reached as far as the shoulder when he was cured. The skin on all this fell off.

The army proceeded without taking any rest, because the provisions had begun to fail by this time. These districts were in rebellion, and so there were not any victuals where the soldiers could get them until they reached Petlatlan, although they made several forays into the cross country in search of

---

[1] There were two settlements in Sonora bearing this name, one occupied by the Eudeve and the other by the Tegui division of the Opata. The latter village, which was probably the one referred to by Castañeda, was situated on the Rio de Oposura, a western tributary of the Yaqui, eight leagues east of San José Matape. It became the seat of the Jesuit mission of Santa María in 1629.

provisions. Petlatlan is in the province of Culiacan, and on this account was at peace, although they had several surprises after this.[1] The army rested here several days to get provisions. After leaving here they were able to travel more quickly than before, for the thirty leagues of the valley of Culiacan, where they were welcomed back again as people who came with their governor, who had suffered ill treatment.

Chapter 6

Of how the general started from Culiacan to give the viceroy an account of the army with which he had been intrusted.

It seemed, indeed, as if the arrival in the valley of Culiacan had ended the labors of this journey, partly because the general was governor there and partly because it was inhabited by Christians. On this account some began to disregard their superiors and the authority which their captains had over them, and some captains even forgot the obedience due to their general. Each one played his own game, so that while the general was marching toward the town, which was still ten leagues away, many of the men, or most of them, left him in order to rest in the valley, and some even proposed not to follow him. The general understood that he was not strong enough to compel them, although his position as governor gave him fresh authority. He determined to accomplish it by a better method, which was to order all the captains to provide food and meat from the stores of several villages that were under his control as governor. He pretended to be sick, keeping his bed, so that those who had any business with him could speak to him or he with them more freely, without hindrance or observation, and he kept sending for his particular friends in order to ask them to be sure to speak to the soldiers and encourage them to accompany him back to New Spain, and to tell them that he would request the viceroy, Don

---

[1] See pp. 346, 347. Petatlan is an Aztec word signifying "place of the petates," or mats, referring to the character of the native dwellings.

Antonio de Mendoza, to show them especial favor, and that he
would do so himself for those who might wish to remain in
his government. After this had been done, he started with his
army at a very bad time, when the rains were beginning, for
it was about Saint John's day,[1] at which season it rains continuously. In the uninhabited country which they passed
through as far as Compostela there are numerous very dangerous rivers, full of large and fierce alligators. While the
army was halting at one of these rivers, a soldier who was
crossing from one side to the other was seized, in sight of
everybody, and carried off by an alligator without its being
possible to help him. The general proceeded, leaving the men
who did not want to follow him all along the way, and reached
Mexico with less than 100 men. He made his report to the
viceroy, Don Antonio de Mendoza, who did not receive him
very graciously, although he gave him his discharge. His
reputation was gone from this time on. He kept the government of New Galicia, which had been entrusted to him, for
only a short time, when the viceroy took it himself, until the
arrival of the court, or audiencia, which still governs it. And
this was the end of those discoveries and of the expedition
which was made to these new lands.

It now remains for us to describe the way in which to enter
the country by a more direct route, although there is never a
short cut without hard work. It is always best to find out
what those know who have prepared the way, who know what
will be needed. This can be found elsewhere, and I will now
tell where Quivira lies, what direction the army took, and the
direction in which Greater India lies, which was what they
pretended to be in search of, when the army started thither.
Today, since Villalobos[2] has discovered that this part of the
coast of the South Sea trends toward the west, it is clearly
seen and acknowledged that, since we were in the north, we
ought to have turned to the west instead of toward the east,
as we did. With this, we will leave this subject and will pro-

[1] June 24, 1542.
[2] See p. 360, note 2.

ceed to finish this treatise, since there are several noteworthy
things of which I must give an account, which I have left to
be treated more extensively in the two following chapters.

Chapter 7

*Of the adventures of Captain Juan Gallego while he was bring-
ing reenforcements through the revolted country.*

One might well have complained when in the last chapter
I passed in silence over the exploits of Captain Juan Gallego
with his twenty companions. I will relate them in the present chapter, so that in times to come those who read about it
or tell of it may have a reliable authority on whom to rely.
I am not writing fables, like some of the things which we read
about nowadays in the books of chivalry. If it were not that
those stories contained enchantments, there are some things
which our Spaniards have done in our own day in these parts,
in their conquests and encounters with the Indians, which,
for deeds worthy of admiration, surpass not only the books
already mentioned, but also those which have been written
about the twelve peers of France, because, if the deadly strength
which the authors of those times attributed to their heroes
and the brilliant and resplendent arms with which they adorned
them, are fully considered, and compared with the small stature
of the men of our time and the few and poor weapons which
they have in these parts, the remarkable things which our
people have undertaken and accomplished with such weapons
are more to be wondered at to-day than those of which the
ancients write, and just because, too, they fought with barbarous naked people, as ours have with Indians, among whom
there are always men who are brave and valiant and very
sure bowmen, for we have seen them pierce the wings while
flying, and hit hares while running after them. I have said
all this in order to show that some things which we consider
fables may be true, because we see greater things every day in
our own times, just as in future times people will greatly

wonder at the deeds of Don Fernando Cortes, who dared to go into the midst of New Spain with 300 men against the vast number of people in Mexico, and who with 500 Spaniards succeeded in subduing it, and made himself lord over it in two years.

The deeds of Don Pedro de Alvarado in the conquest of Guatemala, and those of Montejo in Tabasco, the conquests of the mainland and of Peru, were all such as to make me remain silent concerning what I now wish to relate; but since I have promised to give an account of what happened on this journey, I want the things I am now going to relate to be known as well as those others of which I have spoken.

The captain Juan Gallego, then, reached the town of Culiacan with a very small force. There he collected as many as he could of those who had escaped from the town of Hearts, or, more correctly, from Suya, which made in all twenty-two men, and with these he marched through all of the settled country, across which he travelled 200 leagues with the country in a state of war and the people in rebellion, although they had formerly been friendly toward the Spaniards, having encounters with the enemy almost every day. He always marched with the advance guard, leaving two-thirds of his force behind with the baggage. With six or seven Spaniards, and without any of the Indian allies whom he had with him, he forced his way into their villages, killing and destroying and setting them on fire, coming upon the enemy so suddenly and with such quickness and boldness that they did not have a chance to collect or even to do anything at all, until they became so afraid of him that there was not a town which dared wait for him, but they fled before him as from a powerful army; so much so, that for ten days, while he was passing through the settlements, they did not have an hour's rest. He did all this with his seven companions, so that when the rest of the force came up with the baggage there was nothing for them to do except to pillage, since the others had already killed and captured all the people they could lay their hands on and the rest had fled. They did not pause anywhere, so that although the villages ahead of him received some warning, they were upon them so quickly that they did not have a chance to collect. Especially in the region where the town of Hearts had been, he killed and hung a large number of people to punish them for their rebellion. He did not lose a companion during all this, nor was anyone wounded, except one soldier, who was wounded in the eyelid by an Indian who was almost dead, whom he was stripping. The weapon broke the skin and, as it was poisoned, he would have had to die if he had not been saved by the quince juice; he lost his eye as it was. These deeds of theirs were such that I know those people will remember them as long as they live, and especially four or five friendly Indians who went with them from Corazones, who thought that they were so wonderful that they held them to be something divine rather than human.[1] If he had not fallen in with our army as he did, they would have reached the country of the Indian called Turk, which they expected to march to, and they would have arrived there without danger on account of their good order and the skill with which he was leading them, and their knowledge and ample practice in war. Several of these men are still in this town of Culiacan, where I am now writing this account and narrative, where they, as well as I and the others who have remained in this province, have never lacked for labor in keeping this country quiet, in capturing rebels, and increasing in poverty and need, and more than ever at the present hour, because the country is poorer and more in debt than ever before.

Chapter 8

Which describes some remarkable things that were seen on the plains, with a description of the bulls.

My silence was not without mystery and dissimulation when, in Chapter 7 of the second part of this book, I spoke of

---

[1] The Indians of this vicinity had a similar regard for Cabeza de Vaca and his companions. See the narrative in the present volume.

the plains and of the things of which I will give a detailed account in this chapter, where all these things may be found together; for these things were remarkable and something not seen in other parts. I dare to write of them because I am writing at a time when many men are still living who saw them and who will vouch for my account. Who could believe that 1,000 horses and 500 of our cows and more than 5,000 rams and ewes and more than 1,500 friendly Indians and servants, in travelling over those plains, would leave no more trace where they had passed than if nothing had been there — nothing — so that it was necessary to make piles of bones and cow-dung now and then, so that the rear guard could follow the army. The grass never failed to become erect after it had been trodden down, and, although it was short, it was as fresh and straight as before.

Another thing was a heap of cow bones, a crossbow shot long, or a very little less, almost twice a man's height in places, and some eighteen feet or more wide, which was found on the edge of a salt lake in the southern part, and this in a region where there are no people who could have made it. The only explanation of this which could be suggested was that the waves which the north winds must make in the lake had piled up the bones of the cattle which had died in the lake, when the old and weak ones who went into the water were unable to get out. The noticeable thing is the number of cattle that would be necessary to make such a pile of bones.

Now that I wish to describe the appearance of the bulls, it is to be noticed first that there was not one of the horses that did not take flight when he saw them first, for they have a narrow, short face, the brow two palms across from eye to eye, the eyes sticking out at the side, so that, when they are running, they can see who is following them. They have very long beards, like goats, and when they are running they throw their heads back with the beard dragging on the ground. There is a sort of girdle round the middle of the body. The hair is very woolly, like a sheep's, very fine, and in front of the girdle the hair is very long and rough like a lion's. They

have a great hump, larger than a camel's. The horns are
short and thick, so that they are not seen much above the
hair. In May they change the hair in the middle of the body
for a down, which makes perfect lions of them. They rub
against the small trees in the little ravines to shed their hair,
and they continue this until only the down is left, as a snake
changes his skin. They have a short tail, with a bunch of
hair at the end. When they run, they carry it erect like a
scorpion. It is worth noticing that the little calves are red
and just like ours, but they change their color and appearance with time and age.

Another strange thing was that all the bulls that were
killed had their left ears slit, although these were whole when
young. The reason for this was a puzzle that could not be
guessed. The wool ought to make good cloth on account of its
fineness, although the color is not good, because it is the color
of buriel.[1]

Another thing worth noticing is that the bulls travelled
without cows in such large numbers that nobody could have
counted them, and so far away from the cows that it was
more than forty leagues from where we began to see the bulls
to the place where we began to see the cows. The country
they travelled over was so level and smooth that if one looked
at them the sky could be seen between their legs, so that if
some of them were at a distance they looked like smooth-
trunked pines whose tops joined, and if there was only one bull
it looked as if there were four pines. When one was near
them, it was impossible to see the ground on the other side
of them. The reason for all this was that the country seemed
as round as if a man should imagine himself in a three-pint
measure, and could see the sky at the edge of it, about a

---

[1] The kersey, or coarse woollen cloth out of which the habits of the Franciscan friars were made. Hence the name Grey Friars. (Winship.) Various
attempts were made to manufacture the hair into garments, especially stockings, but the ventures did not prove profitable. See Hornaday, " The Extinc-
tion of the American Bison," *Report of the United States National Museum*
for 1886–1887.

crossbow shot from him, and even if a man only lay down on his back he lost sight of the ground.

I have not written about other things which were seen nor made any mention of them, because they were not of so much importance, although it does not seem right for me to remain silent concerning the fact that they venerate the sign of the cross in the region where the settlements have high houses. For at a spring which was in the plain near Acuco they had a cross two palms high and as thick as a finger, made of wood with a square twig for its crosspiece, and many little sticks decorated with feathers around it, and numerous withered flowers, which were the offerings.[1] In a graveyard outside the village at Tutahaco there appeared to have been a recent burial. Near the head there was another cross made of two little sticks tied with cotton thread, and dry withered flowers.[2] It certainly seems to me that in some way they must have received some light from the cross of Our Redeemer, Christ, and it may have come by way of India, from whence they proceeded.

Chapter 9

Which treats of the direction which the army took, and of how another more direct way might be found, if anyone was to return to that country.

I very much wish that I possessed some knowledge of cosmography or geography, so as to render what I wish to say intelligible, and so that I could reckon up or measure the advantage those people who might go in search of that country would have if they went directly through the centre of the country, instead of following the road the army took. How-

---

[1] The cross is common to the Indians and always has been. It often is symbolic of the morning and the evening stars. Those referred to as having been seen by Coronado's men at Acoma were characteristic prayer-sticks, the downy feathers representing the breath of life. Such are still in common use by the Pueblo Indians.

[2] Probably dried corn-husk.

ever, with the help of the favor of the Lord, I will state it as
well as I can, making it as plain as possible.

It is, I think, already understood that the Portuguese,
Campo, was the soldier who escaped when Friar Juan de
Padilla was killed at Quivira, and that he finally reached New
Spain from Panuco,[1] having travelled across the plains country until he came to cross the North Sea mountain chain,
keeping the country that Don Hernando de Soto discovered
all the time on his left hand, since he did not see the river of
the Holy Spirit (Espiritu Santo) at all.[2] After he had crossed
the North Sea mountains, he found that he was in Panuco, so
that if he had not tried to go to the North Sea, he would have
come out in the neighborhood of the border land, or the country of the Sacatecas,[3] of which we now have some knowledge.

This way would be somewhat better and more direct for
anyone going back there in search of Quivira, since some of
those who came with the Portuguese are still in New Spain
to serve as guides. Nevertheless, I think it would be best to
go through the country of the Guachichules,[4] keeping near the
South Sea mountains all the time, for there are more settlements and a food supply, for it would be suicide to launch
out on to the plains country, because it is so vast and is barren of anything to eat, although, it is true, there would not
be much need of this after coming to the cows. This is only
when one goes in search of Quivira, and of the villages which
were described by the Indian called Turk, for the army of Francisco Vazquez Coronado went the very farthest way round to get
there, since they started from Mexico and went 110 leagues
to the west, and then 100 leagues to the northeast, and 250
to the north, and all this brought them as far as the ravines
where the cows were, and after travelling 850 leagues they
were not more than 400 leagues distant from Mexico by a

[1] The northeastern province of New Spain.
[2] That is, he travelled from the Quivira province, in the present Kansas,
southwestwardly to Mexico.
[3] Zacatecas.
[4] This wild tribe inhabited chiefly the region of the present state of San
Luis Potosí, Mexico. They were known also as Cuachichiles and Quachichiles.

2 c

direct route. If one desires to go to the country of Tiguex, so
as to turn from there toward the west in search of the country
of India, he ought to follow the road taken by the army, for
there is no other, even if one wished to go by a different way,
because the arm of the sea which reaches into this coast toward
the north does not leave room for any. But what might be
done is to have a fleet and cross this gulf and disembark in
the neighborhood of the Island of Negroes [1] and enter the
country from there, crossing the mountain chains in search
of the country from which the people at Tiguex came, or
other peoples of the same sort. As for entering from the country of Florida and from the North Sea, it has already been
observed that the many expeditions which have been undertaken from that side have been unfortunate and not very successful, because that part of the country is full of bogs and
poisonous fruits, barren, and the very worst country that is
warmed by the sun. But they might disembark after passing
the river of the Holy Spirit, as Don Hernando de Soto did.
Nevertheless, despite the fact that I underwent much labor, I
still think that the way I went to that country is the best.
There ought to be river courses, because the necessary supplies can be carried on these more easily in large quantities.
Horses are the most necessary things in the new countries,
and they frighten the enemy most. . . . Artillery is also
much feared by those who do not know how to use it. A
piece of heavy artillery would be very good for settlements
like those which Francisco Vazquez Coronado discovered, in
order to knock them down, because he had nothing but some
small machines for slinging and nobody skilful enough to
make a catapult or some other machine which would frighten
them, which is very necessary. [2]

[1] The dictionary of Dominguez says: "Isla de negros; ó isla del Almirantazgo, en el grande Océano equinoccial; grande isla de la América del Norte,
sobre la costa oeste." Apparently the location of this island gradually
drifted westward with the increase of geographical knowledge, until it was
finally located in the Philippine group. (Winship.)

[2] This would indicate that the bronze cannon which Coronado left at
Sia pueblo were worthless.

I say, then, that with what we now know about the trend of the coast of the South Sea, which has been followed by the ships which explored the western part, and what is known of the North Sea toward Norway, the coast of which extends up from Florida, those who now go to discover the country which Francisco Vasquez entered, and reach the country of Cibola or of Tiguex, will know the direction in which they ought to go in order to discover the true direction of the country which the Marquis of the Valley, Don Hernando Cortes, tried to find, following the direction of the gulf of the Firebrand (Tizon) River.[1]

This will suffice for the conclusion of our narrative. Everything else rests on the powerful Lord of all things, God Omnipotent, who knows how and when these lands will be discovered and for whom He has guarded this good fortune.

Laus Deo.

Finished copying, Saturday the 26th of October, 1596, in Seville.

[1] The Gulf of California (which had been navigated by Cortés) and the Río Colorado.

INDEX

INDEX

Aays, not to be confounded with Ayas, 225 n.; Moscoso at, 243; Indians of, give battle, 243. *See also* Ayas.

Açamor, mentioned, 126.

Acaxes, Indians of Culiacan, 345.

Acela, town of, 155.

Acha, *see* Picuris.

Achese, cacique of, addresses De Soto, 166–167.

Acochis, Indian name for gold, 314, 337 n., 342.

Acoma, identification of Acuco with, 311 n.; visit of Alvarado to, 311; description of, 311–312; visited by Arellano, 316; route to, 316; mentioned, 358; worship of cross at, 384.

Acoma Indians, water supply of, 312.

Acosta, Maria de, wife of Pedro Castañeda, 276.

Acoste, cacique of, comes to De Soto, 180.

Acubadaos Indians, 87.

Acuco, *see* Acoma.

Adai Indians, 76 n.

Adobe, making of, described, 352.

Aguacay, mentioned, 237; Moscoso at, 238.

Aguar, Indian deity, 118.

Aguas Calientes, pueblos of, 359; identification of, 359 n.

Aguenes Indians, 84, 85.

Alabama, 183 n.

Alaniz, Hieronymo, notary, with Narvaez, 22; objects to abandonment of ships, 23; death of, 57.

Alarcon, Diego de, confusion of, with Alcaraz, 324 n.

Alarcon, Hernando de, expedition of by sea, 294; narrative of, 279, 294 n.; message of, found by Diaz, 303.

Alarcon, Pedro de, 294 n.

Albino, Indian, 332 n.

Alcaraz, Diego de, meeting with Cabeza de Vaca, 112–113; his need of food, 113; returns from incursion, 119; lieutenant of Diaz, 303, 324; inefficiency of, 326; death of, 371.

Aleman, Juan, name given Indian of Tiguex, 317, 321.

Alimamos, overtakes De Soto, 177.

Alimamu, an Indian chief, 195, 200.

Alligators, do harm to Indians, 143; in rivers of New Galicia, 378.

Almirantazgo, or Isle of Negroes, 386 n.

Altamaca, *see* Altamaha.

Altamaha, 167 n.

Altamaha River, 167 n.

Alvarado, Hernando de, appointed captain, 293; protects Coronado at Cibola, 301; expedition of, to Rio Grande, 311; report of, 279, 311 n.; visits Acoma, 311; imprisons Pecos chiefs, 315; route of, 316 n.; at Braba, 341.

Alvarado, Pedro de, expedition of, to Peru, 288; deeds of, 380.

Alvarez, death of, 6.

Amaye, Moscoso at, 238.

Aminoya, Spaniards hear of, 248; take quarters at, 249; brigantines built at, 250.

Amushungkwa, a Jemez pueblo, 359 n.

Anagados Indians, 71 n.

Anane, a fruit, 140.

Añasco, Juan de, 135; sent by De Soto to explore harbor in Florida, 145; goes to Espiritu Santo, 162; sent in quest of habitations, 171; finds a town twelve leagues off, 171; makes road through the woods, 172; sent on a reconnoissance, 200, 228, 229; advises Moscoso to put out to sea, 260; and does so with him, 261; meets with opposition from those with him, 261–262; again advises putting out to sea, 264.

391

Anguille River, 215 n.

Anhayca Apalache, De Soto at, 161, 162, 164.

Anhocan, Cabeza de Vaca at, 116.

Anilco, 227, 228, 245, 248, 249. See also Nilco.

Animals, of Apalachen, 29; of Florida, mentioned by the Gentleman of Elvas, 271–272.

Anoixi, De Soto takes many inhabitants of, 222.

Antonio de Santa Maria, Franciscan friar, 288.

Antonio Victoria, friar, accident of, 299.

Apalache, mentioned, 161; has much maize, 156, 226; distance from, to Cutifachiqui, 188; direction and distance of, from Espiritu Santo, 271, 272. See also Apalachen.

Apalachee Indians, war against, by Creeks, 21 n.; by English, 21 n.; overcome by Cabeza de Vaca, 28; attack the Spaniards, 30, 31; eastern tribes of, 330 n.; mentioned, 349 n.

Apalachen, indicated to Narvaez as source of gold, 21–22; taken by the Spanish, 28; region of, described, 29–30; climate of, is cold, 29; animals of, 29.

Apalachicola, town on Savannah River, 21 n.

Appalachian Mountains, origin of name of, 21 n.

Appalachee Bay, origin of name of, 21 n.

Aquiguate, largest town seen by De Soto in Florida, 214; De Soto returns to, 215; country of, described, 215.

Aquixo, 227, 270; direction of, 271.

Aquixo, cacique of, comes to De Soto, 203; loses five or six of his men, shot by crossbowmen, 203; and ten, killed by De Soto's cavalry, 205.

Arache, province of, 365.

Arawakan Indians, 21; dance ceremony of, 52 n.

Arbadaos Indians, 80.

Arche, see Harahey.

Areitos, among Indians of Malhado,

52; held in honor of Cabeza de Vaca, 89.

Arellano, Tristan de, appointment of, as captain, 292; lieutenant to Coronado, 298, 335; at Corazones, 301, 303; arrives at Cibola, 313; route of, 315 n.; at Tiguex, 317, 339; attacks Cicuye, 341.

Arispe, see Arizpe.

Aristotle, quoted, 134.

Arizpe, 347 n.

Arkadelphia, 238 n.

Arkansas city, 227 n.

Arkansas Post, 226 n.

Arkansas River, 222 n., 248 n., 249 n.

Artillery, at Culiacan, 297; used by Indians, 357; usefulness of, in exploration, 386.

Astorga, Marquis of, learns what Cabeza de Vaca relates to the Emperor regarding New Spain, 137.

Astudillo, a native of Çafra, to seek Panuco, 49.

Asturian, the, with Figueroa, 61, 64; seen by the Avavares, 79.

Asturiano, a clergyman, 68, 69.

Astyalakwa, a Jemez pueblo, 359 n.

Atabalipa, lord of Peru, 135, 175.

Atayos Indians, 76, 87.

Atchafalaya, lower course of Red River, 261 n.

Attacapan Indians, 51 n., 363 n.

Audiencia, definition of, 285 n.

Audiencia of Española, report to, 8; edition of report by Oviedo, 8, 10.

Auia, island of, 49; probably not Malhado Island, 49 n.

Aute, town south of Apalachen, 30, 31; reached by Narvaez, 32.

Autiamque, mentioned, 221, 225, 227, 237; De Soto winters in, 222–224; distance to Guacay, 270; direction of, 271.

Avavares Indians, receive Cabeza de Vaca, 73; healed by him, 6–7, 78; ignorant of time, 79.

Avellaneda, killed by an Indian, 32.

Avila, Pedro de, leader in rebellion at Suya, 370.

Awatobi, Hopi pueblo, 307 n., 358 n.

Axille, De Soto at, 161.

Ayas, Moscoso crosses river at, 248.

Ayays, not to be confounded with Aays, 225 n.; De Soto at, 225.

Ayllon, Governor-licentiate, death of, 174.

Aymay, named Socorro, 171; De Soto at, 172; location of, 172 n.

Azores, mentioned, 122.

Bacallaos, Spanish name for Newfoundland, 343 n., 360.

Badthing, story of, 78–79.

Baegert, Father Jacob, on Indians of lower California, 346 n.

Bahíos, 108. See also Buhíos.

Baldwyn, Mississippi, 212 n.

Bandelier, A. F., researches on the Seven Cities, 287 n.; on Topira, 290 n.; on Cicuye, 355 n.

Bandelier, A. F. and Fanny, Journey of Nuñez Cabeza de Vaca, cited, 22 n.; 59, 87 n., 102 n., 103 n.

Baracoa, town in Cuba, 142.

Barbacoa, a store house for maize, 165.

Barbels, native American fish, 349.

Barrionuevo, Francisco de, companion of Coronado, 292; at Tiguex, 319; explorations of, 339–340.

Baskett, James Newton, investigations of, 326 n.

Bastian, Francisco, drowning of, 225.

Batuco, identification of, 376 n.

Báyamo, town in Cuba, 142, 143.

Bayou de Vue, 215 n.

Bayou Macon, 255 n.

Bears, in pueblo region, 357.

Béjar, mentioned, 125.

Bermuda, Cabeza de Vaca at, 121.

Bernalillo, settlement on site of Tiguex, 278, 317 n.

Bidai Indians, 80 n.

Biedma, narrative of, cited, 40 n.; referred to, 130 n.

Big Bayou Meto, 225.

Big Creek, 21, 215 n.

Bigotes, see Whiskers.

Birds, mentioned, 29–30, 272.

Biscayan Indians, 115 n.

Bison, first printed reference to, 68 n.; described by Cicuye Indians, 311; hunted by plains Indians, 330, 362, 363; stampede of, 331; Coronado's army supplied with meat of, 336; piles of bones of, 382; Castañeda's description of, 382–383.

Black Warrior River, 188 n., 189 n.

Blankets, of cotton, 350.

Blizzard, experienced by Coronado, 333.

Bog of Pia, breeds mosquitos, 144.

Boston Mountains, 221 n.; crossed by De Soto, 221.

Boyomo, settlement of, 347.

Braba, see Taos.

Brazos River, 58 n., 244 n., 245 n.

Bread, maize, 271; Indian, 303, 340, 340 n.

Bridge, built by Spaniards across Cicuye River, 329; Indian, across Rio Grande, 340.

Brigantines, built by Spaniards at Aminoya, 250; become separated in the Gulf of Mexico, 263.

Buffalo, see Bison.

Buhíos, Arawak word, 19, 79. See also Bahíos.

Burgos, André de, printer, 134, 272.

Buriel, cloth used by Franciscan friars, 383 n.

Burning of Indians at stake by Spaniards, 320.

Caballos, Bahia de, 37, 162 n. See also Horses, Bay of.

Cabeza de Vaca, Alvar Nuñez, narrative of, 1–126; birth and parentage, 3; significance of name, 3; trades and heals among the Indians, 6–7; line of travel, 7; character of his chronicle, 7; his accomplishment, 8; report to Audiencia of Española, 8; appointed governor of provinces of Rio de la Plata, 8; dies, 9; bibliography of the Relacion, 10–11; salutation to Charles V., 12; duration of his wandering, 13; his idea of the value of his narrative, 13; leaves San Lúcar de Barrameda, 4, 14; is treasurer and high-sheriff, 4, 14; reaches Santo Domingo, 14; proceeds to Trinidad and is overtaken by a terrible storm, 15–17; passes winter at Jagua, 17; explores mainland of Florida, with Narvaez, 4, 20; believes it wiser to return to vessels, 22–23; refuses to sail in charge of them, preferring to share risks of march into the country, 24; goes with forty men to seek a harbor, 25–26; enters Apalachen, 28; goes from Aute to find the sea, 33; embarks in open boat, 36; sufferings of his men, 38–40; is assaulted by Indians, 41; deserted by Narvaez, 42; lands on an island among friendly Indians, 5, 44–45; loses three men, in endeavor to re-embark, 46; destitute condition of the survivors, 46; aid given by Indians, 47–48; is overtaken by Dorantes and Alonzo del Castillo, 48; agrees that four of the party shall try to reach Panuco, 49; learns Indians believe the Christians are sorcerers, 50; names island Malhado, 50; heals the sick by breathing on them, and by prayer, 53; on the mainland, 52, 55; his party now numbers fourteen, 55; suffers great hardships, 56; trafficks among the Indians, 56–57; rescues Oviedo from Malhado, 57; is left by him, 59; finds Dorantes, Castillo, and Estevanico, 59–60; waits six months before attempting to escape, 60, 61, 70; is made a slave, 61; is forced to postpone escape another year, 71; succeeds at last, 73; works more cures among the Indians, 74, 77, 78; goes naked, 80, 81; goes among the Maliacones, 80; eats dogs, 80, 81; barters with Indians, 81; performs more cures, 91; reaches a mountainous country, 92; receives presents from the Indians, 92–93; cuts an arrow head out of a wounded native, 96–97; reaches the Rio Grande, 99; is feared by the Indians because of deaths among them, 101; heals the sick, 101; goes among the Jumanos, 102; calls them the Cow nation, 103; starts in search of maize, 105; touches and blesses both sick and well, 106–107; teaches Christian religion, 107; finds news of Christians, 109; checks fear among his Indian companions, 111; is taken to Diego de Alcaraz, 112; joins

party of Diego and dismisses his Indian followers, 114–115; is received by Melchior Diaz, 116; arrives at Mexico, 120; at Havana, 121; at Lisbon, 123; mentioned as a survivor of Narvaez's party, 125; disagrees with De Soto, 136; mentioned by the Gentleman of Elvas, 136, 221, 246; returns from expedition, 288; narrative of, 288; in Corazones valley, 301; traces of, found by Coronado, 332; regard of Indians for, 381 n.

Cabeza de Vaca, Teresa, mother of Nuñez Cabeza de Vaca, 3, 125.

Cabo Cruz, 15 n.

Cabo de Santa Cruz, 15.

Cabusto, 194.

Caçabe bread, see Cassava bread.

Cache River, 215 n.

Cactus belt, northern limit of, 70 n.

Cahita, synonymous with Sinaloa, 346 n.

Cahoques Indians, 87.

Calahuchi, 161 n.

Calderon, Captain, 155; at Espiritu Santo, 162; commands a brigantine, 265.

Cale, province of, reported to be abundant in gold, 154; mentioned, 162.

California, Gulf of, 109 n.; explored, 304, 346; natives of peninsula of, 346, 346 n.

Caliquen, reached by De Soto, 157.

Calpista, mentioned by Ranjel, 216 n.

Caluça, in northeastern part of Mississippi, 212.

Camolas Indians, 87 n.

Camones Indians, are reported to have killed Peñalosa and Tellez, 72.

Campo, Andres del, Portuguese companion of Padilla, 365, 373, 385; returns to New Spain, 385.

Canarreo shoals, 18.

Canasagua, De Soto at, 178.

Caney creek, 58 n.

Cannibalism in Culiacan, 345.

Cannouchee River, 170 n.

Cantaloupes, as food of Indians, 348.

Capachiqui, De Soto at, 165.

Capoques Indians, 54 n., 55 n., 65 n., 66 n., 87 n.

Capothan, province of New Spain, 364.

Caravallo, appointed lieutenant to sail with ships of Narvaez, 24; mentioned, 124.

Cardenas, Garcia Lopez, appointed captain, 292; protects Coronado at Cibola, 301; visit of, to Colorado River, 309; attacks Indian village, 319; treachery of Indians towards, 321; accident to, 331; summoned to Spain, 367; flight of, from Suya, 369, 370.

Carlos, leaves his wife at Havana, 145; is killed at Manilla, 193.

Carmona, Alonzo de, 131.

Casa de Contratacion, at Seville, 135 n.

Cases, with dead bodies, burned by Xuarez, 21.

Casiste, De Soto at, 187.

Casqui, cacique of, 205; speeches of, to De Soto, 206–207; kneels before the cross, 208; directs De Soto to Pacaha, 208; makes many presents to De Soto, 210; gives his daughter to the governor, 211; begs forgiveness for absenting himself without permission, 212; accepts friendship of the cacique of Pacaha, 212.

Cassava bread, 144, 145.

Castañeda, Pedro de, narrative of Coronado's expedition by, 276, 281–387; facts of life of, 276; value of narrative of, 276; manuscript of, in Lenox library, 277; translations of, 276–277; date of narrative, 282 n.; joins expedition at Culiacan, 296 n.

Castile, mentioned, 124.

Castillo, Doctor, father of Alonzo de Castillo Maldonado, 125.

Castillo Maldonado, Alonzo del, with Cabeza de Vaca, 4, 6; joins in report to Audiencia of Española, 8; returns to New Spain, 9; goes with Cabeza de Vaca to find a harbor, 26; again goes on the same errand, 33; embarks in open boat, 36; loses his boat and overtakes Cabeza de Vaca, 48; on the mainland, 54; returns to Malhado, 55; accompanies Indians to find walnuts, and meets with Cabeza de Vaca, 59–60; stay of, with the Yguazes, 65; mentioned, 72; mentioned by Oviedo, 69, 70;

among Lanegados, 71; escapes, 73; cures afflicted Indians, 74, 76, 77; goes to the Maliacones, 80; makes reconnoissance towards Rio Grande, 102; finds evidence of visit by Europeans, 109; rejoins Cabeza de Vaca and attaches himself to a Spanish exploring party, 113; returns to Spain, 125; mentioned by Castañeda, 288.

Catalte, 236.

Catamaya, De Soto at, 222.

Caya River, 216.

Cayas, De Soto at, 217, 219; mentioned, 225, 227, 238; cacique of, is dismissed, 221.

Cebreros, see Zebreros.

Cedar Lake, 58 n.

Cerda, Alvaro de la, left by Narvaez in charge of a vessel, 18, 20.

Cervantes, Spanish soldier, 328.

Chacan, a fruit, 104.

Chaguate, province of, mentioned, 223 n., 236; cacique of, addresses Moscoso, 237.

Chaguete, 237; Indians come to, in peace, 247; Moscoso leaves, 248. See also Chaguate.

Chalaque, province of, 176.

Charles V, emperor, 12 n.

Charruco, Cabeza de Vaca determines to seek, 56.

Charrucos Indians, 87 n.

Chattahuchi, 161 n.

Chattanooga, 181 n., 182 n.

Chauauares Indians, 87 n. See Chavavares Indians.

Chavavares Indians, 73 n., 80 n., 87.

Chia, see Sia.

Chiaha, province of, 175, 177, 178; nature of the country of, 270; speech of cacique of, 178; cacique of, surrenders himself to De Soto, 180.

Chiametla, death of Samaniego at, 295.

Chicaça, De Soto at, 195, 212 n.; Indians of, make an attack, 197–199.

Chicacilla, 199 n.

Chichilticalli, visited by Fray Marcos, 289; by Diaz, 298; location of, 299 n., 349 n.; Coronado's first view of, 299; description of, 349.

Chichimecas, Mexican name for braves, 357.

Chicot County, Arkansas, 255 n.
Chihuahua, 105 n.
Chilano, mentioned, 249.
Childersburg, 183 n.
Children of sun, Spaniards called, 94.
China, belief in its connection with America, 343, 360.
Chisca, a gold-bearing country, 180, 181, 212; mentioned, 205.
Choctaw Indians, 38 n.
Cholupaha, town of, 157; called Villafarta, 157.
Choualla, see Xualla.
Christianity, taught to the Indians, 107, 117; churches to be built by them, 119.
Churches, to be built by Indians, 119.
Chuse, Bay of, 40 n.
Cibola, reached by expedition of Fray Marcos, 275, 289; Guzman's expedition to, 286; description of, 300; captured by Coronado, 301; army arrives at, 306; Castañeda's description of, 350; pueblos of, 358.
Cicuyc, see Cicuye.
Cicuye, synonymous with Pecos, 329 n. See Pecos.
Cienfuegos, Bay of, 17 n.
Civet-marten skins described by Cabeza de Vaca, 39.
Clark, on Indian sign language, 363 n.
Clark County, 238 n.
Cleburne County, 216 n.
Clothing of Indians, 318, 334, 347, 350, 355.
Coahuiltecan affinities, 61 n.
Coayos Indians, 76.
Coça, province of, 170, 175, 228; speech of cacique of, 183–184; inhabitants of, seized by De Soto, 184; cacique of, taken, 185; is dismissed, 187; distance to Tastaluça, 189; has more maize than Nilco, 226; nature of the country, 270; direction of, 271.
Cocopa Indians, a Yuman tribe, 303 n.
Cocos Indians, 54 n.
Cofaqui, 168.
Cofitachequi, see Cutifachiqui.
Cohani Indians, 59 n.
Coké Indians, 54 n.
Coles, Juan, 131.
Coligoa, De Soto at, 215–216; distance to Autiamque, 270; nature of the country, 270.
Colima, ravines of, 332.
Colorado River, 58 n., 90 n.; visited by Diaz, 303; by Cardenas, 309.
Comos Indians, 80 n., 87.
Compostela, in a hostile country, 120; mentioned, 285 n., 287; rendezvous of Coronado's army, 293; departure of Coronado from, 295.
Comupatrico, settlement of, 347.
Cona, settlement of plains Indians, 333.
Coosa, 183 n.
Copee, used in paying the bottoms of Moscoso's vessels, 263.
Copper, found at Quivira, 337.
Coquite, pueblo of, 356 n., 358 n.
Corazones, Pueblo de los, 108, 115 n.; Coronado's army at, 301; valley of, 347; friendliness of Indians of, 372, 376. See Hearts, town of.
Corn, description of, 350; method of grinding, 354; stores of, kept by Indians, 356. See also Maize.
Coronado, Francisco Vazquez de, on Stake Plains, 7; expedition inspired by journey of Cabeza de Vaca, 8; memoirs of George P. Winship on, 276–277; bibliography of accounts of expedition of, 277–279; Castañeda's narrative of expedition of, 276, 281–387; testimony of companions of, 279; expedition of, mentioned, 97 n., 284, 362 n.; appointed governor of New Galicia, 287; marriage of, 287; accompanies Fray Marcos to Culiacan, 288; makes expedition to Topira, 290; returns to Mexico, 291; friendship of Mendoza for, 291; receives command from Mendoza, 275, 281, 291; Castañeda's criticism of, 291, 293; appointments confirmed by, 292; departure of, from Compostela, 295; receives report of Diaz, at Chiametla, 296; at Culiacan, 297–298; Truxillo brought before, 298; arrives at Chichilticalli, 299; discouragement of, 299; reaches Cibola, 300; letter to Mendoza, 277, 300 n.; attacks Cibola, 300; wounded at Cibola, 301; mention of, 294, 302, 305, 319; finds horn of mountain goat, 306;

joined by Arellano, 306; sends Tovar to Tusayan, 307; sends Cardenas to Colorado River, 308; receives report of Cardenas, 310; gifts to, from Cicuye Indians, 311; sends Alvarado to Cicuye, 311; receives message from Alvarado, 312; departure of, for Tiguex, 313; arrives at Tutahaco, 314; at Tiguex, 314; sends Alvarado to Cicuye, 315; joined by army, 317; demands cloth of Indians, 317–318; gives Cardenas orders to attack Indians, 319; orders of, concerning prisoners, 320; besieges Tiguex, 322; attempts of, to make peace, 323; receives news of death of Diaz, 325; sends Tovar to San Hieronimo, 326; messengers from, to Mendoza, 326; letter of, to king, 278, 329 n.; pacifies Cicuye, 329; departure of, for Quivira, 329; bison seen by, 330, 331; experiences blizzard, 333; divides army, 335; arrives at Quivira, 336; route of, 337 n.; returns from Quivira, 338; crosses route of De Soto, 339; reaches Cicuye and Tiguex, 342; winters at Tiguex, 342, 366; receives letters from Mendoza, 367; accident to, 368; schemes of, to return home, 369; request of, for soldiers to, 370; preparations of, for return, 372, 373; arrives at Cibola, 374; meets Gallego with re-enforcements, 375; feigns illness, 376, 377; at Culiacan, 377; promises of, 378; returns to Mexico, 378; reports to Mendoza, 378; coolness of Mendoza towards, 378; deprived of governorship of New Galicia, 378; route of, 385; inadequacy of equipment of, 386.

Coronado expedition, memoirs of George Parker Winship on, 276–277; Castañeda's narrative of, 276, 281–387; bibliography of other accounts of, 277–280; importance of, 280; date of, 293 n.; reasons given by Mota Padilla for failure of, 366 n.

Corral, death of, 49.

Corrientes, Cape, storm at, 18.

Cortes, Hernando, receives Cabeza de Vaca, 121; mentioned, 283; trial for

murder of wife, 285 n.; given new title, 286 n.; feats of, 380.

Corvo, mentioned, 122 n.

Coste, speech of cacique of, 182.

Cotton, garments of, presented to Cabeza de Vaca, 104; noted by him, 106; cloth of, made at Tusayan, 308; blankets of, 350.

Council Bend, suggested as the place of De Soto's crossing of the Mississippi, 204 n.

Cow nation, Indians so named by Cabeza de Vaca, 103. See Jumanos Indians.

Cows, see Bison.

Creek Indians, 21 n.

Cremation among Zuñi, 351.

Cross, raised at Casqui, 208; sign of, among the Zuñis, 351; venerated by Indians, 384.

Cruz, Bahia de la, 36. See also Tampa Bay.

Cuachichiles, see Guachichules.

Cuba, De Soto in, 141–145.

Cuchendados Indians, 86.

Cuenca de Huete, mentioned, 124.

Culiacan, mentioned, 115 n.; Cabeza de Vaca at, 116.

Culiacan, San Miguel de, foundation of, by Guzman, 276, 286, 344; arrival of Cabeza de Vaca at, 288; location of, 296 n.; Castañeda's description of, 344; return of Coronado to, 377.

Cultalchulches Indians, 76, 78, 80 n., 87.

Cures among Indians wrought by Cabeza de Vaca, 6–7, 53, 73, 74, 76, 77, 78, 91, 101, 106–107, 117; by Alonzo del Castillo, 74, 76, 77.

Cushing, F. H., on Zuñi breadstuff, 354 n.

Cutifachiqui, 172 n., 178, 180; Indians of, 173–174; speech of kinswoman of the cacica of, 172–173; speech of cacica of, 173; cacica of, furnishes pearls, 174; cacica of, is made a slave, 176; escape of cacica of, 177; distance of, to Xualla, 188, 270; lad of, acts as interpreter, 224; nature of the country of, 270; direction of, 271.

Cuyamunque, a Tewa pueblo, 359 n.

Cuzco, city of, 135.

Dances of the Tahus, 344.
Daniel, Franciscan friar, 288.
Dávila, Pedrárias, governor, 135, 136.
Davis, W. W. H., on the fate of Padilla, 373 n.
Daycao, distance of, to Rio Grande, 247; direction of, 271.
Daycao River, 245, 246.
Dead bodies, eaten by members of party with Cabeza de Vaca, 49; Soto-Mayor eaten by Esquivel, 63.
Deaguanes Indians, 59.
Decubadaos Indians, 87 n.
Deer, 350, 363.
Deer-suet, 105.
Deguenes Indians, 87 n.
Descalona, Fray Luis, settles at Cicuye, 365 n., 373.
Desha County, 227 n., 249 n.
Diaz, Melchior, 116 n.; explains to the natives the coming of Cabeza de Vaca, 117; reports of Fray Marcos investigated by, 277, 296; companion of Coronado, 292; position of, 292; reference to, 299; in command at Corazones, 302, exploration of, 303, 324; death of, 325.
Divorce among Indians, 353.
Dogs, eaten by De Soto's men, 167; used by Indians, 330, 334, 362.
Doguenes Indians, 59 n., 84, 87.
Dorantes, Pablo, father of Andrés Dorantes, 125.
Dorantes de Carrança, Andrés, with Cabeza de Vaca, 4, 6; joins in report to Audiencia of Española, 8; later years and death of, 9; goes to find the sea, 33; embarks in open boat, 36; repulses Indians, 39; loses his boat and overtakes Cabeza de Vaca, 48; on the mainland, 54, 55; returns to Malhado, 55; accompanies Indians to find walnuts and meets with Cabeza de Vaca, 59–60; escapes from slavery, 64; escapes from the Yguazes, 65; mentioned by Oviedo, 69, 70; joins Cabeza de Vaca in escape from Indians, 71, 73; mentioned, 72; performs cures among Avavares, 78; goes to the Maliacones, 80; receives a hawk-bell of copper, 95; is presented with over six hundred open hearts of

deer, 108; rejoins Cabeza de Vaca and attaches himself to a Spanish exploring party, 113; returns to Spain, 121, 125; swears not to divulge certain things he has seen in New Spain, 136; a survivor of Narvaez's expedition, 288; traces of, found by Coronado, 332.
Dorantes, Diego, killed by Indians, 58, 64, 69.
Double Mountain fork, 245 n.
Dragoon pass, location of, 349 n.
Dreams, respected by the Indians, 64; citation from Oviedo regarding, 70.
Dulchanchellin, Indian chief, 27.

Eagles, tame, kept by Indians, 348, 348 n.
Earthquakes, near Colorado River, 325.
Elvas, Gentleman of, narrative by, 127–272; may have been Alvaro Fernandez, 130; related narratives, 130–131; bibliography of the Narrative, 131–132.
Emeralds presented to Cabeza de Vaca, 106, 108.
Enequen, used in making rope, 248.
Enriquez, Alonso, comptroller of Narvaez's fleet, 14; lands on island off Florida coast, 19; joins conferences regarding inland exploration, 22; embarks with Xuarez in open boat, 36; boat of, found bottom up, 61; rescued by Narvaez and loses his commission, 62; is cast away on the coast, 72; is mentioned by Oviedo, 70.
Espejo, Antonio de, on the Rio Grande, 7; cited, 102 n.; Mexican Indians at Cibola found by, 374 n.
Espíritu Santo, Bay, 58 n.; mentioned by Oviedo, 70.
Espiritu Santo, port, 153; adjacent country described, 169; distance to Palache, 188; direction from Apalache, 271; distance to Ocute, 270; land between the two places, 270; direction to Apalache and Rio de las Palmas, 272.
Espiritu Santo River identified with Mississippi, 339 n.
Esquivel, Hernando de, among Indians, 62; informs Figueroa of fate

of Narvaez and the others, 62–63; feeds on flesh of Soto-Mayor, 63; is slain because of a dream, 58, 64, 68; mentioned, 72; mentioned by Oviedo, 70.

Estévanico, with Cabeza de Vaca, 4, 6; with Fray Marcos de Niza, 9; put to death by Zuñis, 9; brought by Indians, with Dorantes and Castillo, and meets with Cabeza de Vaca, 59; stay of, with the Yguazes, 65; escapes from Indians, 71, 73; performs cures among Avavares, 78; goes to the Maliacones, 80; cause of death of, 95 n.; accompanies Alonzo de Castillo on reconnoissance towards Rio Grande, 102; is useful in securing information from the Indians, 107; accompanies Cabeza de Vaca in search of Spanish exploring party, 112; acts as guide, 113; mentioned as a survivor of Narvaez's party, 126, 288; guide for Fray Marcos, 275, 288–289; death of, 275, 290.

Estrada, Alonzo de, treasurer for New Spain, 287.

Estremadura, 216, 341.

Estufas, at Braba, 341; at Cibola, 350, 350 n.; description of, 353.

Evora, 272.

Feathers, trade in, 286; use of, in dress, 350; symbolism of, 384 n.

Ferdinand, king of Spain, 287.

Fernandes, Benito, drowned, 166.

Fernandez, Alvaro, a Portuguese sailor to seek Panuco, 49.

Fernandez, Alvaro, may have been the Gentleman of Elvas, 130.

Fernandez, Bartolomé, sailor, 22.

Fewkes, *Aborigines of Porto Rico*, cited, 19 n.

Fifteen-Mile Bayou, 205 n.

Figueroa, a native of Toledo, to seek Panuco, 49; found by the fugitives from Malhado, 58 n., 61; relates his experiences, 62–63, 68; escapes by flight, 64; seen by the Avavares, 79.

Figueroa, Gomez Suarez de, companion of Coronado, 293.

Figueroa, Vasco Porcallo de, *see* Porcallo de Figueroa, Vasco.

Firebrand, use of, by Indians in travelling, 303.

Firebrand River, *see* Colorado.

Fish, taken by De Soto, 209–210.

Fisher County, Texas, 245 n.

Fleet of Narvaez, size of, 14; visited by hurricane on southern coast of Cuba, 3–4, 15–17; brigantine bought in Trinidad, 18; another vessel purchased, 18.

Flint River, 164 n.

Florida, eastern limit of grant to Narvaez, 3, 14; fleet of Narvaez sights, 18; grains, fruits, and nuts of, 271; bad character of country of, 386.

Flowers, use of, in Indian ceremonials, 384.

Food of Indians, 312, 333, 348, 354.

Fort Belknap, 244 n., 245 n.

Fort Prince George, 176 n.

Fort Smith, 222 n.

Fowls, domestic, among the Indians, 348, 354.

Franciscans, with Narvaez, 14; in Cuba, 142; in New Spain, 288; elect Marcos de Niza father provincial, 291.

Fruits of Florida, 271; of the great plains, 364.

Fuentes, De Soto's chamberlain, condemned to death, 197.

Galena, 96 n.

Galeras, Juan, explores Grand Cañon, 309.

Galicia, New Kingdom of, in New Spain, 285 n., 286.

Galisteo, pueblo of, 356, 358 n.

Gallego, Juan, companion of Coronado, 292; messenger from Coronado to Mendoza, 302; sword of, found in Kansas, 302 n.; messenger to Coronado, 371, 372; meets Coronado on his return, 375; exploits of, 380.

Gallegos, Baltasar de, is chief castellan, 138; leaves his wife at Havana, 146; at the town of Ucita, 147; sent into the country, 148; returns with a survivor of the party of Narvaez, 149; is sent to the province of Paracoxi, 154; hears speech on part of the absent cacique, asks where gold may be found, 154; sent in quest of habitations, 171; in affray with Indians at Mauilla, 190; responds to De Soto's dying speech, 233.

Galveston Island, resembles Malhado, in certain particulars, 57 n.

Gamez, Juan de, killed at Mauilla, 193.

Gaytan, Juan, takes an Indian boy of Yupaha, 164.

Giant Indians, 302, 304.

Gibraleon, mentioned, 125.

Gifts, exchange of, on Cabeza de Vaca's line of march, 97 n.

Giralda, great tower of Seville, 309 n.

Giusiwá, a Jemez pueblo, 359 n.

Goat, mountain, seen by Spaniards, 304, 305, 348.

Gold, sought by the Spaniards, 21–22, 145, 154, 164, 180, 181, 205, 212; traces of, found, 19, 21, 111; tales of, at Quivira, 328, 329; discovered at Suya, 371.

Gomera, one of the Canary Islands, 139.

Gorbalan, Francisco, companion of Coronado, 293.

Government of Indians, 308, 347, 351.

Granada, Coronado's name for Hawikuh, 277, 300 n.

Grand or Neosho River, 217 n.

Grand Cañon, discovery of, 309.

Grande River, 201, 202, 205, 208, 209, 215, 224, 227, 245, 246, 247, 248, 249, 270, 271. See also Mississippi River.

Grapes, wild, found by Coronado, 334, 338.

Graves, at Tutahaco, 384.

Great plains, Spaniards lost on, 336; description of, 362.

Great River, the, 202. See Mississippi River and Grande River.

Greene County, Alabama, 189 n.

Grey Friars, origin of name, 385 n.

Guacay, distance of, to Daycao, 270–271; nature of the country, 271.

Guachichules, Indians, 385.

Guachoya, De Soto reaches, 227; cacique of, comes to him, 227; makes an address, 228; and assists in attack of Nilco, 231; death of De Soto at, 233; Spaniards leave, 236; mentioned, 245, 248; cacique

of, plots against Moscoso, 251; exposes plot of caciques of Nilco and Taguanate, 252; and kills Indians of Nilco, 252; direction of, 271.

Guadalajara, beginning of, 285 n., 287.

Guadalaxara, see Guadalajara.

Guadiana, Spanish river, 341.

Guaes, province near Quivira, 328, 328 n., 364.

Guahate, province, mentioned, 222.

Guaniguanico, storm at, 18.

Guasco, see Waco.

Guatemala, conquered by Alvarado, 380.

Guaxulle, De Soto at, 177; mentioned, 178.

Guayaba tree, 141.

Guaycones Indians, 87.

Guaymas Indians, 108 n.

Guevara, Diego de, captures Indian village, 324.

Guevara, Juan de, appointment of son of, 292.

Guevara, Pedro de, appointed captain, 292.

Guevenes Indians, 59 n.

Gutierres, Diego, appointed captain, 292.

Gutierrez, Juan, see Xuarez, Juan, and 14 n.

Guzman, Diego de, 111.

Guzman, Francisco de, goes away with his Indian concubine, 238.

Guzman, Juan de, made captain of infantry, 164; crosses Mississippi with infantry, 204; sent against Indians, 231, 256; is taken by them, 257.

Guzman, Nuño de, position of, in New Spain, 285; career of, 285 n.; cruelty to natives, 285 n.; expedition of, to the Seven Cities, 286; Culiacan settled by, 276, 287; imprisonment of, 287.

Hacanac, cacique of, gives battle, 239.

Hailstones, in Coronado's camp, 333.

Hair dress, of pueblo women, 350.

Halona, Zuñi pueblo, 358 n.; excavations at, 351 n.

Hano, Hopi pueblo, 358 n.

Hans Indians, 54, 87.

Hapaluya, De Soto passes, 160.

Harahey, identification of, 328 n., 365 n.

Havana, fleet of Narvaez nears, 18; Miruelo to return to, if harbor is not found, 20; Cabeza de Vaca at, 121, 122; mentioned, 125, 142.

Hawikuh, scene of Estévan's death, 275; called Granada by Coronado, 277, 300 n.; history of, 300 n., 358 n.

Haxa or Haya, settlement near Mississippi River, 330, 331.

Hearts, town of, 7, 108 n. See Corazones, Pueblo de los.

Hearts of animals, as food, 301.

Hearts Valley, see Corazones.

Hemes, see Jemez.

Hempstead County, 240 n.

Henry, cardinal, archbishop of Evora, 272.

Hermosillo, 109 n.

Hewett, on Pecos, 355 n.

Hirriga, town of Ucita, 147 n.

Hodge, F. W., 11, 280; on route of Coronado, 337 n.

Hope, camp near, 239 n.

Hopi, tribal name of Indians at Tusayan, 307 n.; as cotton growers, 308 n.; pottery of, 340 n.; tame eagles of, 348 n.; hair dress of women, 350 n.; population of pueblos of, 351 n.; pueblos of, 358 n.

Hornachos, mentioned, 124.

Hornaday, W. T., on wool of bison, 383 n.

Horseflesh, eaten by Spaniards, 27, 35, 36, 253.

Horses, Bay of, 37 n., 162 n. See also Caballeros, Bahia de.

Horses, fear of Indians of, 386.

Houses of Indians, 165, 346, 350, 356, 364.

Huelva, Diego de, killed by Indians, 58, 64.

Huhasene, an Indian chief, 255.

Iguaces Indians, 61 n.

Inca, the, see Vega, Garcilaso de la.

India, believed to be connected with America, 343, 360.

Indian Bay, 253 n.

"Indian giving," 100 n.

Indians, stature and proportions of, 32;

fine archery of, 32; customs of, at Malhado, 54; weeping of, 54 n.; as a sign of obedience, 241, 242–243; barter among, 56–57; subsist on walnuts, 59–60; eat prickly pears three months of the year, 60–61; kill even their male children, 64, 70; have great reverence for dreams, 70; call Spaniards children of the sun, 78; marriage relations of, 83; methods of warfare of, 84–86; nations and tongues of, beyond Malhado, 86; peculiar customs of, in drinking a tea of certain leaves, 87–88; method of, in preparing flour of mesquite, 89; plunder those who welcome Cabeza de Vaca, 91, 92; and plunder one another, 97; rabbit hunts of, 98; eat spiders and worms, 98; offer all they have to Cabeza de Vaca, 99; women of, may negotiate in war, 100, 102; chastise children for weeping, 101; have fixed dwellings, 102; go naked, 103; eat powder of straw, 106; languages of, 107; believe Spaniards are from heaven, 107; women of, wear grass and straw, 108; worship the sun, 107–108; promise to be Christians, 118; and to build churches, 119; worship the devil with blood sacrifices, 151; approach, playing on flutes, 158, 183, 189; costumes of, 166; have abundance of meat at Ocute, 168; description of, at Cutifachiqui, 173–174; mortuary customs of, 234, 351; described by the Gentleman of Elvas, 272; use poisoned arrows, 326, 371.

Intoxication, among Indians, 66.

Iron, 93 n., 95 n.

Isleta, 358 n.

Jacona, 359 n.

Jagua, Cabeza de Vaca at, 17 n.; Narvaez reaches with a pilot, 18.

Jaramillo, Juan, narrative of, 279, 337 n., 365 n.

Jefferson County, 225 n.

Jemez, pueblos of, 339 n., 352, 359 n.; visited by Barrionuevo, 339.

Jeréz de la Frontera, 3.

John III., king, 272 n.

Juamanos Indians, 102 n., 103 n.;

know something of Christianity, 102 n.; the Cow nation, 103; method of cooking among, 104–105; have fixed residences, 112.
Juana, Queen of Spain, 292.

Kansas, description of, 364.
Karankawan Indians, 51 n., 57 n., 61 n.
Kaw or Kansa Indians, 328 n., 364 n.
Kiakima, Zuñi pueblo, 358 n.
Kyanawe, Zuñi pueblo, 358 n.

Lacane, Moscoso at, 242.
Lake Michigamia, 214 n.
Lakes, near Apalachen, 29.
Lanegados Indians, hold Castillo captive, 71.
Lara, Alonso Manrique de, companion of Coronado, 293.
Las Navas de Tolosa, battle of, 3.
La Vaca, Bay, 58 n.
League, Spanish, 22 n.
Lee County, Arkansas, 214 n.
Lenox Library, manuscript of Castañeda in, 277.
Leopard, see Wildcat.
Lewis, T. Hayes, 132.
Lions, see Mountain lions.
Lisbon, 123.
Little Red River, 216 n.
Little River, 240 n.
Little Tennessee River, 177 n.
Little Valley, settlement of, 347.
Llano River, 95 n.
Lobillo, Juan Rodriguez, at court, 135; sent by De Soto into the country, 148; returns with four Indian women, 149; sent in quest of habitations, 171; overtakes De Soto, 172.
Lopez, Diego, death of, 49.
Lopez, Diego, appointed captain, 292; succeeds Samaniego, 296; adventure of, at Tiguex, 319; visits Haxa, 331.
Lopez de Cardenas, G., see Cardenas.
Lowery, Woodbury, Spanish Settlements, 1513–1561, cited, 19 n.
Luis, Friar, see Descalona.
Lusitanians, characterized, 134.

Mabila, see Mauilla.
Macaco, 150 n.
Macanoche, presented to De Soto, 213.

Maçaque, see Matsaki.
McGee, W J, account of Seri Indians, 301 n.
Magdalena River, 33.
Mago, a poisonous tree, 108 n.
Maize, shown by Indians to Narvaez, 21; found under cultivation, 22, 25; little seen by Cabeza de Vaca on march to Apalachen, 28; is found growing in that place, 28, 29; secured with difficulty from Indians, 35; mentioned, 94, 96, 102, 103, 104, 105, 108, 110, 113, 114, 247, 248, 271. See also Corn.
Malapaz, town, 156.
Maldonado, Doña Aldonça, 125.
Maldonado, Alonzo del Castillo, see Castillo Maldonado, Alonzo del.
Maldonado, Francisco, ordered to the coast, 163; sent to Havana, 163; at Ochuse, 193; mentioned, 175, 204.
Maldonado, Rodrigo, appointed captain, 292; visits seacoast, 301; Indians attack camp of, 323; receives gift of buffalo skins, 332; horse of, injures Coronado, 368.
Malhado Island, Spaniards at, 5–6; named by Cabeza de Vaca, 50; identification of, 57 n.; Christians leave, losing a part of their number, 61; mentioned, 72.
Maliacones Indians, 80, 87. See also Malicones Indians.
Malicones Indians, 76 n. See also Maliacones Indians.
Mallery, Garrick, on sign language, 363 n.
Mallets, use of, as weapons by Indians, 321.
Mamei, a fruit, 141.
Mançano, is lost, 186.
Mantelets of thread, found at Apalachen, 28.
Marcos, Fray, see Niza.
Margaridetos, a kind of bead, 226.
Mariames Indians, kill even their male children and cast away their daughters, 64; mentioned, 87.
Marian Indians, 61.
Marjoram, wild, 338, 349, 364.
Marquis, Isle of the, name of, given to lower California, 304, 304 n.

Mat;iage, among the Tahus, 344; at Cibola, 350; at Tiguex, 353.
Mats, used in building houses, 346, 357 n.
Matsaki, Zuñi pueblo, 315 n.; description of, 315–316, 350, mentioned, 358 n.
Muuilla, De Soto at, 189; encounter with the Indians at, 190–193; mentioned, 195.
Mayayes Indians, 54 n.
Maye, cacique of, gives battle, 239.
Mayo Indians, 346 n.
Meal, sacred, use of, 307 n.
Meat, scarcity of, among De Soto's men, 167–168.
Meirinho, see Tapile.
Melgosa, Pablo de, appointed captain, 293; explores Colorado River Cañons, 309; at Tiguex, 319.
Melons, native American, 348.
Memphis, near place of De Soto's crossing of the Mississippi, 204 n.
Mendez, to seek Panuco, 49; taken by Indians, 58, 62.
Mendica Indians, 87.
Mendoza, Antonio de, first viceroy of New Spain, 121 n., 281 n.; learns of the arrival of De Soto's men at Panuco, 267; receives them at Mexico, 269; appoints Coronado governor of New Galicia, 287; plans expedition to Cibola, 275, 281; gives command to Coronado, 275, 281, 291; names Compostela as rendezvous, 293; addresses soldiers at Compostela, 294; returns to New Spain, 295; mentioned, 296, 297, 302, 326; letter of, relating progress of expedition, 277; Coronado receives messages from, 367; mentioned, 377; disappointment of, over failure of expedition, 378.
Mesa, Spanish soldier, 538.
Mesquite flour, 89.
Mestitam, Mexico, 268.
Mexico, 97 n.; Cabeza de Vaca at, 120, 121; Moscoso at, 269.
Miakka River, 150 n.
Michoacan, province in New Spain, 286; journey of Mendoza through, 294.
Mico River, 228.

Mills, at Tiguex, 354.
Mindeleff, V., on pueblo architecture, 354 n.
Miruelo, pilot, 18, 20.
Mishongnovi, Hopi pueblo, 358 n.
Mississippi River, reached by Narvaez and Cabeza de Vaca, 41; the Great River, 202; De Soto crosses, 204; nature of country of, from Aquixo to Pacaha and Coligoa, 270; described by Indians, 330; reference to, 339; description of, 365; mentioned, 385, 386. See also Grande River, Great River, and Espiritu Santo River.
Mobile, 40 n.
Mochilagua, settlement of, 347.
Mochilla, presented to De Soto, 213.
Mocoço, town of, 150 n.; speech of cacique of, to De Soto, 153.
Moçulixa, 194 n.
Monroe County, Arkansas, 253 n.
Monroe County, Mississippi, 195.
Montejo, feats of, in Tabasco, 380.
Mortar, substitute for, among Indians, 352.
Moscoso de Alvarado, Luis, direction pursued by, 131; mentioned, 135; joins De Soto at Seville, 137; is master of the camp, 146; lodges with Ucita, 147; at Cale, 156; overtakes De Soto, 157; sent forward to Tastaluça, 187; advises a halt, 189; fails to keep a careful watch over the Indians at Chicaça, 197; succeeds De Soto as governor, 233; holds a conference, 235–236; leaves Guachoya, 236; at Chaguate, 236–237; at Aguacay, 238; at Naguatex, 240–242; reaches the Red River, 241; hangs his Indian guides, 242; marches from Nondaco, 243; encounter with Indians at Aays, 243; hears of other Europeans seen by the Indians of Soacatino, 243; decides that reports are false, 244; holds a council and decides to return to Nilco, 245–246; causes resentment among his followers, 247; reaches Nilco, 248; goes to Aminoya, 249; directs the building of brigantines, 250; learns of Indian plot, 251; commands that right hands of thirty Indians be cut off, 252;

mutilates other Indians, 252; proceeds against Taguanate, 253; embarks with his followers, 253–254; is attacked by Indians, 255–259; puts out to sea, 261; is separated from the other brigantines, 263; after fifty-two days reaches the river Panico, 265–266; is received at the town of the same name, 267; and at Mexico, 269.

Mosquitos, 67, 263.

Mota Padilla, M. de la, cited, 356 n., 365 n., 366 n.

Mountain lions, in Chichilticalli, 349; in Cibola, 350.

Mountains seen by Cabeza de Vaca, 92 n.

Mud Island, 57 n.

Mulberries, wild, 334, 364.

Musetti, Juan Pedro, book merchant, 126.

Musical instruments of Indians, 312, 354.

Muskhogean tribes, 21 n.

Naçacahoz, Moscoso at, 244.

Naguatex, mentioned, 238; Indian advance at, 239; cacique of, addresses Moscoso, 241; found full of maize, 247; pottery made at, 247.

Najera, birthplace of Castañeda, 276.

Nambe, Tewa pueblo, 359 n.

Napetaca, engagement at, between De Soto and the Indians, 158.

Naquiscoça, Moscoso at, 244.

Narvaez, Pámfilo de, receives grant, 3; sets sail, 3, 14; failure of his expedition, 7; size of his fleet, 14; reaches Santo Domingo where one hundred and forty men desert, 14; arrives at Santiago de Cuba, 15; loses ten of his ships and sixty men in storm at Trinidad, 3–4, 15–17; major portion of his fleet reach Trinidad and winter there, 17; at Xagua, 17; sights Florida, 18; reaches the mainland, 19; takes possession of country in the royal name, 4, 19–20; explores inland, 20, 21; holds conference regarding further penetration of interior, 22; takes up march into country, with three hundred men, 4, 25; accepts Indian allies against the Apalachees, 26–27; takes Apalachen, 28; departs for Aute, 31; attacked by Indians, 31; reaches Aute, 32; departs from Aute, 33; calls a council, which decides to build vessels in which to get away, 34–36; loses ten men killed by Indians, and forty, who die of disease, 36; leaves Bay of Horses, and meets with many privations, 37–38; lands and is wounded by Indians, 38–39; embarks once more and proceeds along the coast, 39–41; reaches the Mississippi, 41; exhibits selfishness in saving his life, 42; fate of, narrated by Esquivel, 62; mentioned by Oviedo, 70; is carried out to sea, 72; fate of his voyage foretold, 124; his Panuco fleet, 124–125; mentioned, 157, 288; skulls of his horses found at Ochete, 162; his disaster frightens the followers of Moscoso, 248; survivors of his expedition return to New Spain, 288.

Natividad, departure of Alarcon from, 294.

Nebraska, description of, 364.

Negroes, island of, 386.

Negroes, with Coronado, 333.

Neosho River, 217 n.

New Albany, 200 n.

Newfoundland, Spanish name for, 343 n., 360.

New Galicia, province of New Spain, 113, 285 n., 286, 344; Coronado appointed governor of, 287; Coronado deprived of governorship of, 378.

New Spain, mentioned, 124, 254; direction from Rio de las Palmas, 272.

Nicalasa, an Indian chief, 195 n.

Nilco, mentioned, 224, 225, 228, 230, 231; De Soto at, 226; most populous town that was seen in Florida, 226; attacked, by orders of De Soto, 230–232; cacique of, plots against Moscoso, 251; and comes to make excuses, 252.

Nilco, river of, De Soto crosses, 227.

Nissohone, a poor province, 242; a woman of, acts as guide to Moscoso, 242.

Niza, Marcos de, expedition of, to Cibola, 9, 275, 288–290; narrative of, 277, 290 n.; reports of, verified by Diaz, 277, 296; made father provincial of Franciscans, 291; sermon of, 298; mentioned, 300; return of, to Mexico, 302.

Nondacao, reported to have plenty of maize, 242; mentioned, 243.

North Carolina, 176 n.

Nuñez Cabeza de Vaca, Alvar. See Cabeza de Vaca, Alvar Nuñez.

Nuño de Guzman, 116, 119, 120.

Nut pine, 96.

Nuts, 271.

Oaxaca, Marqués del Valle de, title given to Cortes, 286 n.

Ochete, skulls of horses found at, 162.

Ochus, province, 163; mentioned, 175.

Ochuse, Maldonado at, 193.

Ocilla River, boundary of Muskhogean territory, 21 n.

Oçita, see Ucita.

Ocmulgee River, 166 n.

Oconna-Luftee River, 176 n., 177 n.

Oconee River, 167 n.

Ocute, described to De Soto, 167; De Soto at, 167, 168; mentioned, 179; land is fertile, 270; distance to Cutifachiqui, 270.

Ogechee River, 170 n.

Ohoopee River, 170 n.

Oñate, Christobal de, governor of New Galicia, entertains Coronado, 294.

Oñate, Count of, nephew of, appointed captain, 292.

Oñate, Juan de, settlement made at Yukiwingge by, 340 n.

Opata Indians, 305 n., 348 n.; poisoned arrows of, 326 n.; mentioned, 376 n.

Opossum, first allusion to, 29 n.

Oraibi, Hopi pueblo, 358 n.

Ortiz, Juan, rescued by De Soto, 10; found by De Gallegos, 149; his adventures among the Indians, 149–152; reports Indian plan to attack De Soto, 158; acts as interpreter, 170; not to speak of Maldonado's proximity, 193; secures release of Osorio and Fuentes, 197; dies at Autiamque, 224.

Osorio, Antonio, ascends river at Pacaha with five men, 210, 211.

Osorio, Francisco, condemned to death by De Soto, 197.

Otter, 350, 357.

Ovando, Francisco de, companion of Coronado, 292; treatment of, by Indians, 354.

Oviedo, Gonzalo Fernández de, edits report to Audiencia of Española, 8, 10; edition cited, 21 n., 25 n., 31 n., 39 n., 68–70, 92 n., 112 n.

Oviedo, Lope de, at Malhado, 6; deserts, 6; among the Indians, 44–45; rescued by Cabeza de Vaca, 57; returns, through fear, 59.

Oxitipar, district of, in New Spain, 285.

Oyster creek, 57 n.

Oysters, found by Cabeza de Vaca, 33.

Pacaha, sought by De Soto for its gold, 205, 208; probably to be located in the vicinity of Osceola, in Arkansas, 209 n.; De Soto at, 209–213; cacique of, flees from De Soto, 210; is brought to the governor and submits to him, 211; and accepts friendship of the cacique of Casqui, 212; distance to Aquiguate, 215; mentioned, 227, 270; direction of, 271.

Pacaxes, a tribe in Culiacan, 345.

Padilla, Juan de, companion of Alvarado, 279; accompanies Tovar to Tusayan, 307; remains in Quivira, 372; death of, 364, 373, 385.

Pafalya, 194.

Pajarito Park, 340 n.

Palachen, 22 n.

Palacios, death of, 49.

Palisema, De Soto in, 216.

Palmas, Rio de las, western limit of grant to Narvaez, 3, 14; mentioned, 22, 260, 264, 265, 266; direction from, to New Spain, 272; direction of, from Espiritu Santo, 272.

Palmitos, sustenance of Narvaez and his men, 25.

Palos, Juan de, friar, with Narvaez, 25.

Panico, 268. See also Panuco.

Pantoja, Juan, ordered by Narvaez to proceed to Trinidad, 15; possibly the Pantoja killed by Soto-Mayor, 15 n.; advises Narvaez, 42; made lieutenant, 62; killed by Soto-Mayor, 63.

Pánuco, Narvaez orders ships to find, 4; mentioned, 63; to be sought by four men of Cabeza de Vaca's party, 49; Guzman, governor of, 285 n.; mention of, 385. *See also* Panico.

Pánuco River, 265 n.

Papa, title given priests at Zuñi, 351.

Papagos, tribe of Sonora, 348 n.

Paracoxi, province, 153, 154, 155.

Partidos, seduce one hundred and forty men from Narvaez, 14.

Pasquaro, visited by Mendoza, 294.

Patent, to Narvaez, 3.

Pato, Moscoso at, 238.

Patofa, speech of, 168–169.

Patoqua, Jemez pueblo, 359 n.

Pawnee Indians, mention of, 328 n., 337 n., 365 n.

Paz, Augustin de, printer, 126.

Peace, form of making, at Acoma, 312; at Tiguex, 319.

Pearls, found by De Soto, 174; burned at Mauilla, 193.

Pecos, identification of Cicuye with, 329 n.; visit of Indians from, 310; visited by Alvarado, 312; visit of Coronado to, 327; siege of, 341; route of army to, 361 n.; description of, 355–356; history of, 355 n.; mention of, 359.

Pecos River, crossed by Spaniards, 99 n., 329, 338.

Pedro, Don, lord of Tescuco, killed, 31.

Pedro, Indian guide, is baptized, 174; regarded with suspicion, 176.

Pemmican, used by Indians, 363.

Peñalosa, embarks in open boat, 36; repulses Indians, 39; overtaken by Cabeza de Vaca, 43; reported killed by the Camones, 72.

Pensacola, Muskhogean territory, 21 n.

Pensacola Bay, 38 n., 40 n. *See also* Chuse, Bay of.

People of the Figs, 79, 87.

Peru, exploration of, 380.

Petachan River, *see* Petlatlan.

Petates, or mats used for houses, 346, 377 n.

Petlatlan, description of Indian settlement of, 346; houses at, 346, 377 n.; mention of, 376.

Petlatlan, Rio, identification of, with Rio Sinaloa, 346 n.

Petutan River, 111, 117 n.

Philip II., king of Spain, 288.

Philippine Islands, location of isle of negroes in, 386 n.

Piache, *see* Piachi.

Piache River, 188, 189.

Piachi, 188 n.

Picardo, Juan, printer, 126.

Picones, catfish, 349 n.

Picuris, pueblo of, 352 n.

Pima Indians, 115 n., 348 n.

Pimahaitu Indians, 115 n.

Pine Bluff, 225 n., 248 n.

Pine nuts, used as food, 96, 349, 350.

Piraguas, built by De Soto, 225.

Piros Indians, 104 n.; villages of, 341 n.

Pizarro, Hernando, mentioned, 135.

Plot, against Narvaez, 34.

Pobares, Francisco, death of, 322.

Pojoaque, Tewa pueblo, 359 n.

Pontotoc county, Mississippi, 195.

Porcallo de Figueroa, Vasco, offers provisions to Narvaez, 15; keeps his slaves from hanging themselves, 142; mentioned, 143; is made captain-general, by De Soto, 145; is resisted by Indians, 146; lodges with Ucita, 147; is unable to make seizures of Indians, as slaves, 154; and returns to Cuba, 154.

Pork, allowance of, to De Soto's men, 171.

Portuguese, with Hernando de Soto, leave Elvas, 138; Spanish seek to get among the Portuguese, 139.

Potano, town, 156, 162.

Pottery, glazed, of Indians, 340; where found, 340 n.; made by Indians, 355, 361.

Prairie de Roane, 239 n.

Prairie dogs, seen by Coronado on great plains, 338.

Prentiss County, Mississippi, 212 n.

Prickly pears, 61 n., 66–67, 70, 71, 72, 73, 74, 75–76, 77, 78, 80, 81, 93, 94, 96, 246. *See also* Tuna.

Primahaitu Indians, 114.

Prostitution among the Tahus, 344–345.

Puaray, settlement upon site of Tiguex, 317 n.

Pueblo Indians, 90 n., 104 n.; rabbit hunts among, 98 n.; ceremonials of, 384.

Pueblos, method of building, 352.

Puerto de Luna, 338 n.

Puerto Principe, town in Cuba, 142, 143, 144.

Puje, ruin of pueblo of, 340 n.

Quachichiles, see Guachichules.

Quachita River, 238 n.

Qualla, see Xualla.

Querechos Indians, mode of life of, 330; description of, 362–363.

Queres, pueblos of, 327 n., 352, 358 n.

Quevenes Indians, 59, 62, 85, 87.

Quigaltam, 227; cacique of, sends message to De Soto, 229; arouses the latter's suspicions, 230; mentioned, 235.

Quigualtam, Indians of, attack Moscoso, 255.

Quiguate, 213, 215, 216. See Aquiguate.

Quince juice, use of, as poison antidote, 376, 381.

Quipana, near plains, 222 n.

Quirex, province of, visited by Spaniards, 327.

Quitok Indians, 80 n., 87 n.

Quitoles Indians, 87 n.

Quivira, stories of, told by Turk, 313, 314; mention of, 327; departure of Coronado for, 328; stories of Xabe of, 329; arrival of Coronado at, 336; route to, 337 n.; Indians of, identified with Wichita Indians, 337 n.; Coronado returns from, 341, 342; description of, reference to, 362, 365, 366, 367; return to, planned, 368; Padilla remains in, 372, 373 n.; death of Padilla at, 385; route to, 378, 385.

Quizquiz, De Soto at, 202; Indians of, present skins and shawls, 202; direction of, 271.

Rabbits, on the great plains, 363; skins of, used for garments, 350.

Rafts, use of, in crossing Colorado River, 304; method of making, 304.

Ramirez, Fray Juan, establishes mission at Acoma, 311 n.

Ranjel, Narrative by, 130; cited, 161 n., 165 n., 166 n., 167 n., 172 n., 175 n., 177 n., 178 n., 185 n., 188 n., 189 n., 194 n., 215 n., 216 n., 217 n., 222 n.

Rau, Charles, translator of Baegert's narrative, 346 n.

Redland, 195.

Red River, 225 n., 261 n.; Moscoso at, 241 n.; identification of, with Zuñi River, 299 n.

Relación del Suceso, 278; cited, 337 n., 365 n., 367 n.

Relación Postrera de Síbola, 278.

Riberos, el Factor, companion of Coronado, 293.

Rio Grande, 99 n., 102, 103 n., 104 n.; Indians attempt to cross, 323; pueblos near, 327 n., 335 n.; disappearance underground of, 341; mention of, 339 n., 340 n.; direction of, 359 n., 360.

Ritchey, W. E., cited, 302.

River, the, 228.

River Grande, see Grande River.

Rodriguez, Men., killed at Mauilla, 193.

Rojas, Juan de, made governor's lieutenant of Cuba, 146.

Romo, Alfonso, sent in quest of habitations, 171; overtakes De Soto, 172.

Ruiz, Gonçalo, death of, 49.

Saabedra, Fernandarias de, appointment of, 297.

Saabedra, H. de, mayor of Culiacan, 297, 371, 372.

Sacatecas, see Zacatecas.

St. Clement's Point, landing of Narvaez at, 19 n.

St. Francis County, Arkansas, 205 n., 214 n.

St. Francis River, 213 n., 214 n.

St. Marks, seat of the Apalachee, 21 n., 30 n.

St. Marks Bay, 33 n., 37 n.

St. Marks River, 33 n.

Saline County, 236 n.

Saline River, 236 n.

Salt, made by Spaniards, 218, 238; natural crystals of, in Arizona, 310; lakes of, on great plains, 338, 362.

Salvidar, Juan de, companion of

Coronado, 292; explorations of, 296; mentioned, 299; at Tiguex, 319; captures Indian village, 324; escape of Indian woman from, 339.

Samaniego, Lope de, appointed army-master, 292; death of, 295.

San Antonio Bay, 58 n.

San Antonio Cape, 143.

San Antonio River, 74 n.

San Bernardo River, 58 n.

Sanbenitos, described, 334 n., 347.

Sancti Spiritus, town in Cuba, 142, 144.

Sandia Mountains, 352.

San Gabriel de los Españoles, settlement of, 340 n.

San Hieronimo de los Corazones, founding of, 301; dispatches from, 324; disturbance in, 326; transferred to Suya, 301, 326.

San Ildefonso, Tewa pueblo, 359 n.

San Juan, Tewa pueblo, 340 n., 359 n.

Sanlúcar, Bay of, 139.

Sanlúcar, muster of De Soto's forces at, 139.

San Lúcar de Barrameda, port in Spain, 3, 14 n.

San Luis, island, 57 n.

San Marcos-Guadalupe River, 74 n.

San Miguel, village, 120.

San Miguel Culiacan, 113 n.

San Pedro, river in Sonora, 371 n.

Sant Anton, Cape, westernmost point of Cuba, 18 n.

Santa Clara, Tewa pueblo, 359 n.

Santa Fé, seat of provincial government, 340 n.

Santa Maria, Rio, 105 n.

Santander River, called Rio de los Palmas, 14 n.

Santiago, use of, as war cry, 300 n., 308.

Santiago de Cuba, described by the Gentleman of Elvas, 140–141; bread there made of a root, 141; natural products of, 141.

Sant Miguel, strait, 37.

Santo Domingo, Narvaez reaches, 14; mentioned, 19 n.

Saquechuma, burned by Indians to deceive De Soto, 196.

Savannah River, 21 n., 172 n.

Sebastian, king, 272 n.

Seminole Indians, 19 n.

Senora, see Sonora.

Seri Indians, 108 n., 301 n.

Seven Cities, see Cibola.

Sheep, Rocky Mountain, 305, 348.

Shongopovi, Hopi pueblo, 358 n.

Shupaulovi, Hopi pueblo, 358 n.

Sia, identification of, 327 n., 359 n.; mention of, 359.

Sichomovi, Hopi pueblo, 358 n.

Sierra, dies, 49.

Sierra Madre Mountains, 106 n.

Sign language, used by Querechos, 330; by plains Indians, 363, 363 n.

Silos, Pueblo de los, 356, 358 n.

Silveira, Fernando da, epigram by, 133.

Silver, reports of, at Quivira, 313, 314, 329; use of, in glazing, 340, 355, 361; mine of, at Culiacan, 345.

Silver Bluff, 172 n.

Sinaloa, settlement of, 347.

Sinaloa River, 113, 117 n., 346.

Sipsey River, 194 n.

Slavery, Spanish, among the Indians, 64; Indian, among the Spaniards, 110, 114, 116, 312, 329, 339; Indians sought by Vasco Porcallo de Figueroa, 154; taken by De Soto, 160, 181, 184–185, 186, 195, 205, 206, 208, 209, 215, 216, 217, 218, 219, 222, 223, 225, 227, 232; by Moscoso, 238, 239, 242, 254; five hundred men and women abandoned, 254.

Smith, Buckingham, *Relation of Alvar Nuñez Cabeza de Vaca*, cited, 19 n., 24 n., 25 n., 30 n., 31 n., 71 n., 79 n., 90 n., 92 n.; translation of Oviedo's *Letter*, 68–70; *Coleccion de varios Documentos para la Historia de la Florida*, edited by, 130.

Snakes, worship of, 344.

Soacatino, guide to, furnished to Moscoso, 243; Indians of, report seeing Europeans, 243; Moscoso at, 244.

Sobaipuri, 349 n., 371 n.

Socorro, see Aymay.

Sodomy, among Pacaxes, 345; at Petlatlan, 346; at Suya, 348; absence of, at Cibola, 351.

Solis, Alonso de, distributor and assessor, with Narvaez, 14; enters Apalachen, 28; embarks in open boat, 36; is drowned, 46.

Sonora, Spanish settlement in valley of, 301, 302; San Hieronimo abandoned for, 301, 326; description of, 347; rebellion at, 370–371.

Sonora Indians, 106 n.

Sorcery, among Pacaxes, 345.

Soti, brothers, die at Aminoya, 249.

Soto, Hernando de, wishes services of Cabeza de Vaca, 8, 136; Narrative of expedition of, by the Gentleman of Elvas, 127–272; geographical knowledge afforded by the Narrative, 129; Indian tribes described, 129; places mentioned, 129; parentage of, 135; captain of horse in Peru, 135; marries Doña Ysabel de Bobadilla, 136; is made governor of Cuba, and Adelantado of Florida, 136; members of his company, 136–138; sails with six hundred men and seven ships, 139; reaches Santiago de Cuba, 140; goes to Havana by land, 143; lands in Florida, 146; lodges with Ucita, 147; loses his Indian interpreters, 147; sends vessels to Cuba for provisions, 154; moves toward Cale, in search of gold, 155; finds the town abandoned, 155; orders all the ripe grain in the fields to be secured, 156; loses three men, 156; reaches Caliquen and hears of the distress that overtook Narvaez at Apalache, but decides to go onward, 157; takes cacique, and is attacked by Indians at Napetaca, 158; divides some of the captives among his men and orders execution of the rest, 160; seizes a hundred Indian men and women, 160; starts in search of gold, reported to be at Yupaha, 164; tells the cacique of Achese that he is the child of the Sun, 167; plants a cross, 167; receives four hundred tamemes from the cacique of Ocute, 168; leaves the province of Patofa, 169; an exorcism cures his guide, 169; receives seven hundred tamemes, 170; suffers many privations, 171–172; orders an Indian burned, 172; hears speech of a kinswoman of the cacica of Cutifachiqui, 172–173; hears speech of the cacica, 173; leaves Cutifachiqui, 175; takes the cacica as a slave, 176; distances traversed, 177; begs maize of the cacique of Chiaha, 178; hears speech of cacique of that place, 178; sends men to see if there is gold at Chisca, 181; hears speech of cacique of Coste, 182–183; and speech of cacique of Coça, 183–184; rests at Coça twenty-five days, 185; hears speech at Tallisi, 186–187; hears speech of cacique of Tastaluça, 188; distances traversed to Tastaluça, 188–189; wounded in encounter with Indians at Mauilla, 191; hears that Maldonado is at Ochuse, 193; his losses in the Florida expedition, 194; leaves Mauilla, 194; reaches Chicaça and takes some Indians, 195; cuts off an Indian's hands for theft, 196; repulses Indians, 197–199; leaves Chicaça and sustains two more attacks made by the natives, 199–201; sets out for Quizquiz, 202; crosses the Mississippi, 204; hears speeches of the cacique of Casqui, 206–207; preaches Christianity to the Indians, 207–208; finds many shawls and skins at Pacaha, 209; makes friendship between the caciques of Casqui and Pacaha, 212; burns part of Aquiguate, 214; takes one hundred and forty-one Indians, 215; makes other captures at Coligoa, 216; at Tanico, 217; subdues cacique of Tulla, 218–220; has now been gone three years, 221; has lost two hundred and fifty men, 221; winters at Autiamque, 222–224; goes to Nilco, 226; and thence to Guachoya, 227; sends a message to cacique of Quigaltam, 229; is taken ill, 230; sends expedition against Nilco, 230–231; farewell speech to his men, 232–233; names Moscoso to be his successor, 233; dies, 233; and is secretly buried, 234; sale of his property, 235; reference to discoveries of, 313, 339, 365; crosses route of Coronado, 339; mentioned, 362, 366; route of, 386.

Soto-Mayor, Juan de, companion of Coronado, 293.

Soto-Mayor, kills Juan Pantoja, 15 n., 63; dies and is eaten by Esquivel, 63.

Soto-Mayor, Pedro de, chronicler of Cardenas' expedition, 310.

South Carolina, 176 n.

South Sea, 105, 108, 111, 238. *See also* California, Gulf of.

Staked Plains, 7, 97 n., 245 n., 361 n., 362 n.

Stevens, John, dictionary of, 300 n.

Susola Indians, 76, 80 n., 87.

Suwannee, river, crossed by Narvaez, 27 n.

Suya, *see* Sonora.

Swain County, 176 n.

Tabasco, mention of, 380.

Tabu, among Indians of Malhado, 51–52.

Taguanate, cacique of, plots against Moscoso, 251; comes to make excuses, 252; town assaulted by Moscoso, 252–253.

Tahu Indians, a tribe in Culiacan, 344.

Tali, De Soto at, 182; speech of cacique of, 182–183.

Taliepataua, 194.

Talise, nature of the country, 270. *See also* Tallise.

Talladega County, 183 n.

Tallahassee, seat of the Apalachee, 21 n.

Tallahatchie River, 200 n.

Tallapoosa County, 186.

Tallapoosa River, 186.

Tallimuchose, without inhabitants, 185.

Tallise, 186; cacique of, lends forty men to De Soto, 186; presents the tamemes needed, 187. *See also* Talise.

Tamemes, Indians who carry burdens, 168, 170, 176, 182, 184, 186, 187, 213.

Tampas Bay, reached by Narvaez, 20; mentioned, 36 n., 125 n.

Tanico, De Soto at, 217.

Tanto River, 143.

Taos, identification with Braba, 340 n.; visit of Spaniards to, 340; Valladolid Spanish name for, 340; mention of, 359.

Tapatu River, 228.

Tapile, equivalent of meirinho, 269.

Tarasca, a district in Michoacan, 286.

Tascaluça, De Soto seeks, 185; cacique of, addresses De Soto, 186–187; distance to Mississippi, 215; nature of the country, 270; direction of, 271. *See also* Tastaluça.

Tastaluça, cacique of, sends a chief to De Soto, 186–187; dwelling of, 187; speech to De Soto, 188; is taken by De Soto, 188; asks to be allowed to remain, 189; at Mauilla, 189. *See also* Tascaluça.

Tatalicoya, De Soto at, 217.

Tattooing, among Indians, 348 n.

Tavera, one of Cabeza de Vaca's party, death of, 48–49.

Tejas, *see* Teyas.

Tejo, stories told by, 285–286; death of, 287.

Tellez, captain, embarks in open boat, 36; repulses Indians, 39; overtaken by Cabeza de Vaca, 43; reported killed by the Camones, 72.

Tennessee River, 181 n., 212 n.

Teocomo, settlement of, 347.

Tepoca Indians, 108 n.

Terceira, island, 123; produces batata, 141.

Ternaux-Compans, Henri, translation of Castañeda by, 277, 290 n., 341 n.

Tesuque, Tewa pueblo, 359 n.

Tewa Indians, pottery of, 340 n.; pueblos of, 359 n.

Teyas, tribe of plains Indians, 333; identification with Tejas, or Texas, 333 n.; guides of Coronado to Quivira, 335, 338; Cicuye besieged by, 357; name of, synonymous with braves, 357; mentioned, 362; cannibalism among, 363 n.

Theodoro, a Greek, makes resin, 35; deserts, 40.

Tietiquaquo, chief of, comes to De Soto, 223.

Tiguas, 317 n.; pueblos of, 358 n.

Tiguex, visited by Alvarado, 312; identification of, 317 n.; demands of Spaniards at, 318; revolt of Indians of, 319; Indians of, distrust Spaniards, 321, 328; seige of,

322; description of, 352; pueblos of, 358.

Timucuan Indians, 19 n., 25 n.

Timuquanan or Timucuan Indians, 19 n., 25 n.

Tishomingo County, Mississippi, 212 n.

Tison, Rio del, reason for name of, 301. *See* Colorado River.

Toalli, De Soto at, 165, 166; houses made of grass, 165.

Toasi, 185 n.; De Soto at, 186.

Tobar, Nuño de, at court, 135; accompanies De Soto, 137; is deprived of his rank as captain-general, 145; leaves his wife at Havana, 146; sent against Nilco, 231.

Tobosos Indians, 103 n.

Tocaste, town, 155 n.

Tombigbee River, 189 n., 194 n., 195 n.

Tomson, Robert, cited, 334 n.

Tonala, settlement of, 287.

Tonkawa Indians, Texas tribe, 363 n.

Topia or Tapira in Durango, 290 n.

Topira, expedition of Coronado to, 290.

Torre, Diego Perez de la, replaces Guzman, 287.

Torrejon de Velasco, death of Guzman at, 285 n.

Tovar, Fernando de, position of, 292.

Tovar, Pedro de, appointed ensign-general, 292; visits Tusayan, 307; sent to San Hieronimo, 326; joins Coronado at Tiguex, 367.

Traslado de las Nuevas, 278.

Travois, dog saddles used by plains Indians, 362.

Trees, near Apalachen, 29; of Santiago de Cuba, 140–141; named by Gentleman of Elvas, 206.

Trigeux, *see* Tiguex.

Trinidad, storm at, 15–17; town in Cuba, 144, 145.

Truxillo, adventure of, 298.

Tuasi, *see* Toasi.

Tuckaseegee River, 176 n.

Tula, direction of, 271.

Tulla, De Soto's encounter with Indians at, 218–219; cacique of, offers presents, 220; is dismissed, 221.

Tuna, native American fruit, 347; preserves made from, by Indians, 305 n., 348.

Tunica County, Mississippi, 204 n.

Turk, Indian slave at Pecos, 313, 372; stories of, 314; bracelets of, 315; mentioned, 326, 329, 330, 331; Spaniards grow suspicious of, 328, 334; put in chains, 335; motive of, in misleading Spaniards, 336–337.

Turkeys in pueblo regions, 354.

Turquoises, presented to Cabeza de Vaca, 106, 117; found at Waco, 246; collected by Estevanico, 288, 289: how obtained by Indians, 308 n.; gifts of, made by Indians, 308, 312; of pueblo Indians, 350.

Tusayan, description of, by Zuñi Indians, 307; visited by Tovar, 307; cotton cultivated at, 308 n.; description of, 351; names of pueblos of, 358 n.

Tutahaco, visit of Coronado to, 314; problem of name of, 314 n.; eight pueblos of, 358.

Tutelpinco, De Soto at, 225.

Tyronza River, 206 n., 208 n.

Ucita, an Indian chief, 146 n.; town of, 146, 147; temple thrown down, 147.

Uitachuco, burned by Indians, 161.

Ullibahali, chiefs of, approach De Soto, 185; a fenced town, 185; cacique of, offers tamemes to De Soto, 186.

Union County, Mississippi, 200 n.

Upanguayma Indians, 108.

"Upper Cross Timbers," 244 n.

Urine, use of, as a mordant, 354 n.

Urrea, Lope de, companion of Coronado, 293; envoy of peace to Indians, 323.

Utinama, town, 156.

Uzachil, much food found at, 160.

Uzachil, cacique of, sends embassy to De Soto, 158; presents him with deer, 160.

Uzela, De Soto at, 161.

Vaca, Cabeza de, *see* Cabeza de Vaca.

Vacapan, province crossed by Coronado, 305.

Vacas, Rio de las, 103 n.

Valdevieso, killed by Indians, 58, 64; mentioned by Oviedo, 69.

Valençuela, captain, ordered by Narvaez to follow river to the sea, 26.

Valladolid, Spanish name of Braba, 340, 359.

Valley of Knaves, rebellion of Indians in, 326.

Vargas, Juan de, killed by Indians, 257.

Vargas, Luis Ramierez de, companion of Coronado, 293.

Vasconcelos, André de, of Elvas, 137, 138; commands a ship in De Soto's expedition, 139; slave of, espouses cacica of Cutifachiqui, 177; dies at Aminoya, 249.

Vasconyados Indians, 115 n.

Vazquez, Juan, killed at Mauilla, 193.

Vazquez de Ayllon, Lucas, 21 n.

Vega, Garcilaso de la, "the Inca," author of *Florida del Yunca*, 131; gives distance of Moscoso's journey down the Mississippi, 259 n.

Vegetation of the great plains, 362.

Velasco, island, possibly to be identified with Malhado, 57 n.

Velazquez, Juan, first man of Narvaez' exploring party to be lost, 27; his horse affords supper to many, 27.

Venison, a thing little known, 74.

Vera, Francisco de, father of Nuñez Cabeza de Vaca, 3, 125.

Vera, Pedro de, conqueror of the Canaries, grandfather of Nuñez Cabeza de Vaca, 3, 13 n., 125.

Vera Cruz, Cabeza de Vaca at, 121; mentioned, 265 n., 268.

Vessels, built by men under Narvaez, 34–36; by Spaniards at Aminoya, 250.

Vicksburg Bluffs, 255 n.

Villafarta, named by De Soto, 157.

Villalobos, R. L. de, voyage of, 360, 360 n., 378.

Virgins, treatment of, 355, 356.

Voth, H. R., studies on Oraibi marriage customs, 353 n.

Waco, Moscoso at, 244 n., 245; turquoises and shawls of cotton found at, 246.

Walnut Bend suggested as the place of De Soto's crossing the Mississippi, 204 n.

Walnuts, found by Coronado, 334.

Walpi, Hopi pueblo, 358 n.

Watercress, native American, 349.

Whiskers, captain of Cicuye Indians, 310, 312; taken prisoner by Alvarado, 315; release of, 329.

White Oak shoals, Red River, 242 n.

White River, 216 n., 217 n., 253 n.

Wichita Indians, identified with Indians of Quivira, 337 n.

Wildcat, native American, 349, 350.

Wine, of pitahaya, 348.

Winship, George Parker, memoirs on the Coronado expedition, 276–277, 337 n., 341 n., 360 n., 366 n., 374 n., 386 n.

Witchcraft practised by Pacaxes, 345.

Withlacoochee River crossed by Narvaez, 25 n.

Wolves on great plains, 363.

Women, work of, in pueblo building, 352; functions of, 353.

Woodruff County, Arkansas, 216 n.

Xabe, Indian from Quivira, with Coronado, 329, 342.

Xagua, see Jagua.

Xalisco, establishment of, 287; Alarcon's destination at, 294.

Xeréz de Badajóz, 135.

Xeréz de la Frontera, 126.

Ximena, *see* Galisteo.

Xuala, direction of, 271.

Xualla, mentioned, 176 n., 177; distance to Tastaluça, 188; distance to Coça, 189.

Xuarez, Juan, commissary of Narvaez' fleet, 14; burns cases containing dead men, 21; approves the plan for Spanish to continue inland exploration, 23; joins inland march, 25; one of party that goes to look for the sea, 33.

Yaqui Indians, 118 n., 346 n.

Yaqui River, 376 n.

Yaquimi, settlement of, 347.

Yeguaces Indians, 87 n.

Yguases Indians, *see* Yguazes Indians.

Yguazes Indians, 61, 87; manners and customs of, 65–66; marriage among, 65.

Young County, Texas, 244 n.

Ysabel de Bobadilla, wife of Hernando

de Soto, 136; receives a waiting-maid from the governor of Gomera, 140; and a mule from a gentleman of Santiago de Cuba, 140; sails for Havana, 142; is in much danger, 143; remains in Havana, 145; receives twenty women, sent by Añasco, 162; has not heard from De Soto in three years, 221.

Ysopete, Indian of Quivira, with Coronado, 331; supplants Turk in confidence of Coronado, 334, 337.

Ytara, town, 156, 162.

Ytaua, De Soto at, 185.

Yukiwingge, visited by Barrionuevo, 340; location of, 340 n.; pueblos of, 359 n.

Yuma Indians, description of, 303.

Yupaha, governed by a woman, 164; reported to have much gold, 164.

Yuqueyunque, see Yukiwingge.

Zacatecas, Mexican province, 385.

Zamora, printing press at, 126.

Zebreros, an alcalde, acts as guide to Cabeza de Vaca, 115; goes to Culiacan, 116.

Zuñi Indians, pueblos of, 300, 358 n.; pottery of, 340 n.; tame eagles of, 348 n.; dress of women of, 350 n.; population of pueblos of, 351 n. See also Cibola.

Zuñi River, crossed by Coronado, 299.